THE PUBLICATION OF *TACONITE, NEW LIFE FOR MINNESOTA'S IRON RANGE: THE HISTORY OF ERIE MINING COMPANY* IS MADE POSSIBLE THROUGH MAJOR CONTRIBUTIONS FROM:

Brian Maki, President and CEO

Legislation authored by Senator David Tomassoni and Representative Jason Metsa during the 2017 Minnesota Legislative Session

DEPARTMENT OF IRON RANGE
RESOURCES & REHABILITATION

Mark Phillips, Commissioner

AND OTHERS LISTED AS CONTRIBUTORS

COMPANY

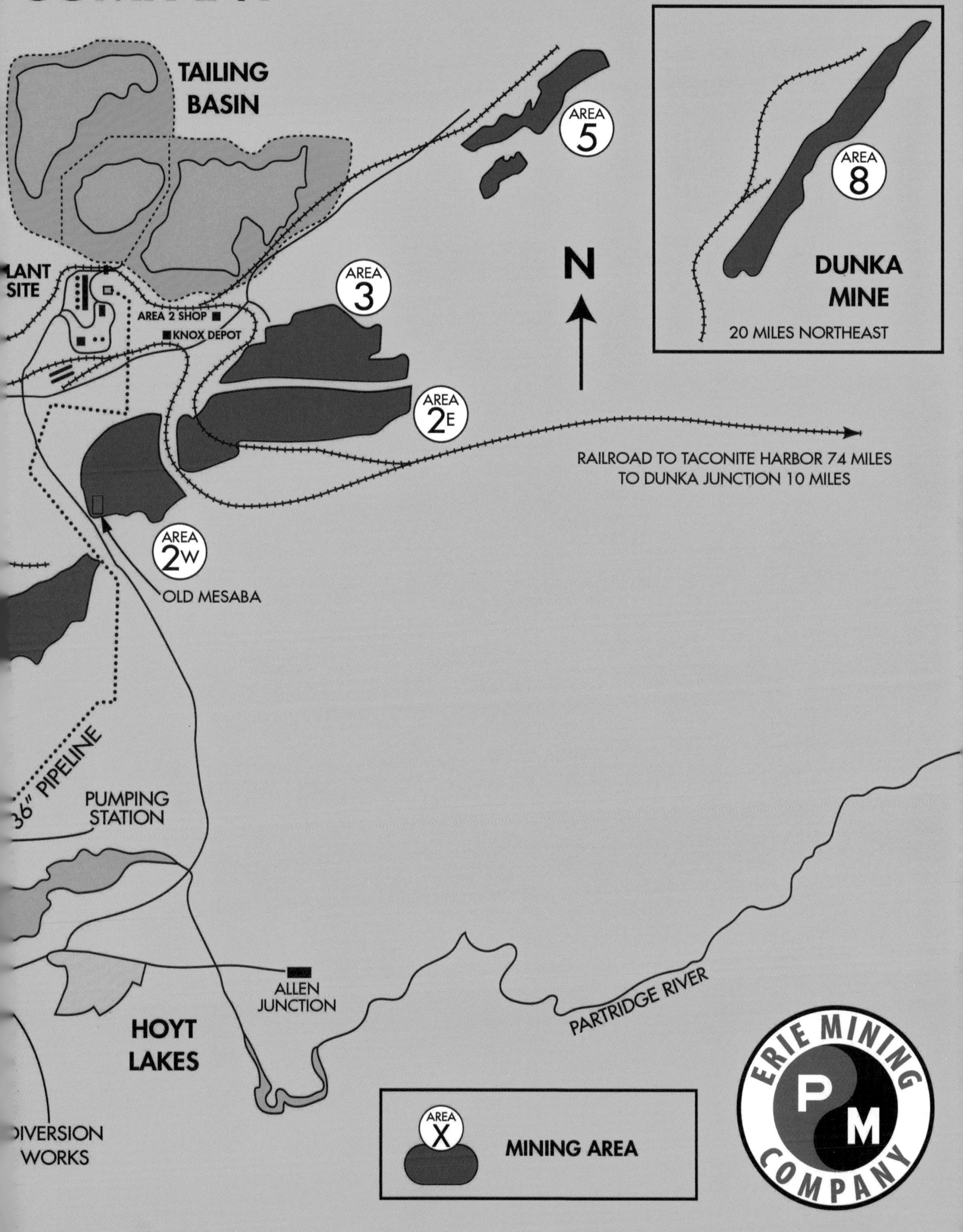

TAILING
BASIN

PLANT
SITE

AREA 2 SHOP

KNOX DEPOT

AREA 3

AREA 2E

AREA 5

N

AREA 8

DUNKA MINE

20 MILES NORTHEAST

RAILROAD TO TACONITE HARBOR 74 MILES
TO DUNKA JUNCTION 10 MILES

AREA 2W

OLD MESABA

36" PIPELINE

PUMPING
STATION

ALLEN
JUNCTION

PARTRIDGE RIVER

**HOYT
LAKES**

DIVERSION
WORKS

AREA X **MINING AREA**

ERIE MINING
P M
COMPANY

TACONITE

New Life for Minnesota's Iron Range

The History of
ERIE
MINING COMPANY

THIS BOOK IS DEDICATED TO ALL ERIE MINING COMPANY
EMPLOYEES AND THEIR FAMILIES AND THOSE WHO
SUPPORTED ERIE THROUGH THE YEARS.

THE
DONNING COMPANY
PUBLISHERS

The Donning Company Publishers

731 S. Brunswick St.

Brookfield, MO 64628

Lex Cavanah, General Manager

Nathan Stufflebean, Production Supervisor

Pamela Koch, Editor

Jeremy Glanville, Graphic Designer

Dusti Merrill, Project Research Coordinator

Katie Gardner, Marketing & Production Coordinator

Barry Haire and Geoffrey Bass, Project Directors

ISBN: 978-1-68184-244-8

Library of Congress Control Number:2019911509

Printed in the United States of America at Walsworth

TABLE OF CONTENTS

FOREWORD

History teaches us that things do not "just happen." The ability to draw minute particles of iron out of an ancient pre-Cambrian rock so lean in iron content that it can't be called ore and put the iron particles back together again in the form of iron rich pellets, equal, if not superior to natural ores used in the making of iron and steel, is one of the great human achievements of the twentieth century—and it didn't "just happen."

By the mid-nineteenth century, the need for steel in America had grown to a point where all its existing iron mines weren't enough to meet the growing steel industry's needs and an intense search for new sources of iron ore began in the Lake Superior District. In 1872 mineralogist and prospector Peter Mitchell evaluated what he called a "mountain of iron" at the eastern end of Minnesota's Mesabi Range. Although at the time it was useless because of its low iron content, the land contained an enormous supply of what came to be known as the hard, iron-bearing rock called taconite. According to Minnesota State Geologist Newton Winchell, "The rock is widely spread over the whole length of the Mesabi."

Taconite's value lay in the fact that the formation was large and more than a billion years old having been exposed to the forces of nature that created oxidized portions. These became the great beds of naturally enriched iron ore, called hematite, that would make the Mesabi Range famous. In 1890 hematite was found near what became the Mesabi Range's first mine, the Mountain Iron Mine. A rash of discoveries soon followed and were quickly turned into mines. Because the ore was soft and the deposits close to the surface, it took little time for a mine to be brought to production. By 1895, the Mesabi Range was producing more ore than any other place in America and would continue to be the major supplier of ore to the nation's steel mills over the next 100 years. America had become dependent on steel—and steel was dependent on iron ore.

However, men with foresight soon realized that the high-grade, natural iron ore was being rapidly depleted and that a time would come when it would be gone. They also recognized that the amount of iron ore produced by every iron ore mine that had ever existed in America was but a small fraction of all the iron that was locked up in the vast taconite deposits of the Mesabi Range. The potential was phenomenal; however, significant challenges lay ahead. If the iron could be separated from the taconite and made marketable like natural ore, the entire formation could be mined and a lasting iron ore mining industry could be established in Minnesota. But before companies would invest in complex plants and mining equipment to make taconite usable, new methods and equipment to mine and process taconite had to be invented. A process had to be developed to separate the fine iron particles from the rock and put them back together in pellet form, economically.

Research using samples of taconite from the eastern Mesabi Range began in 1912 at the University of Minnesota's Mines Experiment Station by Edward Davis and others. This proved that the fine iron particles could be separated from the taconite at a laboratory level. However, it would be up to mining companies to develop the commercial-size equipment necessary for full-scale mining and the production of iron rich pellets that would be equal to or better than natural ore. The challenge was daunting, but urgently important to the nation, as two world wars had proven that self-sufficiency in a strategic material like iron ore was essential.

One of the first mining companies to respond to the challenge and "make it happen" was Pickands Mather. Led by bold men of vision such as Elton Hoyt 2nd, Henry Dalton, John Metcalf, Fred DeVaney, and others, Pickands Mather collaborated with Minnesota's Mines Experiment Station and conducted its own research into taconite. In 1940, under the leadership of Pickands Mather, Erie Mining Company was formed for the purpose of acquiring taconite lands and developing the necessary mining and processing techniques. At Hibbing, an iron ore research laboratory was established and a few years later Erie built a taconite demonstration plant, called PreTac, near Aurora for the purpose of proving the laboratory results with full-scale equipment.

Davis wrote in 1949, "It is very fortunate that such a strong well-financed organization like Pickands Mather decided to investigate Mesabi taconite, because the success or failure of the Erie taconite project will largely determine the future of iron mining in the Lake Superior District." In 1957 Erie spawned a new life for Minnesota's Mesabi Range when its commercial plant, a $300 million investment, began operation. Erie would become a leading employer in the area and one of the largest producers of taconite pellets in the world. Its story is told here, only in the way former employees can tell it—in vivid words, pictures, and diagrams covering its history from the time of its inception to its closure and beyond.

Marvin Lamppa, Author
Minnesota's Iron Country, Rich Ore, Rich Lives

ERIE MINING COMPANY HISTORY PROJECT TEAM

Ted Williams

Front row, left to right: Jim Westbrook, Elroy Rafferty, Dan DeVaney, Doug Buell, Lynn Niemi.
Back row, left to right: Tom Michels, Jim Scott, Ron Hein, Mike Sterk, Tom Niemi

INTRODUCTION

At an annual Erie Mining Company (Erie) employee Christmas party on December 6, 2013, conversation turned to the fact that there were fewer Erie pioneers in attendance and their personal stories and histories needed to be recorded before it was too late. Erie, one of the nation's largest iron mining operations, had closed twelve years earlier.

The group was asked if they thought a booklet or brochure documenting the history of Erie should be developed. All responded with a resounding "Yes!" Individual comments were enthusiastic. One of the fellows said, "I need something to do, so count me in." Another told me, "Ron, if we don't do it now, it will never happen."

This was the beginning of the Erie Mining Company History Project and the start of a five-and-a-half-year journey of research, fund-raising, conducting oral history interviews, writing, rewriting, and many other activities leading to this book. Our goal was to document the sixty-one-year history of Erie from its formation in 1940 to its closure in 2001. Our vision was to pass on to future generations the knowledge of and insight into the vast amount of pioneering work involved to develop an economically feasible method to mine and process a previously worthless low-grade iron ore called taconite. By turning taconite into a high quality product, the development of one of Minnesota's mineral resources was made possible. This ensured Minnesota's continued prominence as the major supplier of the iron ore critical to the nation's security and advancement of its standard of living. The story of Erie and its people deserved its rightful place in Minnesota's documented history.

Our first step was to establish a basic roadmap of the process required to write and publish a book. With the aid of the owners of Duluth's Lake Superior Magazine, we developed an extensive and detailed work plan.

In February 2014, at the first meeting of the volunteer group, the publishing process and time commitment was explained. Then the crucial question was asked, "Should we go ahead with this project?" The answer with a unanimous "Yes."

It was obvious from the start that a nonprofit organization was needed to handle the financial aspects of the project, and the St. Louis County Historical Society in Duluth was contacted. Executive Director JoAnne Coombe was very supportive, and, within a month, the Board of Governors reviewed the project and approved the partnership.

The next many months were busy conducting oral history interviews, fund-raising, selecting a publisher, doing research, and writing and rewriting the manuscript. Two local historians, Marvin Lamppa and Pam Brunfelt, were contacted to review and critique the project. Lamppa, encouraged us to proceed with the project, telling us if we didn't do it, it would never be done. After listening to our presentation, Brunfelt, exclaimed, "I want this book to be relevant 100 years from now." That statement certainly "raised the bar!"

Several former Erie hourly employees, some who had significant involvement with the local United Steel Workers of America (USWA) union, soon joined the original group. This team immediately recognized that the book needed to be accurate and include historical and operational details that could only be known by the people who worked at Erie. Committed to working through that process, over a three-year period, the team showed its dedication by doing their "homework" and meeting weekly to write, review, and rewrite the manuscript and select the graphics for the book.

The Erie Mining Company History Project Team includes the following:

Doug Buell

Doug began his employment with Erie in the summer of 1965 in the Mine Engineering Department. He returned to the University of Wisconsin–Madison to complete his Mine Engineering degree and joined Erie full time in 1966. After a five-month training program, Doug spent two years as a replacement foreman in various Mining Department positions before being assigned to the Mine Engineering Department in 1968. There he held positions in short- and long-range forecasting and mine planning, production reporting, blast monitoring, and mining lease management, retiring as senior mining engineer in 2001. Doug has published several articles on the history and operation of the Erie Mining Company Railroad and has had many of his railroad photographs reprinted. He is currently active with the Archives section of the Lake Superior Railroad Museum. Doug and his wife, Karen, live in Duluth.

Dan DeVaney

Dan is the son of Fred DeVaney, who managed early taconite research for Pickands Mather and developed the taconite concentration and pelletizing processes used at Erie. Dan is a graduate Mining Engineer from the University of Missouri–Rolla and began employment with Pickands Mather in 1952 at its natural ore wash and heavy media plants. He transferred to Erie on the first day of mill operation in 1957, working in the Concentrator. Dan transferred to Pickands Mather's Wabush Mine in Labrador, Canada, in 1965 for three and a half years. He returned to Erie and retired as General Foreman Tailings and Water in 1991. Dan and his wife, Jane, who worked for many years for the East Range Clinic as a nurse at the Erie Dispensary, live in Duluth. Dan's son Steve also worked for Erie in the Purchasing Department, marking three generations of DeVaneys to work for Erie.

Ron Hein

Ron started his career at Erie in 1960 as a welder. In succession he was promoted to Maintenance Foreman, Assistant Training Supervisor, Training Manager, and Director of Organizational Development. He holds an American Society for Quality certification as Manager/Organizational Excellence and is a graduate of the U.S. Army Command and General Staff College. He served in the Army National Guard for thirty-seven years, retiring with the rank of Colonel. In 2015 he was promoted to the rank of Brigadier General (Bvt) in the Minnesota National Guard. In his career at Erie, his work involvement and participation included all the operating and staff departments. Ron is currently a member of the St. Louis County Historical Society Board of Governors where he serves as Treasurer. He and his wife, Joyce, live in Duluth.

Lynn Niemi

Lynn began working for Erie in 1973 in the Accounting Department. Over her twenty-eight years of service, she held various positions in the department, the last fifteen years involved developing Erie's financial statements, budgets, and monthly and annual reports. Between 1997 and 1999, Lynn was assigned as a member of the Cleveland–Cliffs "Beyond 150" group implementing a corporate-wide computer systems network. Lynn and her husband, Tom, live in Aurora.

Tom Niemi

Tom was raised on the Iron Range and graduated from the University of North Dakota with a mechanical engineering degree. He began working for Erie in 1968 in the Plant Engineering Department. Tom completed an Erie sponsored and financed correspondence program in Electrical Engineering. In 1974, he transferred to Taconite Harbor as department engineer and advanced to Assistant General Foreman Yard and Dock. In 1984 Tom was assigned to Supervisor of the Harbor Area and in 1987 was promoted to Superintendent Harbor. In 1990 Tom was promoted to Superintendent Railroad & Harbor and relocated to Hoyt Lakes, retiring in 2000. Tom is a member of the Schroeder Area Historical Society and the St. Louis County Historical Society, and a life member of the Minnesota Historical Society. He and wife, Lynn, live in Aurora.

Tom Michels

Tom arrived in Hoyt Lakes in 1959 from a small farming community in west-central Minnesota when his father took a job at Erie. Tom graduated from Aurora–Hoyt Lakes High School and attended Mesabi Junior College for two years. He started working at Erie in 1969 and held several jobs in different departments until entering the Maintenance Mechanic apprenticeship in 1975. Tom finished that apprenticeship three years later and was assigned as a mechanic (later, by agreement became a Millwright) in the Pellet Plant. He became active in our Local Union in 1983 and remained active until Erie's closure. Along the way, Tom returned to college, receiving a Bachelor of Science degree in Business Administration in 1991 from Bemidji State University. Tom served on the Hoyt Lakes Fire Department for twenty-two years. He continues to remain active in USWA activities as President of the local SOAR (Steelworker Organization of Active Retirees) chapter. Tom and his wife, Vicky, raised two boys and continue to reside in Hoyt Lakes.

Elroy Rafferty

Elroy, a native of Bemidji, Minnesota, moved to Hoyt Lakes and started at Erie in 1960 as a production truck driver in the Mining Department. Over the years, Elroy "rode 'em all" as he experienced a wide range of haul trucks over the years, starting with the 45-ton mechanical drive haul trucks up to the state-of-the-art 240-ton electric drive trucks. He was also instrumental in developing the Mining Department's truck driver training program and served for many years as the mine's truck driver trainer. Elroy was active in the local USWA union from 1972 to 1993, serving one term as Vice President. Elroy retired in 2000 and is a SOAR member. He and his wife, Judy, live in Hoyt Lakes.

Jim Scott

Jim Scott is a third-generation miner, and after graduating from the University of Minnesota, he started at Erie in 1970 as an Electrical Engineer in Plant Engineering and then moved into Maintenance as Electric Shop AGF. He served as Technical Assistant in Maintenance before transferring to Pickands Mathers's central

services staff, working on computer applications in maintenance management and process control, eventually becoming Manager-Process Automation, a position that included managing the Hibbing Lab. Jim returned to Erie as Area Manager Technical Services and remained at the Erie location after closure as Cliffs Erie's Manager. After retiring in 2003, he continued at the Erie location as Assistant Project Manager for PolyMet's NorthMet Project. Jim and his wife, Linda, live in Palo, Minnesota.

Mike Sterk

An Iron Range native, Mike graduated from Michigan Technological University with a mining engineering degree and began working for Jones & Laughlin Steel at their natural iron ore mines in Minnesota. After working several years for the company in Pennsylvania, Mike returned to Minnesota, eventually transferring to Erie in the Mining Department, retiring as Area Manager of Mining in 2000. Mike then began a second career with U.S. Steel at Minntac, eventually becoming Area Manager of the Mine Production Department. Mike is a board member of the Iron Range Historical Society. He, wife Linda, and daughter Lauren live in Hoyt Lakes.

Jim Westbrook

Jim moved from Iowa to Hoyt Lakes in 1960 when his father began working at Erie. Jim graduated from Aurora–Hoyt Lakes High School in 1962 and entered the U.S. Army, completing three years' active duty in West Germany. Jim returned to Hoyt Lakes in 1965 and started his career at Erie shortly thereafter. In 1966 Jim entered Erie's welder apprenticeship program, completing it three years later. He worked in all departments at Erie until retiring in 2001 with thirty-six years' service. Jim continued his military career in 1970 when he joined the Navy Reserve (Seabees), retiring as a Chief Petty Officer after thirty years of service. Jim and his wife, Mary, reside in Hoyt Lakes.

Ted Williams

Ted Williams was a Pennsylvania native and served three years as a Navy veteran during World War II. He attended the University of Pennsylvania and graduated as an Electrical Engineer. Based on previous power plant experience, Ted accepted a position at Erie in 1956 during the construction of the power plant at Taconite Harbor. Ted was assigned to inspect, test, and approve the installation of power plant generating and auxiliary equipment. In 1959 he transferred to the Pellet Plant as General Foreman–Electrical. He held several positions of increasing responsibilities in the Maintenance Department and in 1976 was promoted to Superintendent of Maintenance, where he remained until retiring in 1989. Ted was an original member of the Erie Mining Company History Project and was an enthusiastic, hardworking team member who made a significant contribution to the project. Ted passed away on December 31, 2015, and his spirit is still with us—he will always be part of the team.

This Team spent most of their working lives in Minnesota's iron mining industry, primarily at Erie and represents a cross-section of Erie's workforce from startup to closure. They experienced the highs and lows of the iron mining industry—

strikes, layoffs, evolving technology, process improvements, changes in organizational structure and culture, and ultimately closure. They worked shift work, day shift, holidays, weekends, and in every operating department and most staff departments and are uniquely qualified to write the book you are about to read.

This book was a cumulative effort over a five-year period. While the Team has done its best to prevent errors, some may remain, and for those we accept responsibility.

Our hope is that you will gain a greater appreciation for the vision, dedication and determination that characterized the pioneers who worked at Erie, built a new community, and a new life for Minnesota's Iron Range. This story is intended to keep the memory of Erie Mining Company alive and to serve as an inspiration to you, the next generation of pioneers.

Ronald L Hein

Early on November 7, 2000, the one-billionth ton of ore was delivered to Erie's Coarse Crusher.

ACKNOWLEDGMENTS

Researching, writing, and publishing a history book is a daunting process and requires significant support to be successful. This book is a testimony of that fact. After the formation of the Erie Mining Company History Project Team, we immediately began involving other people.

Special thanks are due **Paul and Cindy Hayden** from *Lake Superior Magazine* for providing a roadmap for the process of getting a book from an idea to print.

We are indebted to the St. Louis County Historical Society Board of Governors and Executive Director **JoAnne Coombe** for partnering with us on this nonprofit project. The Society staff including **Julie Boles, Kathleen Cargill,** and **Charlene Langowski** provided the administrative and financial services that were critical to success.

In preparation for the Project Team to conduct oral history interviews, we are grateful to **Barb Sommer**, an internationally known authority on oral history interviewing, who trained the Team. Her initial assistance was invaluable to help us conduct over 150 interviews.

We are eternally grateful to **all the people who volunteered to give oral history interviews.** Their interviews and the information they provided are invaluable as a source of information for the book and for future research.

We would like to express appreciation and special thanks to transcriptionist **Deb Anderson** for her dedication to ensuring the interview transcriptions were complete, accurate, and correctly formatted.

Fund-raising was essential for completion of the project. Lakehead Constructors Inc. and President **Brian Maki** were instrumental in getting the project off the ground by making the first significant donations. We are grateful for the roles **Bob S. Mars Jr.,** Chairman, Emeritus, W. P. and R. S. Mars Co., **Scott Brown,** President and CEO, Pickands Mather Group, and **Ralph Berge,** Principal, Visualized Energy, LLC, played in hosting meetings for potential contributors in Duluth and Chisholm, Minnesota, and Cleveland, Ohio. Minnesota State Senator **David Tomassoni,** Minnesota State Representative **Jason Metza**, and Iron Mining Association President **Kelsey Johnson** worked diligently to pass a bill in the Minnesota State Legislature that provided a significant grant for the project. **Mark Philips,** the Iron Range Resources and Rehabilitation Board Commissioner, his Board and staff also worked to help us obtain other grants. We give special thanks to the numerous other individuals and companies for their financial support.

The Project Team members did a tremendous amount of research and conducted oral history interviews and that work was passed on to **Bill Beck** and **Larry Sommer**, who, with their own research, produced the basic manuscript for the book. Their work was then reviewed, edited, and rewritten by the Project Team members.

The following individuals and organizations provided primary sources for the Project Team research, including documents, photographs, maps, and charts:

- **Chris Welter**, Archivist at the Iron Range Research Center for the LTV Steel Mining Company Collection and the Henry Whaley Collection.

- **Susan Sowers**, Library Director for the photo and document collection at the Hoyt Lakes Public Library.

- **Ann Sindelar**, Reference Supervisor at the Western Reserve Historical Society, Pickands Mather collection in Cleveland, Ohio.

- **St. Louis County Historical Society** mining industry collection located at the Kathryn A. Martin Library at the University of Minnesota, Duluth.

- **Iron Range Historical Society,** McKinley, Minnesota

- Natural Resources and Research Institute, Duluth, Minnesota, Executive Director **Dr. Rolf Weberg,** Senior Geologist **Dean Peterson**, and External Affairs Manager **June Breneman.**

- **Andy Saur,** Graphic Designer at Krech Ojard and Associates, Duluth, Minnesota. Andy did an exceptional job of creating custom graphics.

- **Terry O'Neil**, Mine Inspector, St. Louis County, for providing safety and production statistics.

We acknowledge and thank **Sandy Karnowski**, District Manager, Public Affairs-Minnesota, Cleveland-Cliffs Inc., for her support of the Project, including securing contributions, a Cliffs Foundation grant, and transfer of Hibbing Lab historical artifacts and graphic materials to St. Louis County Historical Society.

We are particularly grateful to historians **Marvin Lamppa** and **Pam Brunfelt** for their continued support of the project and their encouragement to write a book documenting the history of Erie Mining Company from the unique perspective of a group of former employees.

Katy Lofquist, Director of Operations, Iron Mining Association of Minnesota, has provided encouragement and support, and we are thankful for her willingness to help whenever requested.

The Mayor of Hoyt Lakes **Mark Skelton**, City Clerk/Treasurer **Rebecca "Becky" Burich,** Deputy Clerk **Tammy Snetsinger**, Custodian **Kileen Trueblood**, and other City Hall staff members provided us meeting and working space at City Hall for the past five years. We appreciate their cooperation and support by providing a convenient and functional place to work.

We appreciate the encouragement, technical assistance, and patience provided by our Donning Publishers team, Production Supervisor **Katie Gardner**, Editor **Pam Koch**, Graphic Designer **Jeremy Glanville**, and Publisher Representatives **Barry Haire** and **Geoffrey Bass**.

Lastly, we express our deep gratitude for the support and encouragement of our spouses and families without which this book would not have been written.

"*If gold is precious, iron is priceless.*"

—Andrew Carnegie

Chapter 1

IRON AND STEEL

The history of Minnesota's iron mining industry and that of Erie Mining Company (Erie) is an extraordinary story that forms an important part of the industrial history of Minnesota and of the United States. It is a story that began over a century ago and was directly tied to the economic ebb and flow of the American steel industry, and one that continues today with potential new developments of Minnesota's mineral resources. For more than sixty years, the real story of Erie's immense iron ore mining complex has largely remained hidden in various technical publications and in the hearts and memories of the men and women who worked there and made

it all happen. It is a unique story of a mine, its community, and its people that deserves to be told. A story that seeks to provide a better understanding of the vital ways that Erie and its employees pioneered the methods that shaped Minnesota's iron mining history and produced the essential materials that improve our standard of living.

Most of us take for granted the materials that form the basis of our everyday lives. We seldom contemplate the complicated interactions of finance, technology, labor, markets, environment, and politics required to provide the raw materials necessary to advance our way of life. Mining is the discovery and removal of metals and minerals from the earth that are used in the manufacturing of man's tools and products. One of those minerals, iron ore, is key to modern living and impacts virtually all aspects of life. Iron ore is used to produce iron and steel, critical metals to guarantee a sustainable and healthy economy. Minnesota's iron ore mining industry has been the cornerstone for ensuring the security and economic development of our country since 1884. Erie played a key role in that industry.

The history of Erie can only be understood against the background of the evolution of America's integrated iron and steel industry and the development of iron mining on Minnesota's Mesabi Range. The Erie project was conceived because of the increased raw material needs of the steel industry. Throughout its life, Erie was intimately tied to the economic forces acting on that industry. Erie's only reason for existence was to produce a low-cost, high-quality iron ore product for its customer, the North American steel industry.

STEELMAKING

Steel is one of man's basic materials and the most useful metal known, and as a result, steelmaking has become one of the world's fundamental industries. Every American will utilize nearly fourteen tons of steel during their lifetime. Steel is made from iron, which has three essential raw materials: coal, iron ore, and limestone. Coal is first "cooked" in tall, narrow ovens, which convert the coal into coke.

Large volumes of iron ore, coke, and limestone are proportioned and dumped into the top of a blast furnace and heated by the coke and hot blasts of air to smelt the iron ore into molten iron. As the iron ore and limestone melt and move downward in the furnace, the impurities in the iron ore combine with limestone and float on top of the heavier molten iron. The liquefied impurities, called slag, are removed from the furnace, and the molten iron, called hot metal, is drawn off, collected, and moved to the next step in the steelmaking process.

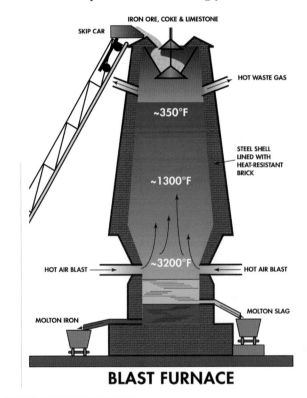

BLAST FURNACE

Blast furnace cross-section.

Above: Typical steel mill with iron ore stockpiles, ca. 1950s.
Left: Aerial photo of Erie Plant Site and Taconite Harbor (insert).

Typical blast furnace layout at a steel mill.

The iron from the blast furnace is made into steel by introducing oxygen into the molten iron to further purify the iron. Other materials are added to produce specific grades and alloys of steel. The steel is then cast into various shapes and formed into sheets, wire, or structural members. Because of the multiple steps and the large quantities of raw materials involved, steel mills have developed into some of the world's largest industrial complexes. A steel company that depends heavily upon its own raw material sources and facilities to produce its high-quality finished steel products is considered an integrated steel company.

Iron has been produced for centuries, but it is only within the last 150 years that an industry has been developed to produce steel in the quantity necessary to advance civilization. Major technological innovations that spurred the creation of the American steel industry occurred in the 1850s when the Bessemer converter and open-hearth steelmaking processes were developed and made possible the conversion of large quantities of iron into steel and at a greatly reduced cost. Following the American Civil War, rapid industrial growth across the country demanded even more iron and steel products and, consequently, new sources of iron ore.

In 1844, iron ore deposits were discovered in northern Michigan. Later exploration revealed even larger quantities of high-grade (i.e., high iron content), low-cost iron ore throughout the Lake Superior Region. It was not until the Soo Locks were constructed at Sault Ste. Marie, Michigan, that ore boats finally were able to travel between Lake Superior and the other Great Lakes. Large volumes of iron ore could now be economically and efficiently shipped from ports on Lake Superior to the nation's steel mills. The introduction of steam-powered ore boats, constructed of steel and capable of carrying large cargos, together with new mechanized unloading equipment at the receiving docks, made possible dramatic increases in the amount of iron ore that could be delivered to the nation's steel mills.

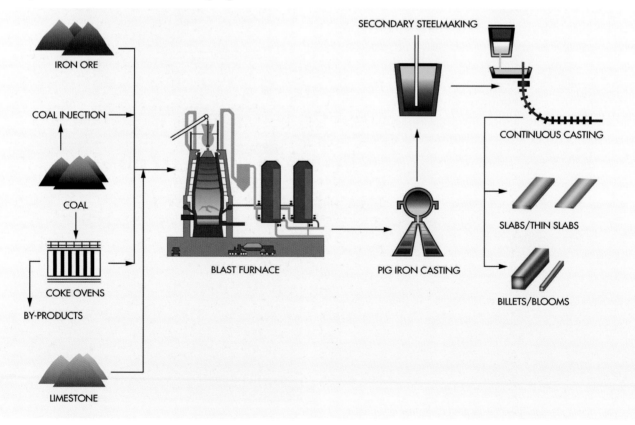

The blast furnace is at the center of the integrated steelmaking process.

The Soo Locks made it possible to inexpensively ship iron ore from the Lake Superior Ranges to the steel mills on the lower Great Lakes.

In the early years, iron ore from the Minnesota Ranges was shipped on ore boats from the ports of Duluth, Superior, and Two Harbors.

Hulett unloaders, introduced in the late nineteenth century, enabled faster unloading of iron ore.

In America, the tremendous demand for steel products, innovations in steelmaking technology, discovery of new raw material sources, and transportation improvements, all occurring simultaneously, contributed to the creation of the world's greatest integrated steel industry.

THE MESABI RANGE— MINNESOTA'S BURIED TREASURE

In the early part of the twentieth century, the land surrounding Lake Superior became one of the world's great mining centers as the region's rich iron ore deposits were being rapidly developed. Although iron occurs naturally and after aluminum is the second most abundant metallic element of the earth's crust, only in certain locations does it occur in sufficient quantity to be considered a resource.

The most common forms of iron ore minerals include, from top to bottom, hematite, magnetite, siderite, and pyrite.

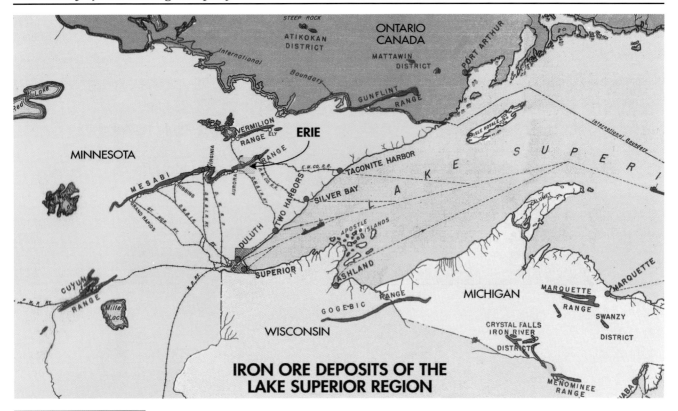

IRON ORE DEPOSITS OF THE
LAKE SUPERIOR REGION

Lake Superior Region showing ore deposits and transportation routes.

Iron is almost always found as a mineral in combination with oxygen, silicon, and other elements. The most common iron minerals occurring in nature are hematite (Fe_2O_3), magnetite (Fe_3O_4), siderite ($FeCO_3$), and pyrite (FeS). However, these iron-bearing rocks are not called ore unless the rock contains enough iron to make its extraction profitable.[1]

About two and a half billion years ago, a shallow sea covered portions of the Lake Superior Region. Over long periods of geologic time, iron-bearing silt, iron, and silica, flowing down from the surrounding hills, settled to the bottom of the sea and formed thick layers of iron-bearing sediments. These sediments were then buried and compressed under more sand, clay, and other sediments to create an iron-bearing sedimentary rock formation. Later, as the land uplifted and the sea receded, the iron formation was subjected to volcanic intrusions, heat, and pressure that transformed it into a hard, flint-like rock called taconite.[2]

Taconite is an extremely hard, abrasive gray-black rock that contains about 30 percent iron in the form of magnetite—a magnetic iron oxide mineral. Taconite is composed chemically of silica, iron silicates, iron oxides, and carbonates in varying proportions. Minnesota state geologist Newton Winchell first used the name taconite in 1891, as a term to generally describe all the rocks that comprise the entire iron formation.[3]

The Mesabi Range, the largest of the Lake Superior Region iron ore mining areas, has produced over two-thirds of the total region's iron ore. It is here where the sedimentary iron formation on the south side of the Giants Range in northeastern Minnesota is near the surface. The Giants Range was once part of an ancient mountain chain that today exists as a series of low ridges forming the divide between the Lake Superior, Mississippi River, and Hudson's Bay drainage systems. The Mesabi Range's iron formation, named the Biwabik Iron Formation, averages about 1.5 miles wide and extends roughly

GEOLOGICAL CROSS SECTIONS

ALGOMAN GRANITE

ELY GREENSTONE

KNIFE LAKE SLATE

VIRGINIA SLATE

GABBRO

IRON FORMATION

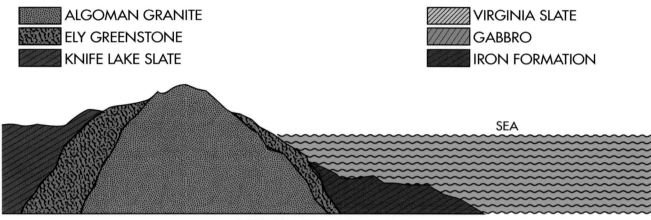

AFTER GIANTS RANGE GRANITE
(2.6 BILLION YEARS OLD)

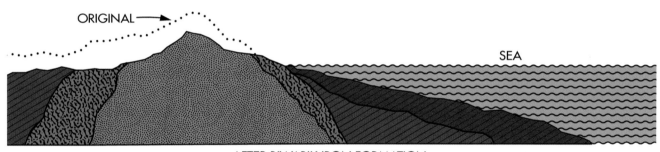

AFTER BIWABIK IRON FORMATION
(1.8 BILLION YEARS OLD)

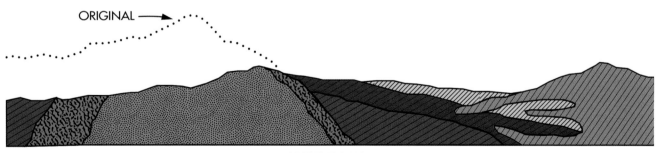

PRESENT DAY

Geological history of the Biwabik iron formation encompasses billions of years.

Taconite formation in a mine with overburden above.

120 miles in length, from north of Birch Lake near Babbitt to west of Pokegama Lake near Grand Rapids. The iron formation dips gradually to the southeast and varies from 500 feet to 700 feet in thickness. Glacial deposits, called overburden, consisting of sand, gravel, boulders, and silt cover most of the formation.

The Biwabik Iron Formation consists of four major taconite layers named from the top down as Upper Slaty, Upper Cherty, Lower Slaty, and Lower Cherty. Each layer and its subdivisions have different chemical and physical properties that produce different types of taconite. Owing to the varying amounts of magnetite present and how the magnetite is combined with other minerals, certain taconite subdivisions are ore while others are not. Contrary to common belief, the entire thickness

of taconite in a given area cannot simply be mined as ore. But, generally across the Biwabik Iron Formation, the Upper Cherty and Lower Cherty taconite layers do contain enough magnetite that these layers can be processed as taconite ore.

Included within the Biwabik Iron Formation are the naturally enriched zones or pockets of iron ore containing much higher iron content than the surrounding taconite. These zones of concentrated iron, like raisins in a cake, formed natural or "red" ore deposits that made the Mesabi Range famous. Natural ore is classified as either high grade, also called direct shipping, or low grade, which required improving before it could be used in a blast furnace. The natural ore deposits were formed within the Biwabik Iron Formation where the silica present in the taconite rock was

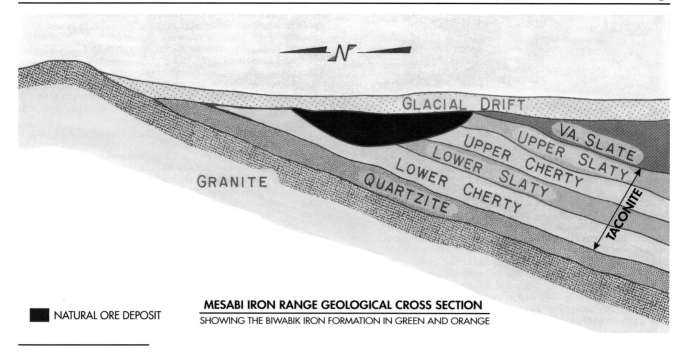

NATURAL ORE DEPOSIT

MESABI IRON RANGE GEOLOGICAL CROSS SECTION
SHOWING THE BIWABIK IRON FORMATION IN GREEN AND ORANGE

The Biwabik Iron Formation showing the four taconite layers with natural ore deposit.

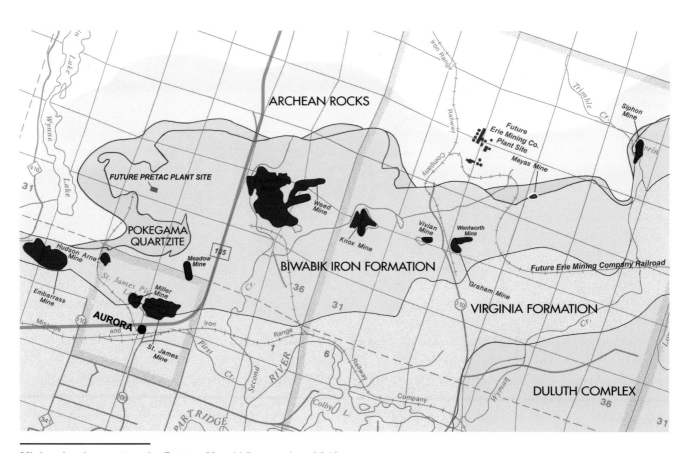

Mining development on the Eastern Mesabi Range, circa 1940.

Typical open pit natural iron ore mine on the Mesabi Range, ca. 1960s.

dissolved and removed by water moving through the rock. This process not only removed the silica but also oxidized the iron minerals, leaving them essentially in place and increasing iron content. The removal of silica created porous, soft iron ore that was easily mined in contrast to the unaltered hard taconite rock. However, across the Mesabi Range this natural enrichment of the taconite was not uniform, but typically occurred in areas where the iron formation had been broken and fractured by geologic actions such as folding and faulting, creating passages for the water to flow. The process of oxidizing the magnetite mineral in the taconite to form hematite occurred over many thousands of years and is like "rusting," which helps explain the "red" color of the natural ores.

Pickands Mather's Embarrass Mine near Biwabik, ca. 1950s.

The Mahoning Mine operated by Pickands Mather near Hibbing was part of Hull Rust complex—the largest open pit natural iron ore mine on the Mesabi Range.

MESABI RANGE NATURAL ORE MINING

Minnesota's iron ore was first noted in 1850 and again in 1865 on lands east of Lake Vermilion in northeastern Minnesota. Following a report of gold in the same area, a new group of prospectors and explorers headed for Lake Vermilion. Although gold was not discovered in commercially minable quantities, iron ores were identified, sampled, and packed out for analysis. Encouraging analytical results eventually led to the development and first shipments from the Soudan Mine on the Vermilion Iron Range on July 31, 1884.

Occurrences of iron formation on the Mesabi Range were first observed at Embarrass Lake near Biwabik in 1866 but were considered too low-grade to be of economic interest. The first large natural iron ore deposit was discovered at Mountain Iron in 1890 and was followed the next year by a natural ore discovery at Biwabik. In 1892, the first Mesabi Range iron ore was shipped from Mountain Iron Mine. In 1894, the large Hull Rust-Mahoning ore body at Hibbing was located, and by the end of the century, extensive mine development across the entire Mesabi Range was under way. Relatively easy to extract and requiring minimal processing, the initial Mesabi Range direct shipping natural ores were ideally suited feed for the blast furnaces of America's early twentieth century steel mills. Minnesota's Mesabi Range fast became the most productive iron mining district in the world and the source of a significant portion of the iron ore used to manufacture iron and steel that formed the basis for modern industrial development of the United States.[4]

The natural ores would be the first to be mined and were key in establishing Minnesota's leading position in the iron mining industry. Taconite would only emerge as the depletion of these natural ores accelerated following two world wars and the industrial growth in the first half of the twentieth century.[5] The story of Erie and its pioneering work in developing taconite on a commercial basis would have to wait to take its place in iron mining history.

Typical of the depletion of Minnesota's natural ore mines, Embarrass Mine, ca. 1960.

PICKANDS MATHER

The rapid increase in demand for steelmaking raw materials during the latter part of the nineteenth century led to the creation of numerous enterprises focused on the development, expansion, and transportation of raw material resources. However, as annual steel production and demand fluctuated, many of these marginally financed, poorly managed raw material companies failed and their assets were taken over by larger, more efficient organizations. Pickands Mather & Co. (Pickands Mather) was founded in 1883 as a partnership between three Ohioans, James Pickands, Samuel Mather, and Jay Morse. The company, headquartered in Cleveland, was an exception and one of the few that survived. Formed to do business in iron ore and blast furnace pig iron, the firm's initial assets amounted only to 1,800 tons of iron ore in stockpile at Ishpeming, Michigan, two small iron ore mines on Michigan's Marquette Range, and part ownership in a wooden ship with a 1,700-ton carrying capacity. From these meager beginnings, Pickands Mather eventually would become a leading worldwide supplier of raw materials and services to the steel industry.

In the 1890s Pickands Mather grew quickly, adding to its iron ore mining and shipping holdings by managing several new ore mines and vessels. Pickands Mather also began serving as sales agent for products from some of the largest blast furnaces and coal mines in Ohio and Pennsylvania. Although Pickands Mather would never retain significant ownership interest in any iron ore mines, it did provide complete management services and operating expertise to mine owners and steel company customers. Pickands Mather would evaluate the feasibility of developing ore deposits on an owner's property and, if viable, would design a detailed plan for mining and processing the ore. The mine owner then could contract with Pickands Mather to manage, construct, and operate the mine for a set fee. Pickands Mather provided all the services necessary, including engineering, technical,

In 1901, the Corsica underground mine was the first iron ore mine developed and managed by Pickands Mather in Minnesota.

and administrative staffing, operating supervision, as well as hiring and training the workforce. Pickands Mather vessels would transport the ore to lower lake ports, provide unloading services at its docks, and coordinate transportation of the ore to the steel mills.

Until the turn of the century, Pickands Mather mined most of its iron ore in Michigan. In 1901, the company assumed management of its first Mesabi Range iron ore mine, the Corsica Mine located near the village of McKinley. Pickands Mather expanded its Minnesota mine management services rapidly, and by the end of the decade, Pickands Mather's Mesabi mines were shipping more than ten million tons annually.

In 1894, after years of leasing and managing the boats of other companies, Pickands Mather formed the Interlake Company to manage its own iron ore and coal shipping and Great Lakes dock activities. Pickands Mather's shipping business also grew rapidly, to the point where by 1912 it managed the second-largest fleet on the Great Lakes, with thirty-seven boats. In 1913, Pickands Mather consolidated its various shipping interests into the Interlake Steamship Company (Interlake Steamship) and by 1916 had expanded the fleet to fifty-two boats.

Pickands Mather's first coal mining venture, Mather Collieries in Pennsylvania, began operation in 1919 and, during the next forty-five years, supplied its American and Canadian steel companies with more than thirty-three million tons of coal.

Corsica underground mine developed into an open pit mine by the 1920s.

The first ore carrier in Pickands Mather's Interlake Steamship Company fleet was the *V. H. Ketcham*.

In 1923, Pickands Mather became manager of one of the Mesabi Range's most famous mines, the Mahoning Mine in Hibbing. By the time it was exhausted in 1973, Pickands Mather produced more than 129 million tons of iron ore from the Mahoning.

By the 1920s, Pickands Mather was the second-largest iron ore mining company in the United States. This was a ranking that the company would hold for several decades. Pickands Mather was the only company actively mining ore from all six of the U.S. iron ranges in the Lake Superior Region and by 1932 operated twenty-three iron ore mines.

Around 1900, Pickands Mather began acquiring blast furnaces to produce pig iron. In 1929, it merged these blast furnace operations into a subsidiary, Interlake Iron Corporation, the world's largest producer of pig iron for sale on the open market. Around this time Pickands Mather also expanded its coal mining interests into West Virginia and Kentucky.

In the early 1930s, Pickands Mather was among the first to recognize that the reserves of Lake Superior Region natural ores were limited and began researching how to commercially mine and process Minnesota's taconite. In 1940, Pickands Mather formed Erie to carry out this work, which continued unabated during World War II at a research laboratory in Hibbing, Minnesota, and by 1946 a flow sheet for processing taconite had been developed (detailed in chapter 2). A demonstration plant to test the process with full-sized equipment was constructed near Aurora, Minnesota (detailed in chapter 3).

By 1953, the taconite pellets produced at the demonstration plant successfully passed blast furnace tests, and in December Pickands Mather announced that it would build a 7.5 million ton per year taconite mine and processing facility. Construction would take more than four years to complete and cost more than $300 million

The Erie Plant Site under construction, ca. 1950s.

(detailed in chapter 4). Erie's success would lead Pickands Mather to expand its iron ore interests in the United States, Canada, and Australia to become one of the world's largest producers of pelletized iron ore.

In 1960 Pickands Mather's partners reorganized the firm into a corporation to provide a more efficient structure for meeting future capital requirements. In 1969, Pickands Mather was sold to Diamond Shamrock Corporation (Diamond Shamrock), a Cleveland-based shipping, chemical manufacturing, and oil refining company. Diamond Shamrock held Pickands Mather for just four years and in 1972 sold Pickands Mather to the Moore-McCormack Company (Moore-McCormack), a shipping company with a large fleet of ocean-going vessels.

Global competition and the high cost to produce and ship steelmaking raw materials adversely affected Pickands Mather's profitability in the 1970s and 1980s. Finally in July 1986, the economic shock of the reorganizational bankruptcy of one of Pickands Mather's largest customers, LTV Steel Corporation (LTV Steel), caused Moore-McCormack to sell the Pickands Mather iron ore and coal business to Cleveland-Cliffs Inc. (Cliffs).

Moore-McCormack retained control of Interlake Steamship until 1987 when it was sold as a private company. Today only segments of the original Pickands Mather remain as part of Cliffs. The Pickands Mather name continues with Pickands Mather Coal Company LLC, which ships coal and other bulk commodities via railroad, truck, and lake vessel. It also purchases coal at the mine and sells it directly to customers, as well as providing technical assistance to coal companies and distributors.

DEVELOPING MINNESOTA'S LOW-GRADE ORES

The recognition of the eventual depletion of Minnesota's natural ores and awareness of the need to improve the low-grade natural ores was evident in the 1920s. The development and application of beneficiation to improve low-grade Mesabi Range natural ores was already underway by several mining companies. But the process of developing a mine and a processing plant for the taconite ores of the Mesabi Range was time-consuming, extraordinarily expensive, and took decades of research to accomplish. To better understand the history of Erie, it is important to be aware of the orderly steps involved in this complex development process.

An ore body is a mineral deposit that contains enough accessible material to be mined and processed to generate enough value to more than cover the cost of mining and processing. The first step in developing a mine is finding the ore body through exploration. Geologists can estimate what is below the ground by studying outcrops where rock is exposed above ground or by digging test pits to access the rock. They also conduct magnetic surveys with instruments that can measure changes in Earth's magnetic field. Many iron-bearing minerals, including taconite, are magnetic and can be located with magnetic surveys.

When a taconite deposit is indicated by these initial surface investigations, exploration drills can be used to sample the solid rock many feet below the surface. These drills utilize a hollow, diamond-embedded bit with an inside diameter ranging from one to two inches, which is connected to hollow drill pipe. As the diamond bit cuts through the hard taconite rock, a sample many feet long is collected inside the drill pipe. This sample is called the drill core. Geologists visually classify the drill core for the presence of various minerals. Because taconite is typically found in identifiable layers with somewhat uniform characteristics, the geologist selects specific sections of the core for analysis. The drill core sections are split or cut lengthwise, with at least one half sent to a laboratory for analysis and the remainder usually saved.

Early core drilling rig on the Mesabi Range, ca. 1890s.

29

Typical drill core showing taconite sample alongside a hollow diamond drill bit.

The first step of taconite sample analysis is to crush the sample so that a well-mixed, smaller representative sample can be obtained. This representative sample is further reduced in size so that tests can be performed to determine the chemical properties of the taconite, such as the amount of iron, silica, and other elements. A Davis Tube (detailed in chapter 2) test is then performed to determine how much of the sample is magnetic.

In the case of Erie, the result of Pickands Mather's exploration and analysis effort was to identify a large, accessible taconite ore body located near the Village of Mesaba (Mesaba) on the eastern Mesabi Range.

The next step in mine development is to determine the type of beneficiation process required to upgrade the taconite to a usable product. Determining the correct processes involves testing samples of taconite in various pieces of laboratory equipment, and then connecting those pieces of equipment in a pilot

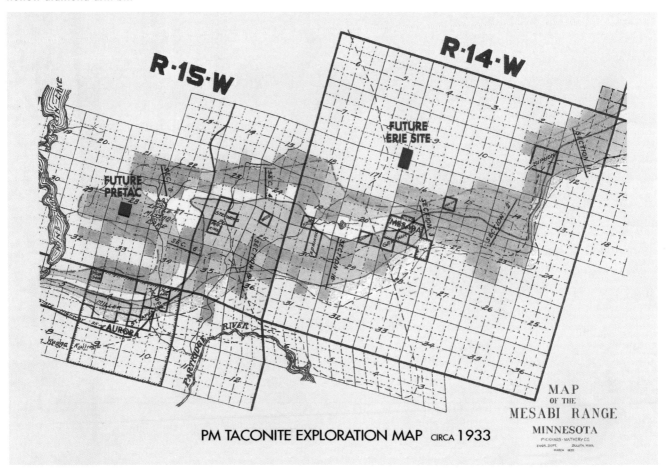

PM TACONITE EXPLORATION MAP CIRCA 1933

MAP OF THE MESABI RANGE MINNESOTA

An early Pickands Mather taconite exploration map of the east Mesabi Range with future Erie sites added in red.

MESABA[14]

Mesaba, locally called "Old Mesaba," was the very first community on the Mesabi Range and was located about a mile south of the future Erie mine and processing complex. In the mid-1880s, Mesaba Station was established as a stop along the Duluth & Iron Range Railroad (D&IR) during construction of the route between Two Harbors on Lake Superior and the Vermillion Iron Range. A short distance away, a sawmill was erected.

The Village of Mesaba was incorporated in 1891 shortly after iron ore was discovered farther west on the Mesabi Range and quickly grew as an outfitting point for prospectors and mine developers. At the time, it was reported that Mesaba had a population of about one thousand residents and around three hundred buildings located on the site, including fifteen hotels, six saloons, a town hall, fire hall, two schools, several general stores, restaurants, and a post office. Later, water and electrical systems were installed, modernizing the village.

However, the fortunes of Mesaba declined rapidly as nearby mining activity was sporadic, lumbering operations moved, and rail lines were extended to new mines and communities being built farther west. In 1947, the last three residents voted to dissolve the Village, and in the late 1990s, the final remnants of "Old Mesaba" were absorbed by Erie's mining operations.

Mesaba station on the D&IR railroad between Two Harbors and Tower.

Plan map of Mesaba town site.

View of Erie Plant Site from remnants of Mesaba.

Last remaining structure in Mesaba—Graham Mine railroad load out pocket.

TACONITE MINING & PROCESSING FLOWCHART

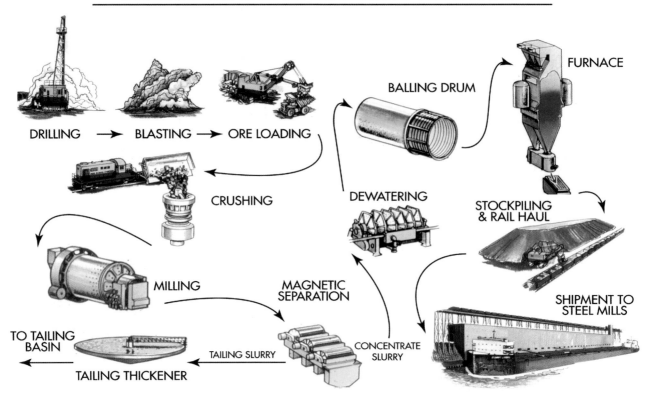

DRILLING → BLASTING → ORE LOADING

CRUSHING

BALLING DRUM

FURNACE

DEWATERING

STOCKPILING & RAIL HAUL

MILLING

MAGNETIC SEPARATION

SHIPMENT TO STEEL MILLS

TO TAILING BASIN

TAILING SLURRY

CONCENTRATE SLURRY

TAILING THICKENER

Typical taconite mining and processing flowsheet.

plant to create a process flow sheet. To determine the most promising flow sheet, multiple configurations of process equipment are tested and evaluated in limited production trials in the pilot plant. Then a single line demonstration plant using commercially available full-size equipment is designed based on the flow sheet developed in the pilot plant. The demonstration plant is constructed to process mined taconite and operate for an extended time to refine operating procedures and to determine full-scale mine and plant operating costs. The demonstration plant eventually could lead to the construction of a commercial plant.

Mineral processing ("ore dressing") is the process of upgrading or beneficiating low-grade ore to a more valuable product. The desired mineral first must be separated from the rock. To do this, the desired mineral must have some characteristic that is different from other minerals in the rock to allow separation. In the case of iron ore, the main characteristic is that iron minerals are heavier than most other minerals in the rock. In the case of taconite, many iron minerals are also magnetic.

Cross-section of a gyratory crusher.

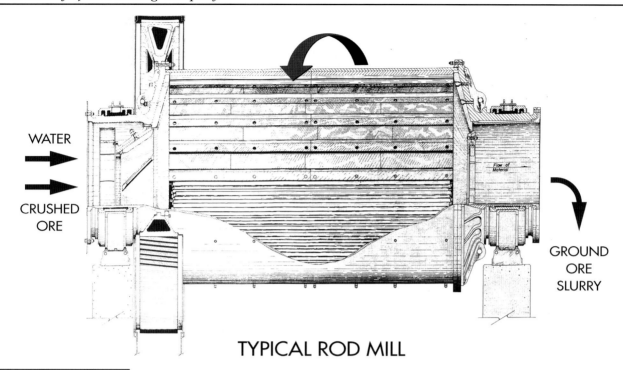

WATER

CRUSHED
ORE

*Flow of
Material*

GROUND
ORE
SLURRY

TYPICAL ROD MILL

Cross-section of a rod mill.

The first step in mineral processing is size reduction, making little rocks out of big rocks. For taconite, size reduction allows subsequent steps in the process to separate the iron particles based on the characteristics that differentiate iron from other minerals in the ore. Size reduction is accomplished by crushing and grinding. Crushers break the ore by squeezing it against itself and metal surfaces so that it fractures into smaller pieces. Taconite crushers typically reduce large, up to five-foot in size, ore down to less than three-quarter-inch in size.

Because further size reduction is required before the separation of iron minerals can take place, grinding mills follow crushing. These mills are large horizontal rotating cylinders that contain grinding media (i.e., hard metal rods, balls, or the ore itself). Ore and water are added, and as the mill rotates, the ore is ground among and between the media and mill wall liners. Grinding mills produce a slurry of ground ore and water that can either flow by gravity or be pumped to further processing steps. Because of the hard, abrasive nature of taconite rock, there are significant costs for electric power,

wear material (i.e., crusher and mill parts and liners), and grinding media in crushing and grinding.

Size classification is used in crushing and grinding to bypass processing of ore particles that are already small enough and recycle ore particles that are too big. Equipment used for size classification includes screens, screw classifiers, trommels, and cyclones.

The next step in mineral processing is concentration, which separates the valuable mineral from other minerals in the ore slurry. Concentration results in two products—one a concentrate containing mostly the desired mineral, and the other a waste product called tailing, mainly consisting of silica. For taconite, magnetic separation is the primary method of concentrating the iron minerals using belt or drum magnetic separators. For nonmagnetic low-grade iron ores, separation based on the different densities of the minerals is used and is called gravity separation. Equipment designed for gravity separation includes jig concentrators, shaker tables, and spiral concentrators.

Another concentration method is flotation. Chemicals are added to the ore slurry in a tank

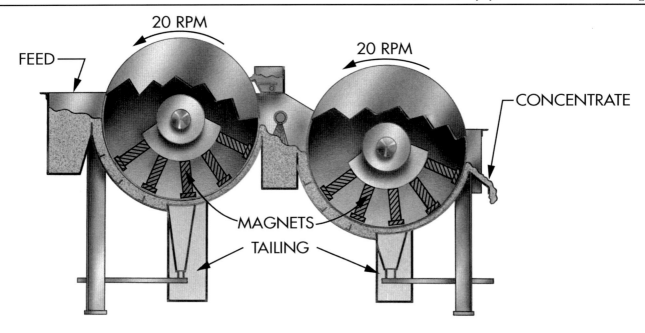

CROSS SECTIONAL VIEW OF MAGNETIC SEPARATOR

Typical magnetic separator consisting of rotating drums with stationary, high-intensity, interior magnets that caused the iron ore slurry feed to be separated into a magnetic concentrate and a nonmagnetic tailing.

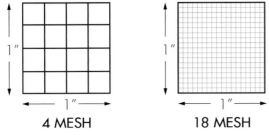

MESH: NUMBER OF SCREEN OPENINGS PER LINEAR INCH

In taconite mineral processing, the ore size is reduced to smaller than 325 mesh (finer than face powder), and the 30 percent iron content of the ore is upgraded to about 65 percent in the final concentrate.

to which air is injected. Typically, two different chemicals are used—a collector that makes air bubbles adhere to a selected mineral and a frother that strengthens the air bubbles. The bubbles with the selected minerals attached float to the top of the tank and are collected as froth. The froth is either the concentrate or the tailing depending on the processing objective—collect the desired mineral or remove impurities. The remaining slurry exits the bottom of the tank as concentrate or tailing. Flotation is a more expensive and more complex process than either gravity or magnetic separation. Flotation of taconite removes additional silica from the final iron concentrate.

Agglomerated iron ore products included sinter, pellets, nodules, and briquets.

34

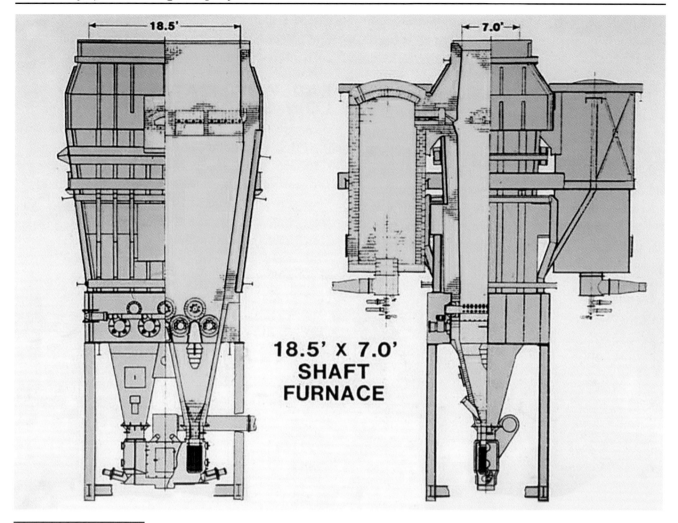

18.5' X 7.0'
**SHAFT
FURNACE**

Cross-section of a vertical shaft pelletizing furnace.

To facilitate further processing, the concentrate slurry must be dewatered, which is accomplished by thickeners and filters. Thickeners are large tanks in which the solids portion of the slurry settles to the bottom and most of the water portion overflows and is recycled. The thickened bottom slurry is collected and goes to the next step in the process.

The thickened slurry is filtered to remove additional water. Filters utilize either vacuum systems or mechanical presses to force the water through a fine screen membrane while retaining the solids on the membrane. Filtered taconite concentrate is typically a very fine size, and the particles must be bound together (agglomerated) to form a more usable product.

The final step in processing taconite is to produce an iron product desirable for the blast furnace. Four types of iron ore agglomerating processes were initially investigated: briquetting, nodulizing, sintering, and pelletizing.

Briquetting consists of adding a binder to the iron concentrate and pressing the concentrate into briquettes using mechanical methods. In nodulizing, coal is added to the concentrate and heated in an inclined rotary kiln. The rotation of the kiln causes the concentrate to clump, and the heat in the kiln improves the adhesion of the clumps. For sintering, a thin bed of a coal, limestone, and concentrate mixture is heated on a traveling grate. Heated air, passing through the grate and bed, fuses the concentrate particles into irregular, solid clumps or clinkers.

The preferred method for agglomeration of taconite concentrate is pelletizing, which is forming the concentrate into small balls and then hardening the balls by heating. The filtered iron concentrate is typically mixed with a binder and then fed into an inclined rotating drum or disk. The rotation and incline results in a "snowball" effect by which the concentrate/binder mixture forms balls—called green balls at this point. The green balls are then hardened in vertical shaft furnaces, traveling grate machines, or grate-kiln machines. In a vertical shaft furnace, green balls move downward against an ascending flow of hot gases, which first dry and then harden the green balls into pellets that exit the bottom of the furnace. A traveling grate carries a bed of green balls through different drying, heating, and cooling zones. In a grate-kiln, green balls are fed onto a moving grate on which the balls are dried and partly hardened. The grate discharges the partially hardened pellets into a heated rotating kiln to complete the hardening. Erie utilized the vertical shaft furnace pelletizing method.

EARLY UTILIZATION OF LOW-GRADE ORE DEPOSITS

As early as 1907, the Oliver Iron Mining Company (OIMC), a subsidiary of U.S. Steel Corporation (U.S. Steel), began experimenting with crushing and washing western Mesabi Range low-grade natural ores to increase their iron content. In 1909, the company constructed Minnesota's first ore concentration plant at Trout Lake near Coleraine. The success of the Trout Lake concentrator eventually led to much of Minnesota's low-grade natural ore being upgraded by washing and concentrating. By the late 1950s, there were eighty concentrating plants scattered across the Mesabi Range.[6] These plants typically produced a coarse

Mesabi Iron Company plant looking north, ca. 1920s

and fine product that were shipped separately. The coarse product could be added directly to the blast furnace. But the fine product had to be processed in a sinter plant before being added to the blast furnace.

Daniel Jackling, a metallurgist and mining promoter, had solved major problems associated with mining low-grade copper ores at the Bingham Canyon Mine in Utah by using large-scale open-pit mining, crushing, and concentrating technology.[7] In 1912, several Duluth businessmen who controlled a large taconite deposit on the eastern Mesabi Range near Birch Lake asked Duluth mining engineer Dwight Woodbridge to investigate ways to mine the deposit. Woodbridge was familiar with Jackling's Utah copper operation and suggested that the same technology might work on Minnesota taconite.[8] Woodbridge met with Jackling to discuss a test. Initially, two railcar loads of taconite were sent to an experimental plant in Moose Mountain, Ontario. The tests showed that fine grinding and magnetic separation could produce a concentrate that contained about 60 percent iron.[9]

Jackling and his backers formed the Mesabi Syndicate and consolidated control of substantial acreage of taconite lands on the eastern Mesabi Range. The group agreed to underwrite the construction of an experimental taconite processing plant in Duluth and to establish a small mine near present-day Babbitt. In 1918, a sample of 1,840 tons of the plant's sintered taconite that contained over 62 percent iron was shipped to eastern steel mills. It was used to make steel for armor-piercing artillery shells for the U.S. military in World War I.[10]

Based on the success of the experimental Duluth plant, the Mesabi Syndicate decided to move ahead with the development of a full-size commercial plant. The estimated cost of the project was $3 million, including construction of a mine, plant, town (later called Babbitt), and power plant. They expected to sell taconite sinter for $7.50 per ton.[11] In November 1919, the Mesabi Iron Company (Mesabi Iron) was organized to succeed the Mesabi Syndicate and construction began in 1920. Equipment from the Duluth experimental plant was salvaged and moved to the new plant.[12] As designed, the plant would have the capacity of 400 tons of sinter a day. To meet this goal, the miners would have to mine 1,200 tons of taconite daily.[13] The blasted taconite ore was loaded into side dump cars and hauled by rail four miles to the crusher where it was crushed in three stages, followed by grinding, magnetic separation, and then sintering.

The Mesabi Iron operated the plant from 1922 to 1924. However, when Lake Superior iron ore prices dramatically decreased, Mesabi Iron could not compete and operations ceased. Although not financially successful, the Mesabi Iron proved that a high-grade iron product could be produced from Minnesota taconite.[14] Nearly thirty years after Mesabi Iron ceased operation, Reserve Mining Company (Reserve) reopened the plant in 1951 and operated it for four years as a demonstration plant.

Mesabi Iron Company plant modified by Reserve, ca. 1950s.

Chapter 2

THE HIBBING LABORATORY

Under the guidance of managing partners Henry Dalton and Elton Hoyt 2nd, Pickands Mather was among the first to research low-grade natural ores and taconite in the 1930s and 1940s. Pickands Mather's interest in the beneficiation of iron ores began in 1931 when the firm recognized that the reserves of natural ores from the Lake Superior Region were limited. Pickands Mather convinced iron ore customers Bethlehem Steel Corporation (Bethlehem), Youngstown Sheet and Tube Corporation (Youngstown), and Interlake Iron Corporation (Interlake) to begin a program to beneficiate low-grade natural ores. It soon became apparent that there were not enough of those ores available to guarantee a long-term iron ore supply, and investigations turned to the study of taconite. The group began acquiring lands north of Aurora where diamond drilling results, confirmed by the University of Minnesota Mines Experiment Station, indicated taconite containing a high magnetic content. During 1938 and 1939, the group conducted extensive geophysical surveys, and collected and analyzed thousands of feet of drill core and test pit samples across the Mesabi Range, from Aurora to Nashwauk. This evaluation indicated that sufficient magnetic taconite reserves existed and resulted in the formation of a new company. In 1940, Erie was formed to develop taconite and find ways to process and utilize the Mesabi Range's vast reserves of taconite commercially.[1]

THE EARLY YEARS

The first step in taconite research was to conduct a costly and wide-ranging core drilling of the taconite formation to determine the chemical and physical characteristics of the material, which is extremely variable. Drill crews worked day and night to obtain numerous drill cores, which were then tested to determine the quantity and characteristics of the taconite. The results of these investigations would govern the type and design of the test equipment used in the next phase of research—pilot plant testing.

The opening of the Hibbing Laboratory (Lab) and the hiring of Fred DeVaney as its director coincided with American entry into World War II. The U.S. War Production Board had assigned critical priority to iron ore production, research, and development, so the new laboratory was in line with U.S. defense aims. The Lab came into being in September 1942 and was tasked with finding a way to process taconite commercially.[2] The Lab expanded with the addition of a large pilot plant building in 1943, which provided room necessary for the installation of various types of machinery required to process taconite ore.[3]

DeVaney assembled a staff of twenty-five chemists, metallurgists, and engineers in 1942 and early 1943. He hired Earl Herkenhoff to assist him with setting up the Lab and Gordy Planck, a pharmacist, to run the chemical analysis portion of the Lab. John Banovich was placed in charge of the pilot plant, and Frank Udovich was hired to supervise the field crew. Udovich and his crew sampled the low-grade ore stockpiles from twenty-three mines that Pickands Mather operated in Minnesota and brought the samples to the Lab for testing. The samples were initially manually crushed to a very fine size (smaller than 100 mesh), screened, and then tested in a Davis Tube Magnetic Separator.

Above: Exploration drilling in northeastern Minnesota.
Left: The Hibbing Lab, ca. 1940s.

Field samples were collected from across the Mesabi Range.

FRED DEVANEY

Fred DeVaney was born in South Dakota and grew up in Minneapolis. In 1923 he graduated from the University of Minnesota in metallurgical engineering, and received his master's degree from the University of Alabama. For several years, he worked for the U.S. Bureau of Mines at the Missouri School of Mines in Rolla, Missouri, developing processes for flotation of iron ore to separate unwanted silica. In 1938 he was transferred to Chamberlain, South Dakota, to build and operate a manganese plant.

DeVaney has been referred to as the driving force of the Lab. Hired by Pickands Mather in 1942 to establish the company's iron ore research facility, DeVaney made significant contributions to the development of taconite beneficiation on

Fred DeVaney at the Lab.

a commercial scale. His background as a metallurgist and his leadership enabled the skilled team he assembled to develop the processes Erie used at its Preliminary Taconite Plant, which eventually made possible the development of Erie's commercial taconite plant.

While at the Lab, DeVaney also worked on flotation processes for treating nonmagnetic iron ores and developed the flow sheets for beneficiation plants that would process ores from Pickands Mather–managed properties on the western Mesabi Range. DeVaney worked closely with Edward Davis at the University of Minnesota Mines Experiment Station to develop and test taconite-processing technology.

As Erie worked to develop and refine the equipment and processes required to beneficiate taconite ore, portions of the process and techniques were patented. Dan DeVaney recounted how his father made many trips to Washington, D.C., where Pickands Mather retained a patent attorney who worked to file all their patent applications. Fred DeVaney was granted thirty U.S. and forty-six foreign patents in the field of mineral processing. DeVaney moved to Pickands Mather's Duluth office in 1956 and retired as the company's Director of Metallurgy and Research in early 1966.

DeVaney was recognized as one of the nation's foremost authorities on low-grade minerals research. In February 1958, the American Institute of Mining, Metallurgical and Petroleum Engineers (AIME) named DeVaney the recipient of the Richards Award for "his contribution in grinding and pelletizing and for his direction of research, metallurgical engineering, and development of methods of taconite beneficiation."[20] In 1960, DeVaney was named an Outstanding Graduate by the University of Minnesota.

In retirement, DeVaney worked as a consulting metallurgist. He and his wife split their time between their home in Duluth and winters in Florida. DeVaney lived to see the development of the second wave of taconite plants on the Mesabi Range in the early 1970s.[21] In 1973, DeVaney was named a recipient of the Legion of Honor Award for fifty continuous years of membership in the AIME.[22]

A year after it opened, the Lab was in full operation. In a report to Alex Chisholm, the general manager of Pickands Mather's mines, the staff reported that 1943 had been extremely productive. Crews had conducted three miles of magnetic surveys north of the Mahoning and Pool mines in the Hibbing area, and had located potential tailings basin sites where the waste generated from processing ores could be disposed. By far the most exciting event at the Lab was the completion of the pilot plant, which was equipped with machines that processed taconite at the rate of five tons per hour.

Magnetic concentration tests conducted on many samples collected from lands near Mesaba revealed that a concentrate averaging 64 percent iron and 7 percent silica could be achieved.[4] The area around Mesaba eventually became the site of Erie's mine and Commercial Plant.

The report stated that flotation testing of iron ores with the intention of concentrating the iron particles had been abandoned because of high costs and the difficulty of filtering (dewatering) the frothy iron concentrate. The concentration of iron particles from the ore using flotation proved inefficient; however, the removal of the silica (waste) was more successful. The Lab stated, "The conclusions to be drawn from our work so far is that the progress has been more rapid than we expected and that the results lead us to believe that the process, metallurgically (ed. technically), will be successful."

The 1944 plan as outlined in the report was ambitious. The staff planned to complete a field map of the Hibbing area, maps to show core drilling, topographic surveys of potential tailing basin sites near Hibbing, Buhl, and Mesaba, and magnetic surveys north of the Mahoning mine to outline a suspected area of high magnetic iron content. Field crews intended to sink test pits to furnish bulk samples for large-scale pilot plant tests and would examine and classify samples from previous core drilling as well as from outcrops on the taconite lands. The Lab staff planned to evaluate various mining methods and equipment, including investigating methods used in mining hard ore and rock, performing tests to determine blast hole drilling costs, and estimating overall mining costs.[5]

Screening and weighing samples.

Testing a sample in a Davis Tube.

DAVIS TUBE

Designed by Edward Davis, the Davis Tube operated on the principle of a strong electromagnetic field surrounding an oscillating two-foot-long glass sample tube in which the magnetic particles from a pulverized ore sample were separated. A weighed sample was placed in the tube and the oscillations started. The magnetic particles were captured by the magnetic field, and the nonmagnetic portion was collected at the bottom. Both the magnetic and nonmagnetic portions were removed, dried, and weighed. With this instrument the percentage of magnetic and nonmagnetic material in an ore sample was determined, and further chemical analysis was performed on these for more detailed information about their composition. The Davis Tube provided iron ore researchers and ultimately plant operators with a quick and easy way to determine the amount of iron that could be recovered from taconite.

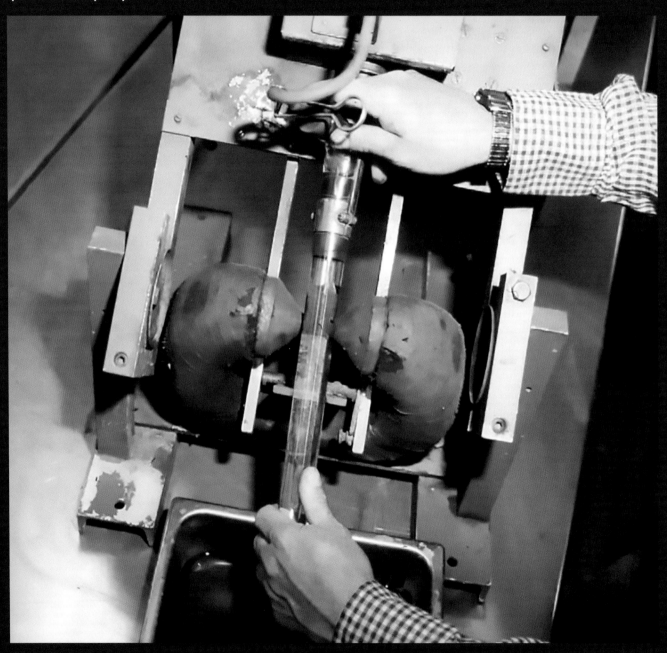

Davis Tube in operation.

Operating an early magnetic separator.

Bench scale flotation testing.

The plan continued the investigation of various concentration methods on low-grade ores and taconite including jigging and tabling, flotation, magnetic separation, roasting (a process for changing nonmagnetic iron particles to magnetic iron, which could then be extracted by magnetic separation), and combinations of these methods.[6] Plant tests would be conducted using the concentration method found to be most effective and then a flow sheet of that method developed. Visits to large concentrating plants already in operation were proposed, followed by a preliminary design of a commercial plant for estimating costs. The staff also planned to investigate all applicable agglomeration methods including sintering, nodulizing, pelletizing, and briquetting. The staff was interested in the work done in a shaft furnace at the Mines Experiment Station; however, heat requirements (fuel required per ton produced) were excessively high. The Lab revised the process, utilizing the idea of heat recuperation with finished pellets serving as a kind of heat exchanger for the incoming air. The idea was further refined by designing a furnace with an upper stove in which raw pellets were heated by the addition of air from a combustion chamber and a lower stove in which ambient air was passed through the hot pellets as they descended through the furnace

to cool them and carry heat to the raw pellets above for easier operation and heat conservation. The Lab built a thirty-inch-diameter circular shaft furnace of this configuration for testing. The furnace ran for many months, producing excellent quality pellets at acceptable heat requirements.

Fred DeVaney's son Dan, who worked at the Lab during summers in the late 1940s, recalled the trials involved in agglomerating the taconite concentrate before processing in the furnace. Dan said, "They tried extruding it like toothpaste. They tried briquetting it. They had all kinds of things that they tried to do and found out that pelletizing was the best."[7] As part of the agglomeration study, the staff planned to make further tests on the most promising process while investigating fuel supply and plant operating costs.[8]

During 1944, the Lab staff was involved in a host of additional studies critical to the operation of a large-scale taconite plant, including methods for stockpiling and reclaiming winter production, water and electric power supply, and sources and costs of supplies, such as grinding media, fuel, explosives, and the like.[9] "As much of this work will be done during 1944 as can be done," the Lab staff pledged to Chisholm.[10]

The Lab's experiments into the beneficiation of taconite ores took many different paths, utilizing various processing techniques and types of equipment, but test work eventually focused on fine grinding followed by magnetic separation of the iron particles as the most effective method. As knowledge and experience progressed with magnetic separation in the pilot plant, the design of equipment and flow sheet for full-scale trials in a future demonstration plant followed. Although there was a virtually unlimited supply of taconite ores in Minnesota, the process of making them commercially usable was recognized as a large and expensive undertaking.

Extracting the microscopic particles of iron from the hard taconite ore was one problem; recombining them in a form suitable for transportation to the nation's blast furnaces and be a more desirable blast furnace feed was another. DeVaney and his team tried various methods and, after years of testing, determined that pelletizing was the best.

Pickands Mather historian Walter Havighurst called the development of magnetic separation of taconite ore at the Lab "hit and miss, trial and error, hope and disappointment. But out of experiment with many mechanisms came the production of efficient magnetic separators."[11] The pellets produced at the Lab were approximately 64 percent iron and actually converted to hot metal in the blast furnace more efficiently than the Mesabi Range's natural ore.[12]

OTHER EARLY TACONITE ACTIVITIES

The rapid depletion of natural ore from the Minnesota iron ranges during World War II sped up investigation into utilizing the taconite of the Mesabi Range. Edward Davis, a researcher at the University of Minnesota Mines Experiment Station, had been working on taconite research since 1915 and was familiar with the wartime work done by DeVaney and his staff at the Lab as well as that being done by Reserve. Davis called the accelerated depletion of natural ores "serious times for the Old Mesabi," but he had great faith in the determination of the iron and steel companies to maintain a domestic supply of iron ore.[13]

Adding green balls into the Lab's circular test furnace.

Engineers evaluate lab results to plan for future ore mining development.

In 1939, Reserve was organized by Oglebay Norton and Company (Oglebay Norton), which had acquired the ore properties and assets of Mesabi Iron, including the mine and plant at Babbitt. Oglebay Norton named their new company "Reserve" because they viewed taconite as a long-term future resource that would not be needed for many years.[14] With the outbreak of World War II, Oglebay Norton investigated the possibility of restarting the Mesabi Iron mine and plant but decided against doing so when it was determined that it would take at least a year to put the plant back in production, and that there were technical problems that could not be solved by using the existing plant machinery.

Erie and Reserve were not the only companies studying the potential utilization of low-grade iron ore during the 1940s. U.S. Steel and its iron-mining subsidiary, OIMC, had a longtime interest in low-grade iron ores. In 1943, U.S. Steel president Benjamin Fairless told reporters that the company had been working on plans to use low-grade iron ores since the mid-1930s, with much of that test work being done in the company's New Jersey Laboratory.[15] Later in 1943, the OIMC acquired a four-story building in West Duluth to house its iron ore research and development activities. Much of the test work involved research into the concentration of low-grade iron ore formations.[16] In 1945, OIMC developed plans for an agglomerating plant on the Mesabi Range, which would later become the Extaca Plant at Virginia.[17]

Taconite processing equipment at the University of Minnesota Mines Experiment Station, ca. 1940s.

In 1945, Butler Brothers, a major independent ore producer on the western Mesabi Range, doubled the size of its ore research laboratory at Cooley. Built in 1933 to test making concentrates from low-grade ore, the Cooley laboratory staff worked closely with E. W. Davis and the Mines Experiment Station during the latter half of the 1930s.

Davis's 1949 observation that the nation's steel companies would protect their domestic source of iron ore by developing methods to mine and process the taconite ores of the Lake Superior District proved true. By that time, Erie, Reserve, and OIMC were all in the process of testing the feasibility of taconite mining and processing on the Mesabi Range.

LEADING THE WAY

In a 1971 paper looking back on the history of iron ore mining and processing, Fred DeVaney stated, "the use of high-grade pellets, closely sized and porous, has provided a major increase in the capacity of the blast furnace and resulted in the reduction in the amount of fuel and flux."[18] He noted that the pellets produced using the taconite processing technology developed by the Lab in the mid-1940s had been widely accepted in the steel industry because their use reduced the operating costs (in terms of dollars per ton of hot metal) at the blast furnace to one-half of what it would have been using natural ores.

TACONITE TAX INCENTIVE

In 1940, Minnesota's iron ore tax laws were structured to apply to the state's natural ore reserves. An annual tax, called *ad valorem*, was essentially a property tax assessed in proportion to the present value of the ore in the ground. The rationale for the tax was that because iron ore was an irreplaceable resource, the mining companies should be taxed on their ore reserves at a higher rate by both state and local governments. This tax in turn provided the primary source of revenue for the communities located adjacent to the reserves. However, it was apparent that if these tax rates were applied to the vast taconite reserves required to justify a commercial taconite operation, taxes alone would prohibit development of Minnesota's taconite.

Recognizing that the state's natural ores would eventually be depleted, and that the large expenditures required for taconite development would not occur unless a favorable tax structure was established, Edward Davis, together with state senator John Blatnik from Chisholm and state representative Thomas Vukelich from Gilbert, proposed a change in Minnesota's iron ore taxes.

During the 1941 Minnesota legislative session, the Mesabi Range representatives worked tirelessly to convince fellow legislators that a change in the tax structure, as applied to taconite, was necessary. The Legislature unanimously passed a bill that stated taconite would be taxed on a production basis, and not on its value in the ground like other iron ores. The production tax was set at five cents per ton with an escalator of one-tenth of a cent for each percent of iron content above 55 percent. The production tax was to be paid in lieu of *ad valorem* taxes, and the proceeds shared equally by the state, county, school districts, and local communities. In addition, a yearly, unmined taconite tax was imposed, which required payment of a dollar per acre on any parcel of taconite land producing less than 1,000 tons of concentrate.

By creating a favorable tax climate, Minnesota had cleared a significant obstacle from the path of taconite development. Erie immediately began acquiring numerous leases on state and private taconite lands, blocking out large areas for potential future taconite mining.

Throughout its history, the Lab conducted research and analytical studies for Pickands Mather iron ore mining operations as well as for others. The Lab also studied and recommended other processes such as washing, float-sink separation, cycloning, sintering, and magnetic roasting that could be utilized at other Pickands Mather properties. The Lab was an essential part of the company's efforts to continuously improve the quality and reduce the costs of the ores it produced.

When it was first established, the Lab was called the Erie Research Laboratory or Erie Lab. At other times, it was known as the Pickands Mather Laboratory and finally the Cliffs Research Laboratory. Using the facilities and equipment at the Lab, the processes for producing a usable commercial product from taconite ore were developed and tested. Once the processes for crushing, grinding, separating, concentrating, and pelletizing taconite ore were perfected at the Lab, the technology and equipment were scaled up, first at the Erie Preliminary Taconite Plant near Aurora and then at Erie's commercial taconite plant at Hoyt Lakes. The Lab closed in 2001 and had a long, rich history leading the way from natural ore to taconite.[19]

The Hibbing Lab, ca. 1970s.

Chapter 3

ERIE PRELIMINARY TACONITE PLANT

By 1946 Erie's test work at the Lab had progressed far enough for the company to authorize construction of a full-scale demonstration plant to beneficiate taconite ore and produce a high-grade iron pellet. The plant was called the Erie Preliminary Taconite Plant (PreTac) and was intended to test the process flow sheets developed at the Lab on a commercial scale.[1] From mid-1948 to mid-1952, PreTac was the world's only commercial-scale taconite processing plant in operation. The demonstration plant closed in 1957 after producing more than a million tons of pellets.[2]

PreTac also provided a test site to refine techniques, train operators in the new process of taconite beneficiation, and guide decision making for the future construction and operation of a large commercial taconite plant under consideration.

PRETAC CONSTRUCTION AND OPERATION

On January 23, 1947, officials of Pickands Mather announced that Erie would begin construction in July of a demonstration plant on the Mesabi Range to process taconite ore into pellets. Pickands Mather stated that the plant would cost $1.5 million to construct and would utilize full-size equipment to produce approximately 200,000 tons of pellets a year from 600,000 tons of taconite ore. The plant was being designed to operate using the magnetic separation and agglomeration processes developed at the Lab.

According to *Skillings Mining Review* (*Skillings*), "Several other mining companies have been conducting extensive experiments along the same line, but this is the first attempt to construct a

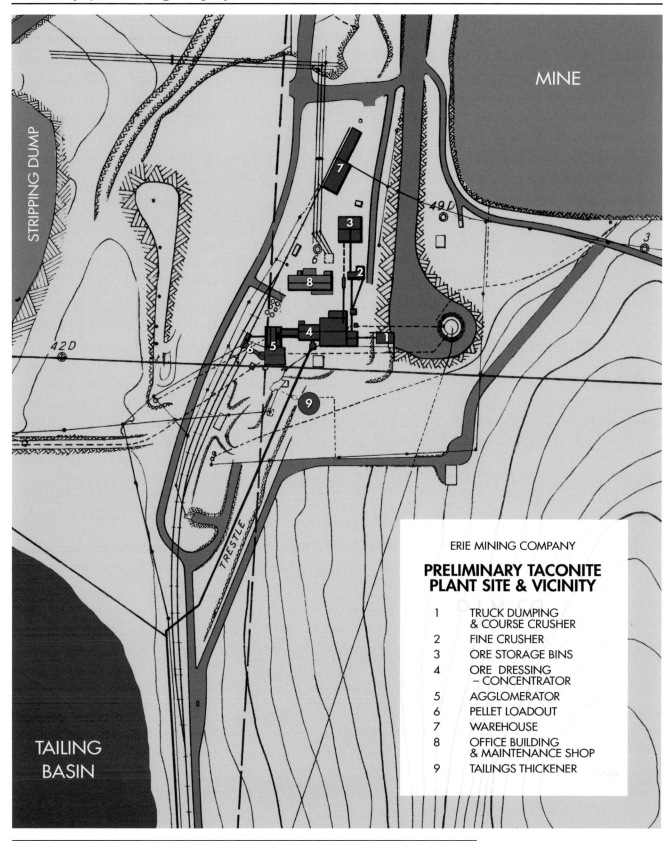

MINE

STRIPPING DUMP

TAILING BASIN

TRESTLE

ERIE MINING COMPANY

PRELIMINARY TACONITE PLANT SITE & VICINITY

1   TRUCK DUMPING & COURSE CRUSHER

2   FINE CRUSHER

3   ORE STORAGE BINS

4   ORE DRESSING – CONCENTRATOR

5   AGGLOMERATOR

6   PELLET LOADOUT

7   WAREHOUSE

8   OFFICE BUILDING & MAINTENANCE SHOP

9   TAILINGS THICKENER

Above: Plan map of PreTac plant area with mine at upper right and tailing basin at lower left.
Left: Aerial photo of PreTac looking southwest with mine in foreground and tailing basin at upper left.

plant with full commercial-sized equipment since the unsuccessful operation of the Babbitt plant (ed. Mesabi Iron) some twenty-five years ago."[3] For its part, Pickands Mather said it had every hope that the new plant would be able to demonstrate that scaling up the processes developed at the Lab would be successful and eventually lead to commercial scale mining and processing of taconite. "If this is the result," one Pickands Mather official stated, "we expect very large investments in plants in Minnesota in the comparatively near future."[4]

PreTac was located about three miles north of Aurora on the eastern end of the Mesabi Range. In the spring of 1947, Erie issued two contracts to start the project. The first was awarded to Peter Kiewit Sons' Co. (Kiewit) to strip 150,000 cubic yards of material to uncover the first 600,000 tons of taconite ore. Kiewit also was tasked with clearing the site for the PreTac facility and building a railroad grade to the mine.[5] The second was to the George F. Cook Construction Co. (Cook) to erect the processing plant buildings, including the circular shaft pelletizing furnace. The Duluth Mesabi and Iron Range Railway (DM&IR) extended a railroad spur from Aurora to the site, and Minnesota Power & Light (MP&L) constructed a 110,000-volt electrical transmission line to service the site.

Construction of pelletizing plant showing vertical shaft furnace with railroad loadout at left.

On June 10, 1947, Erie appeared before the Minnesota Department of Conservation to seek permission to use water from nearby Wynne Lake for the taconite processing at PreTac.[6] It was estimated that approximately 75 percent of PreTac's water needs would be met by recovering water used in the process. By the spring of 1948, Erie had installed the pumps for the water supply from Wynne Lake, a tailing disposal area that was located near the plant and the processing equipment for separating the fine particles of iron from the taconite rock. Three tons of taconite ore would be mined and processed to produce each ton of concentrate.

PreTac construction in late 1947.

PreTac mine in operation with jet piercing drill at left and shovel and trucks at right.

The PreTac process started with drilling and blasting the hard taconite ore. After blasting, the ore was loaded by electric shovel into twenty-two-ton capacity trucks and hauled a short distance to the plant. On July 1, 1948, the first truckload of ore was dumped into the PreTac primary crusher. The date marked the start of an exciting time for the dedicated Erie staff, as the process and equipment in the plant did not work exactly as it had in the Lab. Long months of frustration, disappointment, change, and modification lay ahead.

The plant's flow sheet incorporated three stages of dry crushing (i.e., primary, secondary, and tertiary), which reduced the size of the taconite ore from up to four feet across down to less than five-eighths of an inch. The crushed ore traveled through a series of conveyors to a 6,000-ton capacity storage bin. Because the mine and crushers operated day shift only, this storage was needed to provide a continuous supply of crushed ore for around-the-clock operation of subsequent processes.

The crushed ore was then further reduced in size in two stages of fine, wet grinding, first in a rod mill for primary grinding, followed by a ball mill for secondary grinding. The ground particles from the rod mill entered rougher (or cobber) magnetic separators, which performed initial removal of the usable magnetic iron particles (concentrate) from the nonmagnetic waste material (tailing) to eliminate unnecessary grinding. The magnetic particles from the cobber separators were ground even finer in the ball mill, followed by cleaner magnetic separators, which removed even more nonmagnetic material. The magnetic particles from the cleaner separators then entered a spiral classifier, where the finer particles, typically minus 100 mesh size, overflowed and the larger particles were returned to the ball mill for more grinding. The finer material from the classifier was sent to finisher magnetic separators, designed to reject the remaining nonmagnetic particles and produce the final magnetic iron concentrate. PreTac's grinding and magnetic separation process produced a concentrate analyzing of between 63 and 65 percent iron from taconite ore averaging only about 28 percent iron.

The iron concentrate, now in slurry form, required dewatering with a cylindrical drum filter to achieve the approximately 10 percent moisture needed by the next process. Initially, steel filter cloth, which had worked well in the Lab, was used as the filter medium.

But at PreTac the steel cloth on the filter clogged up and would not dewater the concentrate. Nylon filter cloth was tried with good results and eventually became standard practice for the Commercial Plant.

The filtered concentrate, although usable, required additional processing. Powdered anthracite coal and a binding additive were added to the concentrate, and the mixture fed into a rotating, 8-foot diameter, 24-foot-long drum, where the mud-like concentrate particles were rolled into soft, green balls ranging in size from one-half inch to one and a half inches.

The green balls were then fed into an 11-foot diameter, 60-foot-high circular vertical shaft, oil-fired pelletizing furnace and baked at high temperature for hardening. The furnace, designed by Surface Combustion Corporation (Surface), was the first and only round commercial-sized furnace to be constructed. It had two combustion chambers to provide heat to the furnace and was designed to utilize the heat from the fired pellets before discharge.

PreTac forty-two-inch opening primary crusher.

Interior of concentrator showing the ball mill, spiral classifiers, and magnetic separators.

Drum filter used for dewatering concentrate prior to feeding the balling drum.

Balling drum with trommel screen attached to separate smaller pellets for recycle.

Air was blown into the bottom of the furnace to cool the pellets.[7] The process was intended to produce a finished, hardened pellet that had adequate strength to withstand subsequent loading and unloading during shipment to the blast furnaces as well as being more desirable blast furnace feed.

A seventy-five-ton capacity railroad pellet loading pocket and pumping equipment to handle magnetic separator tailing completed the equipment installation.[8] At the start of operations, PreTac employment totaled approximately 100, consisting of engineers, technicians, and mine and plant workers. Initially, pellets were shipped by rail from PreTac to Erie's owners' steel mills. In June 1950, PreTac shipped its first cargo by boat from Two Harbors.

The PreTac plant showing material flow.

FUTURE PLANT SITE

UPPER PARTRIDGE LAKE

FUTURE SITE OF HOYT LAKES

ALLEN JUNCTION ROAD

PROPOSED SITE OF DIVERSION WORKS

LOWER PARTRIDGE LAKE

Aerial view of Partridge Lakes, Commercial Plant makeup water source, looking north.

First carload of PreTac pellets shipped with the traditional pine tree, signifying the opening of a new mine.

During the remainder of 1948 and early 1949, PreTac operated intermittently as the numerous steps in the process were tested, experiments conducted, procedures refined, and various types and combinations of equipment tried and modified with the objective of producing pellets in the most efficient and cost-effective manner.

By late 1949, the work was showing promise, and the next phase of development would involve performing costly and extensive engineering studies to determine if taconite processing on a larger scale was feasible. In October 1949, Erie asked the Minnesota Department of Conservation for permits to obtain a sufficient water supply for a plant having capacity to produce up to ten million tons of taconite a year on the east end of the Mesabi Range. The application sought permission to build a channel between Upper Partridge Lake (now Colby Lake) and Lower Partridge Lake (now Whitewater Reservoir), along with the construction of a series of dams, spillways, and pumps to create Whitewater Reservoir, capable of providing 12,000 gallons of water per minute for commercial taconite processing.[9]

Elton Hoyt 2nd, president of Erie and managing partner at Pickands Mather, stressed to *Skillings* that "no final decisions have yet been made as to whether the proposed large plants will be built."[10] Hoyt noted, however, that the Commercial Plant absolutely could not proceed until Erie had secured an adequate water supply for the facility. Hoyt also pointed out that the plan did not contemplate changing the normal water level of Upper Partridge Lake and that plant tailing would be deposited on lands that had been acquired north of the proposed Plant Site.[11] Hoyt indicated that if the decision were made to proceed with a commercial operation, "the effect on employment in the Range communities would be substantial."[12]

The successful operation of the PreTac pelletizing furnace was critical to progressing to commercial operation. Aurora native Frank Settimi would spend nearly four decades with Erie and was one of the Erie veterans who worked at PreTac. "At the Preliminary Plant," said Settimi, "they started out with a round furnace, and they were having problems." Feeding the pellets evenly into the round furnace was the major problem because the green balls "had to be handled as carefully as eggs to avoid breakage." The narrow neck between the upper and lower stoves of the furnace sometimes caused bridging, which restricted the movement of pellets and air. Another problem was the formation of clusters of fused pellets (chunks), which caused blockage of the furnace discharge.[13]

Fortunately, Erie partner Bethlehem had been conducting pelletizing experiments of its own since 1942 at its Cornwall, Pennsylvania, iron ore mine. As a result of those experiments, the company had developed a rectangular vertical shaft furnace design incorporating chunk breakers and heat recuperation that was shared with Erie. In 1952, a rectangular shaft furnace, designed by Fred DeVaney and Surface, was installed at PreTac, replacing the circular furnace. Pelletizing operations improved significantly as the rectangular furnace design made for easier feeding of green balls, the minimizing of pellet chunks, and more precise furnace temperature control.[14] The rectangular shaft furnace that Erie eventually adopted for its commercial plant was a combination of the Bethlehem and PreTac designs.

As Fred DeVaney later reminisced, "we were pretty naïve back then, we didn't even have an idea of what size to make our pellets. When we asked the blast furnace operators, they sort of shrugged and said maybe about an inch or so in diameter. So we worked on making pellets of that size, even though it was harder to roll larger pellets than smaller ones. Also, it was taking about 2 million BTU's of heat to fire a ton of finished pellets and we knew that would not be economical. To top it off, our larger green balls were breaking apart in the shaft furnace."[15] By modifying the furnace burner system so that fired pellets preheated the draft air to the burners, PreTac was able to reduce the shaft furnace heat requirements by about 300,00 BTUs per ton of finished pellet.

DeVaney stated, "We continued to make pellets that were about an inch in diameter, and had developed a reciprocating cutter bar for the balling drums that solved a number of problems in rolling the green balls. We continued to fire our pellets in the shaft furnace, but heard that Reserve was having difficulty firing the larger pellets in their traveling grate furnace. They went to a smaller sized green ball that they could fire, and in blast furnace tests these smaller pellets proved to be a better product, and we quickly adopted the smaller pellets because we could roll them more easily. When we were able to produce sufficient tonnage of smaller pellets for a trial, blast furnace production doubled, with a reduction in coke and flux requirements."[16]

Because the low strength and resulting pellet breakage during transit was a significant problem, workers at the Lab focused on the issue and discovered that adding about two to three pounds of starch per ton of concentrate in the balling process gave the pellets a major increase in strength. At PreTac, starch was used effectively to reduce the pellet breakage problem. But starch was expensive, and that was a cost that Erie needed to eliminate from the finished product. In 1950, the Lab began experimenting with using a Wyoming clay mineral called bentonite

Completed PreTac plant.

as a replacement for starch, resulting in pellets with a high strength at a far lower cost. PreTac became the first plant to use bentonite in the pelletizing of taconite—a practice that has since become standard across the industry. One of Fred DeVaney's patents was for this discovery.

At PreTac, the combination of uniformly sized, smaller pellets, with higher iron and lower silica content, and greater control of quality led to a major breakthrough in blast furnace operation.[17]

DEVELOPING JET PIERCING TECHNOLOGY

One of the obstacles to early Minnesota taconite development, as experienced by Mesabi Iron, was the inability to efficiently drill blast holes in the extremely hard taconite rock in a cost-effective manner. During the 1940s, the predominant drilling technology in use on the Mesabi Range centered on churn drilling machines, which essentially chiseled a hole in the rock and was capable of producing blast holes in taconite at a rate of only two to three feet per hour. Because of the large volume of ore needed to supply a commercial taconite operation, this drilling method would not meet requirements.

In addition to making significant advancements to the process of beneficiating and agglomerating taconite, PreTac, in cooperation with the Linde Air

Linde's tricycle-mounted test machine—proved the jet-drilling concept.

Linde's truck-mounted test machine collected operating data for design of a prototype.

Division of Union Carbide (Linde) made a major contribution to future taconite mining with the development of a new drilling technology called jet piercing.

As early as the mid-1930s, Linde, a producer and distributor of industrial gasses and combustion equipment, began experimenting with drilling holes in and cutting stone in much the same way steel plate was cut and pierced with a cutting torch. In 1938, Linde's Robert Atchison began testing this new technique at underground mines located on Minnesota's Vermilion Iron Range. Working with both OIMC and Pickands Mather, Linde was able to use the torch method to produce holes in the harder-than-normal rock in those mines. However, the results were not satisfactory as the smoke and steam created during drilling proved difficult to disperse from the underground workings.[18] It was at this time that Linde first learned about the extensive and extremely hard taconite deposits located on the neighboring Mesabi Range, and of the earlier failed efforts of

Mesabi Iron, in part because of its inability to drill and blast the taconite economically.

After World War II, as interest in taconite development rekindled, Linde's research turned to developing a workable drilling torch for the hard rock of the Mesabi Range. Linde was doing preliminary work on a high-pressure, internal combustion burner that produced a high-velocity flame jet by igniting a mixture of kerosene and oxygen, much like rocket exhaust.

By incorporating this design with the drilling torch, Linde estimated that the drilling rates would increase.[19] It was determined that "thermal spalling" would occur when the high temperature flame jet contacted the rock face, heating the surface rock layer, expanding and breaking it away from the base. The high-velocity jet scoured the rock surface and blew away the broken rock pieces, exposing a fresh surface. Cooling water was inserted near the bottom of the drill hole to cool the combustion chamber and burner, and to increase "spalling" of the heated rock. The water, heated to steam, aided

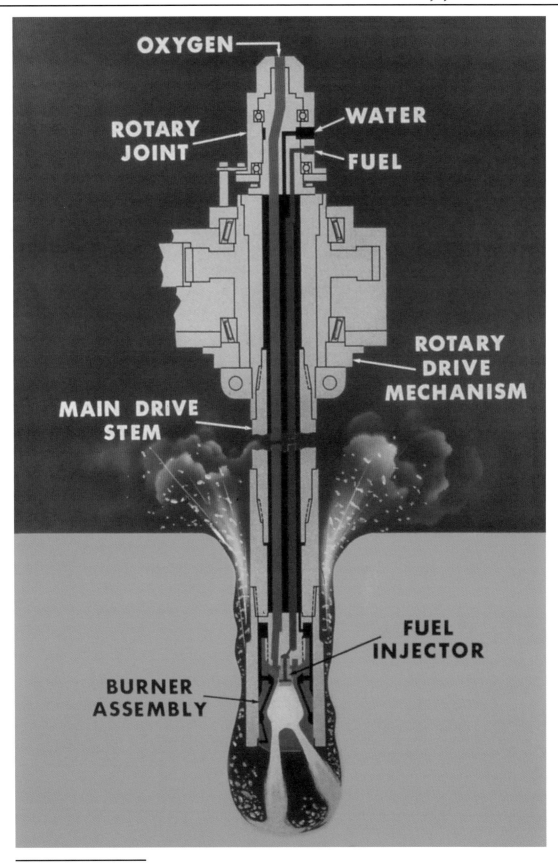

Cross-section of jet piercing assembly in operation.

Prototype Jet Piercing Machine (JPM-1) in operation at PreTac—made taconite mining possible.

in continuously removing the broken rock particles from the drill hole. Drilling tests were conducted at Reserve in the summer of 1947 using this new jet "piercer" burner design.

Pickands Mather, observing the tests at Reserve, expressed interest in testing the new jet piercer drilling method at PreTac. In October 1947, the test results far exceeded expectations, with drilling rates eight to ten times faster than existing churn drills. Blasting performance from jet pierced drill holes was also improved.

George Watts, the PreTac superintendent, and Edward Tyler, pit foreman, were impressed by jet piercing's potential to reduce drilling costs and improve blasting performance. They recommended to Pickands Mather management that a production model jet piercer be acquired for extended tests at PreTac. In early 1948, Linde representatives met with Pickands Mather's Alex Chisholm and members of the company's mining and mechanical engineering departments. Also in attendance were representatives of mining equipment manufacturer Bucyrus-Erie, who would be working with Linde to design the jet piercer machine. At the meeting, the specifications were established. Chisholm authorized Pickands Mather's purchase of the world's first production model jet piercing drill. The new drill, designated Jet Piercing Machine One (JPM-1) was built in Linde's New York factory and delivered on schedule in June 1949 at a cost of $68,919.[20]

The JPM-1 pierced its first hole at PreTac on July 9, 1949. Over the next two years, Erie and Linde improved JPM-1's performance. Drill operating costs were reduced, and personnel were trained in the operation and maintenance of the new machine. Robert Bell, PreTac's assistant mine superintendent, closely monitored the JPM-1 and stated, "The success or failure of operating a large taconite mine depended largely upon efficient drilling and blasting. Not only is it a costly phase of the operation, but the efficiency of the following phases depends upon an adequate supply of well-fragmented material."[21]

With the success of PreTac's JPM-1 established, Erie now had confidence it could deliver the volumes of taconite required to support a commercial taconite facility. JPM-1 was the prototype drilling machine for forty-three subsequent jet piercing drills in service across North America's early taconite mining industry.[22]

START OF THE TACONITE INDUSTRY

Edward Davis, of the Mines Experiment Station, took notice of the work done at PreTac in a 1949 article about the future of taconite development. "Pickands Mather is the second largest mining company operating in the district (ed. Lake Superior) and they have had years of experience in the iron mining business," Davis wrote. "It is very fortunate that such a strong well-financed organization decided to investigate Mesabi taconite because the success or failure of this Erie taconite project will largely determine the future of iron mining in the Lake Superior District."[23] Davis, who was working closely with Reserve on a similar taconite development, had little doubt that the work being done by Erie and Reserve would bear fruit.

Davis stated, "Perhaps within a year or two—certainly within five years," the Mesabi Range could expect a decision on taconite mining. "Much depends on steel production this year and next and upon foreign ore developments and upon the cost of transporting foreign ore to present steel plants and upon the attitude of our government. Foreign traffic is vulnerable during war times, and if tension should increase alarmingly, we can expect taconite developments soon, regardless of economics."[24]

Both Erie and Reserve mining companies supported and benefitted from the research at the Mines Experiment Station where different types of beneficiation processes and pelletizing furnaces were tested. Although both companies selected similar beneficiation processes, Reserve opted for a traveling grate pelletizing furnace while Erie decided on a vertical shaft pelletizing furnace.[25]

Edward Davis.

During the Korean War, from 1950 to 1953, there was another accelerated mining of iron ore from the Lake Superior District. Recognition that the region's remaining reserves of natural ores would soon be unable to meet the demands of the nation's steel industry, and that foreign sources of iron ores were rapidly becoming available, placed added emphasis on quickly developing Minnesota's taconite as a feasible substitute. In 1950, Reserve's ownership was revised with Republic Steel (Republic) and Armco Steel Corporation (Armco) becoming 50 percent joint venture partners. The next year, Reserve began reactivating and modifying the former Mesabi Iron buildings at Babbitt into a preliminary plant for testing processes and equipment, and began permitting and construction activities for a taconite mine and crushing facility at Babbitt with a concentrating and pelletizing facility at Silver Bay, on the north shore of Lake Superior.[26]

Meanwhile, Erie's partners, although encouraged with the progress made at PreTac, were a bit more cautious in committing to the large capital expenditures required to construct a commercial taconite facility in Minnesota. Part of the reason was that Erie's major partners, Bethlehem and Youngstown, were also evaluating foreign sources of iron ore, principally in the newly discovered northern Labrador-Quebec region of Canada. Bethlehem also was actively participating in iron ore projects in Venezuela and Chile. These vast new deposits of iron ore held the potential to displace significant volumes of ore from the Lake Superior District. Simultaneously, Erie's partners were also making substantial investments to upgrade and expand their steelmaking facilities.

The time for Erie to commit to a commercial Minnesota taconite venture was still years away. However, it was at PreTac that the results of the research and experiments performed at the Lab and at the Mines Experiment Station were refined and developed on a commercial scale. PreTac proved that the flow sheets for crushing, concentrating, and pelletizing taconite developed at the Lab were valid and showed that taconite could be economically mined with new jet piercing technology, setting the stage for design and construction of Erie's commercial taconite plant.

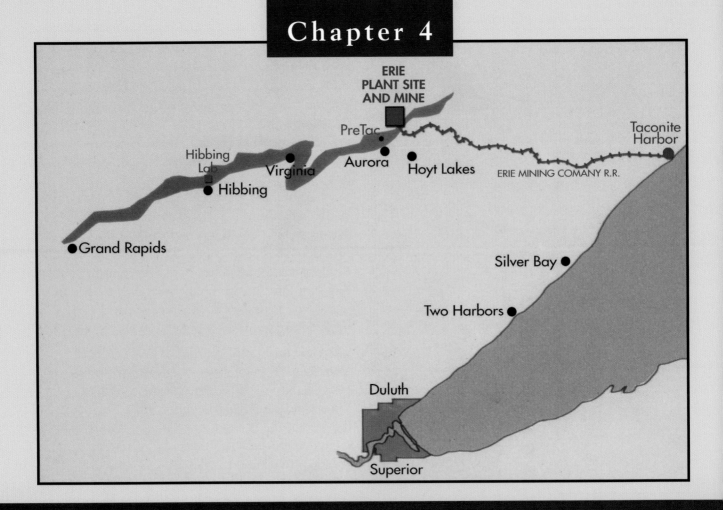

Chapter 4

ERIE
PLANT SITE
AND MINE

PreTac

Taconite
Harbor

Hibbing
Lab

Virginia

Aurora

Hoyt Lakes

ERIE MINING COMANY R.R.

Hibbing

Grand Rapids

Silver Bay

Two Harbors

Duluth

Superior

ERIE COMMERCIAL PLANT—CONSTRUCTION

In 1953, the owners of Erie authorized construction of a $300 million, privately financed project. A commercial taconite mine and processing plant, along with associated maintenance and support facilities, tailing disposal area, and water reservoir, was to be constructed at the Plant Site immediately north of Mesaba and a few miles east of PreTac. The project also included a new harbor, shipping port, and power plant on Lake Superior. A railroad and high voltage power line would connect those facilities to the Plant Site. New communities were to be built to provide housing for the families and thousands of workers required to construct, operate, and maintain this huge new investment. It took nine years to complete the project financing, design, engineering, and construction.

THE DECISION TO BUILD

As iron ore pellets from Minnesota's preliminary taconite plants were being shipped to the nation's steel mills in ever-greater quantities, steel plant engineers were finding that the pellets provided advantages over the typical Mesabi natural ores. Pellets were higher in iron content, more uniformly sized, and had improved smelting properties, which increased blast furnace productivity significantly. However, steel companies were not depending entirely on Minnesota taconite as their sole future iron ore supply. They were developing other iron ore sources of comparable quality and cost to Mesabi ores in Canada, Venezuela, Brazil, Chile, Africa, and elsewhere. If Minnesota taconite was to meet this competition, it was critical that the cost of production be kept to a minimum. The cost of

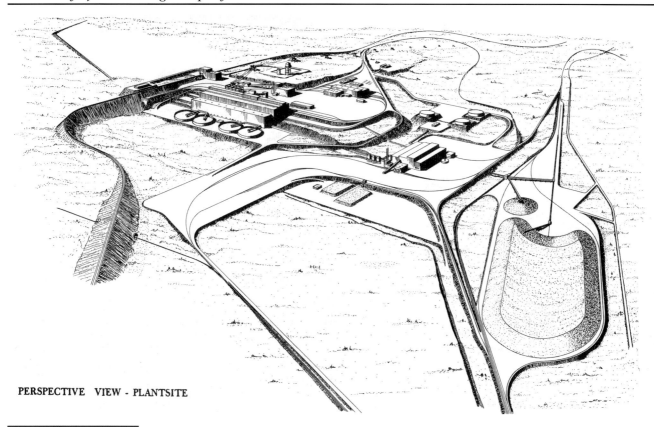

PERSPECTIVE VIEW - PLANTSITE

Above: Perspective view of proposed Erie Commercial Plant.
Left: Map showing location of major Erie Project facilities labeled in red.

3 TONS OF TACONITE = 1 TON OF IRON ORE PELLETS + 2 TONS OF TAILINGS

It requires three tons of taconite to make one ton of pellets.

mining and processing three tons of taconite ore to produce one ton of pellets was recognized early on as an important factor and that only by producing very large volumes could a taconite plant be competitive.

The facilities required to handle these tonnages would be large and complex, and consequently expensive to build and maintain. The extremely hard nature of taconite required special equipment and machinery capable of handling the very abrasive material and standing up to the rugged service, which in turn added to both capital and maintenance costs. The scale for an Erie Commercial Plant would require significant financial commitments by the owners.

In 1952, the ownership of Erie was revised when the Steel Company of Canada (Stelco) became a 10 percent partner, joining Bethlehem (45 percent), Youngstown (35 percent) and Interlake (10 percent). Pickands Mather would continue to manage the operation.

After twenty-two years of exploration, research, plant testing, planning, design, and engineering, as well as an expenditure of more than $22 million, a decision was made. The owners of Erie finally were ready to take on the financial risk and commit to a massive project in Minnesota that would ensure a long-term supply of high-grade pellets. It was confidence in the process and in the future economic growth of the North American steel industry that prompted the decision. On December 4, 1953, Elton Hoyt 2nd, the Senior Managing Partner of Pickands Mather and President of Erie, announced that Erie planned to invest $300 million to build a huge commercial processing plant in northeastern Minnesota, making it one of America's largest privately financed ventures. Erie's operation was planned to produce 7.5 million tons of pellets a year, the highest annual production announced to date.

Hoyt stated that Erie had arranged to sell $207 million of first mortgage bonds at 4.25 percent interest, and that the sale of the bonds was arranged through the investment-banking firm of Kuhn, Loeb & Co. (Kuhn). The bondholders were nine North American insurance firms and Bethlehem.[1]

Elton Hoyt 2nd—Senior Managing Partner of Pickands Mather and President of Erie.

He also noted that Erie's owners had pledged substantial equity capital.[2] Hoyt concluded by stating that the Defense Production Administration the previous year had awarded Erie a "certificate of necessity," allowing the project to produce up to 10.5 million tons of pellets each year. The certificate also carried provisions allowing Erie to take accelerated tax depreciation on up to $298 million of the construction costs,[3] an economic advantage to the owners. Hoyt said the initial annual production of pellets would be 7.5 million tons, but he quickly added that plans were already on the drawing board to increase production.

Pickands Mather's Alex Chisholm told the *Duluth News-Tribune* that he was sure "everyone concerned with the future of our state will see at once the significance of Erie Mining Company's decision to go ahead with its large-scale taconite program. This project, along with the taconite projects of other

FEDERAL GOVERNMENT ASSISTS TACONITE DEVELOPMENT

Appearing before the U.S. House Judiciary Committee in April 1950, Charles White, President of Republic, told the committee members that "we are at the crossroads. Although great new bodies of high-grade [foreign] open-pit ore have been found and commercially feasible methods of reducing known low-grade domestic reserves have been developed, large sums of money are required to develop, mine, and transport such new high-grade ores and to beneficiate low-grade ores on a commercial scale. The expenditure of such sums of money will be encouraged only if the present tax structure on domestic reserves is changed."[30]

White told the Congressional Committee that the industry could not develop the huge taconite reserves of the Lake Superior Region without changes in the tax law. Specifically, he asked Congress to revise tax laws to provide accelerated depreciation (investment write down) of ore-mining facilities and equipment erected to beneficiate taconite ores.[31]

In September 1950, following the start of the Korean War, Congress passed the Defense Production Act of 1950, which granted the President new wartime powers. The Act included provisions to "encourage the exploration, development, and mining of critical and strategic minerals and metals."[32] The government now could allow for quicker depreciation of mining and processing plant capital investments.[33]

The Internal Revenue Service revised the tax code to allow a five-year, rather than the previous twenty-five years, write-down for major portions of approved capital investments required for defense purposes. The accelerated-depreciation tax provisions allowed companies to deduct large portions of capital investments while new facilities were being constructed, which made the expenditures required for new facilities more attractive. The accelerated write-down was exactly what White had recommended and what was needed to spur the significant investments required to advance taconite development.

Erie was the first beneficiary of this tax law change. In the spring of 1952, *Time* magazine reported that "In the drive to expand industrial production, the Defense Production Administration last week ok'd the biggest single quick tax-write-off in its history: a $298 million project for Minnesota's Erie Mining Company."[34]

companies, should allow Minnesota to maintain its position for many years to come as the leading source of iron ore in the United States."[4] Chisholm added that state and local governments would welcome the additional employment and added payrolls generated by the new project. The tax on the Erie bonds alone resulted in a $310,000 revenue windfall for Minnesota's St. Louis, Lake, and Cook Counties.[5]

PREPARING FOR THE PROJECT

Five years prior to Hoyt's announcement, Erie had begun serious planning for a large-scale commercial taconite operation. In the spring of 1948, Pickands Mather began design and engineering work for a

The Two Islands location on Lake Superior's north shore where Taconite Harbor would be constructed.

Clearing and preparation of Plant Site, looking east.

Aerial view of initial west mine area development with Plant Site in background.

proposed railroad line linking the Plant Site located near Aurora to a new harbor, ore dock, and power plant facility on Lake Superior.

Erie's plan to build these new facilities was an important early decision. Erie was unable to

Crews drill holes for blasting rock at the Plant Site prior to construction.

negotiate favorable transportation rates with the DM&IR railroad to haul pellets to the existing ore docks at Two Harbors. The option of shipping through the Reserve dock at Silver Bay was briefly considered but rejected. A new shipping facility was needed, and a site at Two Islands on Lake Superior near the community of Schroeder was selected. The location allowed for construction of a sheltered harbor and provided the shortest lake transportation distance to the owner's steel mills. This facility was later named Taconite Harbor.

In June 1950, because Pickands Mather did not have the expertise to design and build what would be the world's largest ore concentrating plant, Erie negotiated a contract with Anaconda Copper Mining Company (Anaconda), a company with extensive design and operating experience with large-scale ore processing plants in North and South America. The contract included engineering and design, plans and specifications, and construction supervision. Anaconda began work immediately on the project at its New York office and in Minnesota.[6]

Workers excavate rock for the Coarse Crusher foundation.

Walter Williams, Vice President TCC.

As planning and engineering on the Plant Site progressed, Erie initiated the next phase of the project. In 1952, Frederick Snare Corporation (Snare) was contracted for the design of the Taconite Harbor facilities.

At the end of 1952, Erie awarded the first major construction contract to Kiewit, a company with a reputation for completing large construction projects in out-of-the-way places. Kiewit was assigned the task of clearing and preparing the Plant

Leonard Johnston, Project Manager TCC.

Site for construction of the Commercial Plant. The site selected was a granite hill that was one of the higher elevations of the Mesabi Range. Kiewit's work involved excavating 1,240,000 cubic yards of material using a fleet of drills, shovels, and dump trucks, and reshaping over 500 acres of rocky hilltop. The project took over a year to complete as the hard granite hill proved difficult to remove. Extensive cracks in the granite caused blasting to create huge slabs that were difficult to load and haul away.[7]

Work was under way in early 1953 when a small group of field engineers, under the direction of Anaconda, reported to the site. This group supervised Kiewit's Plant Site cut and fill work, and in November 1953 constructed the Commercial Plant's first building, a warehouse.[8]

In June 1953, Col. C. D. Barker was hired as Erie's Director of Industrial Relations. On November 18, 1953, he negotiated a "Taconite Labor Agreement" with the American Federation of Labor that would govern Erie's working relationship with the various union organizations involved in the construction. The project compiled an enviable labor relations record. During the four years that workers were on site, more than twenty-five million man-hours were worked, with fewer than 15,000 man-hours lost to walkouts or strikes.[9]

TACONITE CONTRACTING CORPORATION

Early in 1954, Erie incorporated the Taconite Contracting Corporation (TCC) to manage and coordinate the entire massive project. At the same time, Erie awarded a contract to Foley Constructors of Minnesota, Inc. (Foley) to serve as the prime contractor for Plant Site construction activities, including the erection of Coarse Crusher, Fine Crusher, Concentrator, Pelletizing Plant, General Shops, and Administration buildings as well as warehouses and auxiliary buildings.[10]

Walter Williams was named vice president of TCC and arrived at Pickands Mather's Cleveland office on February 1, 1954, to become familiar with the project scope of work and the companies involved, and to assemble an organization to manage the job.

Plant Site under construction looking southwest with TCC headquarters building at center.

Plant Site under construction looking northeast with General Shops at right center and Warehouse at left center.

Excavation for Coarse Crusher looking south.

Williams first hired Leonard Johnston as Project Manager of TCC. Johnston was formerly Manager of the National Atomic Reactor Testing Station at Idaho Falls, Idaho.[11]

Johnston reported to work at TCC's temporary offices located in the basement of the Aurora City Hall in May, where he joined L. T. Zbanek, Director of Operations, Ray Greenhalgh, Project Accountant, and Glenn Hostetter, Safety Director.

In May 1954, Williams awarded contracts for the expedited construction work to Dravo Corporation (Dravo) for the Taconite Harbor facilities, Arrowhead Constructors (Arrowhead) for the seventy-three-mile long railroad, and J. D. Harrold Company for construction of the first 200 houses to accommodate Erie employees. The houses were to be part of a new, well-planned community called Partridge Lakes Development, later renamed Hoyt Lakes, located six miles south of the Plant Site. Ground was broken and construction began on May 24, 1954.[12]

TCC's headquarters building for the construction project was established on high ground near where the huge plant would be situated. Some called the area "Frustration Hill," but later it was termed just the Old Administration (Old Ad) building.[13] The building served as the nerve center for TCC's employees managing all phases of the construction activities, solving problems and responding to the challenges that the project presented. More than 8,000 engineering design drawings were required for construction, and during the peak period, TCC coordinated the activities of over 245 contractors and approximately 6,200 contract workers, trades people, laborers, engineers, and managers.

PLANT SITE CONSTRUCTION

From the beginning, safety was a watchword on the construction project. TCC's Hostetter designed and implemented a complete fire and safety program, both for TCC employees and on-site contractors. Major contractors were required to establish a central safety committee, and supervisors were required to hold regular safety meetings with their employees. Hostetter and his TCC safety staff also worked closely with the safety inspectors from the State Industrial Commission assigned to the project. TCC investigated all accidents and kept detailed records on accidents and their frequency. The company also purchased four fire engines and provided training for employees who formed the fire brigades.[14]

TCC made great strides in its first year of operation. Walter Williams reported on January 1, 1955, that nearly 14 percent of the entire project was complete. The warehouse building was completed in September 1954, and the General Shops building was 90 percent complete by the end of the year. All topsoil had been removed from the Plant Site, and rock excavation was underway for the foundations of the Coarse Crusher, Fine Crusher, and Concentrator buildings and tunnels for power, piping, and conveyors.

Based on Anaconda's experience in South America, ore from the mine would be hauled by rail up to the dumping level of the primary crusher, where a hydraulically operated system would empty the 85-ton capacity side dump ore cars directly into the primary crusher. The Coarse Crusher building was

Sixty-inch opening primary crusher.

Concentrator excavation and foundation looking south.

Fine Crusher construction looking north.

Concentrator foundations and structural steel erection looking north.

Concentrator building partially enclosed. Note the terrace construction, designed to maximize gravity flow of process materials.

Concentrator interior during construction looking north, showing rod mills at right and ball mills at left.

175 feet long and 110 feet wide and had eight floors with the bottom floor 94 feet below the surface. The building would house a 60-inch primary gyratory crusher, one of the world's largest, followed by four 36-inch secondary gyratory crushers. The crusher foundation, cut deep into solid granite, required removal of 76,400 cubic yards of material.

The broken ore from the Coarse Crusher would travel on conveyor belts a distance of 1,300 feet and up 227 feet to storage at the top of the Fine Crusher building, where the material would be further crushed. The ore would then be conveyed to the Concentrator.

Constructing what would be the world's largest iron ore Concentrator building was a major undertaking. As designed by Anaconda, the 1,100 feet long, 275 feet wide structure would have a rated capacity of 63,000 tons of ore per day and contain ore storage bins, vibrating feeders, conveyors, 27 rod mills and 27 ball mills, 270 magnetic separators, cyclones, thickeners, and pumps.[15]

The Concentrator was designed to fit into the hillside at the Plant Site. During 1954, a total of 450,000 cubic yards of the granite hill was blasted and excavated in a series of long terraces, and concrete foundation piers then set into the rock. Concrete placement was carried on continuously. Temperature checks were performed daily during the concrete curing process, and the structures were enclosed in tarpaulins and plastic sheeting with portable oil, gas, and electric heaters initially providing heat to cure the concrete. During the winter of 1954–1955 as concrete work accelerated, two former Great Northern Railway steam-powered locomotives were purchased, pulled by crawler tractors up a 10 percent grade to the Concentrator level, and used to provide additional heat.[16]

Dan DeVaney explained that the plant was designed to sit on a hillside so that the railroad could dump the ore into the primary crusher and the flow of material was downhill through the Coarse Crusher, then conveyed to the top of

Two steam locomotives provided heat for curing concrete during winter construction.

73

Construction of vertical shaft furnaces.

the Fine Crusher to flow down through the Fine Crusher and then conveyed to the top of the Concentrator. In the Concentrator, the process utilized gravity flow until at the bottom of the plant the final concentrate was pumped to the Pelletizing Plant to be filtered and pelletized.[17]

The construction of the 360-foot-by-350-foot Pelletizing Plant, located south of the Concentrator, was unique in that the twenty-four individual, sixty-foot-high, vertical shaft pelletizing furnaces were erected first, and then the building structure, and thickening, filtering, balling, and additive equipment was assembled around the furnaces. Skilled brick masons,

The Pelletizing Plant was constructed around the vertical shaft furnaces.

The construction of the pellet-loading pocket with emergency conveyor.

required to construct the refractory lining of the shaft furnaces, were in exceedingly high demand in the United States at this time, and as Dan DeVaney stated, TCC made an agreement with the unions and U.S. State Department that allowed TCC to hire skilled masons from Ireland and bring them to Minnesota on three-month visas. "They came over here and all they did was brick furnaces. I couldn't tell you how big the crew was, but there were dozens of people because they were bricking on all twenty-four furnaces at once, so it took an awful lot of brick masons."[18]

Much of the work during construction was manual labor. The jobs attracted workers from all over Minnesota and the surrounding states. Ray Schaefbauer, a South Dakota native, worked for Foley as a laborer. "Just common labor," Schaefbauer said, "helped pour cement and carry pallets and just labor; no skill, no carpenter or anything. I worked on the pelletizer building. I wheeled a lot of cement up on those floors, I'll tell you that. Lots of cement we poured up there. Then I'd take out forms and move them and just help the carpenters and make more forms for more cement and stuff like that."[19]

At the time, this was the world's largest conveyor belt stacking machine.

Construction of the Diversion Works looking south toward the Whitewater Reservoir.

The finished pellets from the furnaces would be conveyed to the Pellet Loading Pocket for direct pellet car loading, emergency storage, or to the world's largest conveyor belt stacking machine for stockpiling. The self-propelled, 416-foot-long, stacker conveyor, weighing 2.3 million pounds, would be used only during winter months when Great Lakes shipping shut down. The stacker, built by Link Belt Corporation (Link Belt) was designed to operate at temperatures as low as 45 degrees below zero and in wind velocities up to sixty-eight miles per hour. The stacker could build the 4.0-million-ton capacity Pellet Stockpile ninety feet high.

Additional plant facilities under construction included a ten-million-gallon capacity, 320-by-320-by-22 feet deep, concrete-lined Plant Reservoir. Located at the highest point of the Plant Site, the reservoir allowed water to flow by gravity through pipes in underground distribution tunnels. Plant operations would require an estimated 90,000 gallons of water per minute, with 95 percent of the water being recycled. The makeup water supply for the plant would be pumped from Colby Lake located about five miles from the Plant Site.

Two large earthen dams were constructed on nearby Whitewater Lake creating the Whitewater Reservoir, which would be filled when Colby Lake levels were high. When Colby Lake levels were low, makeup water pumped from Colby Lake would be replaced by pumping water from Whitewater Reservoir into Colby to maintain the normal level of Colby Lake. North of the Plant Site, a 10,000-acre Tailing Basin was constructed to contain over fifteen million tons per year of tailing and to recycle water back to the plant through a floating pump house.

RAILROAD CONSTRUCTION

Building the seventy-three-mile-long railroad line linking the Plant Site with Taconite Harbor was a major construction project. The railroad right-of-way passed through the heart of the Arrowhead country's forest wilderness on its descent to Lake Superior.

The single track, standard-gauge railroad required installation of more than 200 culverts to direct drainage, construction of eight bridges to cross over streams, roads, or other railroads, excavation of six cuts, and boring of a 1,860-foot tunnel through solid rock.

The railroad was designed for minimal grade for loaded trains with spur sidings for maintenance equipment built at approximate fourteen-mile intervals and a passing siding where trains could meet located near the midpoint. It followed a gradual uphill 0.3 percent grade to a point about forty-four miles from the Plant Site, and then began a gradual descent to a point about eight miles from Lake Superior, where it entered a steep 2 percent downhill grade to the dock.

One of the first tasks in constructing the railroad involved acquiring the land for the right-of-way. The railroad passed through portions of the Superior National Forest. This government land

Installing culverts for the Mainline Railroad.

Excavating railroad cut on steep grade down to Taconite Harbor.

Removing muskeg to construct the railroad subgrade.

Placing backfill for the railroad subgrade.

could not be purchased outright but could only be acquired by trade, with the U.S. Forest Service receiving two acres for each acre transferred to Erie. Overall, Erie had to acquire more than 75,000 acres to obtain the lands necessary to compete for the project. Pickands Mather's Legal Department processed more than 2,000 separate land agreements.

Dan DeVaney explained that Erie land agents "were trying to buy the land without anybody knowing that this was for a massive ore operation." Every once in a while, someone would not sell and that became a big problem. The biggest one

DeVaney recalled was on the railroad. A man refused to sell land that was on the planned route. So, that is when they had to dig the tunnel to complete the railroad. "This completely changed the route of the railroad, simply because someone would not sell their land for any price."[20]

Once the land had been acquired, the railroad right-of-way was surveyed. TCC supervised engineering for the railroad. Railroad construction began in May 1954, with Kiewit constructing the steep railroad subgrade westward from Taconite Harbor. Arrowhead, headquartered at Murphy City located

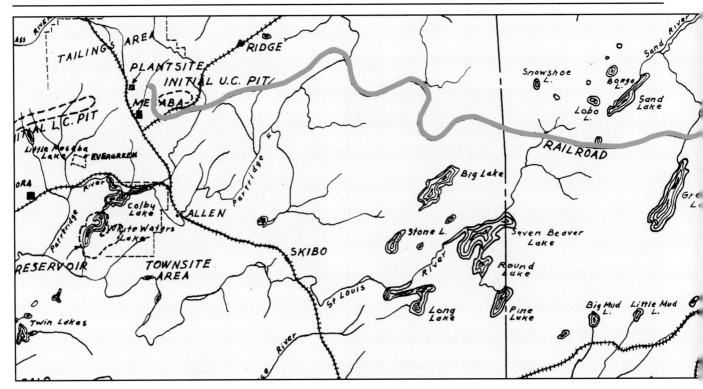

Map of Erie railroad with Plant Site starting at the left and continuing to Taconite Harbor at the right.

where the railroad would cross State Highway 1, built the remaining subgrade to the Plant Site.

Harry Johnson grew up in the Schroeder area and found work on the survey crew of the Erie project at Taconite Harbor. His family had sold twenty acres to Erie for part of the Taconite Harbor facility. Johnson stated that he worked on the railroad and power line survey crew from Murphy City down to Taconite Harbor. Johnson said, "That was not easy country to work in. You had some vertical real estate and some swamp. The swamp would be frozen in the winter and that would help. We'd go so far by a panel [truck] and then we'd get out and put snowshoes on and then we'd walk up to where we had left off the day before. We'd snowshoe and survey and then come back out with snowshoes to the panel truck."[21]

Nothing about building the railroad came easy. After clearing the 125-foot-wide right-of-way, railroad contractors handled more than eight million cubic yards of material over the seventy-three-mile line. This work included removing 1.3 million cubic yards of muskeg, 1.5 million

Typical clearing to allow crews to survey for power line and railroad construction.

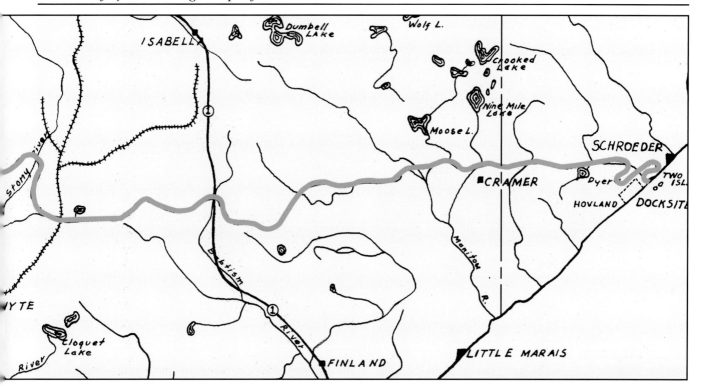

Manitou River bridge under construction—highest bridge on the railroad.

Manitou River bridge beams being hauled to construction site.

The east end of the Cramer Tunnel under construction.

cubic yards of unusable material, and 0.6 million cubic yards of rock from cuts and replacing it with 5.1 million cubic yards of suitable subgrade and embankment materials. Building the railroad across fifteen miles of muskeg swampland provided special challenges. Because the area was impassable during warm weather, most of the grade work occurred during the winter when the soft, sticky muskeg material froze. This provided secure footing for dragline excavators to remove the muskeg down to a solid base. Some of the muskeg removal required excavations up to twenty-eight feet deep. Gravel was then backfilled into the excavations to provide a firm subgrade foundation. At the peak of activity, 430 workers were employed on the railroad grade construction portion of the project.

T. F. Scholes, Inc. (Scholes) was contracted to lay the track, which was built to the highest standard for the time, with 140 pounds per yard rail placed on twenty-three cross ties per thirty-nine feet of rail section. A seven-inch layer of minus three-inch crushed granite was used for the top ballast. A total of 290 employees were engaged in track laying, and their work consistently achieved an average of 1.6 miles of track laid per day.

Gary Hansen, who grew up in Tofte where his father was a resort owner and a commercial fisherman, went to work for a contractor building the Erie railroad. "I worked for Scholes on the railroad grade in the long rock cuts that approached the harbor," Hansen said. "To start out, I was working for a fellow who only laid about 1,500 feet of rail a day, which is not a great deal. Then a fellow came out of Canada and we learned that we could run a train over track with only two ties per (ed. section of) rail. After that we started laying about two miles of rail a day." Hansen spent his entire Erie career working at Taconite Harbor.[22]

The railroad required the construction of a 1,860-foot railroad tunnel. Gibson and Roberts, Inc. (Gibson) was contracted to bore the 16-foot-by-22-foot cross section tunnel, cut through a solid rock hill located about ten miles west of Taconite Harbor at Cramer. The material excavated from the tunnel was used to construct a large approach fill to the eastern end of the tunnel. The "Cramer Tunnel" became the longest railroad tunnel built in Minnesota.

Ron Gervais grew up in Tofte and got a job during high school breaks working on the tunnel. Gervais stated that he was the first one to walk through the

Laying ties on completed railroad grade at Taconite Harbor.

tunnel. "When they made the last blast, they had not had it mucked out (ed. removed the broken rock) yet and the foreman told me to walk over the rock pile and say you're the first one that's walked through this thing after she's blown," Gervais said. "I said thank you. So I did."[23]

A half-dozen rock cuts, ranging in depth from 22 to 63 feet, and in length from 2,000 to 4,200 feet, were drilled and blasted for the railroad subgrade. The broken material was excavated and used for fills along the railroad or for harbor construction.

The railroad also required the construction of eight bridges; the largest spanning the Manitou River was 300 feet long and 100 feet above the riverbed. The steel for the Manitou bridge was supplied by Bethlehem. In the early winter of 1955, crews moved four plate girders and the two main span beams more than twenty miles to the site by lowboy trailers on roads constructed over frozen muskeg. The 10-feet-high-by-100-feet-long, 36-ton beams were then set in place by a 100-foot-high temporary derrick.[24]

Completed in late 1956, the Erie railroad was said to be the longest new railroad built in the United States since early in the twentieth century.[25] Once in operation, the railroad allowed equipment, construction materials, and supplies to arrive by boat and be moved by rail from Taconite Harbor to the Plant Site.

HARBOR AND DOCK CONSTRUCTION

One of the most interesting and extraordinary engineering and construction aspects of the Erie Project was the building of Taconite Harbor. Selecting the site required for the large protected anchorage was itself a challenging task. The rugged, rocky shoreline of the North Shore of Lake Superior, at times susceptible to storms with waves as high as

Delivering construction materials.

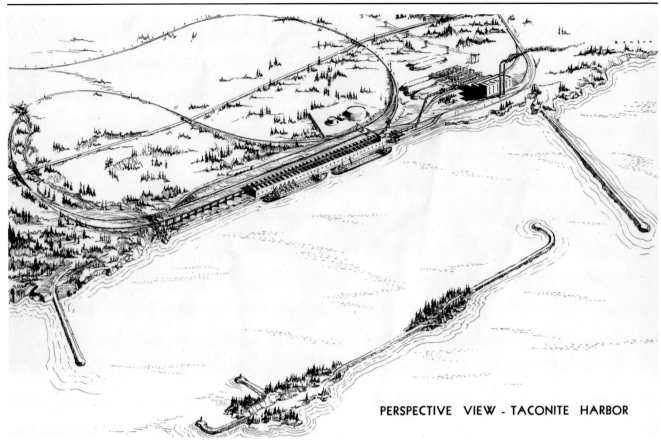

PERSPECTIVE VIEW - TACONITE HARBOR

Perspective view of planned Taconite Harbor facility.

twenty feet, provided few areas capable of supporting the large facility envisioned. The site finally selected was located at Two Islands, about eighty miles northeast of Duluth, and was chosen because Gull and Bear Islands lay only about a quarter-mile off shore and provided some wave protection to the shoreline. The water depth in the area was sufficiently shallow to permit construction of a dock and supplementary breakwaters. The site was seventy-three rail miles directly east from the Plant Site.

The plan for the harbor, Dock, and Power Plant developed by Snare created a harbor approximately 4,500 feet long and 1,300 feet wide, protected by rock breakwaters extending outward from the shore and connecting the two islands. The Dock consisted of a 1,200-foot pellet loading section on the west and an adjacent 510-foot coal unloading area to the east. The loading section with twenty-five pellet bins would have a total storage capacity of 100,000 tons. The Dock face was extended 624 feet to the west to provide for

possible future expansion, resulting in a total dock length of 2,334 feet. The Dock was designed to be parallel to the shoreline, which required cutting into the solid rock to create a 30-foot sheer wall that would be faced with concrete.

Construction began in November 1953 when Kiewit was awarded the contract for site clearing and construction of the initial portion of the 1,900-foot east breakwater, and for the extensive excavation work involved in establishing the steep railroad approaches to the harbor.

In May 1954, Dravo began construction of the 30-foot deep harbor and Dock. Conventional "wet" harbor excavation methods would include drilling the harbor bottom with barge-mounted drills, underwater blasting techniques, and dredging; however, Dravo decided to perform the work "dry." A temporary cofferdam would be built around the work area and the water pumped out. Dravo was also tasked with completing the eastern portion

Construction of the cofferdam allowed water to be removed so that workers could lower the lake bottom and build the dock face.

Aerial view of Taconite Harbor showing cofferdam along shoreline complete with water pumped out and dock construction underway.

Constructing the dock face within the cofferdam thirty feet below the lake level.

Completed dock face.

of the Dock as quickly as possible so that supply vessels could deliver rails and other materials needed for the railroad construction.

Dravo's plan to temporarily wall off a portion of Lake Superior was unique and required installation of two sheet pile cofferdams. The first, approximately 2,000 feet long, extended out into Lake Superior enclosing the work area. The second divided the work area into eastern and western sections. Four specially manufactured, barge-mounted, steam-powered cranes were used to drive more than 7,500 tons of sheet piling into five feet of sand-and-gravel lake bottom. The average lake depth where the piles were driven was thirty-five feet. The fifty-foot diameter cofferdam cells were connected and filled with sand and gravel dredged from the lake, providing a roadway around the perimeter. The cofferdam was twelve feet above the lake level to prevent storm waves from entering the work area and, when completed in December 1954, formed a watertight enclosure. With the first phase of the cofferdam installation completed, crews installed three 5,000 gallons-per-minute pumps to dewater the work area in preparation for deepening the harbor. Once dry, drilling, blasting, and excavation of the lake bottom and dock wall area enclosed by the cofferdam began. The harbor deepening and dock wall excavation required

removal of one million cubic yards of rock from the thirty-five-acre site.[26]

Building of the breakwaters shielding the cofferdams from Lake Superior storms proceeded along with the harbor construction. The rock excavated from the harbor bottom was used to form some of the core for the breakwaters. Trucks dumped the rock from the shoreline, creating a roadway and forming the core of the breakwaters extending out into the lake. At the eastern end of

Placing armor rock on breakwater.

the harbor, the breakwater stretched 1,900 feet out from the shore. On the western end, a temporary roadway was constructed from the shore to Gull Island and then a breakwater was built extending to and beyond Bear Island. The roadway was later removed to create the west harbor entrance. The breakwater cores were designed on a gradual one- (vertical) to two- (horizontal) foot slope on the lake side and slightly steeper on the harbor side. Portions of the breakwater were built in water as deep as 100 feet. To protect the breakwaters from storms, an outer covering of armor rock was placed on top of the breakwater cores. Approximately 325,000 tons of large armor rock was quarried from hard anorthosite rock at Carlton Peak,

located about five miles from Taconite Harbor, and hauled to the site by flatbed trailer trucks. Additionally, 125,000 tons of armor rock was generated during the harbor excavation. The rocks were then barged out to the breakwaters and placed by the cranes. The smaller rocks, ranging in size from two to eight tons, were first placed from the lake bottom up to a point about twenty feet below the lake surface, and larger ones, up to fifteen-ton size, were set from that point to the surface. The tops of the breakwaters were then capped with giant rocks, each weighing more than fifteen tons. In total, more than 1.2 million cubic yards of rock was required to construct the breakwaters.

Aerial view of construction showing temporary road to Gull Island for breakwater construction.

BALDWIN LOCOMOTIVES

When Erie took delivery of its first two Baldwin diesel locomotives in November 1955, there were no railroad tracks on the North Shore between Duluth and Taconite Harbor. Each 125-ton locomotive had to be transferred aboard the deck of a Zenith Dredge Co. derrick barge *Adele* in Duluth and towed up the North Shore by the tug *Essayons* to Taconite Harbor. The locomotives were then unloaded by a 200-ton capacity stiff-leg derrick installed on the dock wall.[37] These locomotives were used on the railroad construction and ultimately worked as switch engines at the Plant Site.

Locomotives arrive by barge for the construction of the eastern portion of the railroad.

Baldwin locomotives at Taconite Harbor

Building the dock wall along the shoreline required special engineering techniques and construction skills to support the forces on the dock face generated by the weight of the storage bins filled with pellets, estimated to be three tons per square foot. The shoreline rock was first drilled vertically on one-foot spacing and then blasted. After the broken rock was removed, a sheer rock face forty-two feet high was established. Next, a machine was set up to drill multiple horizontal holes into the rock face. These holes, some as large as two inches in diameter, were drilled to a depth of thirty-five feet for the purpose of installing steel rods to anchor the concrete dock face to the rock wall, thus creating a solid mass of concrete and rock. The steel rods were secured in the holes with grouting, comprised of cement, sand, and an expanding agent to prevent shrinkage of the grout. Large prefabricated panels were positioned by cranes and attached temporarily to the anchor rods to act as forms for the concrete dock face. A total of 50,000 cubic yards of concrete was required to construct the Dock structure. The structure would contain twenty-five pellet bins, the feeders and boat-loading shuttle conveyors located beneath each bin, the Dock offices, a maintenance area, locker room, sample lab, and an elevator for accessing the various levels of the Dock.

After the eastern end of the Dock and harbor inside the cofferdam was completed, the east cofferdam was removed, permitting boats to tie up and unload steel and supplies at the coal unloading area.

The design of the Dock and figure-eight loop track layout were unique to Erie and permitted continuous forward train movement during car dumping. This tremendously improved train-unloading efficiency compared to other ore docks on Lake Superior. A 2,574-foot-long railroad trestle, constructed with 1,900 tons of steel, was erected high above the pellet bins. Loaded trains were to be positioned on the trestle in up to twenty-five-car groups over the bins and unloaded using wrench cars to open each bottom dump car. The train would then continue moving forward around the loop track returning empty back to the Plant Site. This arrangement eliminated complicated switching and train movements associated with other ore docks.

A Wellman traveling crane equipped with a twelve-ton capacity bucket was erected to unload coal from boats. Conveyor belts transported the coal to a storage area adjacent to the Power Plant.

Two separate complete oil pumping, storage, and transfer systems were also installed at Taconite Harbor. One had a 4.0-million-gallon capacity tank for the "Bunker C" oil required for the Plant Site's pelletizing furnaces, and a second had a 1.6-million-gallon tank for diesel oil.

POWER PLANT CONSTRUCTION

Taconite Harbor was also the site of the Power Plant that supplied electric power for all Plant Site and Dock activities. Anaconda designed the 150,000-kw, coal-fired steam power plant and associated sixty-two-mile-long electric transmission line. Two 75,000-kw boiler turbine generator units were installed. Combustion Engineering (CE) provided the steam-generating system, and Westinghouse Electric Corporation (Westinghouse) provided the steam-driven turbine and electric generator. A substation stepped up the 13,800-volt generator voltage to 138,000 volts for transmission. A total of 310 steel towers and 488 miles of transmission wire were installed on the power transmission line, roughly paralleling the

Power Plant near end of construction.

Power Plant interior looking down on turbine and generator units.

railroad right-of-way, from Taconite Harbor to the Plant Site. United Engineers and Constructors, Inc. (United) was contracted to erect the facility and began construction in the spring of 1955.

The generating capacity for taconite mining and processing was equal to the combined electric needs of the cities of Duluth and neighboring Superior.

Ted Williams, assigned to Taconite Harbor to assist with the Power Plant construction, stated, "I worked with the United Engineers because they were the prime electrical contractors. We would test equipment as it was put in to make sure it was up to specification and if not wouldn't accept it. We worked closely with most of the prime contractors that TCC hired. United was just one."[27]

High voltage transmission towers during construction.

TED WILLIAMS

Ted Williams, an electrical engineer and native of western Pennsylvania, moved to Minnesota in 1956 to work for TCC on the Erie power plant. Williams noted that TCC took care of all the contracts and contractors that built Taconite Harbor and the Plant Site. "It was a huge organization." Williams remembered being astonished by what the construction crews accomplished. "In the dock area, which was amazing to me—the work that they did to make that dock. They drained part of the harbor, built the cofferdam in front of the dock, excavated so the boats would be in 30 feet of water, then they built a big cement wall for the dock face. They also built a huge breakwater and closed in the space between the two islands just off shore. Lake Superior is not very kind when they get an easterly wind on it." Williams also noted that TCC hauled rock that came from the harbor excavation, railroad grade, and tunnel construction and dumped it into the lake and built up the base for the breakwaters. "As they built it up they had to cover it with armor rock. The amazing thing was the size of those slabs of rock. They were anywhere from five to fifteen tons apiece. They hauled these out on trucks. Some of them, they could only haul one at a time, by huge flatbed trailers, and unload them on the edge of the breakwater. Then they would have cranes pick them up and place them on the breakwater."[35]

Williams remembered being even more amazed by the power of Lake Superior. "Before they got the armor rock on, in 1954, they had a bad northeaster storm come in and it washed part of the breakwater out," he said. "What they had built, they lost. They had to rebuild the breakwater before they could start working on constructing the dock."[36]

Workers within the cofferdam deepen the harbor.

Carlton Peak anorthosite quarry where armor rock was mined for breakwater construction.

Skilled linemen erected the transmission towers. David Carlson, a Duluth native, found employment with crews installing power lines. Carlson stated, "I went up to Taconite Harbor as a lineman. That's when they started building the transmission line towers; I worked on the gin pole crew." Gin poles were used in places where access for a regular mobile crane was not possible. The gin pole was a temporary, single-boom crane or derrick that was secured by guy cables and used block and tackle to lift loads. Construction started at the Taconite Harbor end and worked westward. The typical height of the towers was 100 feet. The highest one is right near the railroad tunnel and was erected by the gin pole crew. Carlson recalled, "That tower was 147 feet high. And it was a lousy day to do it, too, if I remember right."[28]

Many North Shore residents got training working at the Power Plant. Ron Gervais got a job as an ironworker at the Power Plant. Gervais recalled, "I couldn't tie rods fast enough because the other guys were experienced ironworkers. I was a new hire and, naturally, you're not going to work like a guy that's been doing it for a living from construction job to construction job. I was put in the labor pool. Then I sorted out lumber after they'd take the forms down. We'd break the forms apart and separate the boards, the pieces of wood that they would use to build more forms."[29]

STARTUP

Construction continued at a hurried pace at the Plant Site, railroad, and Taconite Harbor throughout 1956 and much of 1957. On June 16, 1957, the first coal delivery arrived at Taconite Harbor on Interlake Steamship Company's (Interlake Steamship) vessel *Harvey H. Brown*. The first ore test train was dumped into the Coarse Crusher on August 14, 1957, and full Commercial Plant operations commenced on September 1, 1957. The first test run of pellet train dumping occurred on September 7, and a test run of the dock loading equipment took place on September 26, when Interlake's vessel *J.A. Campbell* was loaded with PreTac pellets. On

September 30, 1957, the first complete boatload of Erie Commercial Plant pellets was loaded into Interlake's *A.B. Wolvin*.

After five years of intensive planning and nearly four years of monumental construction activity, the men and women involved in the project could take pride in achieving a milestone in United States industrial history. Erie, one of the nation's largest, most challenging, and expensive mining projects, was finally in operation, and a new phase of Minnesota's iron mining history had begun.

ERIE COMMERCIAL PLANT CONSTRUCTION STATISTICS	
Total Cost	Over $300,000,000
Construction Period	4 years
Peak Workers	6,200
Structural Steel	50,000 tons
Concrete	370,000 cubic yards
Excavation:	
Plant	5,300,000 cubic yards
Railroad	2,950,000 cubic yards
Power Plant	55,000 cubic yards
Harbor	1,007,500 cubic yards
Fill:	
Plant	2,060,000 cubic yards
Railroad	5,152,000 cubic yards
Power Plant	46,000 cubic yards
Harbor	271,000 cubic yards
Breakwater Rock	1,000,000 cubic yards
Railroad Ballast	750,000 tons
Railroad Track	122 miles

Taconite Harbor Power Plant and Dock ready for operation, 1957.

J.A. Campbell, first boat loaded at Taconite Harbor on September 26, 1957.

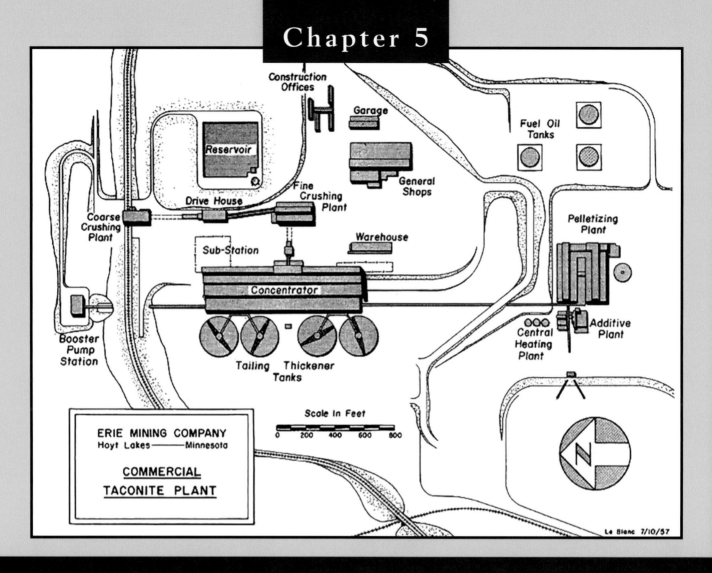

Chapter 5

Construction
Offices

Garage

Fuel Oil
Tanks

Reservoir

Fine
Crushing
Plant

General
Shops

Drive House

Pelletizing
Plant

Coarse
Crushing
Plant

Sub-Station

Warehouse

Concentrator

Booster
Pump
Station

Additive
Plant

Central
Heating
Plant

Tailing   Thickener
Tanks

Scale In Feet

0   200   400   600   800

ERIE MINING COMPANY
Hoyt Lakes ——— Minnesota

COMMERCIAL
TACONITE PLANT

Le Blanc 7/10/57

N

START UP AND EARLY YEARS

⫸ 1957 TO 1965 ⫷

In 1957, the Erie mine and plant complex encompassed an area about nine miles long from east to west and more than one mile wide. The Plant Site, consisting of Coarse Crusher, Fine Crusher, Concentrator, Pelletizing Plant, and General Shops, was centrally located between three initial taconite mining areas, Area 1 west of the Plant Site, Area 2 located southeast, and Area 3 to the east. Mining would eventually expand to encompass twelve separate areas. There were two mine equipment maintenance facilities (Area 1 Shops and Area 2 Shops). The Tailing Basin was located north of the Plant Site, while

the Pellet Loading Pocket and Pellet Stockpile were situated immediately south of the Pelletizing Plant. The Power Plant and Dock were located at Taconite Harbor and connected to the Plant Site by electrical transmission lines and a seventy-three-mile-long railroad.

Operationally, Erie was organized into departments by activity, named Mining, Ore Dressing (crushing and concentrating), Agglomerating (pelletizing), Maintenance, Railroad and Harbor, and Power Plant, which were supported by staff departments that provided administrative and technical support.

MINING

The taconite orebody at Erie dipped generally to the south at an average 8 percent. Because less stripping material (overburden and waste rock) covered the taconite to the north, mining activity typically proceeded in a north-to-south direction. In the east-to-west direction, the orebody was relatively flat, which allowed Erie to originally adopt the practice of direct loading the taconite ore into railcars for delivery to the Coarse Crusher. At the outset, mining areas were developed in a series of long, slender, east and west running benches, following the outcrop of the iron formation.

Above: Overburden stripping.
Left: Plan view of the Plant Site, 1957.

Erie's Mine Engineering Department provided the short- and long-term plans for the Mining Department. These plans were based on Erie's owner's forecast of steel production and iron ore requirements. The engineers used diamond drill hole information, mine and plant production capability, product quality specifications, operating costs, and overall sequencing of material movement to develop the plans. Mine Engineering provided daily direction for the mine operators, measured and reported mining progress and quantities of material mined, and monitored the development of overburden and waste rock stockpiles.

To achieve Erie's rated capacity of 7.5 million tons of pellets per year, it was necessary to mine 37 million tons of material, consisting of 24 million tons of taconite ore and 13 million tons of stripping.[1] This represents an average daily mine movement requirement of 69,000 tons of taconite and 38,000 tons of stripping. Each month, Erie moved more material than the average large Mesabi Range natural ore mine did in a year.

Mining began with removing the overburden that covered the rock. Erie's initial stripping was accomplished by a fleet of small-sized diesel shovels and larger electrically powered shovels loading into end dump trucks, which hauled the material to stockpiles located a short distance away from the mineable iron formation. The overburden

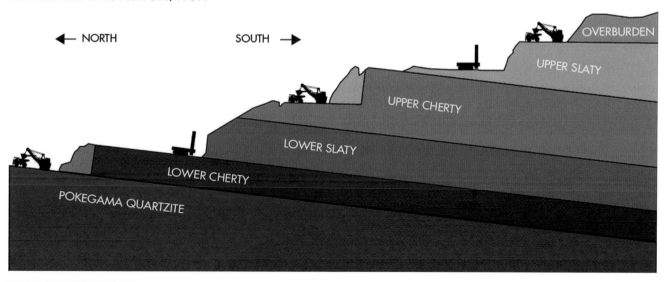

Typical cross-section of Mesabi Range where Erie mined.

stripping at Erie was challenging because glaciers had scoured the top of iron formation, leaving it very uneven, undulating, and rough. In addition, the overburden was interspersed with large granite boulders. As Mining Superintendent Walter Thomte explained in 1963, the stripping operation was difficult and final cleanup involved considerable expense.[2] Stripping shovel operators removed the overburden right down to the bare rock to simplify drilling blast holes.[3]

Before the waste rock (nonmagnetic Virginia Slate and taconite that did not contain enough recoverable iron to be processed economically) or taconite ore could be mined, it had to be drilled and blasted. An important function performed by Mine Engineering was to coordinate drill movements and blast scheduling, and to design the individual blast patterns to meet mine plan requirements. Mining Engineer Doug Buell recalled that the engineer would plan the blast patterns. The blast designs were discussed with the blast foreman and considered location, rock type, hole spacing, and shape of the blast pattern. The agreed-upon plan was plotted on a map and the individual blast holes located on the blast pattern out in the mine.[4]

The blast hole produced by jet piercing averaged about nine inches in diameter but varied from six and a half inches to fourteen inches owing to variations in the characteristics of the rock encountered. Jet drilling rates averaged approximately fifteen feet per hour, but ranged from

Loading blast holes with detonators.

Loading explosive slurry into blast holes from specialized pumper trucks.

Typical jet-piercing drill pattern with water and oxygen trailers to the right.

The end result of the blasting process.

twenty feet per hour in Erie's western mining areas to about twelve feet per hour in denser material toward the east. The average taconite blast consisted of 270 blast holes averaging forty feet in depth and used an average of 320,000 pounds of explosives to break approximately 460,000 tons of ore.[5] One of the difficulties with the jet drilling was that space was needed on the drill pattern for the supporting oxygen and water trailers. The jet drills consumed large amounts of compressed oxygen, water, and fuel each day. According to Drill and Blast Supervisor Tom Barkley, any drill pattern was a logistics chore to get organized and running efficiently. The drill was electric powered, which required a heavy power supply cable. The oxygen and water trailers had hoses running to the drill. The water trailer also had an electric power cable from the drill to run a pump and heaters. All of these hoses and power cables had to be moved as drilling progressed on the pattern and placed to allow vehicle access.[6]

Once the blast holes were drilled, they were loaded with explosives consisting of a waterproof, high-explosive slurry where there was water in the holes or an ammonium nitrate fuel oil mixture where the holes were dry. Detonators were placed in each blast hole. All the blast hole detonators were connected by detonation cord and millisecond timing delays to establish the proper sequence of explosions to efficiently break the rock. Blaster Jim Tossava said, "We would load holes in the rain, would load in the snow, would load in cold weather, and would load in warm weather. The only thing that stopped us was lightning in the area." When lightning was reported near a loaded blast pattern, security was established to keep people away.[7] Drill and Blast Supervisor Joel Evers stated, "There's no second chance in blasting. You've got to get it right the first time."[8]

Once either the waste rock or taconite had been blasted, it was loaded into trucks and railcars by Bucyrus Erie 190B electric shovels equipped with five-cubic-yard dippers. After startup, the original dippers were replaced with eight-cubic-yard dippers, improving productivity. Initially waste rock was hauled by either end dump truck or eighty-five-ton capacity side dump railcar to waste rock stockpiles.

Taconite mining scene with jet-piercing drills and shovel loading blasted ore.

One of two shovels with elevated cab to provide better visibility for the operator.

Loading blasted taconite ore into railroad cars.

ERIE'S RAILROADS

Interestingly, because Erie essentially operated two separate railroads, one to haul the ore to the Crusher and the other, a seventy-three-mile-long Mainline Railroad connecting to the shipping facilities at Taconite Harbor, the locomotives for each sported separate paint jobs. The orange and black paint scheme for the Mine Railroad locomotives was picked by the wife of a department official, while the blue and silver scheme of the Mainline Railroad locomotives reflected the colors of Yale University, the *alma mater* of several of the Pickands Mather executives.[40] In 1963, all Erie Mining Company equipment, including the locomotives, were painted yellow with the distinctive maroon stripe. In 1975, a black roof was added to the paint scheme.[41]

Original paint scheme on a Mine Railroad locomotive.

Original paint scheme on a Mainline Railroad locomotive.

In 1963, the locomotive color scheme for Mine Railroad and Mainline Railroad locomotives was changed to yellow and maroon with the roof color changing to black in 1975.

Taconite was hauled by the railcars about three miles on a maximum grade of 2 percent to the Coarse Crusher. To deliver the 23,000 tons of ore required each shift, and to meet ore quality requirements, an average of six operating shovels and nine ALCO RS-11 diesel electric locomotives, each pulling eight-car ore trains, were operated. Two shovels and twelve trucks were scheduled each shift for moving stripping. According to Shovel Maintenance Supervisor Harlan Nygard, "At one time our shovel fleet was right around about two dozen machines of various types. We used to move those shovels around quite a bit, pretty long moves in those early days. They'd work one mining area for a while and then move to another. It kept you thinking all the time."[9]

Ore mining and the Coarse Crusher activities operated on an eight-hour per shift, twenty shifts per week basis, with one shift per week scheduled for maintenance. Stripping and all plant processing operations beyond the Coarse Crusher operated "round the clock," on a twenty-one shift per week schedule.

Erie initially operated its mine trains with two-man crews, a brakeman and a locomotive engineer. The brakeman's job was to "protect the point" by riding in the end empty ore car as the train proceeded back to the mine from the Crusher, signal the engineer, and dismount and operate switches as required.

Mine train movements were coordinated from a traffic control center where a train director, seated in front of three large steel panels showing the

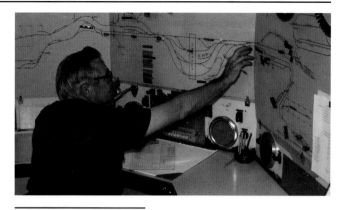

Train director at the traffic control center showing train movement board and communications equipment.

entire track layout, moved numbered magnets to indicate train locations and communicated movement instructions to the locomotive engineers by radio. According to Train Director Mike Hogan, "We understood just how important our job was. The thing that made the job so interesting, so busy, so stressful, was because the trains were not able to move from point A to point B without your giving them verbal clearance, and they then had to repeat those instructions back to you. When you have a dozen or so trains operating, chattering all the time, and you would give them clearance instructions before they could go from point A to point B, and there were probably three or four clearances that you'd have to give each train going up to and returning from the crusher, all done by voice command, it could get pretty hectic."[10]

Hauling taconite to the Coarse Crusher, with Concentrator in background.

A COLD JOB

Mike Hogan remembered just how cold it could be in the winter. "The brakeman would stand in the last car, and he would have a jumper hose to control the air brakes in case something happened, and he would use hand signals to communicate with the engineer," Hogan said. "At night, you would use your railroad lantern, and you would be standing up, or, if you wanted to crouch, just looking over the edge of the car, because when it's below zero, and you are riding in an open car, let me tell you, it's the coldest thing on earth."[43]

"In those early days," Hogan continued, "the brakeman was outside for the ride back empty and to direct train movement while the train was being loaded." At that time, "It seemed like it would take a month of Sundays to load each car . . . and man it would get cold. And then, when the train was loaded, you had to get back to the locomotive. It was never closer to heaven, than when you got into the heated cab of the locomotive."[44]

One of the first things that the train crews discovered with the high, long cabs on the locomotives was that the forward visibility limited communications between the brakeman and engineer and modifications were needed. "So we'd cut the front of the cab off and lowered the nose so you could look right over the top of it," said General Shop welder Gerald "Curly" Rollins. "We did that to all of our ALCO locomotives. We cut them all down, and then the sheet metal guys would make new plates, and we'd weld them back together. The General Shops was an interesting place to work."[45]

The Erie mine railroad brakeman was outside in all sorts of weather.

The ore was brought to the Coarse Crusher where the crusher operator controlled train dumping by activating hydraulic jacks that lifted one side of the railcar to dump the load of ore into the sixty-inch crusher. A series of green and red lights controlled by the crusher operator directed the locomotive engineer to move the train one car length ahead each time a car was dumped.[11]

The delivery of a consistent grade (magnetic iron content) of ore was essential for efficient processing and achieving final product specifications. Because the ore characteristics varied significantly at different shovel locations, ore grading, blending of the ore, was a critical first step. The primary criteria for determining the ore blend were the diamond drill core sample results. The blend was monitored by

Ore car positioned to have its taconite load dumped into the primary crusher.

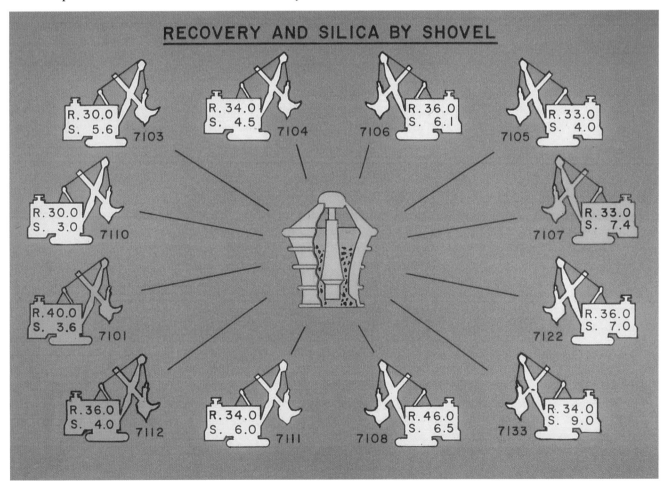

Continuous ore blending at Erie was a complicated process. Recovery (R) and Silica (S) targets at the crusher were achieved by mixing ore delivery from many shovels in various mining areas. Daily blending schedules were developed, actual ore delivery was monitored as each train was dumped, and adjustments were made to stay on target. (White shovels—active, green shovels—spare, yellow shovel—not scheduled.)

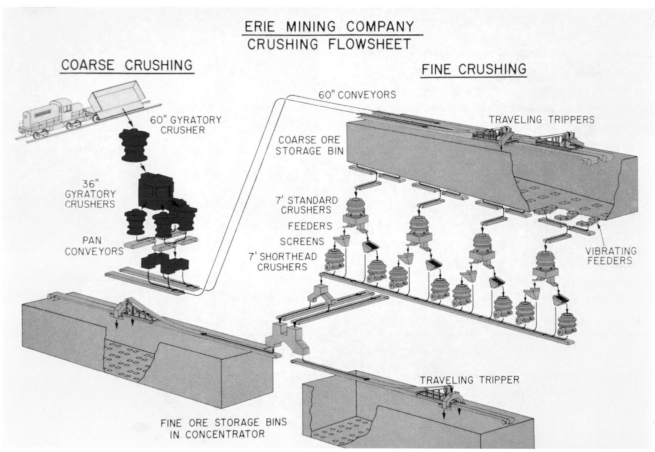

ERIE MINING COMPANY
CRUSHING FLOWSHEET

Crushing flowsheet.

Ramsey Coils (devices that were added after startup and measured the actual magnetic iron content of each trainload of ore after it had passed through the crusher), and ore delivery adjustments were made.[12] Joel Evers said, "We worked pretty closely with the ore graders. They set up an ore grading schedule for every twenty-four hours and that was based on diamond drill data, mine plan, input as to where the shovels were and what direction they were going and what elevation they were digging."[13]

ORE DRESSING

The Ore Dressing department was comprised of three sections—coarse crushing, fine crushing, and concentrating located in separate buildings (Coarse Crusher, Fine Crusher, and Concentrator). There were ore storage facilities in the Fine Crusher and Concentrator. The North Control Room was in the Concentrator building and controlled the switching of power supply from the Power Plant at Taconite Harbor and MP&L as well as power distributed to the mine and plant buildings.

Ore was delivered to the Coarse Crusher building by rail and dumped into a sixty-inch first-stage gyratory crusher (900

Fine crushing line with the standard crusher at the top and one of the two shorthead crushers below.

CONCENTRATING FLOWSHEET

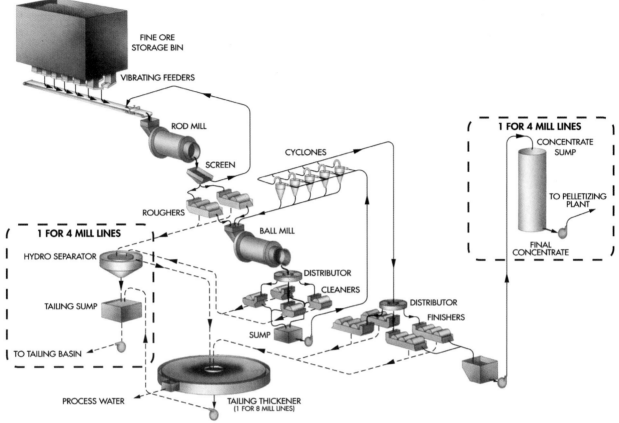

Concentrator flowsheet.

horsepower motor), which fed four thirty-six-inch second-stage gyratory crushers (450 horsepower motor). Immediately after startup, the second parallel coarse crushing line, originally planned for plant expansion, was added to maintain steady production. This process reduced the size of the ore from as large as sixty inches down to six inches. The crushed ore was then moved to the Coarse Ore Bins located at the top of the Fine Crusher building by parallel, sixty-inch wide conveyors where tripper cars distributed the ore to 9,000-ton capacity storage bins feeding the fine crushing lines.

The Fine Crusher was comprised of six parallel lines, each made up of a single first-stage seven-foot standard cone crusher (350 horsepower motor) and two second-stage seven-foot shorthead crushers (350 horsepower motor). A six-foot by ten-foot vibrating screen ahead of each shorthead crusher allowed material crushed smaller than three-fourths of an inch to bypass the shorthead crusher. Fine

Concentrator interior showing the twenty-seven mill lines.

Concentrator mill lines with rod mills at top, cyclones in the center, and ball mills below with 200-ton crane above.

Rougher magnetic separator provides the first separation of magnetic concentrate and nonmagnetic tailing.

Cleaner magnetic separators on the right and finisher magnetic separators on the left. In the Concentrator there were 540 individual magnetic separator drums operating.

Separator attendant inspects finisher magnetic separators.

crushing reduced the size of the ore from six inches in size to smaller than three-fourths of an inch. The crushed ore was conveyed by parallel, sixty-inch-wide conveyors to the Fine Ore Bins located at the top of the Concentrator building, where tripper cars distributed the ore to the storage bins feeding each concentrating line. Enough fine ore inventory was available to operate the Concentrator for twenty hours, approximately 68,000 tons.

The Concentrator consisted of twenty-seven parallel, identical mill lines. A repair bay located in the center of the building separated the operating areas, with twelve mill lines positioned on one side and fifteen on the other. The mill lines were grouped into "sections" of four lines each for ease of handling concentrate and tailing.

Each mill line was equipped with two stages of fine grinding, one rod mill (800 horsepower motor) followed by one ball mill (1250 horsepower motor), to further reduce the three-quarter-inch ore to minus 325 mesh. Erie employed high capacity grate-type ball mills, making it possible to use a one ball mill per rod mill arrangement. "This saved considerable mill space over the more common arrangement of two ball mills to one rod mill," Fred DeVaney wrote.[14] Vibrating feeders fed ore from the Fine Ore Bins to the rod mills and water was added. The mixture of ground ore and water (slurry) exited the rod mill and was passed over a screen where the oversize was returned to the mill and the undersize was sent to a rougher magnetic separator where the initial magnetic separation of iron-bearing particles (concentrate) from the nonmagnetic particles (tailing) occurred. The concentrate flowed to the ball mill for final grinding and the tailing was combined with other tailing streams.

The slurry discharged from the ball mill passed through cleaner magnetic separators where the concentrate was pumped to a bank of cyclones for size classification and the separator tailing was added to the combined tailing stream. The Pickands Mather–designed cyclones performed the same function as the spiral classifier used at PreTac but took up less space and provided improvements in metallurgical efficiency. The cyclones returned the larger sized particles to the ball mill for additional

A 200-ton overhead crane moves a ball mill to the Repair Bay.

grinding, and the smaller particles went to the finisher magnetic separator where concentrate flowed to the concentrate thickener and the tailing to the combined tailing stream. The concentrate thickener performed the final concentrate upgrade before the concentrate was pumped to Concentrate Storage Tanks in the Pelletizing Plant. The concentrating process upgraded the 30 percent iron in the ore to 65 percent iron in the concentrate, and reduced the silica content from 45 percent to 7.5 percent.

Except for the sixty-inch first-stage crusher, all operating machinery was designed for unit replacement. Minor repairs could be done "in place," but extended repairs were done in a Repair Bay with large capacity overhead cranes moving the machinery between the production line and Repair Bay. The mills were moved by a 200-ton overhead crane. The combination of parallel production lines and unit replacement resulted in almost continuous plant production.

A ball mill provided the final stage of grinding with ore recycling through the mill until the desired particle size was achieved.

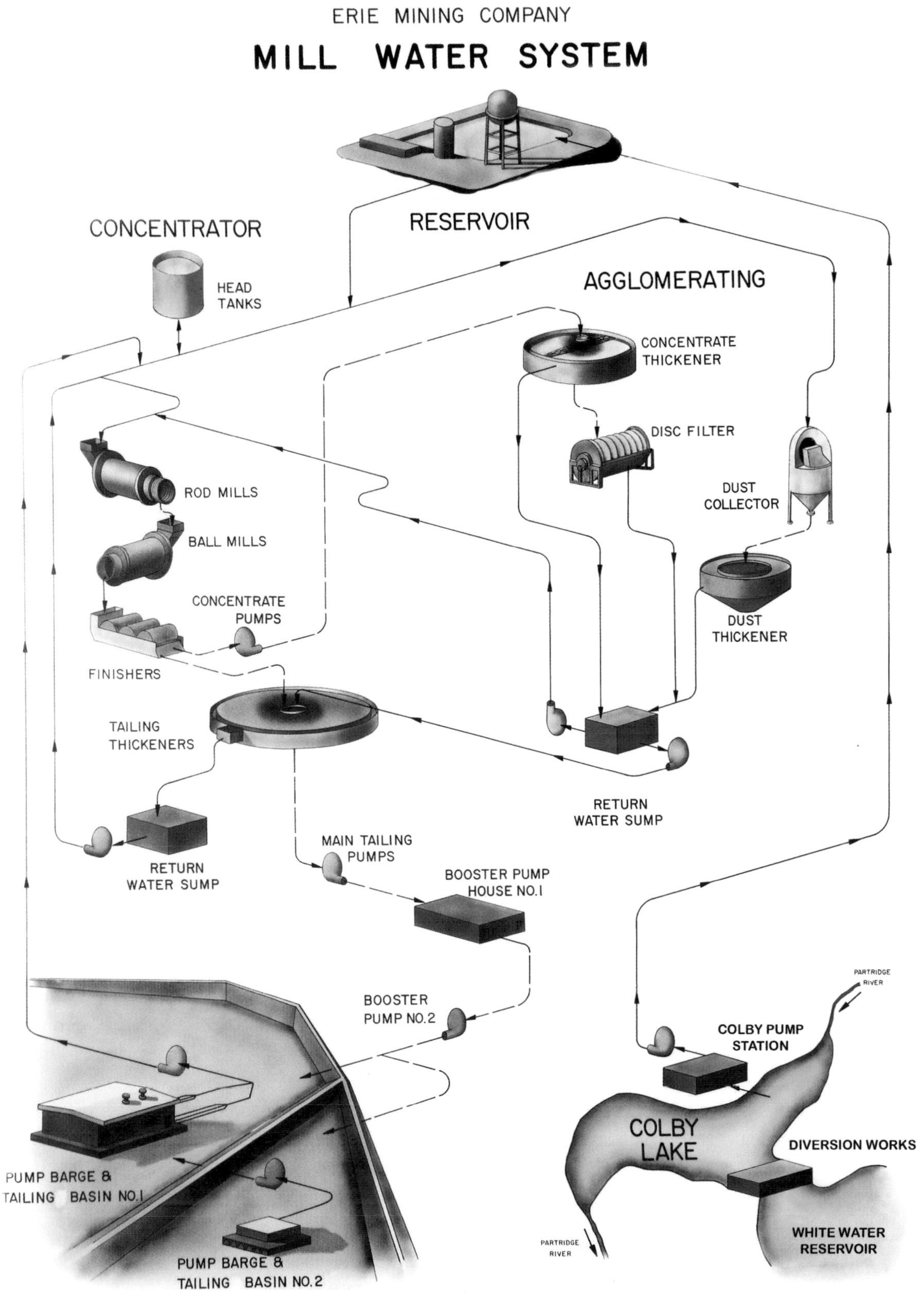

ERIE MINING COMPANY
MILL WATER SYSTEM

CONCENTRATOR

RESERVOIR

HEAD
TANKS

AGGLOMERATING

CONCENTRATE
THICKENER

DISC FILTER

ROD MILLS

DUST
COLLECTOR

BALL MILLS

CONCENTRATE
PUMPS

DUST
THICKENER

FINISHERS

TAILING
THICKENERS

RETURN
WATER SUMP

RETURN
WATER SUMP

MAIN TAILING
PUMPS

BOOSTER PUMP
HOUSE NO.1

COLBY PUMP
STATION

PARTRIDGE
RIVER

BOOSTER
PUMP NO.2

COLBY
LAKE

DIVERSION WORKS

PUMP BARGE &
TAILING BASIN NO.1

PARTRIDGE
RIVER

WHITE WATER
RESERVOIR

PUMP BARGE &
TAILING BASIN NO.2

Erie's mill water system includes recycled Concentrator and Agglomerating process water collected in return water sumps and water returned from the Tailing Basin after solids settled out. Make-up water, amounting to less than 5 percent of requirement, was pumped from Colby Lake. Colby Lake elevation was maintained by pumping from Whitewater Reservoir.

Concentrator building with main tailing thickeners in foreground.

In 1962, the original ten-foot, eight-inch diameter ball mills were replaced with twelve-foot, two-inch diameter mills to achieve the target at least 90 percent minus 325 mesh needed to improve productivity. In 1963, the original ten-foot, eight-inch diameter rod mills were replaced with twelve-foot, two-inch diameter mills to reduce grinding rod consumption and mill liner wear.

About one-third of the ore mined was concentrate that was processed further in the Pelletizing Plant and about two-thirds was tailing. All tailing flowed by gravity to one of four 255-foot diameter main tailing thickeners. The thickened tailing underflow was pumped to the Tailing Basin. The thickener overflow was reused as process water.

Dan DeVaney indicated that water usage at Erie amounted to approximately 130,000 gpm, with about 95 percent of the water reused from the tailing thickeners and Tailing Basin.[15]

Doug Buell remembered how important the design and operation of the Tailing Basin was. Engineers assigned to the Tailing Basin were responsible for designing and monitoring construction of the Tailing Basin and for laying out the tailing pipelines and the discharge spigots where the tailing was to be deposited.[16]

In 1948, as PreTac was beginning operation, Pickands Mather recognized the need to control erosion dust liftoff from the tailing disposal areas, and initiated the first experiments on revegetation of taconite tailing. Years of research work resulted in developing the successful techniques and procedures for establishing vegetation on Erie's Tailing Basin. Operation General Foreman Adrian "Ace" Barker always liked the chance to get out to the Tailing Basin. "It was nice out there," he said, "There was lots of wildlife, and it was just like a park. Erie was kind of a showplace."[17]

Aerial view of Tailing Basin looking south with Plant Site in background. The floating pumphouse on the left pond pumped clarified water back to the Concentrator.

Roger Hull explained what it was like to first start up the plant in 1957. You start up and commission one mill line at a time. The rod mill, ball mill, roughers, cleaners, finishers, pump, cyclone, and tailing system all had to be started in proper sequence and verified for correct operation as the first ore was processed. This had to be done for each of the twenty-seven mill lines. "That's what's amazing about it."

AGGLOMERATING

The concentrate slurry, averaging about 50 percent solids, was pumped 2,500 feet from the Concentrator to a twenty-foot-diameter, twenty-four-foot-deep Concentrate Feed Sump in the Pelletizing Plant. The Concentrate Feed Sump combined the new concentrate, reclaimed storage, dust collector residue, floor spill, and reground undersized pellets, which was then pumped to twelve, forty-foot diameter thickeners.

Disc vacuum filter used to dewater concentrate slurry.

ERIE MINING COMPANY

AGGLOMERATING FLOWSHEET

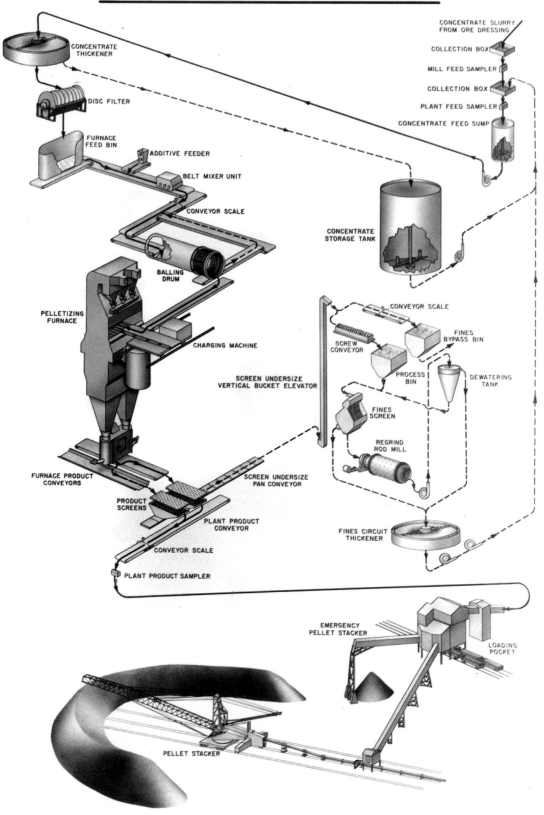

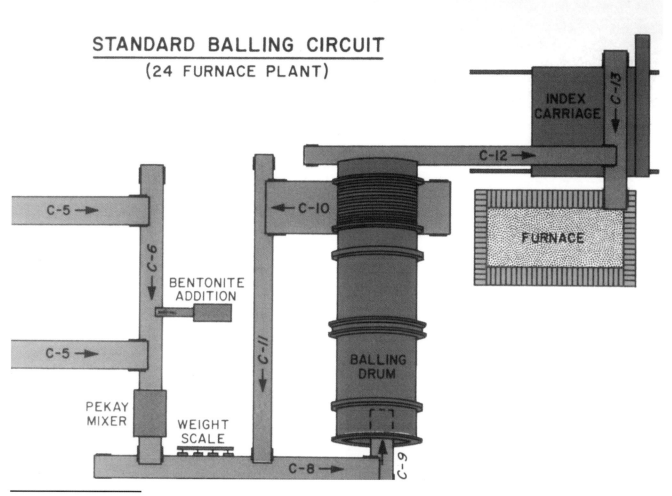

STANDARD BALLING CIRCUIT
(24 FURNACE PLANT)

Schematic of the balling circuit.

Balling drum discharge with trommel screen and properly sized green balls on conveyor to furnace.

Index feeder feeding green balls into the furnace.

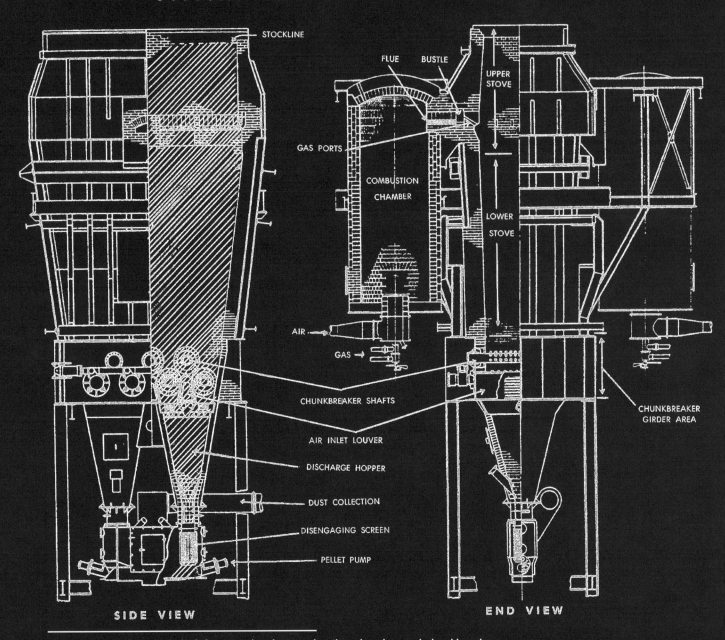

TYPICAL VERTICAL SHAFT FURNACE

STOCKLINE

FLUE   BUSTLE

UPPER STOVE

GAS PORTS

COMBUSTION CHAMBER

LOWER STOVE

AIR

GAS

CHUNKBREAKER SHAFTS

CHUNKBREAKER GIRDER AREA

AIR INLET LOUVER

DISCHARGE HOPPER

DUST COLLECTION

DISENGAGING SCREEN

PELLET PUMP

SIDE VIEW

END VIEW

Cross-section of vertical shaft furnace showing combustion chamber and chunkbreakers.

Furnace operator monitors pelletizing and adjusts furnace controls.

Assistant furnace operator inspects furnace discharge.

The thickeners, located at an elevation in the plant to utilize gravity to flow the material through the process, removed most of the water from the concentrate slurry. Each thickener supplied concentrate, averaging 70 percent solids, to four vacuum disk filters, two per furnace. Any excess concentrate flowed to one of five storage tanks having a total capacity of 7,200 tons. The six-foot-diameter, eight-disk vacuum filters removed more water and produced a filter cake averaging 10 percent moisture.

Bentonite, a binder, was pumped from an additive plant and added to the filter cake. The mixed filter cake was conveyed to the nine-foot-diameter, twenty-two-foot-long balling drums where the green balls were formed. There were twenty-four balling drums each dedicated to a separate rectangular, seven feet wide by fifteen and a half feet in length, and sixty feet high vertical shaft furnace. Because a consistent green ball size was important, trommel screens were attached to the discharge of the balling drums to separate the undersized green balls for return to the balling drum as "seed balls." The sized green balls were conveyed to a furnace.

Pellet stacker in operation.

Each furnace was a steel shell with refractory lining and two tapered discharge legs. There were two external attached combustion chambers and cooling air inlets above the discharge legs and chunkbreakers below the cooling air inlets. The temperature of the air blown into the furnace through the combustion chambers was maintained at 2350 degrees Fahrenheit. One-third or more of the air to the furnace passed through the combustion chambers while the balance was blown up through the cooling air inlets to cool the pellets. Typically pellets traveled down through the furnace to the discharge in less than four hours. Discharged pellets were screened and the screen undersize sent to a regrind mill and the mill product pumped to the Concentrate Feed Sump.

The heat added to the process initially came from the combustion of Bunker C fuel oil, but by 1965 the furnaces were converted to fuel with natural gas.[18] Furnace operator and operations supervisor

Art Lehtonen recalled that every pelletizing furnace would go through a major furnace overhaul periodically.[19] Along with rebricking the furnace, the entire furnace line was repaired from the concentrate thickeners and filters down to the furnace discharges. Erie's multiple-line configuration allowed for planned extended furnace maintenance with minimal impact on production.

During the Great Lakes shipping season, pellets produced were loaded directly into railcars for shipment to Taconite Harbor. During the winter months, pellets were diverted to the Pellet Stockpile Yard that had storage capacity to stockpile more than 4 million tons. Link-Belt had built and installed the largest belt conveyor pellet stacker in the United States. It was equipped with a 280-foot boom conveyor capable of swinging through a 180-degree arc and stacking pellets to a maximum height of ninety feet.[20]

Pellet stockpile yard showing direct railcar loading with cooling water spray racks at bottom.

RAILROAD AND HARBOR

In the spring of 1957, the Mainline Railroad and Dock construction was complete. The Dock could load two boats at a time. The results of early dock operations found train dumping was too slow and required changes. The movement of pellets is discussed in detail in Chapter 7.

Coal was delivered to Taconite Harbor by boat. The coal dock was equipped with a Wellman clam bucket unloader. The coal was then conveyed to a stacker. The stacked coal was reclaimed to long-term outdoor storage, conveyed to the Power Plant, or conveyed to empty pellet cars for shipment to the Plant Site Heating Plant.

The coal handling system worked well. The Heating Plant required delivery of up to 1,200 coal cars annually, but because of the steep rail grade from Taconite Harbor, only 24 cars could be moved at a time.

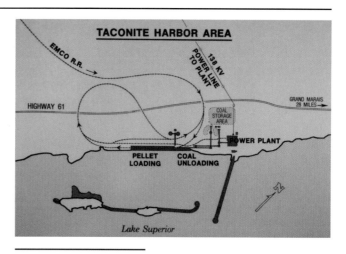

Plan map of Taconite Harbor.

Pellets being loaded into an ore boat.

Aerial view of boat loading.

Rail car dumps pellets into dock storage bins.

The *Samuel Mather* delivers coal to the Taconite Harbor dock.

Wellman unloader in operation.

Loading coal into railcars for delivery to Plant Site Heating Plant.

RAILROAD ROLLING STOCK

Railroad rolling stock included eighteen gondola cars and six 22,000-gallon tank cars, which were used to move material from Taconite Harbor. Vessels carrying rods and balls and other materials would be unloaded into gondola cars for shipment to the Plant Site. Because of the lack of a suitable vessel-unloading crane at Taconite Harbor, the movement of rods and balls via Taconite Harbor was abandoned. Lake tankers would transfer fuel oil into large storage tanks. The oil could then be transferred to the Power Plant or the railroad tank car loading facility. The plan was to attach the loaded tank cars to a returning pellet train and unload them into the Plant Site fuel oil storage tanks. The empty tank cars were then to be returned to Taconite Harbor with a subsequent pellet train. However, oil handling had to be abandoned, as the heavier Bunker C type oil would solidify in the tank cars before being unloaded.

22,000-gallon tank cars.

POWER PLANT

By the summer of 1957, and before the Commercial Plant was ready to operate, the Power Plant was tested to verify its operation. The two generating units were put on line supplying energy to the local utility. Each of the Power Plant units consisted of coal bunkers, a boiler, turbine, generator, and condenser. The boiler was fired with pulverized coal and produced superheated steam for the turbine. The turbine was coupled to a generator that was rated at 75MW at 3600 rpm. A condenser received the turbine exhaust steam, and the condensate was pumped back to the boiler to be recycled. The generator output was 13,800 volts, which was stepped up to 138,000 volts for transmission to the Plant Site. After the short test run during the summer, generation was cut back to match the Plant Site load as it was being increased from September to December.

MAINTENANCE

It was the intent of Erie's designers to make the operation as self-sufficient as possible, and that included providing complete on-site maintenance facilities. Erie understood that every dollar spent on maintenance would be returned many times over in reduced downtime and increased productivity.

Power Plant interior with a view of turbine generator with condenser below.

Bernard "Spike" Borgel, Power Plant superintendent, left, looks on while Leonard Johnston, Erie Works manager, throws the switch to first energize the 138KV power line.

General Shop Building with Rebuild Shop building to the left.

Major maintenance activities were centered at the General Shops building located east of the Concentrator. The General Shops provided services for the entire operation and contained the Car Shop, Machine Shop, Locomotive Shop, Small Tool Repair, Electric Shop, Blacksmith Shop, Weld Shop, and Sheetmetal Shop.

The Locomotive and Car Shops maintained all the railroad rolling stock used at Erie. The Blacksmith, Weld, and Machine Shops fabricated or repaired

components of all mechanical equipment. The Electric Shop serviced and repaired everything from two-way radios to large mill motors. "They had some really good boilermakers and blacksmiths in the General Shop," Maintenance Supervisor Gerald "Curly" Rollins said. "Everything was done in-house. We did all of our own repairing."[21]

The Rebuild Shop, located adjacent to the General Shops, rebuilt engines and maintained the pickups, service trucks, sedans, light plants, forklifts, railroad

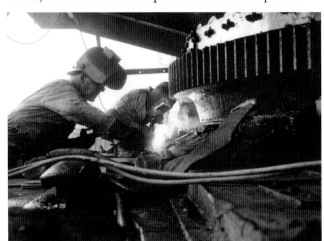

Field repair of a shovel.

Changing a large truck tire.

Shop electricians rebuild a mill motor.

Rebuilding a shovel dipper in the weld shop.

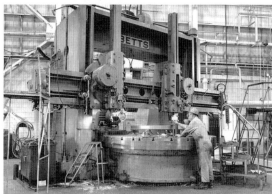

General Shop interior (from top to bottom): Car Shop, Locomotive Shop, vertical boring mill, and Machine Shop.

HINSDALE HIGH BRIDGE

The general arrangement of Erie's commercial plant located north of the Village of Mesaba required that the Mine Railroad cross the existing DM&IR rail line serving the Vermillion Range. Initial plans were for the Mine Railroad track from Mining Area 1 to the Coarse Crusher to cross on fill 100 feet above the DM&IR track near Hinsdale. The DM&IR track would pass through a concrete tunnel and the area surrounding the tunnel back-filled with mine waste rock.

In early 1957, and before the fill on top of the tunnel could be completed, significant and growing cracks were found in the concrete. By June 1957,

Concrete tunnel, looking north, with fill for Erie's Mine Railroad above nearing completion.

it was determined that the tunnel was not structurally sound and that it would have to be replaced with a bridge. The fill was removed and bridge construction begun. By the time the tunnel was removed, the "High Bridge" was in place. This required modification delayed ore delivery from Mining Area 1 until late 1957.

Concrete tunnel, looking south, with fill being removed after concrete cracking developed.

North end of concrete tunnel with fill removed.

Protective shed installed inside the tunnel to protect train traffic during concrete removal.

Installation of High Bridge span to replace concrete tunnel.

Erie mine locomotives on the Hinsdale High Bridge with DM&IR train below.

Interior of the Rebuild Shop where all pickups, sedans, service trucks, and other smaller equipment were maintained.

Aerial view of Area 1 Shop, the mine equipment maintenance facility after expansion.

Interior of Area 1 Truck Shop showing eighty-five-ton-capacity haul trucks.

maintenance equipment, and other small vehicles. Maintenance Supervisor Ron Barteck noted that there were two crews that took turns working day shift and afternoon shift five days a week. At one time, there were more than three hundred pickup trucks plus the sedans to maintain. Erie's operating departments also retained separate maintenance crews that performed scheduled and breakdown repairs on their equipment as necessary.

Repairs and routine maintenance on large mobile mining equipment, such as crawler tractors, front end loaders, and haul trucks, was done at the Mining Department's Area 1 Shops or Area 2 Shops, located respectively about a mile west and a mile east of the Plant Site. Because of the time involved in moving the shovels and drills large distances, repairs were normally performed right where the equipment was located in the mine.

The Area 2 Shops also contained the original Tire Shop, where the repairs and change out of tires used on all the vehicles was done. This included small tires for pickup trucks all the way up to the very large haul truck tires.

Tire repairman Ken Overby described the early days. "You had to do everything with a ratchet and a socket, and it was quite a procedure. Then when they started getting bigger haul trucks, the tires got way bigger. Then you had to use a forklift to wrestle them into position to take them off and put them on. The haul trucks and tires just kept getting bigger and bigger and bigger and bigger."[22] The largest tires on the 240-ton haul trucks weighed about six tons apiece.

"In maintenance, our big problem everywhere was components wearing out," Ted Williams said. "The abrasive taconite wore everything out—ore cars, haul truck dump boxes, dozer blades, shovel teeth, everything."[23] Maintenance crews came up with some innovative solutions to the problem of wear on the mining trucks. "You get a new truck box, it wouldn't last at all unless you did something about it," Williams explained. "Wear bars were welded to the bottom and sides of the truck boxes by trial and error. By changing the pattern and material of the wear bars, good truck box life was developed."[24]

ERIE'S HAUL TRUCKS

Richard Rude, who spent more than thirty years and took great pride in driving trucks in the mine, commented on the changes experienced: "When I started driving trucks in 1962, the trucks were mostly 34- and 45-ton-capacity Euclids (Eucs) and some 50-ton Macks. Then we went to the 55-ton Haulpaks, 85- and 100-ton Unit Rigs, 170-ton Euclids and Lectra-Hauls, and finally to the 240-ton-capacity versions. The moves up in truck size were gradual, taking place over the years. The changes in driving techniques were gradual; in fact, the bigger the trucks got, the easier and safer they were to drive."[42]

The size of the mining trucks increased dramatically from 34-ton capacity of the 1950s (top) to the 240-ton capacity of the 1990s (bottom right).

STAFF DEPARTMENTS

The staff departments that supported the operating and maintenance departments by providing administrative and technical service included Industrial Relations (labor relations, personnel, and training and development), Materials Management (purchasing), Accounting, Public Relations, Safety, Mine Engineering, Plant Engineering, Industrial Engineering, and Process Development.

The first task for the Industrial Relations Department in the late 1950s and early 1960s was hiring the three thousand workers needed to operate and maintain the Commercial Plant. Dan DeVaney said, "They were hiring people from all over the country." There were not enough trained people on the Iron Range to provide the qualified employees needed in just about every occupation."[25]

Recruiters went out to other mining operations in the United States and interviewed people who could be put right on the job. Erie had a lot of success hiring people from the copper industry in Arizona. "They got people from all over," DeVaney said. "They went to Iowa and they got farmers. They hired people from everywhere."[26]

At the same time, Erie was hiring locally. The company opened a hiring hall in Aurora. "Some days they'd open up the door and say, 'Okay, we're hiring today,' and there'd be a line of fifty people out front coming in and signing up to come to work," DeVaney said.[27]

Once all those employees were hired, Industrial Relations faced the more difficult challenge of training them. From its very earliest days, Erie relied on a formal apprenticeship program. Erie also encouraged employees to further their education, reimbursing them upon the successful completion of college and vocational-technical school courses related to their job. The result was a loyal, dedicated workforce that applied the lessons they had learned in training or school to ensure that Erie was an efficient pellet producer.

"Thank goodness the company set up the apprentice program," said Ted Williams. "That is how we developed the craft people. It was a big

program and very effective. We had hundreds of employees that went through it."[28]

Apprentice instructor Gary Paavola remembered thinking that the selection criteria for the apprenticeship system seemed to be fair. "The determination of how an apprentice was selected was based on an aptitude test score, interview, and background experience," he explained.[29] Paavola added that if a candidate interviewed well and their test score showed that they had the ability to learn, that also counted.

Maintenance mechanic Ron Hoechst remembered being impressed when the company reimbursed the money he had paid for apprenticeship textbooks. "Along with that apprenticeship, you had to take an aptitude test and then the interview," he said. "And then you had to go through and take this ICS program. It was a correspondence course, lots of books that you had to pay for and then if you finished them and passed, you got reimbursed all that money back. I think I got $142 back at the time, which was a lot of money for me. That was over two weeks' wages at that time."[30]

Maintenance mechanic Malcolm Stead Jr., an early graduate of the Erie apprenticeship program, recalled, "When we went through the apprenticeship program, we'd spend about six months in each department." This provided a well-rounded background in everything at Erie.[31]

Welder Robert "Bart" Bartholomew remembered his apprenticeship as a "super cool time" of his life. "We started out as welder apprentices," he said. "We actually started to learn how to start the welder to make an arc to get things going. I remember working in those little welding cubicles trying to get an arc running, and I think our first major job that we did was hard surfacing on the inside of pipe spigots. As long as you were in the General Shop, that was basically your job until you got certain skills, and then they put you with a regular welder and you would work together on other projects."[32]

Welder Jim Westbrook signed up for a welding apprenticeship and, with another apprentice welder (Ron Heruth), inquired about GI Bill benefits with a VA representative in Aurora. Erie

Erie Administration Building.

Classroom apprentice training.

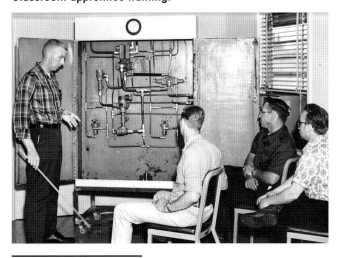

Apprentice training used mockups of actual Erie systems.

Training Department staff assisted with completing the required forms. Before those benefits could be received, apprenticeship-training programs had to be approved by the Minnesota Department of Labor. The GI Bill benefits helped an estimated 60 percent of those in the apprenticeship program.[33]

Manager Greg Walker said the people who staffed the apprenticeship program "were hands-on. There was a real strength of personality, and the training of the craft people, in particular, was outstanding. A very well-developed apprentice-training program had been set up. The maintenance department was a large part of that."[34]

Maintenance Supervisor Darwyn Haveri and Millwright Corinne "Petey" Eden remembered feeling a sense of pride at their accomplishments in the Erie apprenticeship program. "I was the first maintenance mechanic general from Erie Mining Company to complete the correspondence school training that was part of the apprenticeship program," Haveri said. "Once I finished the course, Erie gave me a three job classes raise. That's something I'll always be proud of."[35]

"I was a fulltime millwright," Eden said. "I was the first woman to go through the apprenticeship program—and took pride in getting the job done that we were given at the beginning of the day and doing it well, earning the respect of my coworkers for doing a good job."[36]

On-the-job training for a machinist apprentice.

Maintenance skill training continued as new equipment was acquired.

An electrical apprentice completes his training and receives his graduation certificate.

Industrial Relations also was responsible for labor negotiations on a local and national level; managing seniority, insurance, and pension issues; and administering worker compensation claims. Preparing a weekly work schedule for all employees was a significant ongoing task.

The Materials Management Department was responsible for soliciting and evaluating bids and ordering all equipment, parts, materials, supplies, and services used at Erie. Lynn Niemi's first job was in Materials Management. "What we did was typed purchase orders," she said.[37] One thing Niemi will never forget is the original Erie mailroom operation. She recalled that "in the mailroom there were bags, regular post office heavy canvas bags, and they were locked." "Erie in those days actually had a taxicab," she continued, "and either the taxicab driver or somebody else would bring these mailbags to the various departments."[38] Sometimes the Taconite Harbor mailbags would be delivered by train.

The Accounting Department's function was to track costs, pay bills, prepare reports, develop budgets, and manage warehouses. Warehousing encompassed receiving, properly storing, and

A portion of Erie's Accounting Department.

issuing materials. Erie implemented a detailed cost reporting system where each operating area and piece of equipment was assigned a unique number (cost account). Each cost account was then followed by a cost element number designating labor, materials, or services. Time cards with employee badge number, hours worked, job class, and cost account information tracked labor expenses and were used to process the payroll. Issue tickets with a commodity code number that identified the material, quantity issued, and cost account information tracked where supplies were used and allowed inventories to be adjusted. Initially, several accounting clerks were assigned to each department to manually develop the detailed and summary reports produced at month's end. These reports were used for cost analysis, monthly financial reporting, and, along with planned operating changes, to develop departmental budgets.

The Accounts Payable group made payments to vendors and suppliers as purchase order items were completed. Warehouse receiving would confirm that the materials ordered were received before payment was made. All other expenses required cost accounts and followed a signature approval procedure before they were paid.

Delivery of mail from Taconite Harbor by train.

125

The original Erie telephone operator switchboard.

The Accounting Department also included the typing pool, telephone switchboard, mailroom, and copy room.

The Public Relations Department was responsible for coordinating all official communications with newspapers and public officials as well as the publications of company newsletters. They also planned, organized and coordinated special events such as stockholder tours, apprentice graduation, and service award dinners.

The Safety Department established policies, rules, and procedures to maintain a safe working environment. There were Safety representatives assigned in all major operating departments to facilitate implementation of safety programs and to monitor safety performance. Safety provided talks for supervisors to deliver to workers, coordinated with the Union Safety Committee

Erie's ambulance was parked at the Main Gate and operated by the Safety Department.

and government mine inspectors, and conducted routine safety tours. Most importantly, Safety investigated all accidents or potential near misses with the objective of eliminating possible causes and ensuring a safe work place. Plant Security, the onsite fire brigade, the medical Dispensary, and Erie's ambulance were also managed by Safety.

In the Plant Engineering Department, civil, mechanical, and electrical engineers developed designs and specifications for projects to modify and improve the facilities. Draftsmen made drawings so that the design changes could be implemented. There were also field engineers that monitored the work done on the projects.

The Industrial Engineering Department performed time studies and monitored and evaluated wear part life. The times required for a truck or railcar to be loaded, the load hauled and dumped, and the truck or railcar returning for another load were key elements for determining mine operating costs and productivity. These cycle times were constantly measured and studied for areas of improvement.

The Process Development Department comprised of metallurgists and technicians that researched process equipment performance and recommended flow sheet improvements from crushing to pelletizing. Overall product quality control, including sampling procedures and the many routine laboratory tests conducted on production samples at the on-site labs, was a Process Development function. Process Development also managed the Analytical Lab and coordinated activities with the Hibbing Lab for special projects.

For Roger Hull, there was no question about the secret to Erie's success over nearly a half-century of operations. "The people were what made it work," he said. "I had six hundred people in Ore Dressing at one time, in addition to ninety-five or ninety-six supervisors, including both operations and maintenance. Everybody worked together. The people are what really pulled it off. The people from the area were used to working. They were good people."[39]

The people of Erie had proved they could handle the challenges of the start-up of the largest commercial taconite plant in the world.

Main Gate.

Plant Engineering operated its own reproduction machine that produced blueprints, maps, and photocopies.

NUMBER CRUNCHING TOOLS AT ERIE

Tom Niemi recalled that when he first went into Plant Engineering, many of the engineers were using mechanical Friden calculators. "They were a big, heavy, gray machine that sat on the desk with a huge keyboard on it. The engineers would have their paper all laid out with the calculations they needed, and then they'd be entering these numbers on this machine. Then they'd put the machine into 'go,' and it would be 'boom, boom, bang, bang, crash, grind, grind, grind,' and then out would come the results. They'd be reading numbers off some indicator on the thing." Niemi stayed with his slide rule until Texas Instruments introduced the first handheld pocket calculator in the late 1960s. "I don't know if anybody waited for the engineering department or Erie to get calculators," he said. "I think everybody had them in their pockets immediately when they were available."[46]

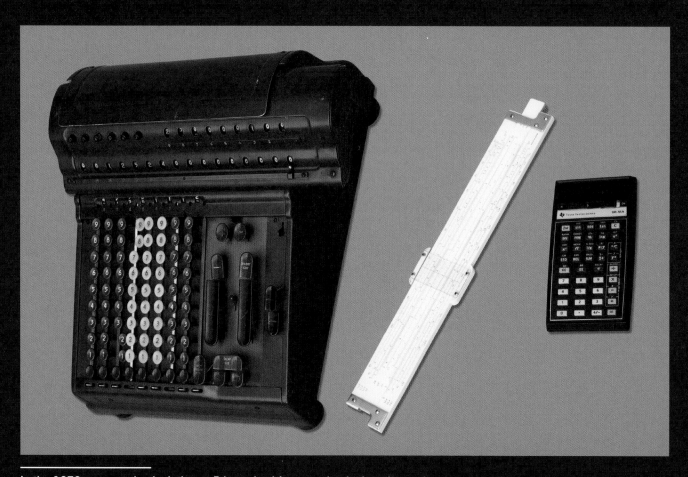

In the 1970s, personal calculating at Erie evolved from mechanical to electronic.

EARLY TACONITE DEVELOPMENT

1865 — Expedition on the way to Lake Vermillion to explore for gold and found significant evidence of iron-bearing rock (taconite) near Babbitt. A group of investors formed Ontonagon Syndicate to acquire the deposit. This was the first investment in iron mining in Minnesota.

1872 — Federal land survey was conducted on the taconite lands near Babbitt, which allowed the Ontonagon Syndicate to acquire the land.

1911 — University of Minnesota Mines Experiment Station was established for the purpose of promoting development of Minnesota's mineral resources.

1913-15 — Mines Experiment Station began work on low grade (-30% iron content) taconite. Laboratory tests of magnetic separation process on samples of taconite ore reduced to 150 mesh produced a concentrate with iron content of more than 60%.

1916-19 — Mesabi Syndicate was organized to develop the former Ontonagon Syndicate lands. A 100 ton/day test plant was established in West Duluth and by the end of 1918 had produced 1,840 tons of sinter.

1919-21 — Mesabi Syndicate established Mesabi Iron Company (Mesabi Iron) to develop a mine and construct a plant at Babbitt to process taconite on a commercial scale.

1922-24 — Mesabi Iron operated for two years, but when the price of iron ore dropped below cost of production, the facility closed.

1931 — Elton Hoyt 2nd, Pickands Mather president, became interested in taconite research and assigned John Metcalf to monitor the Mines Experiment Station's progress.

1933-37 — Mines Experiment Station and Butler Brothers operated an experimental plant for roasting and concentrating of nonmagnetic taconites of the western Mesabi Range.

1930-40 — Research into grinding, concentrating, and further processing of taconite continued at the Mines Experiment Station.

1940 — John Metcalf recommended that Pickands Mather begin its own taconite research program. Elton Hoyt 2nd convinced two steel companies of taconite's potential and organized Erie Mining Company to further that research.

Dunka Loading Pocket

1967
Expansion to
10.3 million
tons annual
production
completed
(announced
in 1964)

1967
Regrind Fine
Screening operational

1971
Closed
Circuit Fine
Screening
operational

1965
Mining started at
Dunka and Area 6

1965
Natural gas replaced
oil as pelletizing fuel

1967
Mining started
at Area 9

1960
Automatic Car
Dumping at Taconite
Harbor operational

1962
Ball Mills enlarged

dded

59
tionwide
eelworkers Strike

1961
Erie achieved design
production capacity

1963
Rod Mills enlarged

1966
TRC organized

1970
Maximum employment
of 3046

1970
Mining started at Area 2W

1970
Total production
reached 100
million tons

LOCAL 4108

Hibbing Lab

1940
Erie formed by
Pickands Mather and
two steel companies

1946
Construction of
PreTac authorized

1949
First Jet Piercer Drill
operational at PreTac

1954
Construction started
on Commercial Plant
and Hoyt Lakes; first
resident moved into
Hoyt Lakes

1958
Second Coarse
Crushing Line a

1942
Hibbing Lab opened

1948
Production started
at PreTac and
continued until 1957

1953
USWA Local Union
4108 organized

1953
7.5 million ton/
year Commercial
Plant announced

1957
Mining started in Area
1 and Area 2. First ore
delivered (Aug 14).
First pellets shipped
from Taconite Harbor
(Sept 26).

19
Na
Ste

PreTac

First PreTac Pellets

First Pellet Cargo

Erie Mining Company Key Statistics

Column	A	B	C	D	E	F	G	H	I	J	K	L	M
Year	Million Tons Surface and Rock Stripping	Million Tons Taconite Ore	Total Million Tons Stripping and Ore	Stripping Ratio	Million Tons Pellets Produced	Million Tons Chips Produced	Million Tons Filter Cake Produced	Total Million Tons Produced	Million Tons Pellets Shipped	Pellet Trains Dumped	Boats Loaded	Million MWH Generated	Million Tons (short) Coal Burned
1957	8.2	1.1	9.3	7.3	0.3	0.0	0.0	0.3	0.1	37	9	0.1	0.1
1958	2.7	9.3	12.0	0.3	2.9	0.1	0.0	3.0	2.7	339	174	0.5	0.2
1959	2.4	12.5	14.9	0.2	4.1	0.0	0.0	4.2	4.1	487	237	0.5	0.2
1960	7.0	21.7	28.7	0.3	7.1	0.0	0.0	7.2	5.7	640	322	0.8	0.3
1961	4.8	21.2	26.0	0.2	6.7	0.0	0.0	6.7	7.6	901	459	0.8	0.3
1962	6.1	24.2	30.2	0.3	7.7	0.0	0.0	7.8	7.7	812	460	0.9	0.4
1963	6.7	24.3	31.0	0.3	7.7	0.0	0.0	7.7	8.2	931	453	1.0	0.4
1964	7.6	24.0	31.5	0.3	7.9	0.0	0.0	7.9	7.9	848	441	0.9	0.4
1965	9.8	23.0	32.7	0.4	8.0	0.0	0.0	8.0	8.0	857	432	0.9	0.4
1966	13.4	24.3	37.7	0.5	8.6	0.0	0.0	8.6	8.6	891	482	1.0	0.4
1967	11.0	29.7	40.7	0.4	9.9	0.0	0.0	9.9	9.6	1,138	523	1.2	0.5
1968	8.8	31.2	40.0	0.3	10.7	0.0	0.0	10.7	10.7	1,347	559	1.2	0.5
1969	8.8	29.7	38.5	0.3	10.2	0.0	0.0	10.2	10.2	1,323	526	1.2	0.5
1970	9.3	30.3	39.6	0.3	10.7	0.0	0.0	10.7	10.4	1,331	548	1.2	0.5
1971	9.2	29.8	39.0	0.3	10.2	0.0	0.0	10.2	9.2	1,143	461	1.2	0.5
1972	9.3	29.3	38.6	0.3	9.8	0.0	0.0	9.8	10.6	1,291	461	1.2	0.5
1973	10.2	32.7	42.8	0.3	11.7	0.0	0.0	11.7	13.1	1,507	569	1.2	0.6
1974	10.3	32.3	42.6	0.3	10.9	0.0	0.0	10.9	11.0	1,282	423	1.2	0.5
1975	8.9	33.6	42.5	0.3	10.9	0.0	0.0	10.9	10.6	1,247	383	1.3	0.6
1976	9.4	33.1	42.6	0.3	10.8	0.0	0.0	10.8	10.3	1,319	258	1.3	0.6
1977	5.1	13.5	18.6	0.4	4.6	0.0	0.0	4.6	3.5	427	103	0.6	0.3
1978	9.0	21.7	30.7	0.4	7.6	0.0	0.0	7.6	9.1	1,105	265	1.0	0.4
1979	10.6	26.0	36.7	0.4	9.8	0.0	0.0	9.8	9.5	1,188	357	1.1	0.5
1980	10.1	16.8	26.9	0.6	5.9	0.0	0.0	5.9	6.1	730	217	0.8	0.3
1981	10.3	23.8	34.1	0.4	8.3	0.0	0.0	8.3	7.6	952	278	1.0	0.4
1982	4.2	11.9	16.1	0.4	4.2	0.0	0.0	4.2	3.6	395	146	0.5	0.2
1983	1.9	5.9	7.8	0.3	2.2	0.0	0.0	2.2	3.9	444	173	0.0	0.0
1984	2.6	14.1	16.7	0.2	4.8	0.0	0.0	4.8	3.4	370	136	0.0	0.0
1985	3.5	14.4	17.8	0.2	5.0	0.0	0.0	5.0	5.0	556	172	0.0	0.0
1986	1.3	13.2	14.4	0.1	4.5	0.0	0.0	4.5	5.5	625	135	0.0	0.0
1987	3.8	21.5	25.3	0.2	6.8	0.1	0.0	7.0	7.0	845	137	0.0	0.0
1988	7.7	30.5	38.3	0.3	7.9	0.2	0.0	8.1	7.1	865	167	0.0	0.0
1989	9.7	24.2	34.0	0.4	7.4	0.2	0.0	7.6	7.6	921	177	0.0	0.0
1990	10.1	25.4	35.4	0.4	7.6	0.4	0.7	8.6	8.2	978	215	0.0	0.0
1991	10.3	22.6	32.8	0.5	6.8	0.3	0.0	7.1	7.2	1,001	179	0.2	0.1
1992	8.3	22.3	30.6	0.4	6.4	0.3	0.0	6.8	7.2	903	172	0.8	0.4
1993	9.2	25.8	35.0	0.4	7.3	0.4	0.0	7.7	7.9	1,009	176	1.1	0.1
1994	10.2	26.7	36.8	0.4	7.4	0.4	0.0	7.8	7.7	903	148	1.0	0.7
1995	13.7	27.5	41.1	0.5	7.4	0.4	0.0	7.8	7.8	915	175	0.7	0.5
1996	30.0	26.2	56.2	1.1	7.1	0.4	0.0	7.5	7.4	910	166	0.6	0.4
1997	32.1	25.8	57.9	1.2	7.3	0.4	0.0	7.7	7.2	988	154	0.9	0.6
1998	34.2	23.7	57.8	1.4	6.7	0.4	0.0	7.1	7.4	865	168	1.1	0.7
1999	31.4	23.2	54.6	1.4	6.6	0.4	0.0	7.0	6.6	780	184	1.0	0.6
2000	6.6	19.2	25.8	0.3	7.3	0.4	0.0	7.8	9.1	998	160	1.2	0.7
2001	0.0	0.4	0.4	0.0	0.1	0.0	0.0	0.1	2.0	271	58	0.0	0.0
Total	440	1,003.3	1,442.9		323.8	4.9	0.7	329.4	330.8	39,615	12,598	33.4	15.3
Average				0.44						880	280		

Column	Description
A	Surface and rock removed to access taconite ore
B	Taconite ore mined
C	Total of stripping and taconite ore mined (A+B)
D	Ratio of stripping removed to ore mined (A/B)
E	Pellets produced
F	Chips (undersized pellets shipped as a product) produced
G	Filter cake (iron concentrate shipped as a product) produced
H	Total pellets, chips and filter cake produced determined by owner requirements and Erie capacity
I	Total pellets shipped
J	Total trains dumped (average 100 car trains)
K	Total Boat Loaded (larger capacity boats in later years)
L	Total power generated - all power purchased from 1983 to 1990
M	Total coal burned to generate power

Source: Erie Mining Company Records except * = St Louis County Mine Inspector's Annual Reports

Erie Mining Company Key Statistics

	Employment		Productivity	Quality				Safety			
	N	O	P	Q	R	S	T	U	V	W	X
Year	Average Number of Employees	Million Manhours Worked	Tons Pellets Produced per Manhour Worked	% Magnetic Iron in Ore	All Material Ratio	% Iron in Pellet	% Silica in Pellet	Lost Time Accidents *	Lost Days *	Lost Time Accident per Million Manhour Worked	Fatality
1957	1,031	2.2	0.12	22.52	34.62	62.53	8.74	7	610	3.2	Truck collision
1958	2,380	4.8	0.62	22.32	4.04	62.53	8.83	7	1,371	1.4	
1959	2,720	4.3	0.98	22.75	3.58	62.02	9.84	9	1,128	2.1	
1960	2,864	5.5	1.30	22.30	4.00	62.11	9.98	14	1,799	2.5	Fall from drill
1961	2,391	4.7	1.43	22.36	3.86	63.01	8.82	8	305	1.7	
1962	2,345	4.7	1.64	22.34	3.89	63.19	8.59	10	568	2.1	
1963	2,269	4.6	1.67	22.70	4.04	63.52	8.11	4	215	0.9	
1964	2,300	4.6	1.72	23.57	3.98	63.49	8.06	3	56	0.6	
1965	2,248	4.7	1.69	24.17	4.09	63.53	8.02	4	364	0.8	
1966	2,544	5.1	1.66	23.80	4.41	63.29	8.00	6	491	1.2	
1967	2,719	5.4	1.83	23.06	4.11	63.71	7.35	5	267	0.9	Brakeman, rail collision
1968	2,723	5.5	1.96	23.69	3.73	63.89	7.19	4	236	0.7	
1969	2,711	5.3	1.93	23.80	3.78	63.91	7.14	12	955	2.3	
1970	2,796	5.7	1.90	24.25	3.69	63.88	7.06	11	681	1.9	
1971	2,800	5.3	1.94	24.24	3.83	64.32	6.50	7	605	1.3	
1972	2,700	5.1	1.91	24.15	3.95	64.36	6.41	9	1,019	1.8	
1973	2,700	5.2	2.24	23.96	3.67	64.42	6.41	8	430	1.5	Train Operator, rail collision
1974	2,700	5.1	2.14	24.12	3.91	64.74	6.02	12	711	2.4	
1975	2,711	5.3	2.04	22.79	3.90	64.70	6.06	12	480	2.2	
1976	2,730	5.6	1.92	22.96	3.95	64.81	5.96	12	928	2.1	Train Conductor, fall
1977	1,821	3.5	1.32	23.91	4.00	64.61	6.18	9	339	2.6	
1978	2,333	4.4	1.74	24.89	4.05	64.56	6.26	9	438	2.1	
1979	2,490	4.8	2.04	24.34	3.74	64.55	6.22	14	448	2.9	
1980	1,900	3.8	1.56	24.11	4.58	64.60	6.19	7	147	1.9	
1981	2,288	4.2	1.98	24.18	4.09	64.60	6.21	10	427	2.4	
1982	1,235	2.5	1.68	24.00	3.85	64.61	6.22	4	235	1.6	
1983	661	1.4	1.56	24.96	3.60	65.40	5.24	2	64	1.4	Welder, fall
1984	1,121	2.4	2.05	24.27	3.44	65.41	5.24	7	169	3.0	
1985	928	1.9	2.68	24.39	3.56	65.38	5.27	3	110	1.6	
1986	994	2.0	2.30	23.53	3.20	65.30	5.25	3	105	1.5	
1987	1,128	2.4	2.89	23.66	3.64	65.28	5.32	4	145	1.7	
1988	1,429	3.1	2.62	22.77	4.72	65.38	5.17	3	106	1.0	
1989	1,520	3.1	2.48	23.36	4.48	65.47	5.05	5	257	1.6	Tractor Operator, drowning
1990	1,721	3.2	2.70	23.12	4.11	65.59	5.02	6	445	1.9	
1991	1,630	3.2	2.19	22.96	4.63	65.61	4.95	4	299	1.2	
1992	1,592	3.1	2.17	22.33	4.52	65.64	4.92	35	1,098	11.2	Safety Statistics Calculation Method Changed in 1992
1993	1,543	3.3	2.34	21.67	4.56	65.56	4.92	41	1,445	12.5	
1994	1,514	3.2	2.43	20.78	4.72	65.45	5.02	23	648	7.1	
1995	1,472	3.1	2.50	19.39	5.30	65.47	4.97	18	520	5.8	
1996	1,433	3.1	2.41	20.19	7.53	65.26	5.23	30	850	9.7	
1997	1,420	3.1	2.53	20.35	7.51	65.20	5.31	32	937	10.5	
1998	1,352	3.0	2.39	21.05	8.14	65.16	5.35	36	723	12.1	
1999	1,314	2.9	2.42	21.16	7.82	65.30	5.20	19	1046	6.6	
2000	1,247	2.7	2.86	na	3.33	na	na	11	391	4.0	
2001	50	0.4	0.34	na	2.89	na	na	0	0	0.0	
Total		172.3									
Average	1,923		1.93	23.05	5.00	64.45	6.46				

Column	Column	Description
N		Average number of employees at Plant Site and Taconite Harbor *
O		Total manhours worked at Plant Site and Taconite Harbor including overtime *
P		Tons per Manhour Worked (H/O)
Q		% Magnetic Iron in Ore (Grade of Ore delivered to Crusher)
R		Tons Ore and Stripping Mined per Tons Pellet Produced (C/H)
S		% Iron in pellets - determines value of pellet
T		% Silica in pellets - contaminant that must be removed in blast furnace
U		Total Lost Time Accidents *
V		Total Days Lost to to Lost Time Accidents *
W		Lost Time Accidents per Million Manhours Worked (R/O)
X		Fatality - worker - type *

Source: Erie Mining Company Records except * = St Louis County Mine Inspector's Annual Reports

0-ton
aul truck,
e Lode,"
rating
ul truck on
Range)

agement
on Teams
d Integrated
ontrol (IPC)
ed

1990
Taconite Harbor townsite closed, houses removed and site landscaped

1990
First Annual LTV Steel Mining Company Employee Picnic

1994
Mine Consolidation Project started—Area 2E Superpocket operational and $26 million for new trucks, shovel, drill

1994
Mining ceased at Dunka

1997
Total production reached 300 million tons

1997
Largest single blast on September 4, 2,854,000 tons of rock

2001
Erie assets sold to Cliffs and Minnesota Power on October 22

2001
Last pellet train to Taconite Harbor on June 23

2001
Last ore dumped on January 4; last pellets produced on January 5

1989
Computerized Truck/Train Dispatch implemented (first integrated truck/ train system)

1993
LTV Steel Corporation emerged from Chapter 11 Bankruptcy

1996
Area 2WX Superpocket operational

1996
Magnetic Separator Replacement Project began

1996
60 degrees below zero at Erie on February 2

2000
On May 24, LTV Steel announced Erie will close in mid-2001

2000
Total ore mined reached 1 billion tons on November 7

2000
LTV Steel declared bankruptcy on December 29 and announced immediate shutdown of Erie

Sample of last Erie pellets

STRIKE VOTE

**LOCAL UNION
4108**

United Steelworkers

Strike Authorization Ballot

1986
Local Union 4108
Work Stoppage began
(8/1/86 to 1/31/87)

1986
LTV Steel Corporation
filed for Chapter 11
(reorganization)
Bankruptcy and
became 100% owner
of Erie as part of
restructuring

1982
28-cubic-yard shovel
acquired (largest on
the Mesabi Range)

1977
Rangewide Strike,
lasted 132 days at Erie

1977
Annual production was
cut to 7.2 million tons

1980
Three-month shutdown

1982
Power Plant
shutdown due to
availibility of lower
cost electrical power
(restarted in 1991)

1986
Pickands Mather
acquired by
Cleveland Cliffs Inc.,
which assumed
management of Erie

1973
Taconite Harbor
shipped record
tonnage of 13.1 million
tons and loaded record
number of boats

1973
Gardner-Denver large
rotary drill operational
—began replacement
of Jet Piercing Drills
(last Jet Piercing Drill
retired in 1982)

1978
Annual production
was cut to 5.75
million tons

1981
Total production
reached 200
million tons

1983
Annual production of
2.1 million tons due to
shutdowns continued
from mid-1982 and at
end of 1983

1987
Flotation opera

1987
Mining started
Area 2WX

1987
Erie's name cha
to LTV Steel
Mining Compar

**LTV Steel
Mining Co.**

Erie in the 1980s

MINNESOTA'S OTHER TACONITE PLANTS

In addition to Erie, seven other taconite plants were developed on the Mesabi Range. Since Erie's PreTac began in 1948, these plants have produced over 2 billion tons of iron ore products. Currently, only six of the taconite plants are in operation, and they have the capacity to produce approximately 40 million tons of iron ore pellets annually, which is about 80 percent of total U.S. iron ore production.

NorthShore Mining Originally developed as Reserve Mining Company, the mine at Babbitt and the processing plant at Silver Bay, began operation in 1956. The plant was expanded to 10.7 million tons annual production in 1966. Reserve closed in 1986 following the bankruptcy of its owners. Cyprus Amax Minerals acquired the property in 1989 and restarted in 1990 as Cyprus Northshore Mining. In 1994, Cleveland-Cliffs Inc. purchased the property and renamed it Northshore Mining, which currently has a rated production capacity of 6.0 million tons per year.

United Taconite Developed as Eveleth Taconite Company (EVTAC), the mine at Eveleth and the processing plant in Forbes began operation in 1965. The facility was expanded in 1976, and in 1996 was restructured and production capacity reduced. The property entered bankruptcy in 2002 and was purchased by Cleveland-Cliffs Inc. and China's Laiwu Steel in 2003 and renamed United Taconite. By 2008, Cleveland-Cliffs Inc. acquired full ownership; United Taconite currently has a rated capacity of 5.4 million tons per year.

Minorca Inland Steel Mining Company developed Minorca near Virginia and began operation in 1977. Currently owned by ArcelorMittal, the world's largest steel company, Minorca has a rated capacity of 2.8 million tons per year.

Minntac U.S. Steel Corporation's Minntac, located in Mt. Iron, is North America's largest taconite operation. Minntac production began in 1967 and was expanded in 1972 and 1978 to a current rated capacity of approximately 16.0 million tons per year.

Hibbing Taconite The mine and processing plant located near Hibbing began production in 1976. Hibbing Taconite has a current rated capacity of 8.0 million tons per year.

Keewatin Taconite (Keetac) Originally developed as National Steel Pellet Plant in 1967, the mine and processing plant located near Keewatin were acquired by U.S. Steel in 2003 and renamed Keetac. The property has a current rated capacity of approximately 6.0 million tons per year.

Butler Taconite (Closed) The mine and processing plant located at Cooley began operation in 1967 at a capacity of 2.0 million tons per year. The property was permanently closed in 1985 due to the bankruptcy of one of its owners, high costs, and reduced demand for its product because of foreign steel imports. Although the Butler Taconite facilities were dismantled, the site holds potential for future mineral development.

ERIE MINING COMPANY

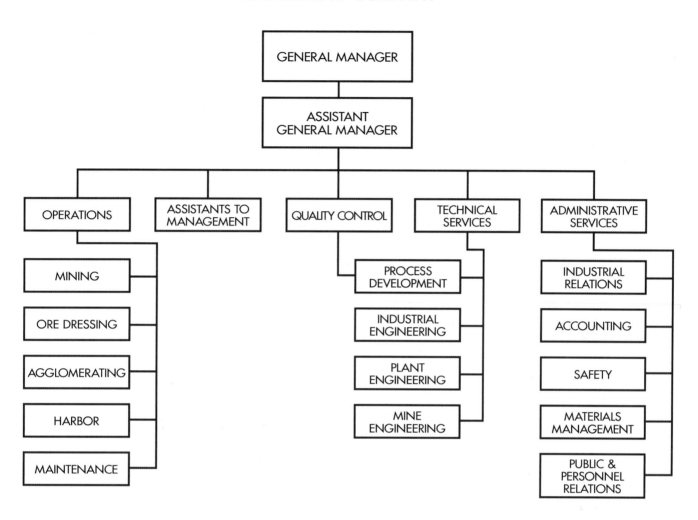

Chapter 6

EXPANSION AND IMPROVEMENTS

Increasing the size and scale of a process conceived in the laboratory, tested in the preliminary plant, and then expanded to the commercial plant designed to produce 7.5 million tons per year of pellets was not without problems. The plant operators had to learn their new jobs "on the fly," and as with any new large processing facility, numerous process flow bottlenecks, equipment capacity limitations, and design problems were encountered. Working with equipment suppliers, they made modifications and changes throughout the entire process. Erie's employees worked long and hard throughout the next several years to solve these production and product quality issues.

In 1958, its first full year of operation, Erie produced 2.95 million tons of pellets. The next year, 4.1 million tons of pellets were produced, despite a 116-day shutdown when the entire domestic iron and steel industry was idled because of a nationwide strike. In 1960, production increased to 7.1 million tons of pellets, followed by 6.7 million tons the next year. Erie achieved its original design capacity in 1962, producing 7.7 million tons of pellets, and this was exceeded annually through the 1967 expansion.

Pellets were clearly more efficient in the steel industry's blast furnaces than natural ore and increased blast furnace iron production by an average of 20 percent. Put another way, "When a plant with five blast furnaces switches to pellets, the effect is the same as adding a sixth blast furnace."[1] To achieve increased iron production, it was more economic for steel companies to invest in additional pelletizing capacity than to construct more blast furnaces.

Steel industry observers noted that iron ore pellets made from taconite surprised the industry, both from a technological and economic perspective. The pellets were more uniform in size and quality than natural ore and melted faster in blast furnaces. They also handled better and could be shipped during early winter. Natural ore no longer represented the future of iron mining in North America; instead, steel would increasingly be produced from iron ore pellets.

Stockpiled pellets at a steel mill.

Left: View of Erie looking northeast after expansion. Above: Erie pellets stockpiled prior to shipment.

THE MINNESOTA TACONITE TAX AMENDMENT

Taxation of iron ore had long been a matter of contention between the steel industry and the State of Minnesota. To promote the development of the vast amounts of taconite that lay under the state, the Minnesota Legislature in 1941 enacted a taconite production tax imposed on taconite pellets when they were produced, rather than being levied against its proven value in the ground as was done with natural ore. Following the initial success of the Erie and Reserve taconite operations in the 1950s, the steel industry was evaluating additional, multimillion-dollar investments in Minnesota taconite. However, they wanted the State to guarantee that the new expanding taconite industry would not be taxed unfairly. In 1964, the Minnesota Legislature negotiated a proposed amendment to the state constitution, which guaranteed that, for a period of twenty-five years, increases in certain taxes on the taconite industry would be limited and would be comparable to tax increases imposed on other manufacturing businesses in the state.

Erie, Pickands Mather, and other industry leaders, together with northern Minnesota legislators, worked hard to gain support for passage of the Taconite Amendment. On November 4, 1964, the voters of Minnesota approved the Taconite Amendment by an overwhelming seven-to-one margin. Confidence in Minnesota taconite was almost immediately rewarded with the announcement of hundreds of millions of dollars in investments for development of long-planned taconite projects and the creation of thousands of new jobs across the Mesabi Range.

Within weeks, U.S. Steel began construction on its huge taconite plant at Mountain Iron. By the end of 1964, Ford Motor Company and Oglebay Norton were employing more than 800 workers at the taconite facility the partners were building near Eveleth.[26] Butler Taconite Company at Nashwauk and National Steel Pellet Company in Keewatin, both managed by Hanna

Mining Company, began producing pellets in 1967.[27] Erie was expanded to 10.3 million tons per year in 1967, and Reserve increased its annual capacity to 10.7 million tons. In the early 1970s, construction of Inland Steel Corporation's Minorca taconite project near Virginia and Pickands Mather–managed Hibbing Taconite Company were announced.

E. W. Davis's prediction that Minnesota taconite producers would be making 40 million tons of pellets by 1975 was correct. The Minnesota industry surpassed that mark in 1973, producing 41.6 million tons of pellets, with almost 30 percent of that total, 11.7 million tons, coming from Erie.

Passage of the Taconite Amendment resulted in multimillion-dollar investments in Minnesota taconite all across the Mesabi Range.

The largest of Minnesota's new taconite plants would be U.S. Steel's Minntac, located at Mt. Iron (original construction shown), near the site of the first Mesabi Range iron ore mine in 1892.

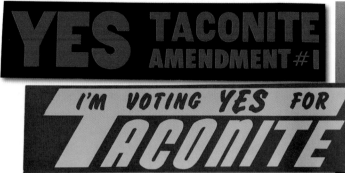

Bumper stickers supporting the Taconite Amendment.

In 1964, the people of Minnesota voted to pass the Taconite Amendment, which was intended to stimulate further investments in developing Minnesota's vast taconite reserves by ensuring that taconite mining would continue to be taxed fairly.

In the wake of the Taconite Amendment passage, Erie's owners decided to expand production capacity. This decision was based on their confidence in the future of Minnesota taconite and the productivity gains realized using pellets in the blast furnaces. In early 1965, Erie announced construction plans to expand its capacity to 10.3 million tons per year.

PRE-EXPANSION

The expansion of Erie was preceded by ten years of continuous operating, maintenance, and process improvements intended to make the operation more efficient and cost effective.

In the mine, changes occurred daily as the mine continuously expanded, and new, larger mining equipment (shovels, haul trucks, and drills) were purchased. Testing was conducted to improve drilling and blasting performance of the extremely hard, abrasive ore. Advances in rotary drilling technology permitted rotary drills to replace higher cost jet drilling in certain areas of the mine. Development of different blast pattern designs and explosive materials improved fragmentation.

Direct rail haulage of ore from the various Mining Areas to the Coarse Crusher was used exclusively until 1965 when mining started at Area 8 (Dunka Mine), located twenty miles northeast from the Plant Site. Dunka Mine taconite had much higher

Erie 7041 rotary drill.

Completed drill pattern with well-blasted ore being loaded in the foreground.

133

Initial mining at Dunka Mine.

Concept for Erie's first truck-to-rail loading pocket.

One of the two Dunka loading pockets in operation.

magnetic iron and lower silica content than ore from the other mine areas. However, because of the narrow, steeply dipping ore body, direct rail haulage was impractical. For the Dunka Mine, engineers designed Erie's first truck-to-rail Loading Pocket that received ore from trucks and transferred it to railcars.[2]

Mining Superintendent Tom Flemal noted that construction began on two Loading Pockets at the Dunka Mine in 1964. The design included a 100-ton capacity rectangular steel bin and a vibrating feeder that conveyed ore from the bin to 85-ton capacity railcars.[3]

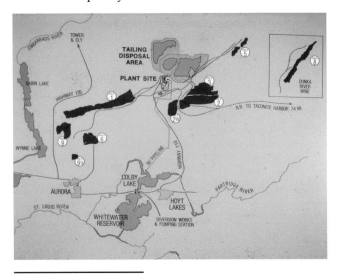

Erie's Mining Areas shown in red ca. 1967.

When Mining Areas 6 and 9, located about six miles west of the Plant Site, opened in 1966 and 1967 respectively, Loading Pockets based upon an improved Dunka Mine design were installed.[4] It was determined that the loading pocket concept was more economical than direct rail haulage, and Loading Pockets were constructed at all new mining areas.[5]

One of the first major design changes occurred in the Coarse Crusher. Because of the abrasiveness of the taconite and the large size of some of the ore delivered, wear on the sixty-inch primary crusher was higher than anticipated, resulting in excessive maintenance downtime. In 1958, a second identical Coarse Crusher line was installed. Both lines incorporated discharge modifications to solve material flow problems. The design capacity of each line exceeded Erie's daily 80,000-ton requirement, and under normal conditions, only one line would operate, with the other line kept on standby.

Other improvements focused on crusher wear material composition and maintenance techniques. Erie engineers designed and patented a concave liner system that sped up the replacement of the worn crusher wear surfaces.[6]

Aerial view of Area 6 Loading Pocket based on the improved design.

Area 2W Loading Pocket with cleanup dozer standing by.

In 1963, Assistant Works Manager–Ore Dressing Henry Whaley noted that the first five years of operation resulted in substantial improvements in operating performance and product quality achieved in the face of formidable obstacles. Changes were made in substantially all phases of the operation. Whaley explained, "The major advances made in Ore Dressing have been the result of improvements in wear steel life, the automation of the fine crushing plant, the automation of the mill grinding circuits,

Original (south) Coarse Crusher dumping track, showing construction of the second (north) crusher at right.

Trains at the North Coarse Crusher.

improvements in concentrating techniques, elimination of material handling bottlenecks, successfully increasing the mill grind from 70 percent minus 325 mesh to the present level, which is finer than 90 percent minus 325 mesh, changes in the grinding mill speeds and the size of mills, improvements in pumping, and improved methods for building tailings dams."[7]

The requirement of the Concentrator to produce a consistent particle size of the concentrate to achieve satisfactory filtering, balling, and pellet firing was recognized when the plant started. In 1960, development began on an automatic grinding control system based on maintaining a

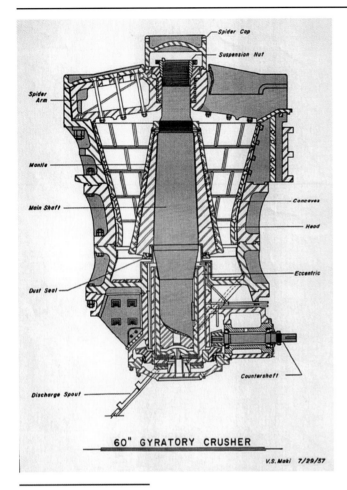

60" GYRATORY CRUSHER

V.S. Maki 7/29/57

Cross-section of sixty-inch crusher.

constant feed density to the cyclones. By 1965, the fine crushing, grinding, and pumping circuits were operated from a common central control room located in the Concentrator. Computer control of grinding mill feed rates and the addition of water ensured the production of concentrate with a more consistent particle size.[8]

A significant reduction of silica in the final concentrate was achieved in 1963 with the installation of hydraulic concentrators, known at Erie as syphon sizers, which removed the less dense mostly silica particles. This reduced concentrate silica by 0.7 percent with no appreciable loss in iron recovery.[9]

A major project in Ore Dressing came in 1962 and 1963 when the original ten-foot, eight-inch diameter rod and ball mill shells were replaced with twelve-foot, two-inch diameter shells on all twenty-seven grinding lines. The mill size change

resulted in additional grinding capacity, which in the rod mills reduced rod consumption and liner wear, and in the ball mills increased the fineness of the ground ore, providing better magnetic separation of iron and silica.[10]

One of the advantages of Erie's multiline design was that it allowed equipment or operating parameter changes to be tested on individual lines without affecting overall production. Because the test lines were operating under those same conditions as other lines, the effects of the changes could be quantified, and the multiple lines allowed coordinated tests. The use of this method of testing multiple process variables simultaneously, called Factorial Design, was used successfully for the first time in the mineral industry at Erie.[11]

Henry Whaley with a new larger diameter grinding mill shell.

In many ways, Erie's pelletizing operations were the best example of pre-expansion continuous improvement and the positive effect it had on the product Erie supplied to its blast furnace customers. Because of an initial production shortfall, Erie's major owner Bethlehem directed the installation of two additional experimental shaft furnaces (G Section) of their design, giving the plant a total of twenty-six furnaces. In 1960 when these furnaces became operational, pellet production was achieved with the original twenty-four furnaces and G Section was not required.[12]

Central Control Room for Crushing, Concentrating, and pumping.

Concentrator showing replacement mills.

CONCENTRATING FLOWSHEET
HYDRAULIC CONCENTRATOR

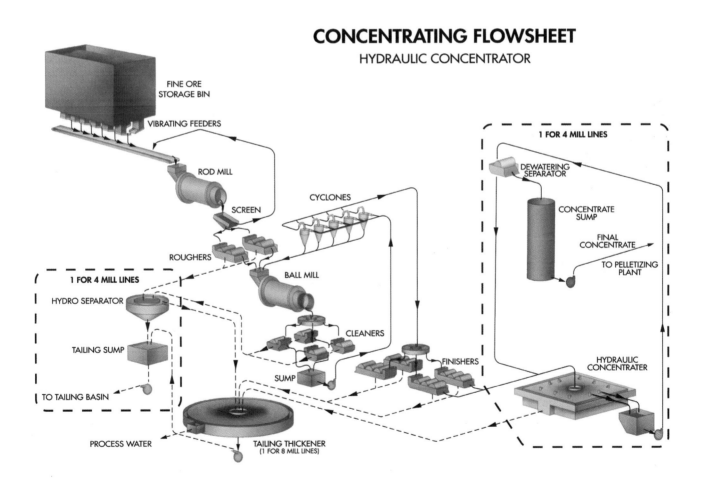

Concentrator flowsheet with changes shown in blue.

Ball mill being moved by 200-ton capacity crane.

Fred Morawski, Assistant Works Manager–Agglomerating, reported in 1963, "Since the first shaft furnace of commercial size was placed in operation by Pickands Mather at Erie's preliminary plant in 1948, many changes have been made to reach the present stage of the development of the units now in operation at the Hoyt Lakes plant."[13] Morawski went on to say that alterations to the original furnace design and support equipment were being made continuously to improve operating efficiencies and the quality and quantity of the product. He noted that changes made in the design of the balling circuits to improve the green ball characteristics and obtain a more uniform sizing was one of the major steps contributing to increased efficiency in shaft furnace operation. Significant improvements were made in green ball size uniformity by (1) increasing the balling drum slope and rotation speed, (2) redesigning the cutter bar and trommel screen, (3) improving concentrate dewatering practices to better control filter cake moisture, and (4) maintaining uniform

Erie's multi-line Concentrator.

G Section furnace addition.

Balling drum discharge showing sized green balls.

feed rates. Furnace improvements resulting from better green ball sizing and a change in furnace feed pattern provided better air distribution within the furnace and resulted in noticeable furnace heat efficiencies and substantial improvements in pellet physical characteristics. As a result of these process improvements, Erie also saw furnace fuel consumption drop from 870,000 BTU per ton of pellet to 500,000 BTU per ton.[14] In addition, the use of coal as a fuel additive to the concentrate was discontinued.

By 1962 other furnace modifications that improved shaft furnace performance included the addition of high temperature air ports in the end walls of the furnace to heat previously cold areas at the stock-line, extending refractory lining down to the furnace discharges, which permitted better movement of pellets through the lower part of the furnace, and incorporating separate automatically controlled air supply to the main furnace inlets, and installing silicon carbide liners in the discharges to reduce wear.

Nobody who worked around the shaft furnaces denied just how challenging a place the Pelletizing Plant was in the early days. "I was transferred to the Pelletizing Plant from Taconite Harbor in the spring of 1959," Ted Williams said. "I left nice, clean working conditions and came to a very dirty plant."[15] Williams recalled that the first major improvement he got involved with was the furnace blow controls.

Sometimes material conditions in the furnace, due to poorly sized green balls, irregular furnace feed, or erratic furnace temperature distributions, would lead to restricted airflow in some areas of the bed and channel higher flows into other areas. This eventually would lead to localized airflow strong enough to carry hot pellets and dust up and out of the furnace and onto the operating floor, resulting in a "blow."[16] The blows affected the Pelletizing Plant operator's safety and work environment, as well as pellet production and quality. In the early days, Frank Settimi said, "The furnaces were spitting out red hot pellets all over."[17]

Williams and Settimi agreed, one of the biggest early improvements was the installation of a pressure sensor in the hood of the furnace to detect an imminent blow and shut the main air blower down. After this system was installed, the blows were significantly reduced, and many other improvements were then made in the Pelletizing Plant.[18]

Another problem was what the operators called "chunking," where pellets would fuse together inside the furnace. "The furnaces would just chunk up and choke," Settimi said. Once the furnace was shut down and cooled sufficiently, workers

Vacuum disc filter for dewatering concentrate.

Index feeder that delivered green balls to the furnace.

Index feeder discharge placing green balls into furnace.

would have to descend into the furnace and use jackhammers to break it up. The working area was very hot, and it might take as long as six days to remove the chunk.[19]

"Many things have contributed to the improvements that Erie has made in pelletizing," Fred DeVaney wrote. "One of these has to do with the making of the green balls. This search for ball improvement has led to an almost completely automated filtering operation to ensure a filter cake of uniform moisture. In the furnace proper, one of the major advances has been in the adoption of a transverse feeder, which deposits the green pellets in twelve ridges, transverse to the furnace rather than feeding the material along the walls."[20]

A significant change in Pelletizing Plant operations was completed in 1965 when the furnace fuel was changed from Bunker C fuel oil to natural gas. Originally, fuel oil was to be delivered to Taconite Harbor and transported by rail to the Plant Site. The tar-like Bunker C required steam heating to flow. Rail delivery proved impractical, so from 1957 to 1965, tanker trucks were used. Approximately 4,100 tanker truck deliveries from area refineries were required each year. The tanker trucks arrived at an unloading station located adjacent to the Rebuild Shop and the heated oil flowed by gravity to three large heated storage tanks that could hold enough fuel for several months of operation. In 1966 after natural gas pipelines were extended

Erie Agglomerating Department managers Charles Matson and Frances "Bebes" Molinaro with furnace model.

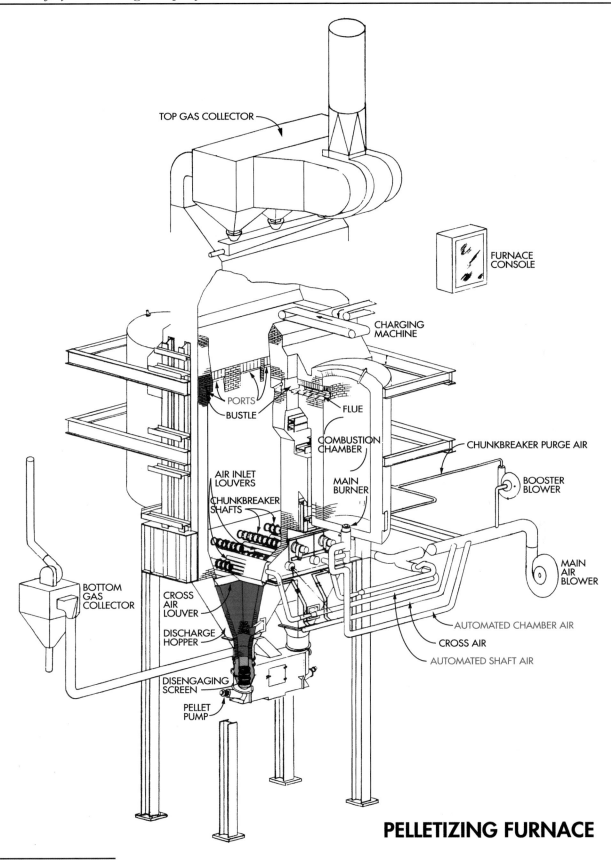

TOP GAS COLLECTOR

FURNACE CONSOLE

CHARGING MACHINE

PORTS

BUSTLE

FLUE

COMBUSTION CHAMBER

CHUNKBREAKER PURGE AIR

AIR INLET LOUVERS

MAIN BURNER

BOOSTER BLOWER

CHUNKBREAKER SHAFTS

MAIN AIR BLOWER

BOTTOM GAS COLLECTOR

CROSS AIR LOUVER

DISCHARGE HOPPER

AUTOMATED CHAMBER AIR

CROSS AIR

AUTOMATED SHAFT AIR

DISENGAGING SCREEN

PELLET PUMP

PELLETIZING FURNACE

Pelletizing furnace with improvements highlighted.

Cleanup on Pelletizing Plant operating floor.

into the area, changes were made to the Pelletizing Plant furnace combustion and piping systems that allowed total conversion to natural gas for furnace fuel. The ability to use fuel oil was retained as a backup. In general, pipeline delivery of natural gas was one-ninth the cost of trucking oil.[21]

1967 EXPANSION

When Erie began planning for expansion in 1965, Pickands Mather was managing iron ore properties across North America that were producing more pellets than any other company in the world. This was a considerable accomplishment considering that it was just fifteen years earlier when Erie decided to move on from PreTac to a commercial pelletizing operation.

In 1965, Pickands Mather negotiated an agreement with the Parsons-Jurden Corporation, successor to Anaconda, to design and construct the $50 million expansion, which increased Erie's annual production capacity to 10.3 million tons. When completed in 1967, the project involved installation of one additional line of fine crushing

Furnace stockline showing improved feeding pattern.

equipment, nine additional Concentrator mill lines, three regrind mills with fine screening, one larger pelletizing shaft furnace (H Furnace), and a third generating unit at Taconite Harbor. At peak construction, about 900 workers were employed on Erie's expansion.

Furnace Bunker C fuel pumphouse and storage tanks.

Fine Crusher expansion.

Bunker C being delivered by tanker truck.

A major process improvement incorporated into the expansion, and one that also was applied by many in the taconite industry, was Erie's installation of regrind fine screening. The company had earlier investigated flotation as a method of reducing concentrate silica levels. The results were favorable, but Erie discovered during testing that the same silica reduction could be achieved more efficiently by fine screening the concentrate and regrinding the oversize. Because about one-half of Erie's concentrate silica occurs in the size fraction that is plus 325 mesh, work was started in 1961 on the development of fine screening to separate the plus 325 mesh size particles.

Three identical regrind fine screening lines were installed, each servicing twelve mill lines, to upgrade the finisher magnetic separator concentrate. Erie preformed fine screening with screens having an opening of three-thousandths of an inch. Primary and secondary fine screens were installed ahead of a regrind ball mill. The

Installation of the natural gas pipeline to Pelletizing Plant.

143

Excavation for Concentrator expansion.

Concentrator expansion mills being installed.

Concentrator expansion foundations under construction.

fine screen oversize material, high in silica content, was reground in a twelve-foot, two-inch by twenty-four-foot long ball mill. The ball mill discharge was rescreened on a final stage of fine screening, with the oversize returning back to the ball mill and the screen undersize going to the regrind magnetic separators to produce a reduced silica concentrate. The regrind separator concentrate was then pumped to the hydraulic concentrator along with the primary and secondary fine screen undersize, with the separator nonmagnetic material combined with other tailing streams. Fred DeVaney called it "an outstanding technical development that may have far-reaching effects in all concentrating plants."[22]

Typical Erie fine screen installation.

CONCENTRATING FLOWSHEET
REGRIND FINE SCREENING

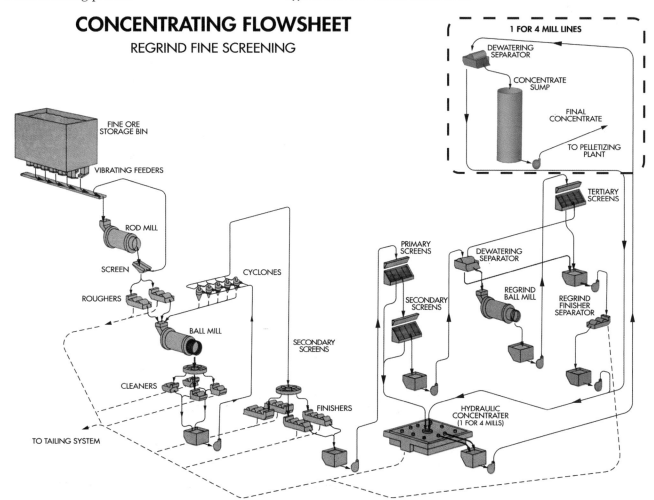

Concentrating flowsheet with regrind fine screening highlighted in blue.

Power Plant showing the third generating unit.

Pelletizing Plant expansion showing H Section furnace construction.

Because of increased ore delivery requirements, at 10.3 million ton annual pellet production, the Mining Department acquired additional blast hole drills, shovels, haul trucks, side dump railcars, and locomotives.

The 1967 expansion also required increasing the capacity of the Taconite Harbor Power Plant with the installation of a third, 75-MW generating unit.[23]

Because sufficient capacity was designed into the original facilities, the expansion was completed without major changes to the Mainline Railroad and Dock.

POST EXPANSION

Following expansion, Erie, its employees, and the entire Minnesota taconite industry experienced ten years of maximum production and full employment. Reserve also expanded, and new operations came on stream. Erie reached a production milestone in November 1970 when cumulative pellet production topped the 100 million ton mark. From 1967 to 1976, Erie produced an average of 10.6 million tons of pellets annually, achieving its greatest tonnage in 1973 when 11.7 million tons of pellets were produced and 13.1 million tons were shipped. This period marked the time when Erie was a taconite industry leader and one of the foremost mining operations in the world. Not only were individual mine production records, such as cars of ore dumped, tons of ore crushed, or tons of ore milled, in a shift, a week, a month, and a year, being routinely set and then broken, but Erie was also recognized nationally for its activities in many areas.

Following the initial success of regrind fine screening, in 1970 Erie installed eighteen additional fine screening units, one for every two of the plant's mill lines, to screen cyclone overflow and recycle the larger particles in the ball mill circuit until they were ground sufficiently to pass through the screen. This closed circuit fine screening modification further reduced the silica content of the pellets from 7.1 percent to 6.5 percent.[24] By 1971, Erie's fine screening concept had been applied to eight other iron ore beneficiation plants and was being tested by other U.S. and foreign companies.

In 1972, the Minnesota Society of Professional Engineers recognized Erie for having one of the best engineering projects in the state. The project was a new, "on stream," ore grading system, which measured the silica content of each ore train as it was dumped. Developed through the Atoms for Peace program, Erie's system, called NOLA (Neutron On Line Analysis), was the result of several years of work. Dust samples from individual trains were collected and the silica content measured using a method called neutron activation. This real-time silica information, as well as the estimated magnetic iron content of each train, was used by Erie's ore graders to adjust ore delivery to maintain target. The system was a "first of a kind" for the iron ore industry and was successful in improving Concentrator operations and stabilizing pellet silica levels.

From the very first day, employee safety and welfare had been the guiding principle for Erie and Pickands Mather. During the 1970s, Erie received several state and national awards recognizing its safety and accident prevention program. In 1973, the National Safety Council presented Erie with its highest industrial safety award, the "Award of Honor," for having outstanding and continuously improving safety performance. In addition, several

Recognizing production of 100 million tons of pellets at Erie on September 29, 1970.

Recognizing shipment of 100 million tons of pellets from Erie on November 17, 1970.

Erie departments earned many Joseph A. Holmes Safety Certificates of Honor.

Erie Union and Management Representatives with Joseph A. Holmes Safety Awards of Honor.

CONSERVATION

In addition to the lands that Erie leased or owned for mining, plant site, Tailing Basin, railroad, power line, dock and power plant, the company also controlled over 60,000 acres of additional lands in northeastern Minnesota. Early on, Erie and Pickands Mather recognized the potential of these lands and committed to a resource conservation policy ensuring the future value of the lands for generations to come. Erie developed a Multiple Resource Management program to guide its activities that included establishing buffer areas around the immediate vicinity of mining operations, harvesting mature timber, conserving water resources, reclaiming inactive Tailing Basin and disturbed mine areas, maintaining wildlife habitat, and providing public recreational opportunities.

View of some of Erie's lands that were part of the Multiple Resource Management program showing Giant's Ridge ski area.

Timber was harvested in areas where mine development would soon take place so that valuable trees would not be wasted. On lands that were never going to be mined, timber was cut on a "sustainable yield basis," where annual harvesting only took and replanted the number of trees that would mature the following year. The timber was sold to local firms who performed the actual logging. Prior to selling the timber, the acreage was inspected by Erie's Lands and Forestry group to evaluate the effect on the environment of harvesting the trees. Only after it was determined that the timber was mature, that there would be no disturbance of any water course, and that the recreational potential of the lands would be enhanced, would the contract be put out for bid. Most of Erie's auxiliary lands were open and available for public recreation purposes, fishing, hunting, camping, snowmobiling, hiking, cross-country skiing, and berry picking. Lands near mining activity were closed for the safety of the public and Erie's employees.

In areas where the trees needed to be cut but were of no commercial value, Erie often issued permits allowing employees to cut trees for firewood. Erie annually issued permits allowing employees to cut Christmas trees on company property.

In 1970, underscoring the fact that conservation and mining can and do go hand in hand, Pickands Mather and Erie were chosen to provide fifty-seven, twelve-foot-high balsam fir trees for the annual Christmas Pageant of Peace in Washington, D.C. Each of Erie's trees would represent a state or territory of the United States and would be arranged just south of the White House around the seventy-eight-foot spruce national Christmas tree from South Dakota.

Erie's foresters, Sam Dickinson and Dave Youngman, personally selected each tree. As Youngman reflected, "It was quite a project because as everybody knows there are very few perfect balsam trees, but we managed to find them. We had a little card that we had to hold up at a certain distance away from the tree and the tree had to fit into that outline. We had a small crawler tractor that pulled a dray, and we would go out with our own crew and cut the trees."

Erie's Sam Dickinson selects trees for the Pageant of Peace.

In early November, Minnesota Eighth District Congressman John Blatnik and the Minnesota Commissioner of Conservation took part in the opening Christmas tree cutting ceremonies by cutting the first tree. Once harvested the trees were wrapped in plastic mesh before being loaded aboard a flat car and taken by train to Taconite Harbor. There, the trees where placed onto pallets and strapped to the deck of Interlake's ore boat Herbert C. Jackson, which was loaded with Erie pellets and headed for Cleveland, Ohio. At Cleveland, the trees were loaded onto a tractor-trailer for the final leg of the journey to Washington, D.C., arriving on December 7. After being decorated, the trees were lighted by U.S. President Richard M. Nixon during the annual National Christmas tree lighting ceremony on December 16.

Erie's 1,200-acre Whitewater Reservoir was developed as a storage area for process make-up water and also provided an attractive public recreation lake for fishing, boating, camping, and duck hunting. Overnight and seasonal camping sites, fishing docks, boat launching ramps, and picnic areas were built by the City of Hoyt Lakes on land made available by Erie.

The needs of wildlife were an important part of Erie's multiple resource management program. The orderly logging of areas gave Erie the opportunity to improve wildlife habitat. According to Dave Youngman, "Wildlife benefited from all of the reclamation work that Erie did. We planted grasses and legumes that were good browse for animals. At one point, we contracted with a logger to cut a large area in strips and brought in a ruffed grouse expert from the University of Minnesota and had him help us with the management program. We also developed hunting trails with different age classes of aspen that provided good habit for ruffed grouse. Erie was probably the only mining company that allowed the public to come on company lands. The only restriction was that areas anywhere close to the mine were off limits."

U.S. Eighth District Congressman John Blatnik and Minnesota Commissioner of Conservation Jarle Leirfalom cut the first Christmas tree.

Erie workers, General Manager Clyde Keith, Congressman Blatnik, and Commissioner Leirfalom help wrap the trees for rail shipment to Taconite Harbor.

Erie's Christmas trees arrived in Cleveland and were loaded into a tractor-trailer for the trip to Washington, D.C.

Erie trees on display at the 1970 Pageant of Peace.

Erie's Whitewater Reservoir provided wildlife habitat and recreational opportunities.

Erie was an early leader in mine land reclamation, bringing value back to lands disturbed by the mining and processing activity. Returning these areas to future use is accomplished through the process of reclamation. Early on Pickands Mather recognized that for Erie to be truly successful, a method for growing vegetation on the barren taconite tailing that would be generated needed to be found. In 1948, Erie contracted with a soil scientist at the University of Minnesota who eventually determined that with proper preparation taconite tailing alone certain types of vegetation could grow without first being covered with topsoil. Erie's Supervisor of Lands and Forestry, Sam Dickinson, continued to run experiments on small plots of tailing, using not only native grasses and legumes, but also those more tolerant to the low-nutrient and dry conditions of the tailing. Tests were run to determine the specific fertilizer combination that would provide the best plant growth. This was followed by large-scale plantings on areas of Erie's

Tailing Basin. The growth of grasses on the Tailing Basin was important because it not only stabilized the slopes against erosion but also substantially reduced dust emissions. Dickinson's steady progress eventually led to gaining the knowledge and establishing the procedures necessary to successfully vegetate taconite tailing. This effort was followed by developing methods for reclamation of mine pits and stockpiles.

Erie's conservation efforts were in place before any state or federal mine land reclamations rules were implemented. In fact, much of Erie's work was used by the State of Minnesota when developing its regulations.

As stated by Youngman and echoed by others, "Sam Dickinson should be considered the Father of Mineland Reclamation of the Mesabi Iron Range. His employment with Erie spanned the period from initial research, through all of the experimental plantings and choosing of plant

Vegetation success on the slopes of the Erie's Tailing Basin.

species that would grow in taconite tailing, and brought it through to the large-scale plantings where we were planting hundreds of acres on the Tailing Basin annually and many acres in the mining areas."

In 1977, Sam Dickinson's efforts in tailing reclamation were recognized nationally when Erie received the very first National Environmental Industry Award for Excellence in Land Reclamation, sponsored by the Environmental Protection Agency, the President's Council on Environmental Quality, and the Environmental Industry Council.

From the beginning, Erie demonstrated sincere stewardship for its lands with a balanced program of multiple resource management. This program was well in advance of regulatory requirements and was accomplished with the desire to make Minnesota mining compatible with the environment.

Sam Dickinson, Erie's Father of Mineland Reclamation, examines the growth of plantings on the Tailing Basin.

Pickands Mather's President Elton Hoyt III (left) accepts the first National Environmental Industry Award for Erie's Tailing Basin reclamation.

of Erie's departments received individual safety awards. The national Joseph A Holmes Safety Association presented Erie and several departments with Certificates of Honor for completing nearly fifty-one million man-hours without a disabling injury for the period January 1973 through December 1975. The Minnesota Safety Council also recognized Erie with its highest safety award. Erie received the Sentinels of Safety Award four times as the safest large open-pit mine in the United States.

In 1977, the Veterans of Foreign Wars and the American Legion both recognized Erie as the "Minnesota Employer of the Year" for its record of hiring veterans. At the time, more than 50 percent of Erie's 2,900 employees were veterans. Employee time spent in military service was also credited to company retirement.

Erie also received the very first national land reclamation award from the Environmental Industrial Council of America for its long-standing work on the successful establishment of vegetation at its tailing basin to control dust and erosion.

During the 1970s, fuel oil and natural gas supply uncertainty resulted in dramatic price increases of 400 to 500 percent by the end of the decade. At Erie, the Pelletizing Plant was the largest consumer of these fuels and the area where extensive energy studies were conducted. Tests determined that the greatest heat or energy loss was through the furnace's top gas exhaust, and plans were developed to reintroduce this wasted heat back into the process.

Preliminary plant testing began in 1976 to determine if heating the concentrate slurry before filtering would capture some of the heat loss and result in improved furnace operation. The successful plant tests were followed by a 1979 prototype design and subsequent 24-furnace plant installation. The design incorporated a top gas heat recuperation unit installed above the furnace exhaust, with concentrate pumped to the top of the heat recuperation unit, cascading down through a series of baffles, and picking up heat as it flowed by gravity to a distributor feeding the filters. The top gas heat recuperation unit installation resulted in a significant 15 percent fuel savings (averaging 75,000 BTU per ton of pellets), with the added benefit of the heated filter feed also reducing bentonite (green ball binder) consumption. On an annual plantwide basis, the energy savings at Erie owing to this improvement were equivalent to the energy required to heat all the homes in a city of 12,000 people for one year.

In 1977, a 133-day Iron Range-wide labor strike reduced Erie's production to 4.7 million tons. When operations resumed in 1978, production had been curtailed, and Erie's annual production never exceeded 8.8 million tons of pellets for the remainder of its operating life.

On June 23, 1981, Erie produced its 200 millionth ton of pellets. Recognizing the achievement, Henry Whaley, then Group Vice President of Pickands Mather, stated, "Erie's 200 millionth ton of taconite pellets is a milestone without equal in Pickands Mather's history. This accomplishment becomes more impressive when one remembers that Erie and its employees played a pioneering role in the taconite industry. Dedicated employees with the skills and talents to match their enthusiasm made Erie work, and work well. That dedication is still evident today, and all of us look forward to even greater accomplishments at Erie."[25]

Reclamation hydroseeding to the Tailing Basin slopes.

Vegetated area at the interior of the Tailing Basin.

Aerial view of Tailing Basin with vegetated exterior slopes.

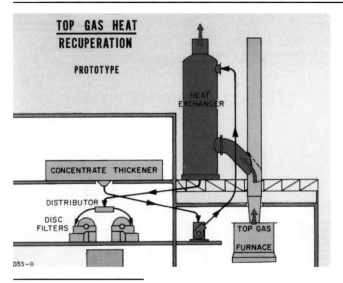

Wasted heat was recaptured in top gas heat recuperation.

A top gas heat recuperation installation at the Pelletizing Plant.

CONCENTRATING FLOWSHEET

CLOSED CIRCUIT FINE SCREENING
(1 CIRCUIT FOR 2 MILL LINES)

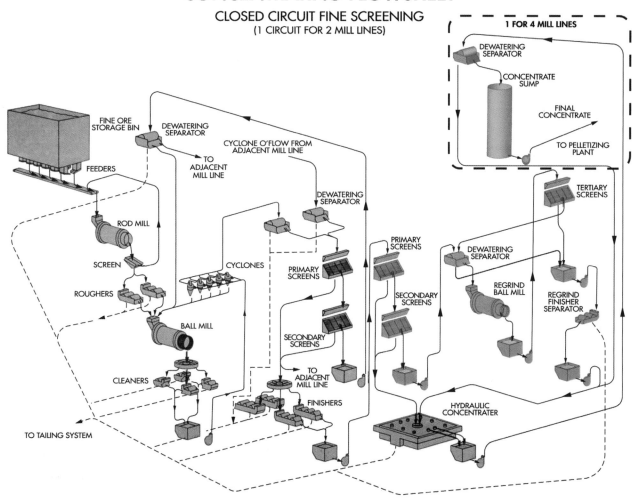

Concentrating flowsheet with closed circuit fine screening highlighted in blue.

A collection system captured the dust generated during car dumping at the sixty-inch crusher. Some of that dust was used for silica analysis.

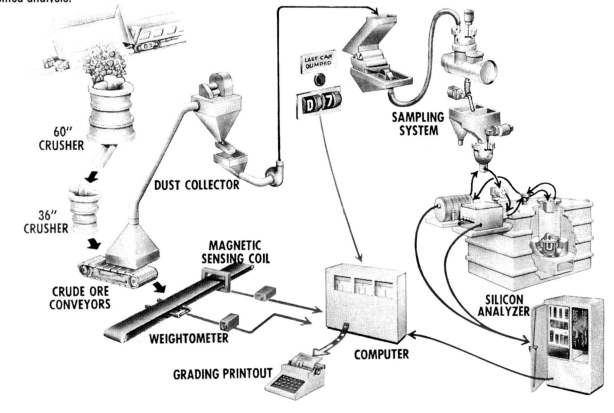

On line silica analyzer, NOLA, flowsheet.

Erie earned the highest annual National Open Pit Mining Safety Award (Sentinels of Safety) four times.

Erie participated in Minnesota's Iron Range Trail Tourism effort by offering public bus tours during the summer and maintaining a mine viewing area.

Erie's Robert Rojeski, Jim Kozar, Ed Karkoska, John "Jack" Healy, Charles Stiles, and Robert Guiliani with the Sentinels of Safety Award.

John "Jack" Healy, Jim Kozar, and Jim Bowen receive one of many Joseph A. Holmes Safety Awards of Honor that Erie earned.

As the 1980s began, some of the advantages that helped Erie succeed during its first twenty years of operation now posed challenges for the aging, first-generation facility. Competition from newer, more modern taconite plants and lower cost foreign ore sources, combined with increased fuel cost, higher labor costs, and decreasing ore quality, forced Erie to make continuous process improvement and cost control watchwords in its mission to remain a pellet provider to its customers. A restructuring of the North American steel industry occurred simultaneously as competition from imported steel products forced the closing of some of the industry's older, less-efficient facilities, reducing the demand for pellets.

The period 1982 through 1986 was particularly challenging for Erie as it was forced to operate in a survival mode with production never exceeding 4.9 million tons of pellets annually. To reduce costs, stripping tonnages were reduced dramatically and maintenance was deferred. In June 1982, the Taconite Harbor Power Plant was shut down because low cost electric power became available for purchase owing to production curtailments at many local mines.

A major change took place on May 2, 1986, when Erie's multiple ownership structure was revised with LTV Steel acquiring 100 percent ownership of Erie. On July 17, 1986, LTV Steel filed for bankruptcy and began reorganizing. Then on December 31, 1986, Cliffs purchased Pickands Mather and assumed management of Erie. LTV Steel announced on February 20, 1987,

that Erie's name would be changed from Erie Mining Company to LTV Steel Mining Company (LTVSMC) to more accurately reflect the new ownership. *This book will continue to use Erie as the company name to avoid confusion.*

The change to a single owner provided some advantages as annual pellet production capacity was established at 8.0 million tons, pellet quality specifications were refined to meet a single customer's requirements, and funding became available for improvement initiatives at Erie.

In 1987, as the higher recovery, lower silica ores from Mining Areas 1, 5, 8 (Dunka Mine), and 9, were being depleted, flotation cells were added into the Concentrator flow sheet after the hydraulic concentrators (replacing two mill lines) to produce a lower and more consistent pellet silica level. In the flotation cells, concentrate was

Flag of Erie's new owner.

158

Some of Erie's employees who served as members of the Minnesota Army National Guard are shown here.

Idled Power Plant.

LTV STEEL CORPORATION

In the 1960s, during a period of low interest rates, the combining of companies operating in entirely different, multi-industry businesses into a conglomerate became a popular business structure. The assumption was that by combining several different businesses a conglomerate would continue to generate profits during any individual industry business downturn. James Ling, a Dallas, Texas, businessman, founded one of the largest conglomerates of the period, combining aerospace, electronics, steel manufacturing, sporting goods, airline, meat packing, car rental, and pharmaceutical industries.

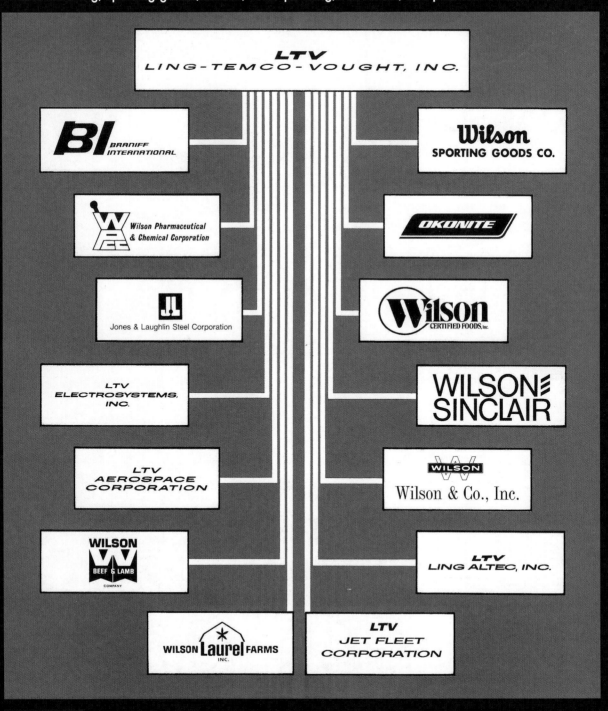

LTV was one of the first and largest conglomerates.

Beginning in 1947 as Ling Electric Company and acquiring ownership positions in several small electronic firms during the 1950s, Ling merged with Tempco Aircraft in 1960 and acquired Chance Vought, an aerospace company, in a hostile takeover in 1961. The combined companies were named Ling-Tempco-Vought. In 1965 Okonite, a wire and cable manufacturer, was added, and in 1967 Wilson and Company (meat packing, sporting goods, and pharmaceutical) was taken over. In 1968 Ling-Tempco-Vought ventured into the steel business when a 63 percent ownership position in Jones and Laughlin Steel Corporation (J&L Steel) was acquired. That year, Braniff International Airways and National Rental Car were also added. By 1969, Ling-Tempco-Vought comprised of fourteen separate companies. However, a slowdown in the economy led investors to discover that conglomerates were not generating profits any better than individual companies, and their attraction waned. Additionally, in 1969, the Department of Justice filed an antitrust suit seeking divestiture of J&L Steel. James Ling was forced to step down as Chairman of the Board and Chief Executive Officer and subsequently left the company.[28]

In 1971, as part of the antitrust settlement, the Braniff and Okonite companies were sold and J&L Steel was retained. The company name was changed from Ling-Tempco-Vought to the LTV Corporation. Later the Wilson group of companies were spun off separately, leaving basically the steel and aerospace industries.

In 1978, J&L Steel acquired Youngstown and the 35 percent ownership in Erie, and in 1984 merged with Republic to form LTV Steel. In July 1986, LTV Corporation filed for Chapter 11 bankruptcy protection to allow for potential reorganization. This was the largest and most complicated corporate bankruptcy in U.S. history to that point. The bankruptcy resulted in divestiture of the aerospace business, leaving primarily the steel business. LTV Corporation emerged from bankruptcy in June 1993, renamed itself LTV Steel, and relocated its headquarters from Dallas to Cleveland, Ohio.

LTV Steel filed a second bankruptcy on December 28, 2000, and received authorization from the bankruptcy court to implement a "hot idle" asset protection plan, which maintained the facilities while attempting to either restructure or sell the business. Unable to secure financing or negotiate a new labor agreement with the USWA, the steel assets were sold on February 27, 2002, and LTV Steel ceased to exist.

treated with two chemical reagents: one that strengthened air bubbles generated in the cells, and a second that coated the silica particles so that they selectively attached to the bubbles. The bubbles formed froth on the top of the cell where they were removed from the final concentrate.

Flotation cells in operation showing agitator froth overflow.

The froth was sent to the regrind fine screening circuit to capture the remaining iron.

Another attempt to improve Erie's pellets was an effort to produce "fluxed pellets" in shaft furnaces. Fluxed pellets include a small percentage of finely ground limestone, which permits more efficient melting of the pellets in the blast furnace. The majority of Minnesota's other taconite plants included limestone in their pellets, and LTV Steel wanted Erie's pellets to provide similar benefits. Beginning in 1987, two furnaces in C section (C-1 and C-2) were dedicated to testing fluxed pellet production. At the time, Erie was operating North America's only remaining shaft furnaces. Over the next two years, numerous modifications were made to these test furnaces. Although more than 120,000 tons of fluxed pellets were shipped for blast furnace trials, the effort was eventually discontinued because shaft furnace operation could not be stabilized.

Flotation cells installation in Concentrator.

Two other major operating changes occurred in the Pelletizing Plant. The first was the replacement of the original vibrating furnace discharge conveyors with belt conveyors. This significantly improved the furnace availability and workplace environment by reducing noise, dust, and spillage associated with moving hot pellets from the furnaces. The second change was the installation of Furnace Mass Air Computer Control, which converted pelletizing furnace operation from manual to automatic control. Computers continuously monitored furnace conditions and adjusted the airflow and feed rates to each furnace.

In 1988, an outgrowth of an existing LTV Steel corporate-wide quality management system called Integrated Process Control (IPC) began to increase employee involvement. The IPC program began with training on statistical analysis methods, which led to the development of process mapping and establishment of standard operating procedures. IPC incorporated employee teamwork and a structured process to identify and solve problems and improve quality and operating efficiency. Operators monitored, recorded, and charted key process variables on graphs, which indicated trends and process deviations, and provided statistical information for problem solving. At Erie, IPC increased operator involvement and ownership of the process by promoting individual action within operating standards, resulting in reduced variability in the process. The program was implemented throughout Erie and audited by both internal and independent auditors.

As the pellet production increased, it became obvious that the mine's development was being adversely affected by the reduced stripping done

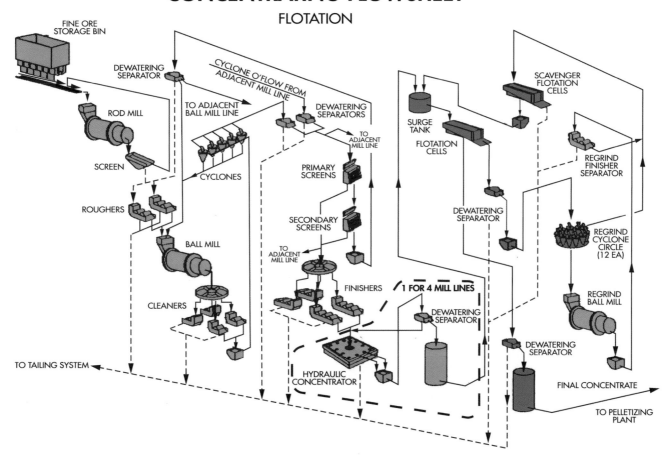

CONCENTRATING FLOWSHEET

FLOTATION

Concentrating flowsheet with flotation highlighted in blue.

in prior years to defer costs, the exhaustion of two major Mining Areas, plant metallurgical and recovery problems associated with certain fine-grained ore, and new pellet chemistry specifications. To address these challenges, a mine improvement plan was developed that included mine plan revisions, additional mining equipment to address the stripping deficit, and productivity improvements achievable from technological and operating changes.

The increased stripping required replacement of the mine's existing fleet of aging 85-ton capacity haul trucks with 170-ton and later 240-ton capacity trucks. To match the new trucks, larger shovels replaced the mine's original units. Additional drills, front-end loaders, crawler tractors, and mine support equipment also were purchased.

An important aspect of the mine improvement plan occurred in 1989 with the $2 million installation of the computerized truck-and-train dispatch system, designed to utilize GPS technology to improve the mine's ore grading and increase operating efficiency and productivity by reducing delays. The system was the first completely integrated truck-and-train dispatch system installed in North America. The system continuously monitored the location and activity of more than ninety production units, trucks, shovels, drills, locomotives, and front-end loaders as well as train loading at Loading Pockets and train dumping at the Coarse Crusher. This information was stored, analyzed, reported, and used to optimize truck and rail haulage that resulted in significant productivity and ore grading improvements.

A company-wide information network was established consisting of the truck-and-train dispatch system, mine planning software, and Concentrator and Pelletizing Plant process control computers and business systems on a mainframe computer. The mainframe stored more than 2,500 daily operating and quality statistics and supported a computerized maintenance management system intended to standardize and streamline maintenance practices on all mine and plant equipment. Terminals and printers were installed throughout Erie for personnel to access spare parts inventory, maintenance inspection schedules, maintenance history, and to originate work orders. Both hourly and salaried personnel entered and retrieved operating and maintenance data as close to the source as possible, and that information was immediately available.

In 1991, the mine employees, recognizing the need to further reduce delays and improve mining performance, approved "Hot Relief" shift change. The practice, which increased equipment utilization and operating time, involved paying equipment operators fifteen minutes overtime per shift to be relieved at the equipment rather than

Pelletizing furnace control console located at each furnace.

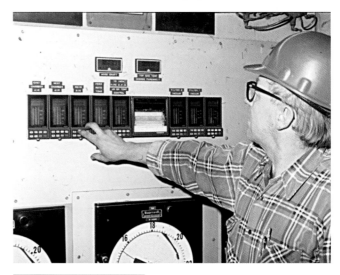

Furnace operator with mass air control equipment that was adjusted by the computer system.

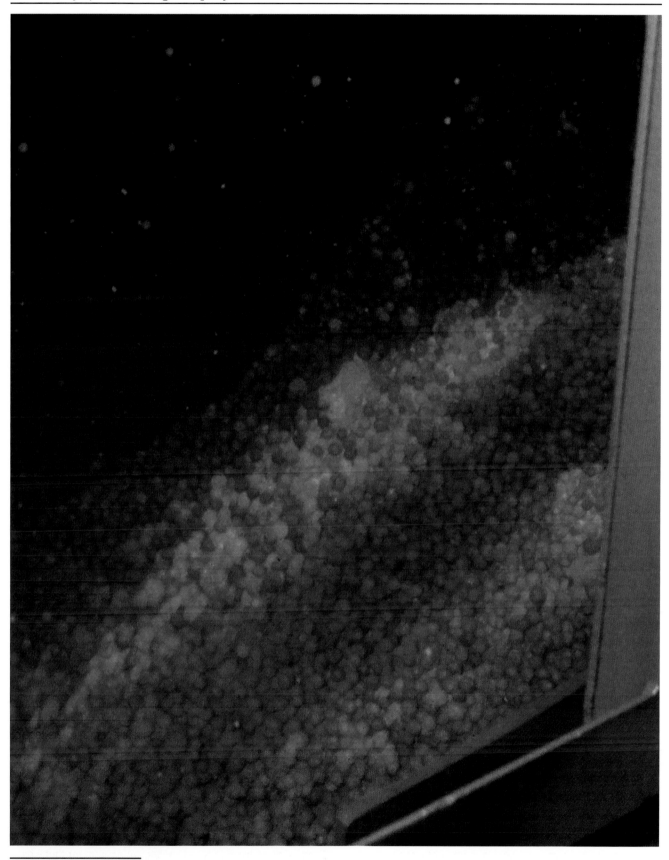

Hot pellets at furnace discharge.

Rubber belt conveyors with hot pellets (foreground) replaced the original vibrating conveyors (background).

Erie employees received a stainless steel plate commemorating the 200th million ton produced.

Aerial view of overburden stripping.

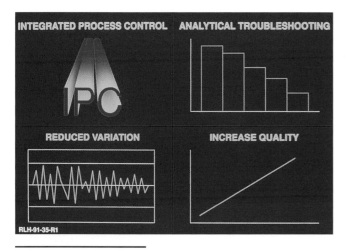

IPC—Monitor the process, analyze results, solve problems, and implement solutions to reduce variability.

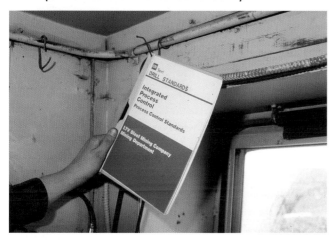

Each department at Erie developed its own IPC process control standards.

Process statistics were posted throughout Erie so all employees could monitor improvement.

shutting the equipment down while operators were transported to and from the mine reporting buildings during shift change.

In July 1991, as the cost of purchased power increased, the Taconite Harbor Power Plant resumed operation complying with new environmental regulations and power interchange requirements. In 1994, combustion controls were updated and computerized to reduce fuel consumption.

Solar-powered signposts monitored equipment locations.

Operator Interface Panels in each piece of equipment communicated between the equipment operator and the dispatchers.

With the exhaustion of high-recovery, low-silica ores from the Dunka Mine and Mining Area 5, Erie was forced to develop a mine consolidation plan maximizing production from the lower quality ore mining areas located near the Plant Site, and reducing the number of active mining areas from five to three. It was recognized that delivering

A significant improvement to mine operations was truck-and-train dispatch installation.

Computer terminals were available everywhere at Erie, and employees were trained to enter maintenance work orders.

the required amount of ore utilizing the mine's existing truck-to-rail Loading Pockets, with limited storage capacity and designed for 85-ton capacity trucks, was not practical. As the mine's haul truck fleet size increased to 240-ton capacity, there was considerable truck delay time at the pockets as the larger trucks could only dump a partial load,

and then had to wait until space was available in the pocket before dumping the remainder. The solution was to construct a larger Loading Pocket that would reduce delays at shovels, trucks, trains, and the Coarse Crusher.

In June 1993, Erie received approval to construct the first "Super Pocket" in Mining Area 2 East, at a cost of $5.6 million. This was the largest single capital project since the 1967 plant expansion. Compared to the original Loading Pockets, the Super Pocket had ten times the usable storage capacity and was capable of loading railcars three times faster. An interesting aspect of the Super Pocket was that part of the project funding was obtained through an Iron Range Resources and Rehabilitation Board (IRRRB) Taconite Assistance Program, which provided for a $2 million grant for each taconite producer for projects jointly submitted by a company and union committee.

On May 5, 1994, the first phase of the mine consolidation plan was completed when the Area 2 East Super Pocket, a world-class taconite loading system, began operating.

Hot relief in the mine increased productivity by reducing shift change delays.

Construction of Erie's first Super Pocket in Area 2 East.

Upgrading mining equipment continued in 1994 with a $26 million capital-spending program for a new shovel, 240-ton capacity haul trucks, a drill, and large front-end loader. This represented the largest single annual outlay to replace and upgrade mine equipment in the mine's history.

In 1995, another element of the mine's consolidation plan occurred when approval was received to construct a second Super Pocket at Mining Area 2 West Extension (2WX). The 2WX Super Pocket began operating ahead of schedule on March 14, 1996. By the time the mine consolidation plan was completed in 1999, more than $50 million had been spent on mine equipment.

As the characteristics of the ore began to change during 1994 and 1995, Concentrator personnel looked for ways to improve magnetic iron recovery. In late 1996, prototype magnetic drum separators were installed on two mill lines. The larger, more efficient separators streamlined the flow sheet by reducing the number of rougher, cleaner, and finisher separators installed on each mill line from twenty to four. The two test lines showed a significant increase in iron recovery and maintenance cost savings. This was the first time that large, four-foot diameter by ten feet long, magnetic separators were used in a Mesabi Range taconite plant, and these soon became the model for other plants. In 1997, the Concentrator

received approval for a $6 million project, also partially funded by an IRRRB grant, to convert an additional eight mill lines to the new separators.

In the fall of 1999, a flow sheet change with significant positive implications for production, quality, and maintenance took place at the Fine Crusher with the test installation of a large new-style crusher. The new test line consisted of one crusher, one screen, and one feeder replacing the original line of three crushers, two screens, and two feeders. Although this was not implemented plantwide, this installation would become the prototype for other plants.

ENVIRONMENTAL ACTIVITIES

In addition to operating improvements, significant investments were made to improve working conditions and to respond to ever-increasing environmental requirements throughout the years.

From 1972 to 1976, electrostatic precipitators were installed at the Taconite Harbor Power Plant on the exhaust stack of the three generating units to bring particulate emissions into compliance with new Minnesota Pollution Control Agency (MPCA) requirements.

In 1991, a locomotive pulled away from the Knox fueling station with a fuel hose still attached, resulting in a large oil spill. The spill was reported and cleaned up, but subsequent testing revealed

170-ton capacity haul trucks (right) replaced Erie's 85-ton capacity trucks (left).

The 170-ton truck fleet was made up of both Euclid and Unit Rig models.

The first 240-ton capacity truck on the Mesabi Range, Erie's Wiseda #7465.

In the 1990s, 240-ton trucks and larger shovels replaced Erie's forty-year-old fleets.

Unit Rig's MT 4000, 240-ton truck formed the nucleus of Erie's new truck fleet.

Additional Gardner Denver rotary drills and a new P&H drill (shown) were added to the roster.

New mining support equipment included front-end loaders and dozers.

Erie was the first mine on the Mesabi Range to acquire Caterpillar's largest D-10 and D-11 crawler tractors.

Erie operated three large Caterpillar 994 front-end loaders, the most of any mine on the Mesabi Range.

The Area 2 East Super Pocket was an operating success.

Area 2 East Super Pocket operator station.

The dedication of the first Super Pocket involved union, political, and corporate leaders.

Super Pocket system loaded ore cars three times faster than the earlier style loading pockets.

Two Bucyrus-Erie 395 BII shovels were acquired, one in 1992 and another in 1994, to address increased stripping demands.

Original Concentrator flowsheet incorporated twenty magnetic separators per mill line.

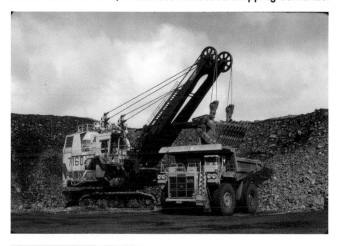

The Bucyrus-Erie 395 BII shovels were equipped with 33-cubic-yard dippers and could load a 240-ton truck in four passes.

A picture of the Erie's last new shovel, #7153 (P&H 2300), and 240-ton haul truck, #7458 (Unit Rig MT 4400), both acquired in 1999.

a substantial amount of oil-saturated ground in the area from years of use. This resulted in the removal and treatment of contaminated soil and the implementation of preventive measures, including installing a new fuel tank and containment dike, covering the fueling area with collection drip pans, and training employees in fueling and spill response procedures. This led to improved equipment fueling practices on the Mainline Railroad and in the mine, as three mine pit equipment and two mine locomotive enclosed fueling stations were constructed.

On July 28, 1993, a major landslide occurred at the coal ash pile located about a half-mile above the Taconite Harbor Power Plant. Ash and water flowed downhill through the railroad cut, across Highway 61 and into the coal yard, the substation, and the fuel tank area. Only a minor amount of ash flowed into Lake Superior. The company immediately activated its Emergency Response Team to deal with the situation and begin cleanup activities. Working with the MPCA and Minnesota Department of Natural Resources (MDNR), plans were developed to address short- and long-term environmental problems associated with the incident. A revised ash disposal site was constructed based on a design that included channeling water away from the pile, consolidating and compacting the ash, building a shallower stockpile slope, installing a water drainage system,

Erie's second Super Pocket at Area 2WX ready for operation.

New, large, 4' x 10' magnetic separators awaiting installation.

Four new large separators installed on a mill line replaced twenty old smaller separators.

Power Plant exhaust stacks with precipitators installed.

and capping the stockpile with impermeable materials. The final environmental cleanup included fertilizing and seeding the impacted areas.

In 1994, a $2.2 million system was installed at Taconite Harbor to prevent water from surface runoff at the dock and dust control operations during train dumping from entering Lake Superior. The water collected by the system was pumped to a settling pond and reused as dust control water.

On August 26, 1994, after thirty years of providing high-recovery and low-silica ore, the last ore train left the Dunka Mine and it was closed. In the early 1960s as the Dunka Mine was being developed, the unique geology occurring on the east end of the Mesabi Range required the removal of millions of tons of Duluth Complex material to access the taconite. This material contained copper, nickel, cobalt, and zinc sulfide minerals, and was stockpiled separately because of its potential future use. In the 1970s and early 1980s, problems were detected with concentrations of metals in the water seeping from the stockpiles. Erie, working with the MPCA and MNDR, studied the situation and eventually proposed a combination of methods for handling the water seeping from these stockpiles. The mine closure plan eventually included seepage treatment wetlands, stockpile capping, and ditching to divert water away from the stockpile.

In 1997, a $1.4 million program to reduce particulate emissions at the Plant Site was initiated. The forty-year-old dust collectors in the Fine Crusher, Concentrator, and Pelletizing Plant were replaced with newer, more-efficient units.

Right up until the closure of the mine was announced in May 2000, the dedicated, hardworking employees of Erie proposed and implemented changes and modifications to the operation, and many millions of dollars were spent to improve the costs, quality, production, and the environment.

Knox reporting building and Mainline Railroad locomotive fuel and service station.

Erie Mainline Railroad locomotives were fueled and serviced before each trip to Taconite Harbor.

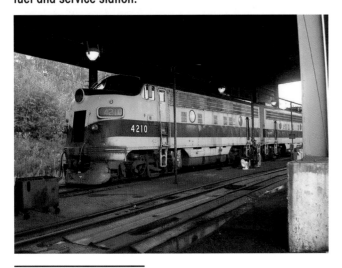

Covered fueling area showing drip containment pans.

Enclosed mine locomotive fueling and service building at Area 2.

Aerial of Taconite Harbor Power Plant coal ash pile slide.

View of ash cleanup beginning at Taconite Harbor Power Plant area.

Dennis Koschak, Erie's last General Manager, was instrumental in the success of the Dunka stockpile seep water treatment facility.

Aerial view of Dunka Mine and Birch Lake in the background.

WEATHER

The start of Erie's operation in the fall of 1957 ushered in a new era of large-scale, year-round mining operations in Minnesota. Until then, most of the Mesabi Range's iron ore mines would shut down in late October when the first of winter's freezing weather arrived and would not start up until the following April. Because Erie was designed to operate "around the clock," 365 days a year, changing weather conditions provided many challenges for its employees, particularly those working in the mine, railroad, and Tailing Basin.

At times, the snow and extreme cold temperatures of Minnesota winters made it difficult for employees working "outside" to keep equipment operating and the mine running smoothly. A heavy snowfall caused the mine to slow down as visibility decreased, haul roads iced up and became slippery, and railroad switches clogged with snow.

Keeping employees safe and taconite delivery moving during a storm was the mine's objective.

But according to Maintenance Supervisor Harland Nygard, "the biggest problem was the extreme cold weather. Getting vehicles moving was difficult because batteries ran down, hydraulic and engine oil got stiff, and even the metal on the shovels got cold and brittle and became hard to repair. Our repair work just slowed down in the cold."

Harlan: "Some days the weather was so cold that the metal on the shovels became cold and brittle and hard to repair."

Erie employees braved the cold temperatures by wearing extra layers of clothing, insulated work boots, wool stocking caps, face masks, and heavy gloves, but it was their determination to "keep the mine running," that showed through the most.

Mike Long: "The cold weather alone is irrelevant, but with the wind it can be unbearable."
Dennis Peterson: "Watching Dwight shiver keeps me warm."
Dwight Husby: "We like real cold weather . . . there are no mosquitoes."

The "Halloween" blizzard of 1991 was particularly challenging. Snow started falling around noon on October 31 and did not stop for three days. Northern Minnesota accumulated over thirty inches of snow during the storm. Once it became evident that a major storm was underway, Erie's "storm plan" was implemented. All activities then focused on keeping taconite delivery going. Stripping operations were shut down, and the employees were reassigned to keep haul roads and track switches open. During the first shift after the snow started, snow built up so fast, causing clogged switches and derailments, that only nine carloads of ore were dumped at the Coarse Crusher, compared to a normal delivery schedule of 270 to 300 cars. Gradually ore delivery improved as Erie's employees gained the upper hand. Because some area roads were impassable, many employees remained at Erie for several days to keep production going—sleeping in drys and eating overtime lunches from onsite supplies.

The Jordan spreader clears a heavy snowfall from Erie's railroad.

On February 2, 1996, cold weather arrived in earnest, and employees' dedication and perseverance were tested again as record cold temperatures of minus 60 degrees descended on the area. According to Bill Moraski, Section Manager in the Pelletizing Plant, "during the minus-sixty-degree weather, we were working at the Stacker trying to get the transfer belt operating after a belt repair. The belt got so cold and stiff that it would not start . . . a long cable was attached to the belt and a large front-end loader was used to pull and assist starting the belt moving."

A cold morning on the Mesabi Range.

Erie's Stacker and conveyor on a cold winter's day.

Not all the weather problems occurred during the winter. Over the years Erie experienced several "100-year" rainstorms that flooded mine areas and washed out portions of the railroad.

Another "100-year storm" on July 4, 1999, knocked out electrical power to Mining Area 6 and caused temporary flooding in lower portions of the mine.

To ensure that proper safe responses were followed when any type of extreme weather or emergency was encountered, Erie developed and issued Standard Practice Procedure manuals, containing detailed and very specific written instructions for handling adverse events, such as the Snow Storm Plan; Tornado Alert Plan; Forest Fire Prevention, Reporting and Suppression Plan; and Oil Spill Reporting, Containment and Cleanup Plan.

Through it all, Erie employees always answered the call and put in the extra effort necessary to keep the operation running.

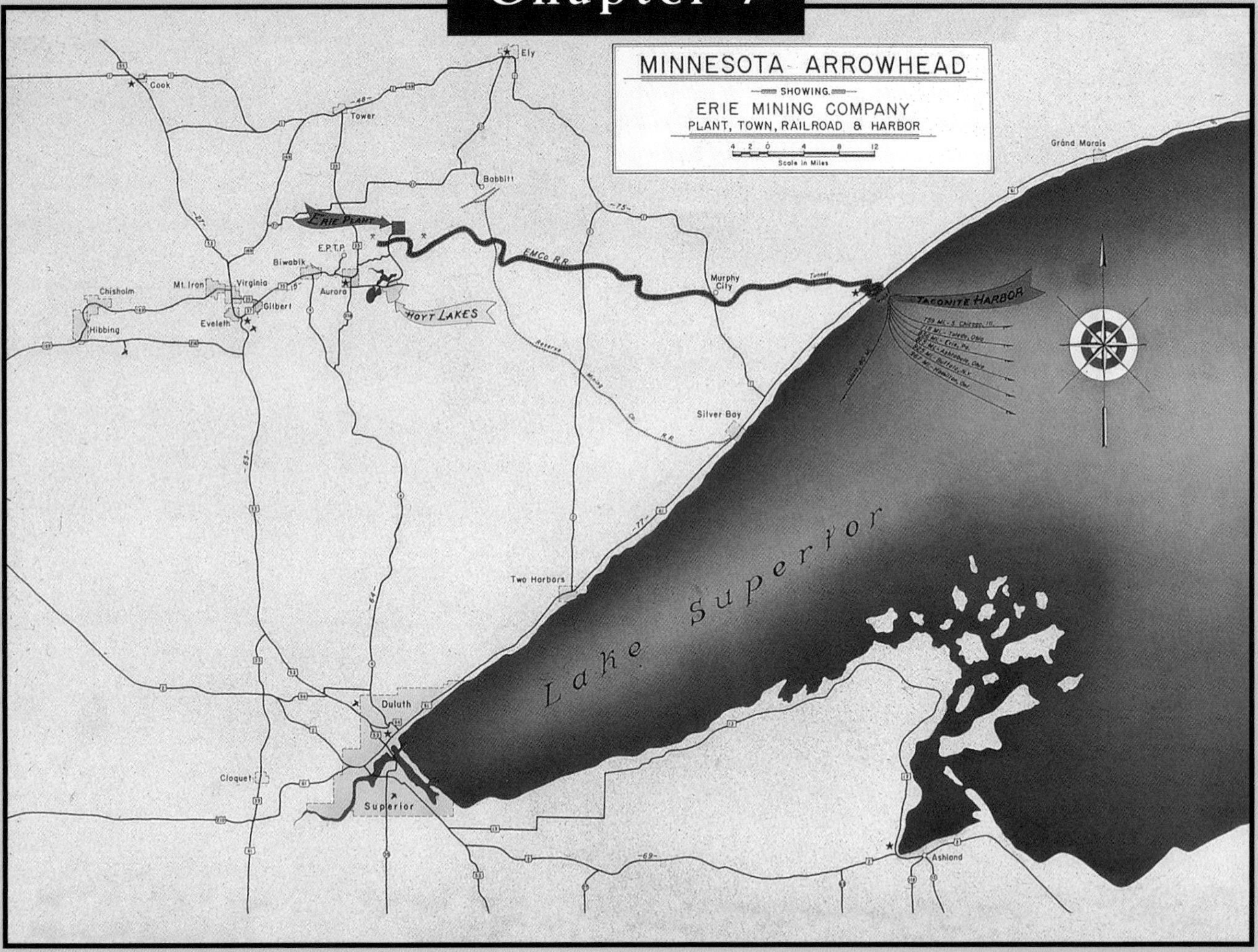

Chapter 7

MINNESOTA ARROWHEAD
SHOWING
ERIE MINING COMPANY
PLANT, TOWN, RAILROAD & HARBOR

MOVING PELLETS

rie moved taconite pellets from its Plant Site near Hoyt Lakes on a seventy-three-mile long, single-track Mainline Railroad across the Minnesota Arrowhead including parts of the Superior National Forest to its Dock at Taconite Harbor on the North Shore of Lake Superior. At the Dock the pellets were loaded into ore boats for transport down the Great Lakes to the steel mills' blast furnaces. The railroad and Dock were an integral part of Erie during its forty-three years of operation. Erie's railroad provided three main functions: Plant Switching, Mine Railroad ore haulage to the Coarse Crusher, and Mainline Railroad pellet haulage.[1]

The original Plant Switching equipment (switchers) was four 1,200-horsepower Baldwin S-12 locomotives. Railcars carrying bentonite, grinding rods and balls, and other materials were delivered by DM&IR to Hinsdale, Erie's only rail interchange.[2] Plant Switching personnel would move the railcars to their unloading locations in the Plant Site and return them to Hinsdale. Switchers also moved Erie's railcars and locomotives in and out of the General Shops for maintenance.

The Mine Railroad originally operated fifteen 1,800-horsepower ALCO RS-11 locomotives on nearly fifty miles of permanent track for

Plant switcher moving commercial railcars from Hinsdale interchange.

Bentonite cars being switched at Additive Plant.

A nine-car ore train heading to Coarse Crusher.

transporting ore from the mining areas to the crusher. Mine Railroad trains were comprised of nine or eighteen ore cars pulled by one or two locomotives, respectively.

Trains of thirty-six ore cars from Dunka Mine, located twenty miles east of the Plant Site, traveled over a 5.6-mile section of Mainline Railroad track between Balsam and Dunka Junctions. This section of track was under the direction of the railroad dispatcher using the only Central Traffic Control (CTC) section installed at Erie. Ore haulage from the Dunka Mine was normally with a dedicated 2,400-horsepower ALCO C-424 locomotive (#7230) to the Marshalling Yard where the thirty-six-car trains were split into eighteen-car trains for delivery up to the Coarse Crusher pulled by two RS-11 locomotives.

Mainline Railroad locomotives consisted of eleven 1,750-horsepower EMD F9 units—five A's and six B's (a power unit with no operator cab) were used for pellet movement. The original mainline equipment consisted of three bay window cabooses, 389 custom-built 85-ton capacity pellet cars, two 45-ton capacity American Locomotive cranes for track maintenance, and a 250-ton Brownhoist Crane for wrecker service.[3]

Subsequent acquisitions include two Pullman sleepers for conversion to work train service and a solarium observation car for transporting dignitaries and guests. Erie renamed the observation car, the Taconite Trail.[4] This car was sold in 1961, and Erie rented passenger cars after that when required. The two work train sleepers were sold for scrap in 1971.

An eighteen-car ore train heading to Coarse Crusher.

Locomotive 7230 pulling a thirty-six-car Dunka ore train to the Marshalling Yard with Baldwin switcher being brought to General Shop for maintenance.

Typical Mainline Railroad train—lead locomotive is an F9A, next two are F9Bs, and the fourth is an F9A.

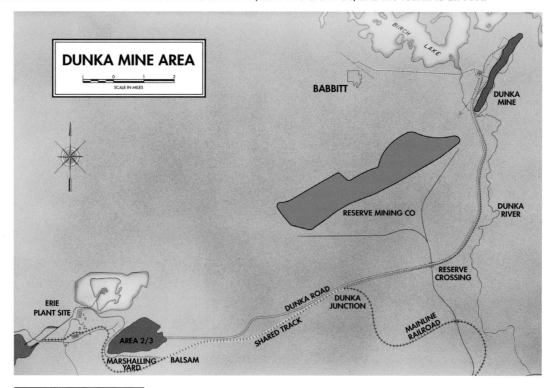

Dunka is located at the eastern end of the Mesabi Range.

Original bay window cabooses.

One of Erie's 389 custom bottom-dump pellet cars.

One of two original 45-ton American locomotive cranes used mainly to handle temporary mine track.

Erie's 250-ton capacity Brownhoist crane re-railing a locomotive—the largest railroad crane on the Mesabi Range.

One of two Pullman sleepers converted for track maintenance service.

Erie's business car, Taconite Trail.

Interior of Taconite Trail observation car.

ERIE'S PASSENGER TRAINS

Erie's railroads were very busy throughout the year. Typically, the Mainline Railroad operated six pellet trains per day during the shipping season while the Mine Railroad operated ten 9- or 18-car ore trains round the clock all year long. Added to this, track maintenance and plant switching activities were scheduled five days a week. Once in a while, these activities would take a secondary role as the railroad and all of Erie geared up to handle a special passenger train.

Throughout the years, senior representatives from Erie's owners and Pickands Mather executives would meet at the mine to review plans and projects, and conduct a tour of Erie. These visits, called "stockholders tours" by Erie personnel, were the impetus for a company-wide house cleaning. Several busy weeks of preparation work took place in all departments beforehand; areas were straightened up, hand railings painted, roadways graded, and presentations prepared. In addition to the meeting and Plant Site tour, the stockholders would occasionally board Erie's observation car, Taconite Trail, for a scenic trip to Taconite Harbor. For a few hours, the stockholders train had priority over other traffic on the railroad. After the Taconite Trail was sold, several passenger cars would be rented to make up these stockholder tour trains.

In the fall of 1989, Erie hosted its first-ever nonemployee rail trip on the Mainline Railroad. The American Institute of Mining Engineers (AIME) sponsored the trip from the Plant Site to Taconite Harbor for more than

Erie's Mainline Railroad operated through some of the most wild and scenic land in Minnesota.

Stockholder train with rented passenger cars.

Stockholder train heading toward Taconite Harbor.

Stockholder train touring the mine.

AIME train approaching Knox.

400 members and guests. Three of Erie's F9 locomotives pulling nine rented passenger cars traveled the seventy-three-mile route and returned in slightly under six hours. The trip proved so popular that the AIME repeated it a few years later.

The final passenger trains on Erie's railroad were fall color rail fan trips on September 21 and 22, 2002, almost two years after the mine had shut down. The trips were promoted as Farewell to Erie Mining Railroad as a fundraising effort for the Lake Superior Railroad Museum and Friends of the Milwaukee Road #261 steam locomotive and included the formal transfer of F9A locomotive #4211 to the museum. The passenger train was led by #4211 together with two of the museum's diesel locomotives.

The AIME train returning from Taconite Harbor.

"Farewell to the Erie Mining Co. Railroad" train on the Taconite Harbor trestle.

Official transfer of #4211 from Cliffs to the Lake Superior Railroad Museum.

Retail Value $1.00

"FAREWELL TO THE ERIE MINING CO. RAILROAD"
SEPTEMBER 21-22, 2002
PRESENTED BY THE LAKE SUPERIOR RAILROAD MUSEUM
AND THE "FRIENDS OF THE 261" WITH THE COOPERATION OF
CLEVELAND-CLIFFS INC

An A-B-B-B-A set of F9s bursts out of 1,800-foot Cramer Tunnel and into the morning sunshine on August 27, 1989. The loaded taconite train is led by F9A 4211 (formerly EMCO 101) which would lead the last trains over the railroad in July 2001. The unit will be formally donated to the Lake Superior Railroad Museum by Cleveland-Cliffs, Inc at a brief ceremony prior to departure on September 21, and will be the lead locomotive on the two excursion trains. — *Lori Van Oosbree photo.*

Brochure cover for "Farewell to the Erie Mining Co. Railroad" train excursion.

LOADING TRAINS

The fired pellets were conveyed to the Pellet Loading Pocket south of the Pelletizing Plant. From there the pellets could be stockpiled via the Stacker, direct loaded into pellet cars, or transferred to emergency storage. During the shipping season, pellet cars were loaded based on the ore boat schedule; otherwise, pellets were directed to the Pellet Stockpile. Emergency storage was only used when pellet cars and the Stacker were not available. In the winter pellets were stockpiled.

The pellet loading area consisted of two Empty Tracks, three Load Tracks, and a Thoroughfare Track. Returning pellet trains brought pellet cars to the Empty Tracks.

Two Trackmobiles (i.e., small vehicle that can travel on rails or roads) operated twenty-four hours a day during shipping season, moving twelve-car strings from the Empty Tracks through the Pellet Loading Pocket and then to the Load Tracks.

A Trackmobile pulling pellet cars through the Loading Pocket.

Initially, reciprocating pan feeders were installed to load pellet cars. These feeders caused structural problems with the Pellet Loading Pocket and were replaced with a series of gates and chutes that automatically loaded each car. The gate action was controlled by sensors that detected a car's position as the Trackmobiles moved the pellet cars under the pocket.

Aerial of pellet stacking and train loading area.

Original Loading Pocket pan feeder and belt.

After loading, the individual twelve-car strings were moved to water spray racks for pellet cooling and dust control before delivery to the Load Tracks. If the pellets were too hot, pellet cars, dock structure, and even ore boats could be damaged. After 1986, pellet direct car loading and associated cooling water spray was discontinued to improve pellet quality by allowing pellets to cool slowly in the Pellet Stockpile.

When reclaiming pellets from the Pellet Stockpile, a switcher pulled forty-eight-car strings for loading by shovel or front-end loader. The loaded pellet cars were then moved to the Load Track. Crews on the Load Track assembled loaded pellet cars into ninety-six-car trains. An engineer, brakeman, and conductor manned the trains. An air brake test was conducted, and the train was inspected for defects before being released for the trip to Taconite Harbor.

Schematic of gate and chute modification that replaced the pan feeders and belts.

Pellet cooling spray racks.

Pellet train being loaded from stockpile by shovel and front-end loader.

THE MAINLINE RAILROAD ROUTE

The Mainline Railroad started counting miles at Knox designated Mile Post 0 (MP 0) and continued to the entry of the Taconite Harbor yard (MP 72.2). Along its route the Mainline Railroad crossed under the DM&IR Eastern Mesaba Branch (MP 1.5), reached Balsam Junction (MP 3.8) and Dunka Junction (MP 9.4), crossed over the Reserve mainline (MP 14.7), crossed Highway 2 (MP 28.3), bridged Stony River (MP 37), and passed under the DM&IR Wales Branch (MP 39.1). At Trow (MP 42) there is a full train-length passing track, named in honor of Conrad Trowbridge, the manager of railroad and harbor construction. The railroad reached its high point of elevation of 1,937 feet above sea level at MP 44 having climbed 400 feet above the starting point at Knox without ascending any grade greater than 0.53 percent. The railroad passed Murphy City and crossed Highway 1 at MP 49 and began a steeper 1.25 percent descent at MP 56. The railroad crossed the Manitou River (MP 58.9) on the tallest bridge on the route and then passed through the 1,860-foot Cramer Tunnel (MP 62). The 2 percent descending grade began at MP 65 and continued for nearly eight miles to the Dock. From its highest point, the railroad dropped 1,246 feet down to the Dock without descending any grade steeper than 2 percent.

Balsam Junction, where Dunka ore trains leave the Mainline Railroad for the Marshalling Yard (left track in photo).

Westbound Dunka ore train entering the Mainline Railroad at Dunka Junction. The Mainline Railroad can be seen curving away under the Dunka JCT sign on the right.

Loaded pellet train ready to leave Knox, beginning trip to Taconite Harbor.

View looking west at the 785-foot-long siding at Reserve.

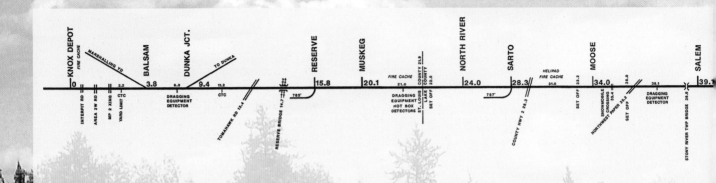

Schematic of Mainline Railroad locations (stations and mileposts).

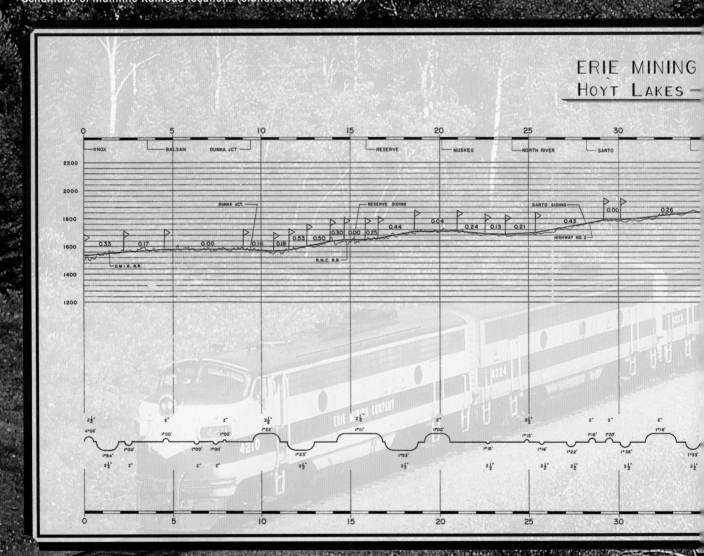

Mainline Railroad elevation profile and plan.

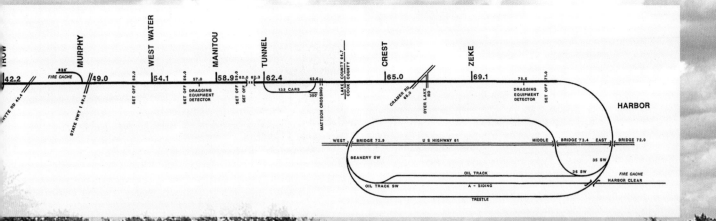

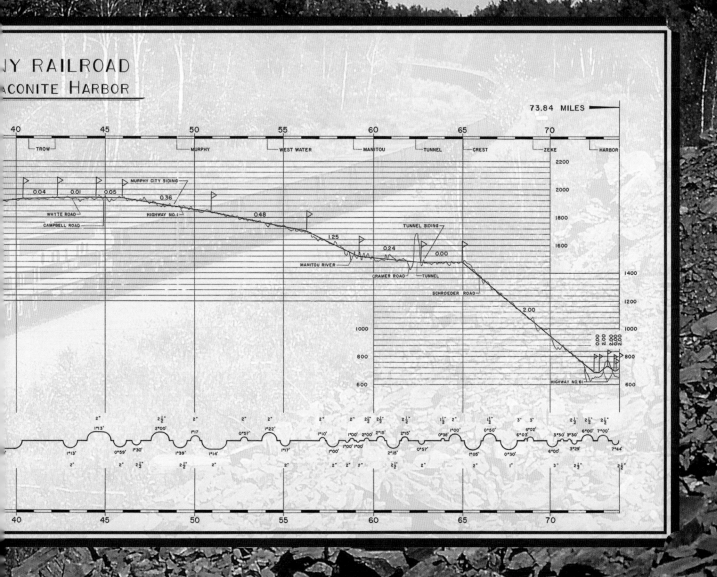

State Highway 2 crossing (called Sarto).

Three culverts under the Mainline Railroad at Stony River.

DM&IR's Wales Branch passed over the Mainline Railroad at Salem Bridge.

The passing track at Trow that allowed full-length pellet trains to meet also had a 490-foot siding for rail maintenance equipment.

At Murphy the Mainline Railroad crossed Highway 1 and had an 836-foot siding with a shop, office, warehouse, and reporting center.

Manitou Bridge was 100 feet above the Manitou River.

Approaching the 1,860-foot-long Cramer Tunnel.

Descending the 2 percent grade, the Mainline Railroad passed Two Island River waterfall.

View approaching Highway 61 Bridge; Power Plant and Lake Superior in distance.

After crossing Highway 61 Bridge, view of East Breakwater (background) and 35 Switch (foreground).

MAINLINE RAILROAD STARTUP AND OPERATION

Before the Mainline Railroad could begin operation, the train brake equipment needed to be tested and braking procedures established. To accomplish this, the brake equipment manufacturer, Westinghouse Air Brake Company, conducted 261 braking tests on Erie trains of varying length and weight from June through September of 1957. Because of Erie's heavy train loads and steep grades, many railroads, including Southern Pacific, New York Central, Erie, Frisco, Canadian National, Canadian Pacific, Reading, DM&IR, Northern Pacific, Great Northern, and Lake Superior & Ishpeming, were interested and sent observers. Erie employees with railroad operating experience that were involved in the tests included Paul Giesking, S. Ward Huntley, Roy Johnson, R. Korby, N. Schwach, G. Gialnetz, Ted Stevens, C. Denney, Chester Walczak, Leonard Marsh, and R. Novlan. At the end of each brake test, the pellets were dumped into the Dock. Once there were enough pellets in the Dock, the first ore boat, the *J. Campbell*, was loaded with 10,909 tons on September 26, 1957. By the end of the year, the Mainline Railroad had hauled slightly more than 137,000 tons of Pre-Tac and the Commercial Plant pellets.[5]

Erie's Railroad Operating Rules books, 1957 to 1995.

Experienced railroad employees also participated in the development of the operating rules that governed all phases of Erie's railroad activities. These rules were published in a handbook given to each railroad employee. Erie railroad employees were required to pass a written test to demonstrate their knowledge and understanding of the rules. The handbook was updated to accommodate changes on the railroad.

The initial Mainline Railroad operating plan called for three 120-car trains to Taconite Harbor daily. This schedule became unsustainable because of the excessive time required to open and close the bottom dump doors on the pellet cars using wrench cars that ran on narrower gauge tracks parallel to the train. The train had to be repositioned several times to complete unloading. Overall pellet delivery was improved when train length was reduced to ninety-six pellet cars.

The typical pellet train consisted of four locomotives, providing 7,000 horsepower, and ninety-six pellet cars, each loaded with 80 tons of pellets for a train total of 7,680 tons. The trip from the Plant Site to Taconite Harbor and back took about eight hours. In early years, three round trips per day were sufficient. Later, as production increased, as many as seven trips per day were required.

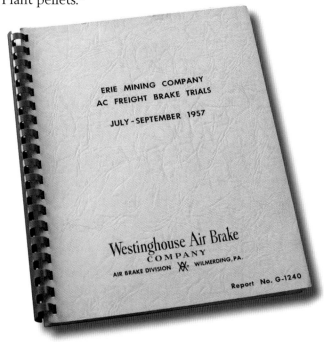

Report of the 1957 brake tests.

PRESERVING ERIE RAILROAD EQUIPMENT

On August 13, 1975, Erie's General Manager Clyde Keith presented the keys for a 1957 Pontiac Hy-Rail station wagon to Don Shank, President of the Lake Superior Transportation Museum since renamed the Lake Superior Railroad Museum. The Pontiac was modified by Fairmont Hy-Rail Company with the addition of hydraulic guide wheel positioning equipment, which allowed transition between highway travel and railroad operation. The vehicle was used to make routine inspections of the Mainline Railroad. During its life it had traveled enough miles to make a trip from the Plant Site to Taconite Harbor and back every week. After seventeen years of use, it was removed from service and donated to the museum.

Pontiac Hy-Rail with guide wheels lowered.

In October 1992 Erie donated a Baldwin S-12 locomotive (#7243) to the museum. This was the last Baldwin locomotive to leave the Baldwin factory.

By the mid-1990s, Erie's EMD F9 units were the last of their kind still operating in their original commercial service, with each having traveled more than 1.5 million miles.[34] These locomotives were known worldwide to rail fans who would find vantage points to photograph the F9s in action.[35] When Erie closed in 2001, these forty-three-year-old locomotives were still making two and sometimes three round trips per day.[36] EMD F9A locomotive (#4211) and EMD F9B locomotive (#4222) were donated to the museum in June 29, 2002, and August 1, 2009, respectively.

Baldwin Locomotive (#7243) donated to the Lake Superior Railroad Museum.

F9A (#4211) and F9B (#4222) on the North Shore Scenic Railroad, which is operated by the Lake Superior Railroad Museum.

A typical four-locomotive Mainline Railroad train returns from Taconite Harbor.

With a few exceptions, Erie's locomotives were able to meet pellet movement requirements. In 1973 when annual shipping reached over thirteen million tons, it became necessary to rent three 2,750-horsepower ALCO C-628 locomotives from the Delaware & Hudson Railroad. Two were rented for six months and one for four months for a total of sixteen locomotive months. Erie's locomotive fleet was all four-axel units, and these were the first six-axle locomotives to be used. During this period excessive rail wear on curves was observed; some thought this was due to the six-axel locomotives, and others believed it was due to the higher traffic and track super elevation (i.e., banking on curves) issues. From 1993 to 1996, because of reduced availability of the aging locomotive fleet, SD-9s and SD-18s were rented from the DM&IR for a total of fifteen locomotive months. In 1997 a major derailment at Taconite Harbor resulted in the loss of four locomotives and ninety-three pellet cars, requiring rentals of thirty-five locomotive months until replacement locomotives were delivered. Rentals of sixteen, eighteen, and twenty-six locomotive months were required in 1998, 1999, and 2000, respectively.

Train with all rented locomotives.

Erie locomotives with two EMD SD9 DM&IR rentals.

One of three ALCO C-628 Delaware & Hudson rentals.

MAINTAINING THE MAINLINE RAILROAD

The Mainline Railroad right-of-way consisted of rails, ties, ballast, culverts, ditches, bridges, grade crossing signals, the Cramer Tunnel, and cuts and fills. Erie employees inspected the right-of-way on a continuous basis, and Track Crews were immediately dispatched for urgent repairs and performed routine maintenance, such as tamping ballast and replacing switch parts, rails, and ties.

There were also major construction projects, such as continuous welded rail installation and replacement of large numbers of ties. Continuous welded rail installation consisted of 1,500-foot-long sections called ribbon rail delivered by special trains that were then installed.

A train carrying ribbon rail on its way to be installed.

Removing a 1,500-foot-long ribbon rail from train for installation.

Installing ribbon rail.

Installing ribbon rail.

BIGGEST TRAIN WRECK

On January 13, 1997, the last pellet train of the shipping season was involved in a major accident. The last ore boat was waiting for one more train to complete its cargo. The train was due to arrive at Taconite Harbor early in the morning, and the Taconite Harbor–based Track Crew was waiting for the train so they could get on the track. Radio transmissions from the train operators indicated it was out of control—traveling too fast on the 2 percent descending grade (a runaway). The track crew immediately reacted to protect the public by blocking traffic on U.S. Highway 61. The original Mainline Railroad design included a speed detector at MP 71.17 that automatically aligned 35 Switch to protect the Dock from runaway trains. As the train passed MP 71, its speed was excessive, and the 35 Switch was activated diverting the train to bypass the Dock. The runaway train passed over the Highway 61 bridge and continued to the 35 Switch where the leading two locomotives left the track, overturned, and came to rest between the return loop track and dock track. The following two locomotives and all ninety-three cars of the train left the track before they reached the Dock. Fortunately, there were no serious injuries although this was the most significant accident at Erie in terms of equipment damage. Immediately, Taconite Harbor personnel cleared pellet cars, pellets, and debris from Highway 61 so traffic could safely resume. In addition to the four locomotives and ninety-three pellet cars destroyed, one-third of a mile of track had to be rebuilt. The cause of this accident was attributed to improper brake operation when the train reached the descending grade.

One of the two trailing locomotives being recovered from outside curve.

Pellet cars on outside curve at the bottom of the fill.

Two lead locomotives lying between the return loop track and dock track.

White vehicle near the wreckage cleared from Highway 61.

The tie changer removed old ties and inserted new ones without moving the rail.

The spiker gauger set spikes so that the correct rail spacing was maintained.

The ballast regulator was used to spread and level the track ballast.

The tamper aligned the track to the correct geometry.

Continuous welded rail replaced the original thirty-nine-foot-long rails sections, which eliminated rail joints and thereby reduced track maintenance. The ribbons were made from new rail or from reused thirty-nine-foot rail sections that were sent to a rail welding plant to be welded together. Track welder Robert "Bart" Bartholomew remembered being impressed by the continuous welded rail. "It came out on . . . flat cars," he said. "The crane would pick it up and set it in, and that was awesome to see that done. When you see all these tons of rail come in . . . It was great."[6]

The Track Crew typically planned to replace up to 10,000 of the Mainline Railroad's approximately

Maintenance crews originally used speeders like this to get to work sites.

Hy-Rail vehicles replaced speeders for transporting track maintenance crews and equipment.

Moose as seen from a locomotive cab.

225,000 ties each year. But in 1998 and 1999, to make up for prior shortfalls, there was a major program to replace 32,000 ties each year using a contractor. Originally maintenance equipment set offs were built every few miles along the mainline track to allow Track Crews to clear the track for pellet trains. With the installation of continuous welded rail and addition of more Hy-Rail maintenance equipment (i.e., vehicle that has both flanged guide wheels for rail operation and rubber tires for road operation), the set offs were seldom used.

Initially Track Crews used rail transportation vehicles [motor cars (speeders), gang cars, and motor car flats] to get to work sites and sidings where specialized track maintenance equipment (tampers, spike pullers, ballast spreaders, tie changers) were located. The slow-moving transportation vehicles contributed to track maintenance inefficiencies and had to move to and from sidings or set-offs to allow trains to pass. Hy-Rail vehicles worked well for track inspection and at the same time could transport crews and tools faster and had more flexibility to get off the track. Over time more than a dozen Hy-Rail vehicles were acquired. These, unlike the original Hy-Rail Pontiac Station Wagon, had manually deployed guide wheels, which were quicker, lighter weight, and cheaper.

Ron Gervais experienced both good and tough days during his career working on the Track Crew. Because of his seniority, he could almost pick his job from Trackman to Track Boss. One of the tougher jobs was Tamper Operator. "I ran the tamper for basically one summer on the railroad," he said. "That's a nasty job. You get tired of watching those things (tongs) go down alongside the ties after a while, but it's a job you've got to do. You lift the track up and make sure the alignment is good and the level is right. The better the job you do there, the less times you're going to have to come back and work on that spot."[7]

For Tom Niemi, rail inspection on the Hy-Rail was one of the more pleasant memories of his time with Erie. "Some of the scenery was amazing," he said. "Around Milepost 71, there are some waterfalls. You go over Manitou Bridge, which is over 100 feet above the Manitou River, so it's kind of exciting to stop there and look down over the edge."[8] Wolves, deer, and moose were frequently observed along the Mainline Railroad.

During dry periods, the forests surrounding the Mainline Railroad became a serious fire risk. As a result, Erie maintained a "Fire Train." Mike Salo recalled that the Fire Train had a caboose, a flat car with ramps for loading a D4 or D6 crawler tractor, and an 8,000-gallon tank trailer and a 22,000-gallon tank car with a water cannon and nozzles that sprayed straight down onto the track to save the ties.[9]

Early fire train with fixed water sprays.

New version of fire train with swivel-mounted water cannons plus side and tie sprays.

U.S. Forest Service drops fire retardant near Erie Mainline Railroad.

In addition, caches of firefighting equipment were located at Knox, MP 21, MP 30.9, Murphy, Tunnel, and Harbor. A helicopter landing pad was also established at MP 30.9. During dry periods, a Track Crew would follow trains with firefighting equipment to extinguish any fire started by hot sparks from the locomotive exhaust. Erie coordinated its fire prevention and fighting activities with the Minnesota Department of Natural Resources and U.S. Forest Service.

THE CRAMER TUNNEL

The view when approaching the Cramer Tunnel from the west was quite spectacular. The track crossed a bridge high above the Cramer Road and Nine Mile Creek and disappeared into the tunnel. To reduce ice buildup, both ends of the tunnel had doors that were closed when shipping stopped. Traveling from the Plant Site to Taconite Harbor by Hy-Rail during the non-shipping season required manually cranking the doors open and closed, a very fatiguing task. When the doors were required to be closed during the shipping season, the Track Crew would operate them using power wrenches.

In the fall of 1956, Erie had taken delivery of twenty-seven diesel electric locomotives. The manufacturer's recommendations were to store the new units in heated sheds during the harsh Minnesota winter. Each of the twenty-seven locomotives was fifty to sixty feet in length, and there wasn't enough covered rail storage anywhere in northeastern Minnesota. At 1,860 feet in length, the Cramer Tunnel could accommodate all twenty-seven locomotives with more than 500 feet to spare. Erie decided to use the tunnel as a storage shed, solving the problem.[10]

Crews quickly began installing giant doors at each end of the seventeen-foot-wide by twenty-two-foot-high tunnel opening. Two 450,000-BTU hot air heaters, in a fabricated building on a flat car at the east end of the tunnel provided heating. A 22,000-gallon fuel tank car supplied diesel fuel for the heaters and a light plant.[11]

Approaching Cramer Tunnel from the west.

Looking out the east end of Cramer Tunnel.

Cramer Tunnel interior showing excavation through solid rock.

Opening tunnel swing doors in the spring of 1957.

Locomotives leave the tunnel after winter storage in 1957.

Winter locomotive storage at Knox.

The locomotives were moved into the tunnel in November and December, and the doors were closed. The heaters maintained a temperature in the tunnel above forty degrees. Two men who operated the heaters and checked on the locomotives lived in heated cabooses parked near the tunnel.[12]

In subsequent years, locomotives were not stored in the tunnel. The Mine Railroad locomotives operated year-round, and the Mainline Railroad units were shut down and stored outside with car body openings closed or covered to prevent snow entering, water drained, and batteries disconnected.[13]

Aerial showing Taconite Harbor and track layout designed for nonstop dumping into Dock.

Diagram showing the flow of pellets from the railroad car into the boat.

When a loaded train arrived at Taconite Harbor, it traveled on a wide curve to cross over U.S. Highway 61 and then to the trestle that spanned the pellet storage bins. The pellet cars would be dumped under the direction of the Dock Foreman, and the empty train would loop back across the highway three more times before the return trip to the Plant Site.[14] After dumping, the empty pellet cars were inspected for door closure.

Trackman Darwyn Haveri recalled a September day in 1957 when the first ore boat was loaded. "I was on the railroad when the first boat came in, and the first trainload of pellets went down," he said. "They did not have a crew at the dock at that time, and the train . . . stopped at Murphy and picked the whole Track Crew up. Some of us rode the engine down, some of them rode the caboose down."[15]

When the train arrived at the Dock, the pellet cars had to be dumped by manually opening the bottom doors with hand wheels and hand cranks because there was no wrench car (motorized car door opener). Haveri said, "It was dusty, dusty, dusty. We were quite black by the time we got done dumping."[16] That first production train was only seventy-five pellet cars. Haveri added, "Everything was new, new ideas and everything. It was a lot of work to go down there and dump a train. But it was terribly interesting."[17]

Towerman in control tower.

THE MV *STEWART J. CORT*

The MV *Stewart J. Cort* was the first of a new fleet of larger self-unloading ore boats that revolutionized bulk shipping on the Great Lakes and was specifically designed for loading pellets at Taconite Harbor and transporting them through the expanded Poe Lock at Sault Ste. Marie to Bethlehem's new 4.2 million ton per year steel mill at Burns Harbor, Indiana. The *Cort* was 1,000 feet in length and was 105 feet wide, limited by the dimensions of the Poe Lock. It was built for Bethlehem by Litton Industries (Litton) in Erie, Pennsylvania, and Pascagoula, Mississippi. Litton built the bow and stern sections in Mississippi, welded them together, and then sailed the 185-foot-combined sections up the East Coast and down the St. Lawrence River to the Litton shipyard in Erie, Pennsylvania. There, the bow and stern sections were cut apart and welded to an 815-foot midsection built at the Erie shipyard to form what would become the first "thousand-footer" on the Great Lakes.[30] Following the completion of the *Cort,* an additional dozen thousand-footers were built.

Cort positioned to be loaded with train approaching to dump.

Cort loading with shuttle conveyors positioned above small hatches associated with its unique self-centering cargo hold design.

The *Cort* was christened in May 1971 in honor of a Bethlehem vice president. The *Cort* loaded its first cargo of 58,300 tons of pellets at Taconite Harbor on April 27, 1972, and sailed for Burns Harbor.[31] The *Cort* had a capacity of 65,000 tons of pellets, double that of the next largest ore boat on the Great Lakes and was 20 percent faster than any other ore boat on the Lakes, which combined with self-unloading allowed a seven-day turnaround to and from Burns Harbor.[32]

Scheduled for forty trips a year between Burns Harbor and Taconite Harbor, the *Cort* by itself could supply 2.5 million tons of pellets each year. During its first four years of operation, the *Cort* traveled exclusively between Taconite Harbor and Burns Harbor.

Mike Salo remembered the sense of pride the dock crew had of loading the thousand-footers. "'If they had two of those big boats coming in back to back, the bins were plumb full," he said. "You had one train sitting at the dock loaded, and the other one was sitting at the tunnel. They never had to move the boat—three hours and forty minutes to load a thousand-foot vessel."[33]

Indicator lights (circled) showing degree of list.

Shuttle conveyors at different positions to provide level boat loading.

Each of the Dock's twenty-five, 4,000-ton capacity pellet storage bins had a forty-two-inch-wide shuttle conveyor beneath each bin. Pellets were fed from the pellet storage bins to each conveyor by a reciprocating two-speed pan feeder. The conveyors were forty-eight feet apart, which matched the hatch spacing on an ore boat. With an ore boat positioned along the Dock beneath the shuttle conveyors, operators (Towermen) in one or two Control Towers above the Dock monitored and controlled the loading operation based on a plan developed in conjunction with the ore boat Captain. Each shuttle conveyor could extend out forty-four feet from the Dock and was capable of loading pellets at rates of either 750 or 1,500 tons per hour based on conveyor speed. The Towerman, who was in constant radio communication with a Mate on the ore boat, could load and trim a boat in three to four hours depending on how fast the boat's ballast water could be pumped out.[18] The Towerman maintained proper loading by observing lights on the ore boat that indicated crosswise level (list).

Ted Williams recalled an interesting thing about the shuttle conveyors: "They were designed to run at two speeds." When the shuttle conveyor was completely extended, it could operate at the higher speed (tonnage rate) increasing the trajectory of the pellets so they reached the far side of the ore boat. When the shuttle conveyor was retracted, it could be slowed down, so the pellets were not thrown so far. "They got even loading in the ore boats that way."[19]

Every shuttle conveyor also had a weigh scale. Once a week, Dockmen would calibrate these scales using a calibrating chain of a known weight made up of rollers that was moved onto each conveyor. The Dockmen would set the chain on the stopped conveyor, roll the chain out, and then start the conveyor to calibrate the scale. The calibrating chains were weighed and certified monthly by the State of Minnesota Department of Weights and Measures.[20]

Completion of ore boat loading (trimming) was extremely important and was as much an art as a science. A typical target draft (depth of the boat below the surface of the water) was twenty-six feet, ten inches because the harbor depth was twenty-seven feet. If after initial loading, the draft could be increased by an inch, more tons were added. Ron

Numbers on the boat show the draft.

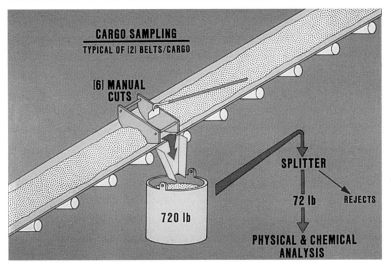

Schematic cargo sampling procedure.

Collecting sample from the cutter.

The 720-pound sample was split to a 72-pound sample shown.

This splitter reduced the 72-pound sample for laboratory testing.

Laboratory samples were dried and screened (screens shown on left).

Typical tumble drum for pellet durability testing.

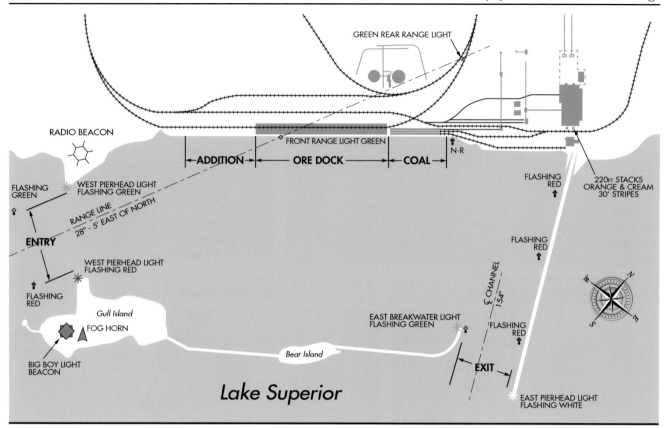

TACONITE HARBOR AIDS TO NAVIGATION

✳ FLASHING LIGHT
⚑ FLOATING BOUY
⚑ N-R RED NUN BOUY

Gervais, who worked as a Towerman early in his career, recalled that "the Mate would call me and say, 'Give me 100 tons in hatch fourteen.' We called it trimming, trimming the boat. So, then I would give him his 100 tons. Meanwhile, he's got a guy down on the dock face watching the draft marks on the rudder and when it hits his mark he'd give a shout, and the first mate would say, 'Shut it off.'"[21]

"When the boat was loaded, you reported a tonnage to the vessel by radio," Dock Foreman Gary Hansen said. The total ore boat tonnage was calculated from the readings from each of the shuttle conveyor scales used on that boat. The ore boat arrival, loading, and departure times and cargo tonnage was reported to the vessel agent in Duluth by teletype.[22]

During ore boat loading, the Dockman took multiple pellet samples manually. To take a sample, a loaded conveyor was stopped, a sample cutter was used to isolate pellets and fines from the total cross section of the conveyor, and that material was collected, processed into smaller portions, and

brought to the Dock's lab. At the lab the individual samples were combined into a cargo sample. Part of the cargo sample was tested for size, moisture, and durability (tumble test), part was sent to an offsite lab for chemical analysis, and part was saved. The cargo analysis was transmitted to the customer.

Barge used for buoy maintenance.

Erie's Dock workforce was constant through the years of operation. Around-the-clock coverage by four crews, each consisting of a Towerman, three Dockmen, and a Foreman was provided during the Great Lakes navigation season.

To ensure safe ore boat movement and to conform to U.S. Coast Guard requirements, there were several navigational aids. Small beacons were mounted on towers located at the lake ends of the east and west breakwaters and at the east and west ends of the inter-island breakwater. Seven lighted buoys initially marked the limits of the safe channel depths. These five- and seven-ton buoys contained rechargeable batteries and automatic bulb changers. The buoys were removed in the winter to prevent ice damage. One unlit buoy, called a "nun buoy," marked the east end of the coal dock safe depths. Range lights helped guide vessels along the west entry channel center line.

The front range light was located on the B Control Tower roof, and the rear light was on top of a fifty-foot tower located along the incoming railroad track. There were diamonds located at the range lights that served as visual indicators and radar reflectors.

Front range diamond near B Control Tower with rear range light and diamond in the distance at upper left.

A large beacon identifying Taconite Harbor that could be seen far out on the lake at night and a foghorn were located on Gull Island. There was also a radio beacon to guide boats to Taconite Harbor from miles away. As ore boat navigation technology evolved, the aids were modified.

Navigation buoys in winter storage.

The rear range light and diamond located near the 35 Switch.

211

US Coast Guard Ice Breaker *Mackinac* opens Taconite Harbor.

Train with end-of-train monitor equipment attached.

IMPROVEMENTS

The three original bay window cabooses provided limited visibility, and the forward-facing windows were subject to being broken by pellets falling from the pellet cars. Erie returned these cabooses to the manufacturer for modification to extended vision cupola cabooses.

In 1983, Erie started using end-of-train monitors on pellet trains, which reduced the size of the train crew and eliminated the cabooses.[23] The end-of-train monitor measured the brake line pressures and transmitted that information by radio to the Locomotive Engineer and marked the end of the train with a blinking light.

Initially, four wrench cars (manufactured by Elwell Parker) were used to open and close the doors of the pellet cars. The wrench cars rode on narrow gauge track located beside the track on the trestle above the pellet storage bins. This unloading method required that the train be stopped and repositioned numerous times and resulted in excessive delays. In 1958, when production was just

Close-up of end-of-train monitor equipment.

Erie caboose with extended vision cupola.

End-of-train monitor panel installed in locomotive.

MESABI MINER

As Erie's managing agent, Pickands Mather instilled in employees a sense of organization, professionalism, and pride in doing a job well. Nowhere was that more evident than in the preparation required before scheduled meetings with owner representatives or public presentations. Typically, preliminary meetings were held with senior management to establish the meeting agenda, and then one or more working sessions with the department heads and presenters took place to review in detail the information to be presented. The maps, graphs, drawings, slides, overheads, and handouts were prepared, reviewed, modified, and reviewed again. At times, all the preparation appeared a bit excessive, but in the end Erie employees were ready to handle any complication and the meetings, presentations, and events went off with flawless precision.

Loading pellets into the *Mesabi Miner* at Taconite Harbor.

An example of a major Pickands Mather's public relations event occurred in 1977, with the christening of Interlake Steamship's MV *Mesabi Miner*.

Mesabi Miner at Taconite Harbor Dock.

The first boat completed for Interlake was the *James R. Barker* in 1976, and the second, the *Mesabi Miner*, was launched in 1977. Virtually identical, at 1,004 feet long and 105 feet wide, these two boats reigned together as "Queens of the Lakes," the longest vessels traveling the Great Lakes.

They would be the first of the 1,000-foot-long boats built entirely on the Great Lakes and would establish the design for other large boats to follow by having the pilothouse, engine room, unloading conveyor, and crew accommodations all located at the aft end of the boat.

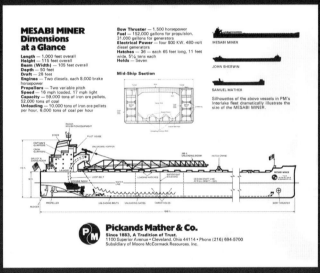

Pickands Mather, rather than name the new boat after an ore company or steel company executive as most boats were, chose to name it *Mesabi Miner* instead. The company recognized that it was important to pay tribute to the many men and women, past and present, who are undeniably proud to live and work on the Mesabi Range, and whose contributions through the years to the state, nation, and world are much greater than any one man, one company, or one city.

The christening of the *Mesabi Miner* was to be held at the Port Terminal in Duluth, Minnesota, at 11:30 a.m. on Saturday, June 11, 1977, with former U.S. Vice President and Minnesota Senator Hubert H. Humphrey in attendance and making the

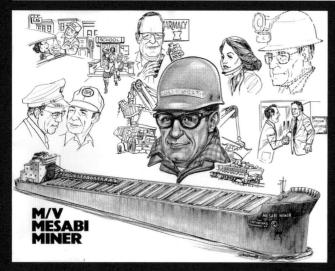

M/V MESABI MINER

keynote address. The plan was for Mrs. Humphrey to christen the boat with more than 1,000 company and customer executives, board directors, state and local politicians, other dignitaries, guests, and news media in attendance.

Local involvement began with a meeting at Erie on June 8, where responsibilities were assigned to a group of seventeen Pickands Mather employees who would serve as hosts. Ten were from Erie, and the rest from other Pickands Mather mines and offices. The following day the group met in Duluth for another meeting and then made a tour of every point involved in the upcoming christening event. This practice (dry) run went from the Duluth airport, where the invited guests would be arriving, to the hotels where they would be staying, to the harbor where the *Mesabi Miner* would be docked. According to Safety Coordinator Jim Stauber, who was one of the hosts, "dry runs, of course, normally go off perfectly. Nothing is out of order and nothing happens. We finished the dry run without incident." Another meeting was held that night to go over any concerns, answer questions, and review the written schedule, which according to Stauber, "listed by time and date, almost by hour, where each named person was supposed to be and what he's supposed to be doing."

On Friday, Pickands Mather, Interlake Steamship, and Moore McCormack Resources executives began arriving at the airport, on both commercial and private flights, and as expected, the schedule began to fall behind as some flights were delayed. Hotel reservations and transportation arrangements had been made for those staying overnight.

On Saturday, the day of the christening, the hosts met for breakfast to review responsibilities one last time before heading to the airport. To transport the approximately 300 invited guests who would be arriving and attending the event, Pickands Mather chartered nine busses, two vans, and two limousines, as well as using its own staff vehicles. Each bus was assigned a guide who was given a script and instructed to point out places of interest along the route from the airport to the christening site.

As the group was waiting at the airport for the dozen or so flights to arrive, the schedule began to unravel. The Pickands Mather corporate jet arrived at 9:00 a.m. from Washington, D.C., with Senator Humphrey but not his wife, who had remained in Minneapolis. Immediately, the plane was dispatched to Minneapolis for Mrs. Humphrey.

Around 10:00 a.m., three chartered airliners, carrying most of the guests, began arriving ten minutes apart at the main terminal. Busses and hosts were waiting. During the trip from the airport to the Port Terminal, the last bus in line got separated from the rest at a stoplight. Traveling down toward the harbor, the bus missed the turn to the Port Terminal and ended up on the Blatnik High Bridge and proceeded to Superior, Wisconsin. Looking down from the bus, the guests could see the *Mesabi Miner* and the other eight busses at the dock below. After a quick turnaround in Superior, and a few anxious moments by the host, the bus finally arrived, no worse for wear and just in time, at the christening site.

The event began on time at 11:30 a.m. with a welcome by Elton Hoyt III, Pickands Mather's President and Chief Operating Officer, and speeches by Richard Mayr, President of American Ship Building; James Barker, President and Chief Executive Officer of Moore McCormack;

Muriel Humphrey, Elton Hoyt III, former U.S. Vice President and Minnesota Senator Hubert H. Humphrey (front), and other dignitaries at the christening.

and Minnesota's Eighth District Representative James Oberstar. Senator Humphrey, who was in ill health, followed, and his sentiments were especially poignant. He acknowledged the tradition of hard work, creativity, spirit, and perseverance of the people of the Mesabi Range and the Port of Duluth that laid a solid foundation for expanding economic development of the region. Humphrey also paid special tribute to Hoyt and Barker, stating, "These two outstanding business leaders represent a corporate effort which has resulted in the construction of the two largest vessels built entirely on the Great Lakes, and the first of a new generation of 'thousand-footers.'"

Following Senator Humphrey's speech, and as Mrs. Humphrey broke the bottle of champagne against the big red hull christening the *Mesabi Miner*, one

James Barker operates Coarse Crusher dump controls during a visit to Erie.

hatch cover was lifted off and thousands of red, white, and blue balloons rose into the sky. The boat was then opened for tours and the invited guests were treated to a reception and luncheon.

Later that afternoon and continuing the next morning, the *Mesabi Miner* was open to public tours, and thousands of people from Duluth and the surrounding area toured the new boat. After the tours ended, the *Mesabi Miner* moved to the Burlington Northern ore docks in Superior for its first load of iron ore pellets, beginning its long career hauling pellets and coal on the Great Lakes.

Mesabi Miner leaves Taconite Harbor loaded with 60,000 tons of pellets.

A follow-up meeting was held at Erie on Monday to review the weekend's big event. According to Stauber, "Things don't work smoothly if you don't have a team effort, and I think we had an excellent team. I really thought that everyone did their job well, over and above. At that type of event things change, and you may have to adapt and bend a little bit."

This was a major event involving hundreds of executives and dignitaries from across the country that was executed without any major problems through the extensive planning and organization that was part of all Pickands Mather and Erie public presentations.

Stockholders, Pickands Mather and Erie executives prepare to leave the Administration Building for a tour of the property.

over two million tons of pellets, the average time to unload a train was more than three hours. With Erie's planned annual production rate of 7.5 million tons, this unloading time was clearly unacceptable.

The solution was innovative. Paul Giesking, Superintendent of Railroad and Harbor, devised a new automatic pellet car dumping system that allowed the train to dump without stopping. The automatic pellet car dumping system involved mounting an automobile wheel and tire connected to the car door–operating mechanism on the sides of the car. As the car crossed the trestle, the Towerman activated pneumatic jacks that raised a rail. The rail engaged the right-side tire, which turned the door-opening mechanism as the train pulled ahead along the dock. The pellets flowed out of the car into the pellet storage bins. As the car reached the far end of the Dock, a rail contacted the left-side tire, closing the doors.[24] The Dock Foreman observed train unloading and determined jack operation based on pellet storage bin levels and ore boat requirements and communicated that to the Towerman by radio. The Dock Foreman would verify that all the car doors were closed. If an open door was observed, the train was stopped, and the door was manually closed.

Narrow gauge wrench car track to the left of dumping track with a wrench car below the dump bridge.

Dock foreman inspects an empty train as it leaves Taconite Harbor.

Euclid dump trucks working at Taconite Harbor.

ERIE'S EARLY AID TO NAVIGATION

It takes a stretch of the imagination to visualize a big Euclid off-highway dump truck serving as an aid to navigation, but that is exactly what happened on June 21,1954, during the construction of Taconite Harbor. The first two construction equipment barges, being towed by a tugboat, were traveling across Lake Superior. Because this was the tugboat crew's first trip to the construction site, they were not exactly sure where the landing was to be made, and complicating matters a heavy fog had set in and the tugboat's radar was malfunctioning.

This is where the Euclid dump truck came to the rescue. Through ship-to-shore radio conversation, arrangements were made to have one of the dump trucks that were working in the area driven out onto the end of a breakwater that extended into Lake Superior. The operator was instructed to blow the truck's air horn in a prescribed series of blasts, which would serve as a foghorn. By homing in on this improvised "aid to navigation," the tugboat and barges made it safely into the harbor.[37]

Construction equipment and material arrives by barge at Taconite Harbor.

Construction equipment arrives at Taconite Harbor. Note the Euclid truck dumping at the end of the breakwater.

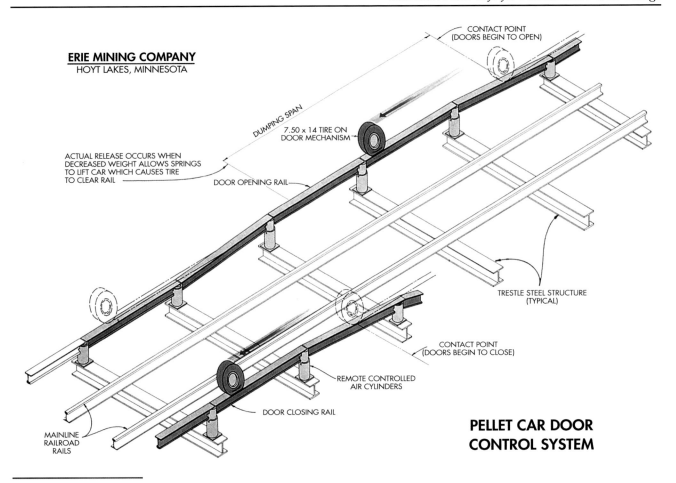

ERIE MINING COMPANY
HOYT LAKES, MINNESOTA

CONTACT POINT
(DOORS BEGIN TO OPEN)

DUMPING SPAN

7.50 x 14 TIRE ON
DOOR MECHANISM

ACTUAL RELEASE OCCURS WHEN
DECREASED WEIGHT ALLOWS SPRINGS
TO LIFT CAR WHICH CAUSES TIRE
TO CLEAR RAIL

DOOR OPENING RAIL

TRESTLE STEEL STRUCTURE
(TYPICAL)

CONTACT POINT
(DOORS BEGIN TO CLOSE)

REMOTE CONTROLLED
AIR CYLINDERS

DOOR CLOSING RAIL

MAINLINE
RAILROAD
RAILS

**PELLET CAR DOOR
CONTROL SYSTEM**

Diagram of Dock portion of the railcar dumping system.

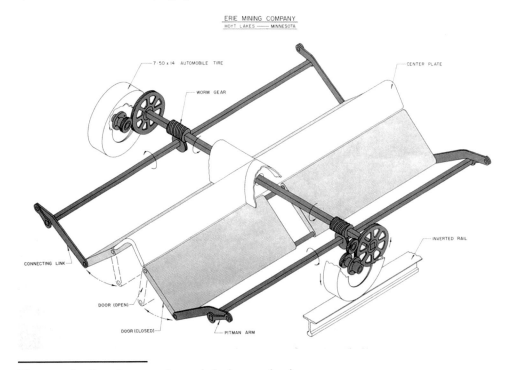

ERIE MINING COMPANY
HOYT LAKES —— MINNESOTA

7.50 x 14 AUTOMOBILE TIRE

CENTER PLATE

WORM GEAR

CONNECTING LINK

INVERTED RAIL

DOOR (OPEN)

DOOR (CLOSED)

PITMAN ARM

Diagram of railcar door opening and closing mechanism.

Door opening tire contacting raised activating rail.

Giesking's automatic pellet car dumping system was operational in 1960 and patented by Erie in 1963.[25] Taconite Harbor successfully reduced the unloading time from hours to minutes. Without ever slowing to less than eight miles per hour, a 120-car pellet train could unload 9,600 tons into the pellet storage bins in less than twenty minutes.[26]

To eliminate unnecessary pellet car weight and maintenance, the brake systems (shoes and beams) were changed from two brake shoes per wheel to one, which allowed the heavy wheel mounting frames to be shortened. Brake tests had proven that a single brake shoe per wheel was safe. This improvement was completed in the late 1960s.

The Westinghouse automatic train braking system on Erie's trains provided controlled brake application and total brake release. To give the Locomotive Engineer flexible train braking capability while handling the heavy trains on the steep grade approaching Taconite Harbor, a second system to provide controlled release of the brakes was installed. The installation started in 1970 was completed in 1974 and was called straight air or variable retainer brake system.

Original pellet car wheel frame and brake shoe arrangement (outlined).

Modified wheel frame with single brake shoe (outlined).

Straight air brake system pipe installed on pellet car.

In the late 1970s, modifications had to be made at the Dock to accommodate the new larger ore boats. "We had to raise the shuttle conveyors," explained Tom Niemi. "They ran perfectly horizontally in the original design, but in later years, they had to be raised so they could clear the side of the new thousand-footers."[27] In addition the Control Tower roofs had to be trimmed back.

In the late 1980s and early 1990s, other improvements were made to the Dock. The dock loading system was computerized so that either of the two Control Towers could control all twenty-five shuttles. The computer communicated ore boat loading information to systems throughout Erie. Electronic scales replaced the mechanical scales on the shuttle conveyors to improve accuracy and reliability. To reduce maintenance the reciprocating pan feeders were converted to pneumatically actuated gates, which eliminated motors, gearboxes, and linkages. The original automatic pellet car dumping system jacks were also replaced.

Between 1987 and 1994, Taconite Harbor handled four million tons of natural ore from LTV's McKinley Extension Mine. The first seven pellet storage bins on the Dock were designated for this ore, which did not flow as easily as the pellets. Because the seven pellet storage bins did not have sufficient live storage, ore from three trains was required to fill an ore boat. Erie constructed a new passing siding just east of the tunnel so a loaded train could be staged near the harbor.[28]

The unique orientation of the Dock parallel to the lakeshore, coupled with the automatic pellet car dumping system, allowed nonstop pellet car unloading and resulted in rapid loading times. The 100,000-ton capacity Dock and the twenty-five shuttle conveyors could efficiently load even the largest ore boat, making Taconite Harbor one of the fastest loading inland ore docks in the world.[29]

Giesking's automatic pellet car dumping system at the Dock was just one example of how Erie's employees used innovative approaches to solve complex problems and kept Erie competitive.

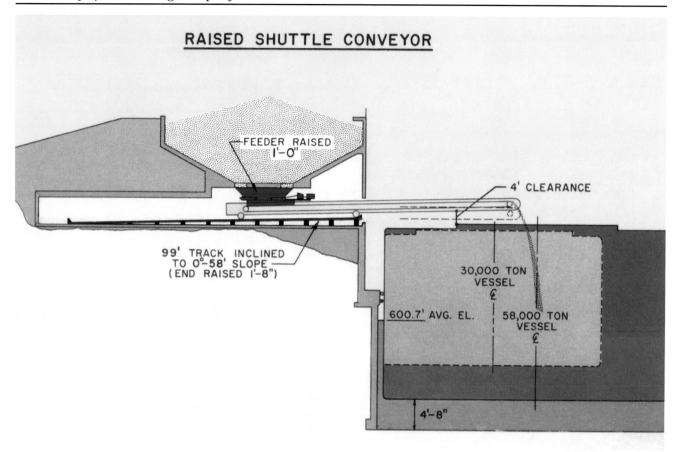

Diagram of raised shuttle conveyor modification.

Computerized controls in Control Tower.

STORM DAMAGE

During the summer and fall of 1977, Erie was not operating because of a strike. Weeks of wet weather followed by torrential rains on September 24, 1977, caused the Two Island River to overflow its banks and resulted in significant washout damage to the Mainline Railroad at three places where it crossed the Two Island River. U.S. Highway 61, the only highway access to the area, was also washed out at Caribou River and near Grand Marais, isolating Taconite Harbor and surrounding communities of Schroeder, Tofte, and Lutsen for several days. Required repairs to 5,830 feet of track consisted of fill and ballast as well as culvert repositioning

Eleven-foot culvert washout at MP 68.8.

and new track as needed at three culvert locations (one with three four-foot diameter and two with eleven-foot diameter culverts). Following discussion with the local union, agreement was reached for a contractor to begin repair of one of the eleven-foot culverts. This work started on September 29 and was completed October 6. Because of the strike, salaried personnel completed the storm damage repair work on October 28. The Mainline Railroad was ready for pellet movement when the strike ended.

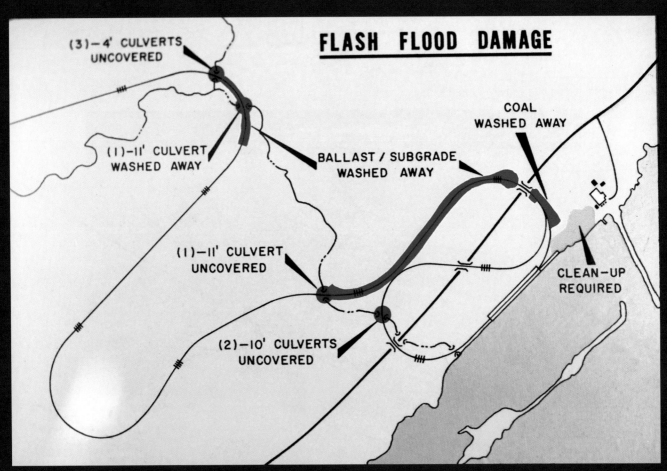

Map highlighting areas of flood damage.

Nearly a mile of track washout.

Washout at approach to bridge over Highway 61.

Contractor repairing subgrade at MP 68.8.

Erie employees rebuilding track.

Manual adjustments to track alignment.

Original pan feeder installation with motor and gear box.

New pneumatic gate system.

Natural ore being loaded into a boat.

Natural ore being dumped.

Chapter 8

IN UNION WE ARE STRONG

By the 1930s, most hourly workers at Minnesota's natural ore mines were represented by unions. Initially, each mine had its own union that negotiated with the company on hours, wages, benefits, and working conditions. Later the individual unions became affiliated with the United Steelworkers of America (USWA), which collectively bargained for all workers on a national level. At Erie, union representation started at the Lab and continued at PreTac in 1953 with the formation of USWA Local Union 4108 (LU 4108), which carried over to the Commercial Plant. This association provided the structure for the orderly resolution of labor issues at Erie during its years of operation.

Erie workers were members of the United Steelworkers of America union that was established in 1942.

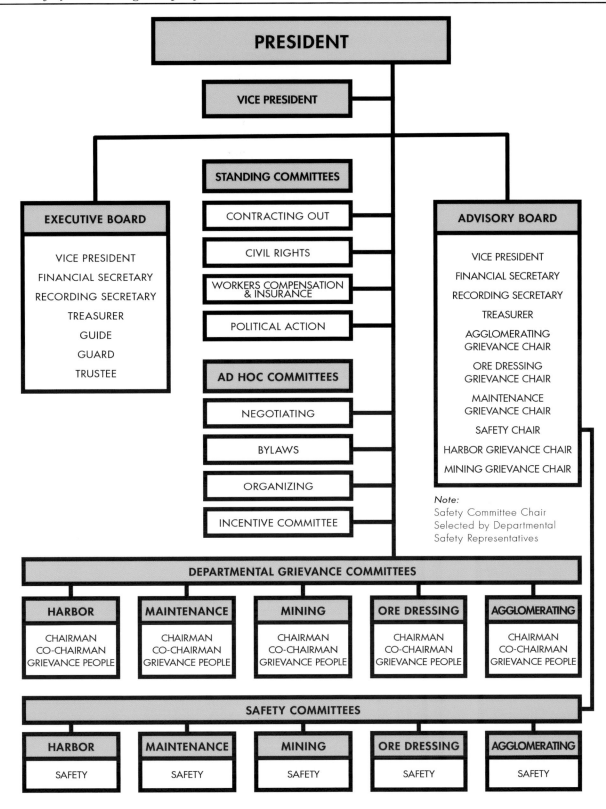

PRESIDENT

VICE PRESIDENT

STANDING COMMITTEES

CONTRACTING OUT

CIVIL RIGHTS

WORKERS COMPENSATION & INSURANCE

POLITICAL ACTION

AD HOC COMMITTEES

NEGOTIATING

BYLAWS

ORGANIZING

INCENTIVE COMMITTEE

EXECUTIVE BOARD

VICE PRESIDENT
FINANCIAL SECRETARY
RECORDING SECRETARY
TREASURER
GUIDE
GUARD
TRUSTEE

ADVISORY BOARD

VICE PRESIDENT
FINANCIAL SECRETARY
RECORDING SECRETARY
TREASURER
AGGLOMERATING GRIEVANCE CHAIR
ORE DRESSING GRIEVANCE CHAIR
MAINTENANCE GRIEVANCE CHAIR
SAFETY CHAIR
HARBOR GRIEVANCE CHAIR
MINING GRIEVANCE CHAIR

Note:
Safety Committee Chair
Selected by Departmental
Safety Representatives

DEPARTMENTAL GRIEVANCE COMMITTEES

HARBOR	MAINTENANCE	MINING	ORE DRESSING	AGGLOMERATING
CHAIRMAN CO-CHAIRMAN GRIEVANCE PEOPLE	CHAIRMAN CO-CHAIRMAN GRIEVANCE PEOPLE	CHAIRMAN CO-CHAIRMAN GRIEVANCE PEOPLE	CHAIRMAN CO-CHAIRMAN GRIEVANCE PEOPLE	CHAIRMAN CO-CHAIRMAN GRIEVANCE PEOPLE

SAFETY COMMITTEES

HARBOR	MAINTENANCE	MINING	ORE DRESSING	AGGLOMERATING
SAFETY	SAFETY	SAFETY	SAFETY	SAFETY

LOCAL UNION 4108 ORGANIZATIONAL CHART

Above: LU 4108 leadership was organized and structured.
Left: Erie was a large complex facility that required thousands of skilled and talented employees.

Erie recognized that the large, complex commercial project utilizing new mineral processing technology would require many skilled workers. To attract these workers Erie negotiated with the union on wages, working conditions, and benefits, some of which included vacations, health insurance, and pension. In addition, Erie made affordable housing available and provided job training.

The USWA organization consisted of International (national), District (regional), and Local (mine) levels. The local unions were typically organized into an Executive Board, an Advisory Board, and Standing and Ad Hoc Committees.

Participation in union leadership activity began at the department level with membership on the Grievance Committee or by election as an officer. Grievance Committee members were appointed by the local union president based on a desire to serve and union meeting attendance. The major role of the Grievance Committee was to represent the union members and attempt to resolve work-related issues with departmental management.

Union elections were held every three years to elect International, District, and Local union officers. For LU 4108, these elections established the Executive Board, which was responsible for all local union activities. An organizational meeting, attended by members of all Grievance Committees, was held the month after the election, where the department Grievance Committees elected their chairmen and these chairmen became part of the Advisory Board.

The union organization provided a framework for day-to-day labor/management interaction at Erie. Industry-wide issues such as basic wage rates, including shift differential, Sunday premium, and cost-of-living adjustments, and benefits, including vacations, holidays, allowed time off, seniority, safety and health, savings plan, and supplemental unemployment, were negotiated at the national level by the USWA resulting in a Basic Labor Agreement (BLA), covering all union members. Issues unique to Erie were negotiated by LU 4108 and were called Local Issues and resulted in Local Agreements.

Union members voted by secret ballot at the Union Hall in Aurora.

LU 4108 leadership monitored compliance with BLA and the Local Agreements and handled disputes through the grievance procedure, a structured, four-step process, agreed to by the parties. Most issues were resolved at the worker/supervisor level, but if that did not happen, the following grievance procedure was initiated:

- Step 1 was the filing of a written complaint requiring a company response and a meeting with the department head. If there was no agreement, the process advanced.

- Step 2 brought upper management into the discussion and required notification to the USWA District Representative if there was no agreement.

- Step 3 was a final attempt led by a USWA District Representative and a management designee to jointly resolve the dispute. If this failed, the process continued to binding arbitration.

- Step 4 consisted of both parties presenting their case to an outside arbitrator, who evaluated the facts and issued a final, binding decision on the matter.

All the steps had time limits and were documented to show that every effort was made to resolve the dispute prior to arbitration.

STRIKES AND NEGOTIATIONS

The BLA was typically a three-year labor contract. Near the end date of the contract, negotiations began at both the national and the local level. The national negotiations were referred to as "pattern bargaining," and involved a team from the USWA International negotiating for all union members and representatives of one targeted steel company, usually the largest—U.S. Steel. "Whatever U.S. Steel got, we got," said LU 4108 President Jim Kozar. "We were known as *me too's*."[1]

To further the USWA's objective to improve union member wages and benefits, nationwide strikes could be called if BLA negotiations were stalemated. Erie workers participated in two major strikes, a nationwide steelworker strike in 1959 and an iron ore miner strike in 1977.

According to Jim Kozar, anyone who was at Erie in the early days vividly recalls the 116-day strike in the summer of 1959. The main disagreement that caused that strike was contract language involving job security. On October 7, 1959, President Eisenhower invoked the Taft-Hartley Act to force an end to the strike. The USWA sued on the basis that the Taft-Hartley Act was unconstitutional. However, on November 9, 1959, the Supreme Court ruled that the Act was constitutional, and work resumed for an 80-day cooling off period. The new BLA was signed on January 15, 1960, and provided agreement on management's rights, an increase in wages, and an automatic Cost-of-Living Adjustment (COLA) and improved health and pension benefits.[2]

In addition, at Erie, a Local Agreement on working conditions became the basis for seniority, work and location assignments, job descriptions, and work rules. However, the contract language wasn't fully implemented until 1962, when agreement was finally reached on establishing union job progression within Erie's five departments (Mining, Ore Dressing, Agglomerating, Maintenance, and Harbor) and job classifications that determined pay rates for various jobs. The job classifications allowed application of the standard job class wage rates established in the BLA to be applied to the respective jobs at Erie. Ultimately over three hundred different jobs were identified and evaluated.

STRIKE VOTE

LOCAL UNION
4108

United Steelworkers

LU 4108 had the right to strike based on a ratification vote by members.

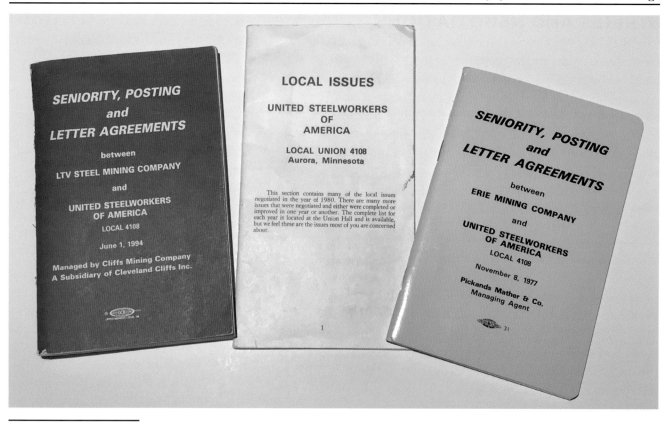

Local Issues and Seniority Agreements specific to Erie were negotiated by LU 4108.

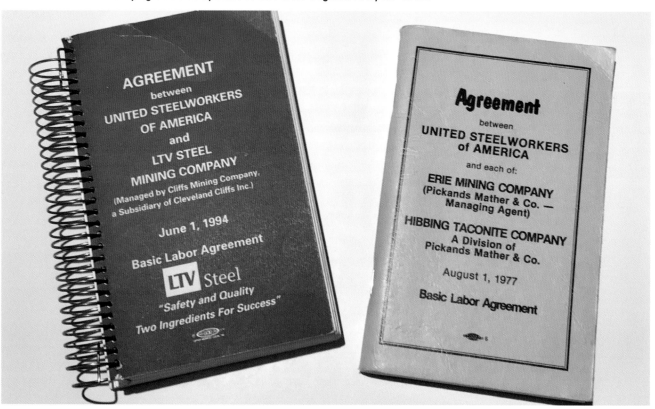

Basic Labor Agreements (BLA) were negotiated every three years at the national level.

Article XI. Adjustment of Grievances

(2) to establish procedures for the processing and settlement of grievances as defined in Section 2 of this Section.

Section 2. Definition of Grievance

"Grievance" as used in this Agreement is limited [246] to a complaint or request of an employee which involves the interpretation or application of, or compliance with, the provisions of this Agreement.

Section 3. Grievance Procedure

Should any employee believe that he has a [247] justifiable request or complaint, there shall be no suspension of work on account of such requests or complaints, but an earnest effort shall be made to settle them promptly under the provisions of this Article. Reasonable effort shall be made to settle such difference between the aggrieved employee and his foreman. A Grievance Committeeman may accompany such employee if requested by him. However, any such employee may instead, if he so desires, report the matter directly to his Grievance Committeeman and in such event the Grievance Committeeman, if he believes the request or complaint merits discussion, shall take it up with the employee's foreman in a sincere effort to resolve the problem. The employee involved may be present in such discussion, if he so desires. For those requests or complaints that cannot be resolved immediately, a mutually convenient time to continue such discussions shall be agreed upon.

If the foreman and the Grievance Committeeman, [248] after full discussion, feel the need for aid in arriving at a solution, they may by agreement, invite such additional Company or Union representatives from the mine as may be necessary and available to participate in

82

further discussion, but such additional participants shall not relieve the foreman and Grievance Committeeman from responsibility for solving the problem.

The foregoing procedure, if followed in good faith [249] by both parties should lead to a fair and speedy solution of most of the complaints arising out of the day-to-day operations of the mine. However, if a complaint or request has not been satisfactorily resolved during such discussion, it can be presented in writing and processed in Step 1 if the Grievance Committeeman determines that it constitutes a meritorious grievance. If the complaint or request concerns only the individual or individuals involved, and its settlement will have no effect upon the rights of other employees, the individual or individuals involved may effectively request that the matter be dropped.

A grievance to be considered further, must be filed [250] in writing with the foreman on forms, furnished by the Company, promptly after the conclusion of the above discussion. It shall be dated and signed by the Grievance Committeeman and employee (or other employee affected) and should include such information and facts as may be of aid to the Company and the Union in arriving at a fair, prompt, and informed decision. The foreman should write on the grievance forms: "The Grievance Committeeman and/or employee and I have fully discussed this grievance and I have determined as follows_____," indicate the date he received the grievance form, sign it and deliver it to his mine superintendent. Such grievances shall be numbered consecutively (three copies to the Company) and processed in the following manner:

Step 1. Between the aggrieved employee [251] and/or a member or members of the

83

The Basic Labor Agreement (BLA) established the grievance procedure.

Ted Williams viewed strikes from a management perspective, and 1959 stood out. "Nobody working," he said. "That was in 1959. That was the worst one. . . . But we all went through this. Strikes were not good, not good at all."[3]

In 1963, LU 4108 and Erie welcomed David McDonald, president of the USWA International, with headquarters in Pittsburgh, Pennsylvania, on a visit to observe the operation and be updated on the implementation of the 1960 BLA and Local Agreements. McDonald served as president of the USWA from 1953 until 1965.

In 1974, after decades of using the possibility of nationwide strikes as a collective bargaining tool, the USWA entered into to an Experimental Negotiating Agreement (ENA) with the major steel companies. Under the ENA, if agreement on

USWA President McDonald tours Erie's Coarse Crusher.

USWA President McDonald meets with Erie union members.

USWA President McDonald is shown a pelletizing furnace operator's control panel.

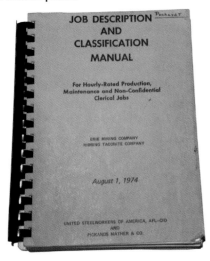

LU 4108 and Erie jointly developed and periodically updated a detailed Job Description and Classification Manual that covered all jobs. The job classifications allowed application of the standard job class wage rates established in the BLA to be applied to the respective jobs at Erie.

a BLA could not be reached, the dispute would be resolved through binding arbitration, and there would be no disruptive nationwide strike; however, the union reserved the right for Local Issue strikes. The companies also agreed to a 7 percent wage increase over the three-year contract term and to end stockpiling finished steel products. This was the first time that a key labor union and an entire industry agreed to settle their disputes through binding arbitration. The agreement occurred at a time of growing foreign competition in the steel industry. The BLA included the following language:

> *It is mutually agreed:*
>
> *Except as otherwise provided in ENA-77, the Union on behalf of Union-represented employees of the Company agrees not to engage in strikes, work stoppages, or concerted refusals to work in support of its bargaining demands, and the Company agrees not to resort to lockouts of employees to support its bargaining position.*
>
> *If Local Issues remain unresolved under ENA-77, our members will have the right to invoke the procedures set forth in the ENA, in order to obtain satisfactory settlements, which includes the right to strike.*

The first test of the ENA occurred during 1977 negotiations with iron ore mine unions over incentive pay. Steel mill workers were offered an incentive bonus based on production (averaging $0.90 per hour) while iron ore miners were offered an attendance bonus plan of $0.30 per hour in lieu of incentives. The iron ore mine union's ability to strike depended on the definition of a Local Issue. The ore miners contended that their right to incentive pay was a Local Issue, and the companies argued that it was included in the BLA and therefore not a Local Issue.

A federal judge decided that incentive pay was a Local Issue because incentive plans were unique to each operating facility. On August 1, 1977, the iron ore mine local unions voted to strike to receive incentive pay based on production rather than the offered attendance bonus. The strike at Erie lasted until December 11, 1977, when the LU 4108 voted to accept a new contract that included production

WAGES AND BENEFITS

Erie union members were paid a basic hourly wage rate based on a Job Description of the work to be performed. All Job Descriptions were assigned an agreed Job Class number from 2 to 20 based on a 12-point evaluation system, and the wage rate was based on the Job Class. The starting job was laborer at Job Class 2. Job Classes increased as work performed became more complex or required specialized skills. There was also a benefits package that evolved over the years. Paychecks in addition to having pay for hours worked included dollars for paid vacations, paid holidays, overtime, shift differential, holiday premium, Sunday premium, paid funeral leave, paid jury duty, paid time for annual physical, incentives, cost-of-living adjustment, and safety shoe allowance. There were other benefits including medical/dental insurance, pension, safety glasses, and overtime lunches. In later years, the benefit package would equate to more than 40 percent over the worker's base wage. As an example, in 2000, an Erie employee working Job Class 2 could receive nearly $30,000 in base wages and $12,000 in benefits.

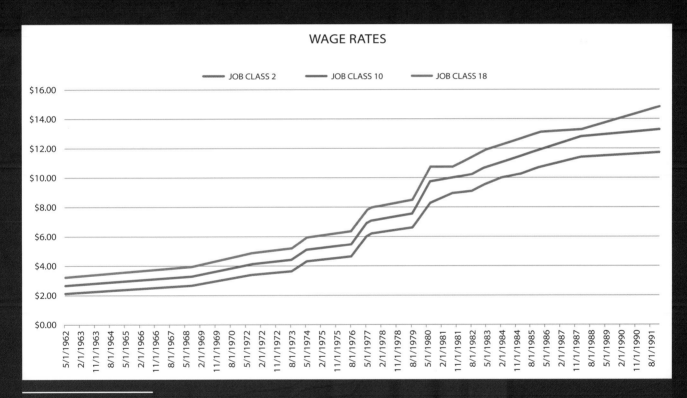

This graph depicts changes in hourly wage rates for three different job classes—2 (laborer), 10 (rotary drill operator), and 18 (shovel operator)—for the twenty-year period 1962 to 1991.

FORM NO. 807

JOB DESCRIPTION_____ ERIE MINING COMPANY_____

BENCH MARK JOB
9

COMPANY

DEPARTMENT_____ MINING _____

STANDARD TITLE_____ GENERAL LABOR – SURFACE _____

MINE_____

MINE TITLE_____

DATE_____ 8-1-74 _____

CODE_____

PRIMARY FUNCTION

To do general manual labor.

TOOLS & EQUIPMENT:

Picks, shovels, wheelbarrow, axes, brush hooks, brooms, mops, lawn mowers, post hole diggers, rakes, simple hand tools, etc.

MATERIALS:

Earth, rock, ore, snow, plant equipment and supplies, grass, wood, brush, waste materials, rags, waste, water, etc.

SOURCE OF SUPERVISION:

Foreman.

DIRECTION EXERCISED:

None.

WORKING PROCEDURE

1. Receives instructions from supervision.
2. Cleans up surface grounds and buildings performing such tasks as mowing lawns, digging ditches and post holes, cutting brush and weeds, washing windows and floors, shoveling snow, chopping ice, sanding walkways, etc.
3. Loads, unloads or moves plant equipment and supplies from service trucks, railroad cars, etc.
4. Washes and cleans storm doors, storm windows, screens, etc.
5. Keeps equipment clean.

The job description which appears above is intended to be sufficient merely to identify the position, and should not be construed as a detailed description of all of the work requirements that may be inherent in the job.

Typical Job Class evaluation form (example for Job Class 2).

JOB CLASSIFICATION _____ Erie Mining Company _____

9

STANDARD TITLE _____ GENERAL LABOR – SURFACE _____ MINE TITLE _____

FACTOR	REASON FOR CLASSIFICATION	CODE	Classifi- cation
1. PRE-EMPLOYMENT TRAINING (This job requires the mentality to learn to): Perform simple repetitive manual tasks or closely supervised non-repetitive tasks.		A	Base
2. EMPLOYMENT TRAINING AND EXPERIENCE. (This job requires experience on this and related work of) Up to and including 2 months.		A	Base
3. MENTAL SKILL Performs simple repetitive routine tasks such as digging, shoveling, loading and unloading materials.		A	Base
4. MANUAL SKILL Uses ordinary tools such as bars, shovels, picks, brooms on simple tasks, handles ordinary materials manually.		A	Base
5. RESPONSIBILITY FOR MATERIAL Works with materials difficult to damage such as earth, timber, scrap and waste materials.	Estimated Cost Under $50	A	Base
6. RESPONSIBILITY FOR TOOLS AND EQUIPMENT Uses simple hand tools such as shovels, picks, brooms, rakes, etc.		A	Base
7. RESPONSIBILITY FOR OPERATIONS Works alone or as a member of a crew on simple work closely directed.		A	Base
8. RESPONSIBILITY FOR SAFETY OF OTHERS Ordinary care and attention required to prevent injury to others when working as a member of a crew.		B	.4
9. MENTAL EFFORT Minimum mental application required for performing simple or closely directed work. Uses simple tools. Loads and unloads materials manually. Cleans up.		A	Base
10. PHYSICAL EFFORT Moderate physical exertion required in loading and unloading materials, shoveling and wheeling materials, digging, sweeping and cleaning.		C	.8
11. SURROUNDINGS Works inside and outside.		B	.4
12. HAZARD Accident hazard moderate and probable injuries consist of severe cuts, bruises, or fractures in picking, shoveling and handling materials.		B	.4

REMARKS:	JOB CLASS 2	TOTAL	2.0
	DESCRIBED BY:		DATE
	CLASSIFIED BY:		
	APPROVED BY:		

Typical Job Class evaluation form (example for Job Class 2).

Erie's empty parking lot during the 1977 strike.

incentive bonus language and end the 133-day strike, the longest work stoppage in Erie's history. Joe Smilanich, president of LU 4108, said that the "'return to work' would start as soon as possible."[4] However, the company did not recall all workers until Erie resumed production in April 1978. Production startup was deferred owing to owner requirements and difficulty of winter startup. Glenn Peterson recalled, "It took a huge toll on the plant. Those were extremely difficult times."[5] As a result of the 1977 strike, comprehensive incentive plans were to be established for all jobs at Erie. The implementation language was included in the BLA.

Incentives were one broad area where labor and management could often find common ground. Initially, nineteen different incentive plans were developed at Erie. Jim Kozar explained, "Most of the incentive plans were designed around tonnage (production)." In Maintenance, plans were based on completing work using fewer than the standard amount of manhours.[6]

On August 1, 1986, failure to reach agreement on a new contract resulted in the start of another long nationwide steel industry work stoppage. Because the USWA had offered to continue working under the terms of the expired agreement while negotiations continued, the federal courts eventually determined the work stoppage to be a lockout and not a strike, and workers were able to collect unemployment benefits. After several months of discussions, agreement on a new contract was reached on January 31, 1987.

LU 4108 and USWA District Representatives negotiate local issues with Erie and LTV Steel management.

LOCAL AGREEMENTS

Local Agreement negotiations included issues such as incentives, job combinations and job classifications, safety, grievances, and overtime procedures.

The company could combine production jobs based on technological change, and the grievance process would address any issues not resolved. The 1988 BLA included language to cover craft job (maintenance) combinations but gave local unions and management the latitude to negotiate those combinations to fit their needs.

Grievance Chairman Tom Michels recalled that in the late 1980s and into the 1990s, after the first LTV Steel bankruptcy, management "wanted to combine jobs throughout the plant, and obviously we were in a bad position because of the bankruptcy. We unsuccessfully arbitrated several job combination proposals. So, we wound up agreeing to a lot of these plant-wide job combinations."[7]

The practice of hiring a vendor or contractor to perform work normally performed by LU 4108 members was called "Contracting Out." Contracting Out was always a contentious issue between labor and management. LU 4108 Contracting Out Chairman Ed Casey's view was "We didn't want anything contracted out because we had men here that were qualified to perform any duties that the company wanted them to do. What made us unique was our General Shops. We could build anything. We could make anything up there. We could repair anything. Of course, the company didn't agree with that. Our position was, somebody's got to do it, and we wanted a steelworker to do it. It didn't have to be a contractor coming in here and doing work we could perform."[8]

Regarding Contracting Out differences, Manager Railroad and Harbor Tom Niemi remembered that on the Mainline Railroad in 1998 "when we were going to change a massive number of ties [ed: over 60,000 in a two-year period], we said we'd have to bring a contractor to do that. The union filed a grievance immediately that argued we've historically changed ties here since 1957, so there was no way.

LU 4108's Contracting Out Chairman Ed Casey felt that Erie's employees could make or repair anything. General Shop's large lathe is shown.

A General Shop electrician rebuilds a large electric motor.

Last shovel construction crew.

Erie employees rebuild a shovel crawler frame.

Erie employees assemble new equipment.

Erie's tie change project.

Well, yes, we said that's fine. You still will change ties, but this project is of such a scope that if you try to do it with our equipment, you're going to be here for the next thirty years trying to do it. Anyway, that grievance went to arbitration. The company won, and we were able to contract out the tie job."[9] The contractor completed the project, and simultaneously Erie's existing Track Crew was fully utilized doing their normal annual tie changes.

Safety was an area in which the two sides would always work together. Jim Kozar began his involvement in LU 4108 on the Safety Committee in the Mining Department and later became Chairman of the LU 4108 Safety Committee. Kozar noted that the committee consisted of representatives from each department whose responsibility it was to monitor and address safety issues. The Safety Committee toured each department once a month with management representatives and accompanied the county and

U.S. Department of Labor
MSHA
Mine Safety & Health Administration

LU 4108 and Erie assisted MSHA in establishing miner safety standards.

federal mine inspectors on their periodic site inspections. The federal mine inspectors were under the Mine Safety and Health Administration (MSHA), which established safety standards that applied to the mining industry nationwide. When MSHA was established in 1977, Erie's Joint (labor and management) Safety Committee made recommendations to be considered in developing uniform safety criteria, and many were included in the final published standards.[10]

Wise Owl.

Wise Owl.

Turtle Club.

Golden Shoe.

To increase on-the-job safety awareness, LU 4108 members participated in several Erie programs that recognized the employee's safe work performance and their proper use of Personal Protection Equipment (PPE). Recognition included awards for preventing injuries by wearing eye protection (Wise Owl Award), hard hats (Turtle Club), and steel-toed boots (Golden Shoe Award).

Along with the PPE awards, employees were eligible to receive award points based on each department's monthly and overall Erie year-end safety performance. These points, as well as points awarded through the Service Awards Program that recognized the employee's years of continuous service, could be accumulated and redeemed for items from a catalog.

In 1972, to reduce property damage accidents that had significant potential for employee injury and resulted in spiraling costs, Erie instituted a Property Damage Control program. The program focused on identifying the specific reasons for accidents and eliminating the causes, and not placing blame on the employee. In the Mining Department, a Safe Operator Award Program issued points and awarded prizes to mobile equipment operators who operated an entire year without an accident.

Recognizing early on that its employees knew best how to improve efficiency and reduce costs, in 1968 Erie implemented the "Dollars for Sense" suggestion program that awarded monetary payments, ranging from $15 to $15,000, to employees whose suggestions resulted in tangible savings.

Mine Superintendent Ed Karkoska and General Foreman Bob Miklausich review safe equipment operator records.

Dollars for Sense

1131 ACCEPTED SUGGESTIONS TO DATE $193,777 Total AWARDS PAID

CONGRATULATING ONE ANOTHER for receiving over $5200 in Suggestion Program payoffs are Wayne (Butch) Hakala, Jr. (left) and Glenn Root. The two Agglomerating Department maintenance men submitted suggestions that earned Butch $3995 and Glenn $1275.

Wayne (Butch) Hakala	Agglomerating	Install load level detection probes on all N.F. Conveyor drives to eliminate overloaded conveyor systems resulting in reduced labor and material costs.	$3,995.00
Glen Root	Agglomerating	Eliminate wheels with bronze bushings on the index driveshaft and install one additional carrying roller assembly to carry the index feeder resulting in reduced labor and material costs.	$1,275.00
Ron Bullis and Louis Gambucci	Public and Personnel Relations Maintenance	Revise the procedure for aligning and erecting new haulage truck boxes resulting in reduced labor costs.	$ 200.00
Arnold Maki	Maintenance	Modify the loader/dozer pivoting brake plate guide so that brake shoes cannot come beyond the guide resulting in reduced labor and material costs.	150.00
Jacob Specht George Wheelock Art Thoreson	Maintenance Maintenance Maintenance	Prepare a supplementary guide for timing the cam on locomotives and incorporate it in the hand maintenance manual resulting in reduced labor costs.	105.00
Lowell Severson	Ore Dressing	Modify concentrator transweigh instruments for ease of calibration and improve grind and density control of the grinding circuit.	* 95.00
Ed Holcomb Ken Kangas	Maintenance Maintenance	Lighten oil rings on ball mill motors by decreasing outside diameter by ⅛" resulting in increased oil to bearings and longer bearing life.	* 90.00
Philip Skarp	Maintenance	Split and hinge conveyor brake cover doors resulting in	* 55.00

Erie employee suggestions are highlighted monthly.

Erie General Manager Clyde Keith presents the highest Dollars for Sense Award totaling $15,000 to Rudy Ceglar.

LMPT Steering Committee.

LMPT brought hourly and salaried employees together to solve problems.

The 1980 BLA included an experimental Labor Management Participation Team (LMPT) agreement. This agreement eventually led to the development of Erie's LMPT program in 1988. The LMPT program was guided by the Steering Committee consisting of the General Manager and the LU 4108 President and their appointees.

The Steering Committee selected departmental facilitators and approved team-generated projects. The facilitators received special training to prepare them to train, coach, and advise departmental teams. LMPT brought volunteer hourly and salaried employees together to solve problems. Locally called *Let's Make Pellets Together*, LMPT combined the knowledge and experience of all Erie's employees, promoted communication and team building, and resulted in specific improvements and many intangible benefits. Later, Labor Management Safety Teams (LMST) were formed to solely address safety-related issues within each department. At one time, approximately 20 percent of Erie's employees were involved in employee participation problem-solving efforts.

LU 4108 officers were recognized as leaders at the USWA District and International level. As an example, LU 4108 Vice President David Ebnet made several trips to Pittsburgh and Cleveland to help negotiate local and national agreements. That experience gave him exposure to high-level labor/

Every LMPT/LMST Team member participated in three days of preparatory team building and problem-solving training.

management relations. Ebnet recalled, "District Director Dave Foster called me to represent the USWA on a trip to England to meet with the Minister of Labour and several committees. They were having issues with safety violations. People were being injured and released from employment because the company didn't want to deal with it. So, I spent a week in England. I gave a talk to Parliament and met with several local union officials."[11]

The 1993 BLA included language establishing a Career Development Program (CDP). The language read:

> *In recognition of the world-wide competitive challenges that confront the Company and the entire work force, the United Steelworkers of America and LTV Steel Company have agreed to initiate a major new venture of training and educating workers—The LTV Steel/United Steelworkers Career Development Program. The purpose of the CDP is to provide support services for the education, training and personal development of the employees of LTV Steel.*[12]

The CDP provided Erie's employees the opportunity to learn new skills whether applicable to their current jobs or future careers. The structure of the CDP began with the corporate Steering Committee at the USWA/LTV Steel level that established guidelines. The next level was the

LU 4108 and Erie management review CDP activities at the Aurora facility.

Steering Committee at Erie that included the LU 4108 president (or designee) and Erie's general manager (or designee), who selected the rest of the Steering Committee to oversee the program including selecting a CDP Coordinator and approving budgets and course offerings.

The LU 4108 CDP began in the fall of 1994 in an office and classroom facility at the Mesabi East School in Aurora, Minnesota. The program also offered tuition assistance for college and vocational curriculums and classes in computers and other subjects tailored to the interests of Erie's employees.

The relationship between Erie management and LU 4108 wasn't as adversarial as that at some of the other taconite operations. Manager Greg Walker recalled that there was a high level of cooperation and "can do" attitude at Erie. "I had friends at other mines and I think there's maybe an envy," said Walker.[13]

Erie's union employees were a real asset, as good as any and better than most.

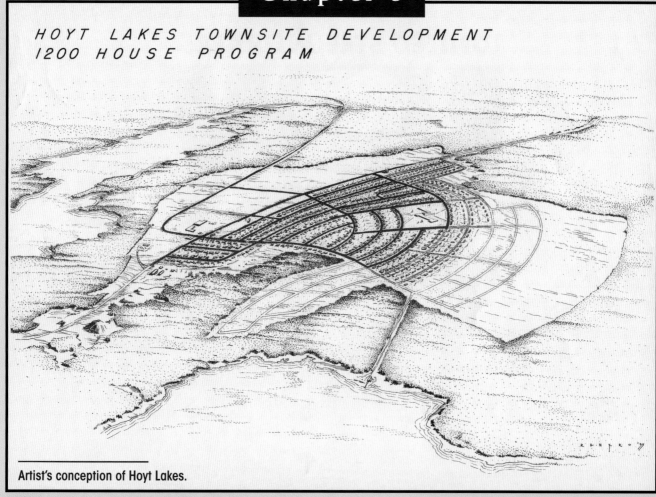

Chapter 9

HOYT LAKES TOWNSITE DEVELOPMENT
1200 HOUSE PROGRAM

Artist's conception of Hoyt Lakes.

PEOPLE AND COMMUNITY

The building of Erie's Commercial Plant required numerous contractors and thousands of construction workers, reaching a peak of over 6,000. Many of them would bring their families to northeastern Minnesota, an area with limited housing, schools, shopping, and medical facilities. Anticipating these needs Erie planned and constructed temporary contractor housing, the Evergreen Trailer Park near the Plant Site and the Hovland Trailer Park near the Dock and Power Plant. Erie also recognized that permanent housing and facilities would be required for many of the families of the employees needed to operate the new mine, plant, railroad, dock and power plant, and two new towns, Hoyt Lakes and Taconite Harbor, were planned and built. The development of Hoyt Lakes and Taconite Harbor was a significant step in creating a strong sense of community and shared experiences among the people of Erie. In general, about one-third of Erie's employees lived in the new towns, with the surrounding communities initially providing the schools, hospitals, and shopping for the residents.

TEMPORARY HOUSING (EVERGREEN AND HOVLAND)

Two trailer parks were built to provide housing for some of the workers needed to construct Erie. The largest, Evergreen Trailer Park, was established in 1954 and was designed to accommodate 1,000 trailer homes.

The park included dormitories for men, cafeteria, shopping center, community church, laundromat, barbershop, post office, police station, administration office, playgrounds, water and sanitary facilities, and a gas station.

Aerial view of Evergreen Trailer Park showing men's dormitories and shopping center at top.

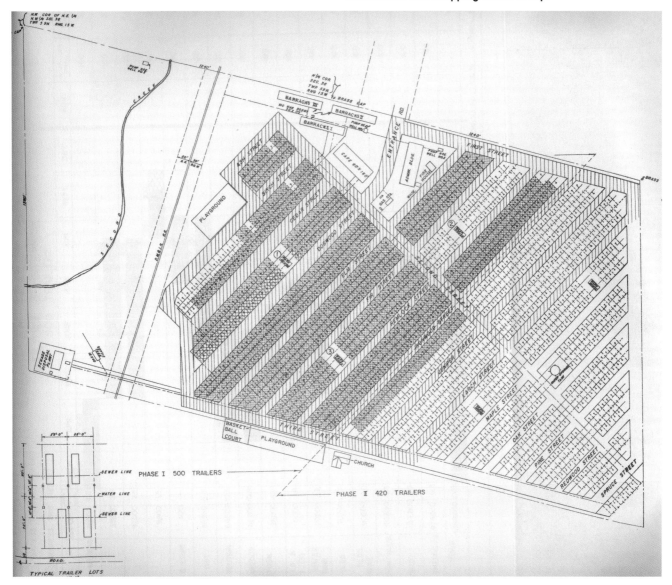

Plan map for Evergreen Trailer Park.

Aerial view of Evergreen Trailer Park with approximately 1,000 trailers.

Trailer homes in Evergreen Trailer Park.

One of Evergreen's four 200-man dormitory units showing the cafeteria at right.

248

Evergreen shopping center and community offices.

Entrance to post office and police department at Evergreen shopping center.

One of several Evergreen laundromat buildings that also contained shower facilities.

Typical Evergreen street scene.

Evergreen's wide streets and narrow alleys with laundromat building at left.

The Hovland Trailer Park, a smaller but similarly configured temporary housing facility, was established adjacent to construction activities at Taconite Harbor. Initially, construction workers stayed at resorts or with local residents while the trailer park was being built. During the winter of 1953, infrastructure for 30 trailers was established and then was expanded the following year to accommodate more than 500 trailers. At the end of 1954, there were 220 Erie trailers and 29 private contractor trailers occupied.[1]

Hovland looking west with the concrete batch plant in the foreground and two-story shopping center building behind.

Early aerial view of Hovland Trailer Park showing Bear and Gull Island in the background.

Erie Taconite Harbor ambulance at Hovland Trailer Park.

Taconite Harbor Shopping Center (restaurant, laundromat, and general store).

Aerial view of Hovland Trailer Park at capacity.

Interior view of shopping center.

Family home converted to classrooms.

As construction workers arrived with families, it was necessary to provide schools for their children. Initially, the Aurora schools were large enough to provide classroom space, but some of the classrooms needed to be updated. Erie worked closely with the Aurora School Board to accommodate the influx of additional students. At Taconite Harbor, the company worked with the Cook County School Board to fund the renovation to the school at Lutsen, which had not been used for several years. Erie also helped to remodel an existing family dwelling on the Hovland Trailer Park site for use as kindergarten and primary grade classrooms.

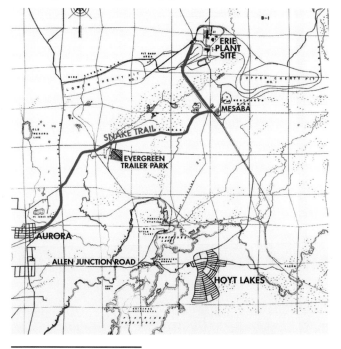

Map showing route from Aurora to Erie (Snake Trail).

Evergreen Trailer Park was located near the Plant Site, about three miles east of Aurora, along an existing road connecting Aurora to several small natural ore mines and to Old Mesaba. For several years the four-and-a-half-mile-long road called the Snake Trail, because of its twists and turns, became the main thoroughfare connecting the Plant Site construction to the outside world.

Erie purchased more than a thousand custom-built Mon-O-Coach trailers. Each identical aluminum trailer was twenty-eight feet long by eight feet wide, with one bedroom, kitchen, an eating/sitting area, and a bath. The first Erie trailers arrived in July 1954, and by the end of the year, 970 were in place. In addition, there were numerous private trailers belonging to contractor employees.

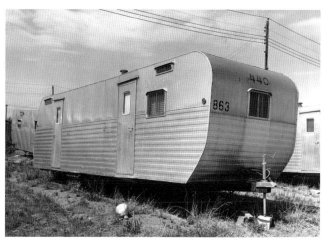

Typical Mon-O-Coach trailer home provided by Erie.

The experience of living in the "little silver boxes" left many indelible family memories. For the children especially, the temporary housing provided its share of daily excitement: taking turns eating meals because the kitchens were so small, sharing the beds by sleeping crosswise, and the cold morning walks to the school bus stop. Young Evergreen Trailer Park resident and eventual Erie employee Art Lee remembered getting off the school bus at the entrance to the trailer park, after a harrowing ride down the Snake Trail, and finding his way home among the hundreds of identical trailers by "turning left, counting six rows of trailers then turning right, and counting trailers on the right side of the street, and the thirteenth trailer would be [his]." In addition to providing housing for contractor workers and their families, the trailers also housed some of the first Erie employees, who were required to work a thirty-shift probationary period before becoming eligible to purchase housing in Hoyt Lakes or Taconite Harbor.

By 1957, the Commercial Plant construction was nearing completion, and as more housing in the Hoyt Lakes and Taconite Harbor townsites became available, Erie's trailer parks began to close. Many of the silver trailers were sold locally, beginning second lives in the northland as lake cabins or hunting shacks. Although the Evergreen and Hovland Trailer Parks were short-lived, with somewhat primitive living conditions, the workers and their families were together. In later years they would take pride in being part of a unique episode in Erie's history.

NEW TOWNS
Hoyt Lakes

Erie recognized early in the planning stages that the existing northeastern Minnesota communities near its Commercial Taconite facilities did not have the population or infrastructure needed to provide and support its projected workforce. Erie first looked at Aurora and proposed an expansion to the town on the east side to include construction of 1,500 houses and a new water and sewer system for the entire community. Aurora's officials declined this proposal, and Erie decided to construct a separate new town. Erie sought expert advice in planning and building the communities that would provide permanent housing for the families of its employees. Two communities were designed and constructed. The larger, Hoyt Lakes, was located six miles south of the Plant Site, and Taconite Harbor was situated near the shore of Lake Superior west of the Dock and Power Plant.

Aerial view of Hoyt Lakes looking west, ca. 1960s.

Clearing land for Hoyt Lakes.

Cleared townsite with Allen Junction Road running through.

Early aerial view of Hoyt Lakes construction with water tower in lower right.

Originally called Partridge Lakes Development, Hoyt Lakes was renamed in honor of Pickands Mather's Elton Hoyt 2nd. The model community was designed for 1,200 houses and an eventual population of 4,000 to 5,000 people. The plan included a semicircular residential street design, water and sewage treatment facilities, buildings for local government, police and fire departments, schools, shopping center, and recreational areas. Although constructed by Erie and the residents would largely be Erie employees, the community was not intended to be a "company town." Residents would own their homes, and the community would be self-governing.[2] The John W. Galbreath & Company (Galbreath), of Columbus, Ohio, was contracted to manage the construction, with J.D. Harrold Company (Harrold), of Duluth, Minnesota, building the houses.

Work began in 1954 with clearing the townsite out of the northern Minnesota wilderness and starting construction of the first 200 houses. Connection to the outside world was an existing gravel road between Aurora and Allen Junction located on the DM&IR.

Carol Weiberg, a resident of Allen Junction, watched that dirt road become the gateway to Hoyt Lakes. "There was a dirt road that we traveled on before Hoyt Lakes was there," Weiberg said. "We saw loggers coming in and cutting down all the trees. I remember my dad saying, 'There's going to be a town here.' And, of course, we thought, no, can't be. But little by little, the material for the houses started coming in. Later, they were putting them up so fast that you could go by one day and there'd be two or three houses built; the next day there'd be five or six; it just came up so fast. It was amazing to watch."[3]

Basement for the first house constructed in Hoyt Lakes.

Hoyt Lakes under construction.

Street curbs being poured in Hoyt Lakes.

Aerial view of the first phase of Hoyt Lakes construction, eighty-eight houses were occupied by the end of 1954.

Dan DeVaney remembers the decision-making that went into the design of the homes. It began in the late 1940s during the construction of PreTac. Erie management knew that if PreTac proved successful, they were going to need housing for employees. To determine what kind of housing would be best, they built ten houses in Aurora, each with slightly different design, for personnel working at PreTac. Each month, the occupants had to report what was good or bad about the houses. Erie received important feedback that was incorporated into the designs for the Hoyt Lakes and Taconite Harbor homes.

Most of the Erie housing incorporated two basic styles: a single-story home floor plan with two or three bedrooms and a detached one-stall garage, or a story-and-a-half style with either three or four bedrooms and an attached garage. There were also a few models of slightly larger "staff" homes originally built for management, which were interspersed throughout the community. All the homes had many features in common, including full basements with poured concrete walls, oil-fueled hot-air furnaces, electric water heaters, steel kitchen cabinets, and garbage disposals.

DeVaney recalled that Harrold had separate crews that poured the basements and framed the houses. There were also roofing, electrical, plumbing, and finishing crews. It was an organized process, and the houses went up quickly.[4]

The first residents, Mr. & Mrs. Harvey Sandstrom, purchased their new house at 102 Suffolk Drive on September 15, 1954, as construction began on the Erie Commercial Plant. Mrs. Sandstrom later recalled seeing only one light in town their first night, the one from the

Partridge Lakes Development office a few hundred yards away.[5] The Sandstroms were joined in a matter of days by the Melvin Dunkleys, Charles Stiles, and Stanley Tregillis families moving into their newly finished houses. At the time, there was no telephone service, paved streets, or stores available in the town, leaving the new residents feeling like real pioneers. By October 1954, all the houses in Phase I of the planned community were occupied, and the houses in Phase II were being occupied as fast as they could be completed. Hoyt Lakes was growing rapidly, and the atmosphere of the town reflected the attitudes, youth, and vigor of its residents and the new taconite industry it was supporting.

Hoyt Lakes resident Elaine Melby-Moen remembered the thrill of having a choice of homes in Hoyt Lakes when her husband took a job at Erie in 1958. Melby-Moen said, "We went to Hoyt Lakes and got keys to try the one-story house and the story-and-a-half house, and we liked the story-and-a-half house with the two bedrooms upstairs for our children and a bathroom upstairs."[6]

ONE STORY—THREE BEDROOM HOUSE

1 LIVING ROOM
2 DINING-KITCHEN
3 BATH ROOM
4 BEDROOM
5 BEDROOM
6 BEDROOM
7 GARAGE

ONE STORY - 3 BEDROOM HOUSE

ONE and ONE HALF STORY HOUSE

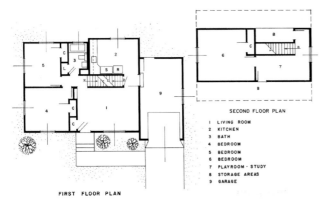

SECOND FLOOR PLAN

1 LIVING ROOM
2 KITCHEN
3 BATH
4 BEDROOM
5 BEDROOM
6 BEDROOM
7 PLAYROOM - STUDY
8 STORAGE AREAS
9 GARAGE

FIRST FLOOR PLAN

ONE & ONE HALF STORY - 3 BEDROOM HOUSE

Typical kitchen in a Hoyt Lakes home.

Street scene in Hoyt Lakes showing single-story homes in foreground.

Aerial view of Phase III Hoyt Lakes construction with shopping center and schools completed, ca. 1958. Fire hall, and city offices in foreground.

Original Hoyt Lakes post office.

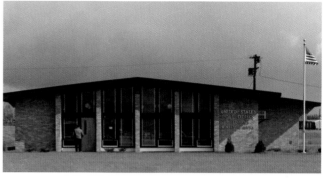

New Hoyt Lakes post office constructed in 1969.

Hoyt Lakes story-and-a-half, four-bedroom home.

Initially the purchase price for the houses ranged from $12,500 to $14,500, with a down payment of $400 for a thirty-year mortgage at 5 percent interest. Monthly house payments averaged less than $100 and included principal, interest, taxes, and insurance.[7]

At first, there was no road directly connecting Hoyt Lakes to the Plant Site. Until County Road #666 was built, employees living in town had to take a roundabout route to work, traveling the Allen Junction Road back to Aurora and then taking the Snake Trail to the Plant Site.[8]

MUDDERS & PACKSACKERS

The Hoyt Lakes streets were not paved and had no lawns. Because of that, the first residents took to calling themselves "mudders" as a badge of honor.[18] The Partridge Lakes Development provided a new homeowner with grass seed, fertilizer, and several truckloads of black dirt. The homeowner did the work. Soon Hoyt Lakes had the luxury of paved streets, sidewalks, and grass lawns.

The residents of the established East Range communities like Aurora and Biwabik called the newcomers to northeastern Minnesota "packsackers," meaning someone who was not born there, and the connotation wasn't exactly endearing. "We were 'packsackers,' if you ever heard that terminology," explained Ed Casey. "They accepted you after twenty-five years; you were not a packsacker anymore, and I had good friends who were from the Range, and that's what they explained to me. But when I first came up here, like I was saying, it was kind of

a nasty terminology—packsacker. We didn't like to be called that, but the local boys thought we were taking their jobs. If you weren't from the Iron Range, you were considered a packsacker. I was from Minnesota, but I was still a packsacker."[19]

Hoyt Lakes house before streets were paved and grass was planted.

Sign listing the Hoyt Lakes churches.

Trinity United Methodist Church.

St. Stephen's Episcopal Church.

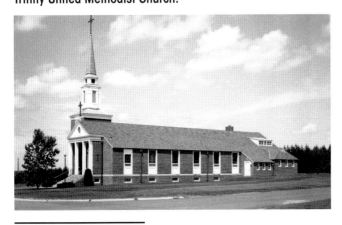

Queen of Peace Catholic Church.

Faith Lutheran Church.

The Hoyt Lakes Municipal Building housed city offices and public library. The building was originally used as a cafeteria during construction of Hoyt Lakes.

First Hoyt Lakes council—Standing: Attorney Fred Cina, Clerk Mrs. Eugene Edwards, Treasurer Orrin Weir; Seated: Harvey Sandstrom, Norman Amtower, Mayor Richard Peterson, Robert Scott, John Holst.

Anna Keefe Elementary School students at recess

Story time at the Hoyt Lakes Public Library.

Gertrude Boase Elementary School students at recess.

Robinson's Café was an early Hoyt Lakes business that served construction workers and also housed church services on Sundays. Hoyt Lakes' first permanent business, the Shell Service Station, opened in August 1955. In 1955, residential telephone service was provided utilizing a DM&IR telephone system with the switchboard in Two Harbors. The first telephone directory for Hoyt Lakes listed about eighty names.[9] The first post office also opened in 1955 with Olive Brown serving as the postmistress in a building so small only three patrons could fit inside at a time.[10] The post office was moved into the shopping center in 1956 and to a new separate building in 1969.

Hoyt Lakes was officially incorporated in 1955 and had an elected mayor, four elected city councilors, and an appointed city clerk, constables, justice of the peace, assessor, treasurer, attorney, and a superintendent of streets, utilities, and equipment maintenance.

HOSPITAL

In 1953, local medical services were provided at a doctor's office situated in the basement of the Aurora High School, with a small hospital facility in Aurora and larger hospital facilities in Eveleth and Virginia. As the area's population grew, more accessible medical facilities were required, and initially the East Range Clinic built a day clinic in Aurora in 1955 that had two full-time doctors, Drs. Richard Barnes and Raymond Chittum. This was followed in 1959 with the construction of the White Community Hospital, also in Aurora. The hospital was staffed by East Range Clinic physicians and provided a full range of medical services locally.

White Community Hospital was dedicated in 1960.

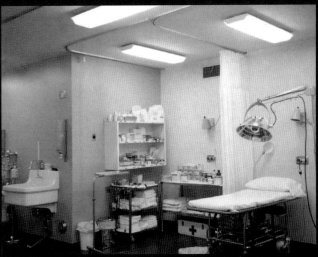

Emergency room at the hospital.

Early view of the west end of Hoyt Lakes shopping center showing a bank, bowling alley, and drug store.

View of the east end of Hoyt Lakes shopping center showing grocery store, Montgomery Ward's catalog store, Dairy Bar, The Mart, and several other small businesses.

One of two service stations in Hoyt Lakes.

Interior of the Dairy Bar.

Howard Ostergaard was the original manager and later owner of The Mart.

One of two apartment motels in Hoyt Lakes.

The role played by churches and schools was important in helping shape the community, as was the establishment of recreational leagues and civic clubs. Four churches and the shopping center were added in 1956 and 1957. To support the growing population, two elementary schools were built in Hoyt Lakes—the Gertrude Boase School in 1956 and the Anna Keefe School in 1958, with the older students bussed to the Aurora High School.

Fire Hall No. 1 was the first permanent nonresidential building constructed in Hoyt Lakes.

Hoyt Lakes' first rescue truck.

Joint Erie/Hoyt Lakes firefighting training.

Hoyt Lakes Arena.

Construction of the Hoyt Lakes Golf Course.

Hoyt Lakes Golf Course clubhouse was purchased from Erie. The clubhouse consisted of construction trailers moved from Taconite Harbor.

Patrick McGauley moved to Hoyt Lakes in September 1954 as a seventh-grader and was among the first five students from the community to attend the middle and high school in Aurora. Reflecting on how rapidly the town grew, McGauley stated, "There was a Chevrolet Suburban that took the five of us to school in Aurora that first year, and by the time I graduated in 1960, there were about a half a dozen seventy-two passenger school buses transporting students from Hoyt Lakes."[11]

The shopping center had a bank, grocery store, hardware store, bowling alley, restaurant, drug store, beauty shop, barbershop, TV repair shop/jewelry store, and two gas stations. The hardware store, called "The Mart," was built and stocked by W.P. & R.S. Mars Company (Mars) of Duluth, Minnesota, and carried all the parts and pieces necessary to repair and maintain the standard Hoyt Lakes house. Pickands Mather requested that Mars provide the hardware store for the town, and in exchange, Mars would supply small tools for Erie.

Aerial view of Hoyt Lakes surrounded by forests and lakes.

Aerial of Fisherman's Point Campground built on Erie-donated land.

BOAT CLUB/WATER CARNIVAL

The Colby Lake Water Ski and Boat Club was formed to provide opportunities to participate in water sports, including boating and waterskiing. A clubhouse was built on Smolich Island in the middle of Colby Lake. The 1958 family picnic with club members performing a water ski show has now evolved into the annual Hoyt Lakes Water Carnival. The event has grown into Hoyt Lakes' biggest annual celebration, which includes a water ski show, concessions, parade, firefighter's Olympics, carnival rides, softball, volleyball, tennis and golf tournaments, a 5K race, bandstand performances, Miss Hoyt Lakes contest, and a fireworks show.

All funds raised are used for improvements in the community, scholarships, and other charities. As boat club membership declined, the Fire Department and later citizen committees assumed responsibility for the Water Carnival and now hire professional water ski show performers.

Colby Lake Water Ski and Boat Club performs at the Water Carnival.

Water skiers practice very early in the season—even with snow along the shore.

WATER CARNIVAL ACTIVITES

Activities during Hoyt Lakes Water Carnival.

POP-A-LONG

The "Pop-A-Long" popcorn truck was started by Al and Muriel Josephson in the early 1960s. Other owners included the Hoyt Lakes Fire Department, Kitty Jenkins and Gail Archambo. The final owners were Carrol Storbeck and his wife, Belle.

Storbeck was a locomotive mechanic at Erie, and Belle was an elementary school teacher and taught in the Aurora/Hoyt Lakes School System. As part of their planning for saving money for their children's education, they first started a cotton candy concession in 1971 and attended local area celebrations and events such as the Hoyt Lakes Water Carnival, the 4th of July celebration in Biwabik, and the Embarrass Fair.

In 1975 they had the opportunity to buy Pop-A-Long, and this was the beginning of their very popular and successful Sno-Cone, popcorn, soft drinks, ice cream bars, and snacks business, which they operated for almost fifteen years.

The memory of Pop-A-Long is forever etched in the minds of Hoyt Lakes children who grew up in the 1960s, '70s, and '80s.

From left to right: Robin, Kristen, Curtis, Belle, Carrol, and Angie Storbeck.

Fire Hall No 1 was the first permanent nonresidential building in Hoyt Lakes, and Erie provided a fire truck and firefighting equipment to the volunteer department, which was formed in 1954. The Hoyt Lakes Fire Department added ambulance service in 1960 and the area's first Rescue Truck in 1965. Erie employees formed the core of the Department's volunteers and many were also members of Erie's Fire Brigade. The Hoyt Lakes and Erie fire departments provided mutual assistance during emergencies.

Surrounded by forests and lakes, Hoyt Lakes was an outdoor recreation paradise. Residents hunted, fished, camped, picked berries, snowmobiled, cross-country skied, and hiked. In 1956 a group of residents formed the Hoyt Lakes Recreation Board to provide recreational activities for the new town and organize activities for the children that included sports, arts and crafts, dancing, and figure skating.[12]

Families had access to many outdoor facilities including skating rinks, a ski jump, tennis courts, rifle range, archery range, trap range, ball fields, go-cart track, Fisherman's Point campground, Birch Cove swimming beach, and playgrounds. The Hoyt Lakes Arena with a hockey rink and gymnasium was built in 1967.

Over a three-year period, from 1966 to 1969, volunteers constructed the nine-hole Hoyt Lakes Golf Course on land provided and using equipment loaned by Erie.

Community recreational opportunities around Hoyt Lakes.

Taconite Harbor townsite with seventeen homes built on the west end of the Hovland Trailer Park.

SAFE HARBOR

The Minnesota Department of Natural Resources (MDNR) program to provide public access and safe harbors on the North Shore of Lake Superior had reached the area between Silver Bay and Grand Marais by the early 1990s. Local landowner and former Minnesota Governor Elmer Anderson met with Erie to discuss the possibility of locating a safe harbor at Taconite Harbor. Erie agreed and by 1996 a lease was signed granting the MDNR a portion of the abandoned townsite for the public access with shoreline for safe harbor installation. Detail design work was commenced by the Army Corps of Engineers, Erie, and the MDNR. Construction was started in 1999, completed in 2000, and the site opened to the public in the spring of 2001.

Installing the safe harbor breakwater with Gull Island in the background.

Taconite Harbor bounded by Highway 61 and Lake Superior.

TACONITE HARBOR

Erie also built housing for employees at Taconite Harbor. Ted Williams moved from Grand Marais to Taconite Harbor in 1957. "They built homes for us," he said. "They were very reasonably priced." Erie furnished sewer and water, but residents paid for electric power.[13] Seventeen houses based on the single-story three-bedroom Hoyt Lakes house designs were originally constructed. Three existing area houses were purchased and moved to the townsite and five more homes were built by 1967. Williams recalled that the houses at Taconite Harbor "were very nice. They were single level, poured basements, and had sod installed, sidewalks and a paved street. We had a three-bedroom, bath and a half."[14]

Taconite Harbor had an active social life with block parties and organized family activities including Cub Scouts, Little League, volleyball, basketball, baseball, sliding, and ice skating. At its prime, as many as seventy students from Taconite Harbor attended schools in Tofte and Grand Marais. The shutdown of the Power Plant in 1982 resulted in many residents leaving Taconite Harbor. Later Erie purchased all the homes and closed the town. By 1990 all the homes had been moved away.

TRC

On February 6, 1966, seven Erie employees formed a recreational organization for employees and their families that was funded by profits from vending machines placed throughout Erie. The organization was called the Taconite Recreational Club, Inc. (TRC).

From the time that Alvin Miller's name was drawn at the original membership meeting to

Taconite Harbor house being moved out.

First elected Board of Directors for the Taconite Recreation Club (TRC): Bernie Sarich, Joe Marcella, Sheldon Porthan, Louie Karish, Robert Woods, and George Coombs.

be member number one, TRC grew to a peak of over a thousand members and their families. Through the years, TRC organized numerous events and activities including holiday parties, dances, card parties, bridge and smear tournaments, bowling leagues, softball leagues, an annual golf tournament, basketball leagues, volleyball leagues, snowmobiling, skiing, a curling bonspiel, an annual picnic and barbecue, hunting and fishing contests, and shopping, baseball, and hockey trips. TRC introduced slow-pitch softball to the area.

The idea of TRC was so new to the area that the club was asked to lecture on its concept and activities at Mesabi Community College. TRC continued for thirty-five years serving the employees of Erie. Following Erie's closure, TRC held its last scheduled event, a summer barbecue in Hoyt Lakes, on Saturday, August 4, 2001.

TRC ice fishing contest on Whitewater Reservoir.

TRC activities.

Annual TRC barbeque at Taconite Harbor.

Annual TRC Barbeque at Hoyt Lakes.

GIANTS RIDGE

In 1958 a group of Hoyt Lakes area skiers, led by Erie Superintendent Ed Karkoska and his wife, Gretchen, wanted to participate in the winter sport closer to home. They selected a hilly, forested area that is now called Giants Ridge, along the west side of Wynne Lake outside of Aurora. By selling shares in the project to friends and co-workers at $100 a share, they went to work with axes, ropes, and equipment borrowed from elsewhere to blaze a ski run out of the woods. The original ski chalet, a converted laundromat and shower building from Evergreen, was purchased from Erie. The building was cleaned, repaired, and repainted, with wooden benches made for seating and wooden cable spools used for tables. Heat for the first chalet was provided by oil burning stoves. Erie also donated a thirty-by-forty-foot wooden contractors building for storage of the group's equipment and supplies. Development of the ski hill progressed, and in 1962 a new chalet building comprising two former Evergreen construction worker dormitories were purchased from Erie. The 170-foot-long, 30-foot-wide buildings provided expanded change and warming areas on the lower level. Sleeping rooms on the upper floor accommodated visitors from outside the area who were coming to the new hill. The contributions from Erie and the hard work of its talented employees made the ski hill successful. The Iron Range Resources & Rehabilitation Board (IRRRB) acquired the facility in 1984 and ultimately expanded it to a major ski and golf resort.[20]

First chalet at Giant's Ridge. The building was purchased from Erie and was originally a laundromat/shower facility at Evergreen.

One of many ski runs at Giant's Ridge, with Erie's mine activity in right background.

Early rope-tow lift at Giant's Ridge.

Two-story chalet in upper right.

ERIE COMMUNITY EVENTS/ SCHOLARSHIPS/TOURS/PICNICS

Erie and Pickands Mather recognized the value of higher education and provided eligible college-aged sons and daughters of Erie employees the opportunity to apply for scholarships under the annual Pickands Mather–Lake Superior Scholarship Program, and many were recipients of these renewing awards. In addition, several sons and daughters of Erie employees received the prestigious Pickands Mather's Harry Coulby Scholarship, which was a "full ride" award, covering tuition, books, board, and room, and included a small cash stipend. Two Coulby scholarships were granted each year to children of Pickands Mather employees.

Erie periodically offered summer employment to sons and daughters of its employees, allowing them to earn substantial money to offset college expenses, as well as permitting these young people to experience firsthand the work environment and challenges that their parents faced daily.

Summer student hires.

Erie display of new shovel.

Open house August 15, 1992.

Erie tours of operation.

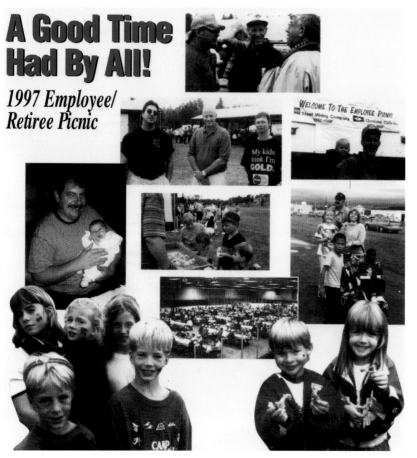

A Good Time Had By All!

1997 Employee/ Retiree Picnic

In the early 1990s, Erie sponsored several employee picnics in Hoyt Lakes and open house events for past and present employees and their families. On July 14, 1990, over 3,500 people attended the First Annual Employee Picnic, which was scheduled throughout the day. This allowed employees from all three shifts to take part in the event that featured food, live bands, games, and a water ski show. The undertaking was the result of a year's worth of planning by a joint committee of employees, retirees, and officials from Hoyt Lakes. Retirees attended from all over the United States. The next year, over 4,000 members of the Erie family attended the picnic.

In the late summer of 1992, the company hosted an open house for the community at Mining Area 6 to showcase new mining equipment, including a new Bucyrus Erie thirty-three-cubic-yard shovel with a sixty-three-foot-high boom. Many of the more than two thousand visitors marveled at the shovel's size. Its dipper had the

capability of filling a large 240-ton truck with as few as four passes.[15] Mine Superintendent Ron Rolando said, "The new shovel represents a major investment in the mine and is the first step in a long-range plan to modernize the mine and ensure its competitiveness for the future."[16] Other equipment on display included Erie's 240-ton Wiseda haul truck and a Caterpillar D-11 crawler tractor. At the time, this equipment was some of the largest iron mining equipment working. Visitors spent the day taking photographs of the equipment and gathering around picnic tables in the food tent before returning to town on the shuttle bus.

For many years Erie opened its doors during the summer to the general public by offering bus tours. Annually, approximately 2,500 visitors would board Erie's thirty-two-passenger bus for a two-hour tour of all phases of the operation. These tours were extremely popular with both local residents and area visitors from across the United States and numerous foreign countries. Erie also routinely hosted school groups (primary, secondary, and college), as well as various professional and historical organizations.

Erie and its employees supported not only east Mesabi Range communities but also the entire northeastern Minnesota area through participation in the United Way's annual fund drive. Erie's campaigns, led entirely by employee volunteers, always were near the top in total amount contributed and in percentage of employees participating. Several Erie employees, including longtime volunteers Donald Micklich and John Kemppainen, also served on the area United Way Board of Directors. The company recognized the efforts of its volunteer employees with a special luncheon following each successful United Way campaign.

As stated by former Hoyt Lakes resident Merrie Healy, "Erie has over and over been generous in its sharing of monies, equipment, and expertise with the community."[17]

Hoyt Lakes' greatest asset was the commitment of its residents to make the best possible community to raise a family by providing opportunities for youth as well as future generations. According to Dan DeVaney, "One of the most stabilizing aspects of Hoyt Lakes was that everyone was from somewhere else. There was no local population to form cliques. There was a feeling that it was all temporary. It took about ten years for people to stop saying 'we are going home for the weekend' and realize that this was their permanent home. The feeling was this is new—we are all in the same boat—let's make it work."

Erie employees' donations to the United Way set a record in January 1999 of $70,350.

United Way volunteers.

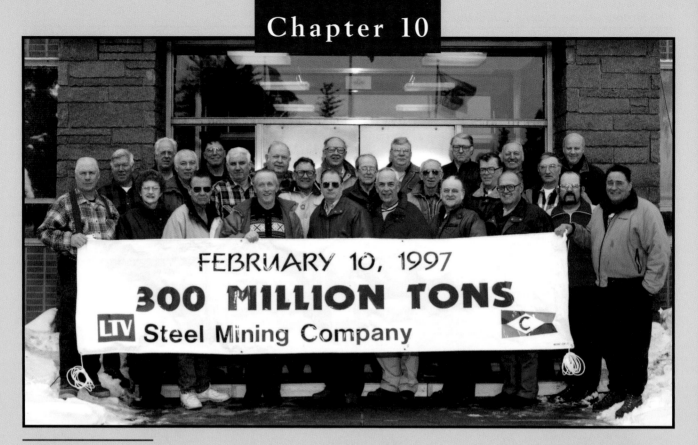

General Manager at the time (John "Jack" Toumi) and some of Erie's original employees celebrate the production of 300 million tons. Front row: Ken Kallio, Ruth Kokko, Al Wallis Jr., Donald Micklich, Bob Litchy, Paul Haskins, Larry Houdek, Bill Schoonover, Orlyn Anderson, and Doc Holliday. Middle row: Jim Seme, Jerry Frey, John Lessar, Art Lehtonen, Neil Shields, Ron Witzman, Geno Halberg, and Ray Park. Back row: Arnie Krueger, John Plesha, Bob Perpich, Tom Pakkala, Norm Condit, Ard Haugen, Chuck Prigge, and General Manager Toumi.

LAST YEARS AND CLOSURE

During the 1980s and 1990s, the North American iron ore and steel industry was challenged by high labor, energy, legacy, and transportation costs, as well as increased government regulation, high interest rates, imports, aging facilities, and global overcapacity all at the same time. This would be the most difficult period in Erie's history. Erie's employees worked hard to stay competitive, and many innovative changes and significant investments were made, but external forces and Erie's first-generation facilities eventually led to closure.

THE FIRST DOWNTURN (1982)

In 1982, restructuring of the steel industry was underway, and companies including two of Erie's owners, Bethlehem and J&L Steel, began closing aging mills and blast furnaces, which lowered demand for pellets. Pellet shipments from the Mesabi Range were reduced to about half of the previous year. Erie's production in 1982 fell to slightly over four million tons for the first time since 1958 and dropped further to just above two million tons the following year. From 1984 to 1986, Erie's annual production averaged about five million tons.[1]

Steel industry restructuring included dismantling of older facilities.

Erie Annual Production
(1980 Thru 2000)

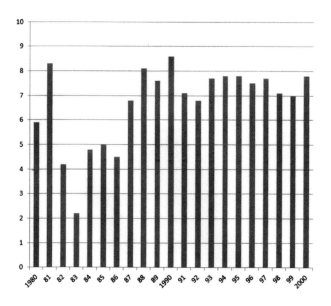

Before 1980 there were about 16,000 workers employed in Minnesota's taconite industry, but by 1982 reduced production demand lowered employment to nearly 6,000.[2] At Erie, the workforce was reduced by over a thousand employees. Assistant General Manager Greg Walker pointed out that, because of its older workforce, Erie took advantage of retirements to reduce employment level as opposed to relying exclusively on layoffs.[3] This preserved the jobs of some younger workers.

THE FIRST BANKRUPTCY (1986)

LTV Steel had been formed in June 1984 through a merger of J&L Steel and Republic. The new company was part owner of Erie and Reserve, as well as several other taconite operations. As a result of the merger, LTV Steel acquired substantial debt, and the lackluster recovery of the steel industry never allowed it to become profitable. On July 17, 1986, LTV Steel filed for federal bankruptcy protection, listing more than $4 billion in debt, making this the largest bankruptcy in U.S. history up to that time.[4] During the bankruptcy process, LTV Steel restructured its iron ore interests, which resulted in its 100 percent ownership of Erie and the shutdown of Reserve.

LTV Steel's first bankruptcy was announced on July 17, 1986.

The bankruptcy allowed Erie to reduce costs because vendor contracts could be terminated and renegotiated. The BLA was later renegotiated as part of the restructuring plan. Erie was directed to increase annual production and shipped 6.8 million tons of pellets in 1987.[5] Production would increase to 7.9 million tons of pellets in 1988 and hold steady at an average of 7.5 million tons of pellets for 1989 and 1990.[6]

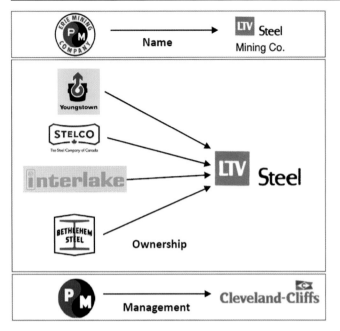

Comparing the previous multiple-ownership structure at Erie to single-owner LTV Steel, LU 4108 President Jim Kozar said, "In terms of collective bargaining, I think the company became more cooperative."[7] LU 4108 official Ed Casey agreed. "The way I looked at it," he said, "it was a benefit to us that we could get things settled without having to go to two or three other owners to get agreements put in place."[8]

THE 1990S

LTV Steel had been making much-needed investments at Erie in the period prior to emerging from bankruptcy in June 1993. These investments (as discussed in Chapter 6) were the first step in a long-range plan to modernize Erie and ensure its future in a very competitive industry.

However, as Greg Walker noted, in 1993 there were still about 100 million tons of excess steelmaking capacity in the world. Some of that was imported into the United States and replaced domestic steel production, resulting in a corresponding decrease in pellet demand.[9] In addition, by the mid-1990s, electric arc furnace (EAF) steel production had steadily increased

its share of total domestic steel output, further reducing the demand for pellets. EAFs do not use pellets but consume scrap iron or alternative iron products like direct reduced iron (DRI), pig iron, or hot briquetted iron (HBI).

Foreign steel rolls are being unloaded from a ship.

This reduced pellet demand drove all North American pellet producers to reduce costs and improve pellet quality with the end result of lowering blast furnace costs. Erie began the 1990s as the lowest cost pellet producer and although pellet production remained relatively constant, and despite significant investments and productivity improvements, ended the decade as the highest cost producer.[10]

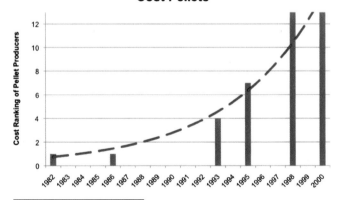

Erie pellet cost ranking among North American producers from lowest cost in 1982 to highest cost in 1998.

CLOSURE ANNOUNCEMENT

On May 24, 2000, LTV Steel announced its decision to close Erie after forty-three years of operation. The company said the orderly shutdown would take about one year with initial layoffs, related to the immediate suspension of stripping operations, at the end of May.[11]

News coverage of Erie's closure announcement.

The reasons behind the closure decision were complex. Richard Hipple, president of LTV Steel, said, "Operations have reached the end of their economic life and are faced with poor quality ore and pellets, high costs, and a need for significant recapitalization."[12] Hipple also noted that LTV Steel's blast furnaces were experiencing lower productivity and higher costs as a result of operating problems related to poor pellet quality.[13] Erie operated the only remaining shaft furnaces in the North American taconite industry. These maintenance-intensive furnaces could not compete with modern straight grate or grate kiln furnaces, which could produce higher quality pellets at a lower cost. Replacement of Erie's furnaces would cost upwards of $500 million. Continued development of Erie's ore body required the most stripping per ton of ore of any mine on the Mesabi Range, and the silica and phosphorous levels in the ore were high.[14] These factors combined with the availability of better quality and lower cost North American pellets resulted in the decision to close.

LTV Steel raw materials financial manager, Jim Janzig, recalled thinking that there were a number of reasons LTV Steel had decided to close Erie. "But I think the biggest thing was lack of future capital [money to invest at Erie]. They couldn't improve the process because there was too much demand for capital; the rest of the company [LTV Steel] wanted it, too."[15]

By 2000 Erie operated the only remaining North American shaft furnace pellet plant.

Erie's higher stripping requirements added additional cost.

Hipple paid tribute to the fourteen hundred people employed at Erie and their efforts. "The employees have done their utmost to maximize the performance of this mine," he said. "They are skilled, dedicated people."[16]

Action to limit the impact on Erie employees began immediately. LTV Steel met with the local and national representatives of the USWA to discuss the closure.[17] Cliffs announced its subsidiaries would offer preferred hiring at their Minnesota and Michigan facilities to former workers from Erie. LTV Steel noted there would be opportunities for employees of Erie willing to relocate to other LTV Steel facilities.[18] LTV Steel also said it would work with the State of Minnesota and local communities to attempt to lessen the impact of the closure.

LTV Steel noted that it intended to purchase replacement pellets, primarily from Cliffs. Cliffs expressed an interest in seeking alternative uses for the Erie site, and LTV Steel said it would cooperate in any effort to find uses for the facilities.

Minnesota Governor Jesse Ventura, who met with LTV Steel executives on the day of the announcement, stated, "We will do all we can to help the displaced employees find jobs." Minnesota's United States Senator Paul Wellstone's sincere expression of concern for Erie's workers and their families will long be remembered by the people of northeastern Minnesota. Wellstone became an outspoken advocate for the workers whose lives had been disrupted by the closure announcement. He initiated legislation that ensured eligible laid off Erie workers would have health insurance through a Health Care Tax Credit and secured federal funding for a retraining program for Erie employees and a three-month extension of unemployment benefits.

For Erie's employees, the announcement that the mine was closing was a life-changing event. Paul Maki reported, "I've always kept a log book. And I put in parentheses that it was truly a sad day here."[19]

Eugene Saumer remembered that the realization the mine was closing hit him one day soon after the announcement. "I was standing in the north end

SENATOR PAUL WELLSTONE MEMORIAL

On October 25, 2002, an aircraft accident just south of the Eveleth-Virginia Municipal Airport took the lives of Senator Paul Wellstone, his wife and daughter, three staffers and two pilots. A memorial recognizing the Senator's dedication to the people of Northeastern Minnesota has been constructed near the crash site and features monuments made from Erie taconite.[39]

of the concentrator," Saumer said, "and you look at these huge buildings, all the mechanical things, all of what's going on there, and thinking they can't shut this down . . . and it just didn't seem right. It doesn't seem like it could be, but there were tears in my eyes a couple times back then."[20]

Speaking of the challenges that faced Erie, Area Manager Mike McGinnis recognized that the people of Erie had given their best but still couldn't affect the outcome.[21]

"I worked other places in my career," Area Manager Mike Johnson said, "but I've never worked with a group of people as fine as the group that was there . . . That was really a sad day."[22]

Joel Evers immediately started planning for mining equipment to be parked for closure. "I had thirty years in, and I didn't think I wanted to be part of that," Evers said. "I didn't want to see it go down so I chose to retire."[23]

For Area Manager Mike Sterk, the most difficult part of the closure was parting company with people he had worked with for years. "The hardest thing to do was to go out and talk to the people and tell them that their job was going to end in a year, some sooner," he said. "I did that with all the crews, and that was difficult because you've fought and worked and sweated with these folks for years and you cared about them."[24]

Area Manager Bruce Gerlach recalled, "During that year a lot of people who worked at the mine had opportunities to get jobs elsewhere, so they left. I have to say that the people who remained at the mine . . . took pride in keeping it going."[25] Erie's safety performance that last year was excellent, and production, cost, and quality met expectations even with reduced manpower.

"One of the most important responsibilities early on was to get approval of closure plans from the State of Minnesota," Gerlach explained. "A twelve-year closure plan accounted for remediation of environmental issues in the various areas of the mine, demolition of structures and so on."[26] Area Manager Jim Scott led the team that developed and implemented the closure plan—"It is tens of millions of dollars to do the closure."[27]

SECOND BANKRUPTCY AND CLOSURE

After emerging from its first bankruptcy in 1993, LTV Steel, then the nation's third-largest steelmaker, faced the challenge of increasing competition. LTV focused efforts on working to improve productivity and quality, reduce costs, and streamline the organization. As part of this, LTV Steel invested in a multiyear corporate-wide information technology project that cost more than $400 million and never met expectations. LTV Steel also formed the $500 million joint venture called Trico Steel Company LLC to construct a non-union EAF and mini-mill in Alabama. The new facility would process HBI product from an LTV Steel/Cliffs/Lurgi joint venture on the Caribbean island of Trinidad using South American iron ore.[28] None of these projects provided the expected benefits and contributed significantly to LTV Steel's continuing financial losses. These factors along with the declining economic condition of the North American steel industry resulted in LTV Steel filing for bankruptcy a second time on December 29, 2000, and its eventual liquidation.

For IRRRB employee and Hoyt Lakes mayor at the time, Marlene Pospeck, the closure was a heavy blow. She recalled coming into work to the news that LTV Steel had filed a second bankruptcy and was immediately shutting down Erie. "That was quite a shock to everybody because we did think that we had a little bit of leeway [before the originally planned closure date]. I walked into work that morning and the Commissioner of IRRRB met me at the door, and he said, 'I have some bad news. They're closing the doors at Erie today. You go home and do what you need to do.'"[29]

At 7:15 a.m. on January 2, 2001, Erie's General Manager Dennis Koschak, received notification from LTV Steel that operations at the mine were to cease. Koschak scheduled meetings that morning with the salaried workforce and officials from LU 4108.

About noon on January 4, the last crude ore was dumped at the Coarse Crusher. At approximately 4:00 a.m. on January 5, the last operating mill line was shut down, and at 11:30 a.m. the last operating furnace (B-4) was shut down.[30] As equipment was shut down, the workforce was reduced with fewer than two hundred employees working for an extra week on various orderly shutdown tasks. Shipping from the pellet stockpile was scheduled to resume in April and to be completed no later than July.[31]

The upside-down broom signifies the last car of ore to be dumped at Erie.

Erie employees gather at the Coarse Crusher for the dumping of the last ore car.

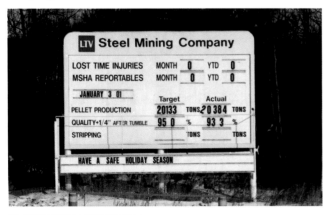

Erie's production board at the plant entrance reflects the last day of full production.

Paul Maki noted in his log book on January 3, 2001: "I documented that I packed up my stuff and I left the property permanently. I also wrote that, since 1986, I've seen the best of times and I've seen the worst of times at this place of employment. It was a sad day."[32]

Corinne "Petey" Eden recalled: "It seemed unreal at the time. Very sad saying goodbye to these people. Sad watching some that had been there thirty years, wondering what they were going to do because they're too young to retire . . . wanting to run to every building so I could make sure I said goodbye to everybody that I had worked with . . . not knowing when I'd see them again . . . You just don't have a job. It's very sad."[33]

Parking of Erie mine equipment.

LTV STEEL MINING COMPANY

WEEKLY MANAGEMENT REPORT   **JANUARY 10, 2001**

GENERAL
Shutdown of the LTV Steel Mining Company began on 01/03. At noon, 01/04, the last trainload of crude ore was dumped at the coarse crusher. At approximately 4 AM on 01/05 the last mill line was shut down. At 11:30 AM, the last operating furnace (B-4) was shut down.

SAFETY
Safe Production was recorded this week with no MSHA reportable injuries.

Representatives from MSHA were on site to discuss closure initiatives and conduct inspections. A closeout meeting will be held 01/12.

Congratulations to all employees for achieving an outstanding safety record in the year 2000. The MSHA reportable rate improved by 35%, the lost time frequency rate improved by 28%, and the lost time severity rate improved by 59%.

In addition, 4 of the 5 departments improved their MSHA reportable rate from 1999, and the only department that didn't improve only had 3 reportables.

MINING
All of the shovels and drills are out of the pits and parked with the exception of the 7152 shovel in Area 6. It lost a propel, which will be repaired to the extent to make it possible to move out of the pit.

The dewatering pumps are out of Area 2W. All explosive inventories were destroyed in a blast in 2W.

MAINTENANCE/CRUSHING
The coarse and fine crushers have been drained and final work is under way to take power off next week.

CONCENTRATING
The return water barge has been shut down. All of the mill water has essentially been drained from the building. The firewater is being drained.

PELLETIZING
The water is drained. The heating plant will continue to provide minimum heat to the concentrator as the isolation valves are bad order. PCB capacitor is underway.

POWER PLANT/RAILROAD
The last boat of the 2000/2001 shipping season was loaded out on 01/06. The JR Barker left with 49,619 tons for Indiana Harbor.

Final weekly summary of Erie operations.

THE ODE TO ERIE MINING COMPANY

By Peter "Mack" Makowski, an Erie employee and proud member of LU 4108.
Written shortly after the May 2000 announcement that Erie Mining was closing.

We started making pellets in 1957,
A new technology, hundreds of jobs, it
    seemed like Heaven.
Brand new equipment, bright and shining,
It was a glorious start to Erie Mining.

And through the 60's, we developed our plant,
We proved there was no such word as "can't".
Sure, with this new technology, we made
    some mistakes,
But we also built a new town; its name was
    Hoyt Lakes.

We worked day and night to produce a high
    quality pellet,
Great for customers, it was easy to sell it.
Into the 70's, the taconite industry roared,
Things were great; the company's
    profits soared.

We set a record in 1973,
Over 11 million tons, to be exact, it was 11.3.
Yes, in the 70's we were moving along,
It seemed that nothing could ever go wrong.

And then came the 80's and things started
    to change,
There were lay-offs and cutbacks all across
    the Range.
Things looked bleak and times were rough,
But you can't stop Iron Rangers because we
    are tough.

In 1986 a new owner came, it was LTV,
We all wondered what would come to be.
The company was in trouble. Reserve Mining
    went down,
Were we next? Would we also drown?

But rather than just scream and shout,
Everyone got together and bailed the
    company out.
And in the 90's, thing started to improve,
Production and employment were up; we
    were back in the groove.

The economy got better; spirits were 'rising',
But there was trouble out on the horizon.
It came this year 2000, on May 24,
When LTV announced it was closing the door.

They said the ore was poor, the pellets
    are bad.
The whole situation is mighty sad.
What now is our future? Will our plant die?
Will there be a new owner, copper-nickel,
    or DRI?

Is the story of Erie Mining and LTV about
    to end?
We can't close the book yet, for this place is
    our friend.
This taconite mine and plant helped to raise
    our Standard of Living,
It provided for our communities and our spirit
    of giving.

While we may feel sad, we're not at the end
    of the rope,
For Iron Rangers everywhere, never give
    up hope.
Perhaps, yes perhaps, there will be a miracle,
    maybe out of heaven.
Just like when we started making pellets
    in 1957.

Koschak paid tribute to all the employees in a February 8, 2001, letter. "Until the end," he said, "you remained a dedicated group, focused on safe production of the best product the plant was capable of producing."[34]

The closure would impact the communities across the Mesabi Range for years to come. Hoyt Lakes business owner James Welch understood that Hoyt Lakes would never be the same again and knew that the closure would create difficulties for the community he had come to call home. "Well, the streets got kind of empty because a lot of the young people had to move someplace to get a job," he said. "So, we've become a community of older people."[35]

Rebecca "Becky" Burich worked as the general manager's secretary and later as clerk for the City of Hoyt Lakes. She remembered thinking that "the plant closing was devastating for the East Range. Hoyt Lakes was built planning for a lot more people than the two thousand–plus that there are

today. A lot of people had to move away. It was a very sad time." But Burich said Iron Rangers are resilient. "What I am proud of is the way people rebound and make a good life for themselves," she said. "They do what they need to do."[36]

On June 22, 2001, a small group of employees and retirees gathered to watch the last load of pellets leave for the Dock. Erie retiree Herb Meckola was there, and he had been there nearly forty-four years before to watch the first load of pellets from Hoyt Lakes begin its journey to Taconite Harbor. Meckola and his colleagues Dan DeVaney and Adrian "Ace" Barker watched as a traditional upside-down broom was inserted in the last carload of pellets to signify a clean sweep. These last 9,234 tons of pellets went into the hold of the *Lee A. Tregurtha* on June 23. By the end of July, the final 150,000 tons of broken pellets (chips) were shipped through Taconite Harbor.[37]

Letter to Erie employees from General Manager Dennis Koschak thanking them for their dedicated service.

Sample of Erie's final pellet production.

LIQUIDATION

Shortly after Erie announced its closure, an East Range Emergency Response Team was formed with representatives from the state, IRRRB, and local communities to deal with the immediate effects of the closure. One of the group's first actions was to publish a prospectus describing Erie's facilities at Hoyt Lakes and Taconite Harbor including 73,000 acres of land. IRRRB Assistant Commissioner Brian Hiti said, "We had three goals, preserve the assets, bring some jobs back, and take care of some of the environmental liabilities."[38]

This resulted in several offers being received. One proposal was to purchase the entire property, demolish the structures, and sell material as scrap. American Electric Power of Columbus, Ohio, made an offer to buy the power plant, transformer yard, and transmission lines only. The winning proposal supported by the State of Minnesota was a joint offer from Cliffs and MP&L for all the facilities.

MP&L obtained the Power Plant and 138KV transmission lines between Taconite Harbor and the Plant Site as well as 30,000 acres of non-mining lands. Cliffs obtained all mining- and plant-related assets, including the Mainline Railroad and Dock, and formed Cliffs Erie LLC with the mission of handling the environmental obligations, performing reclamation, and recovering assets.

With the completion of the sale on October 22, 2001, Erie Mining Company's sixty-one-year story (from its formation in 1940 to its sale) came to an end.

Last Erie pellet train with yard and train crews.

Full circle: *Some who saw first shipment leave LTV return for the last*

LTV retirees (from left) Herb Meckola, Dan DeVaney and Adrian Barker, all of Hoyt Lakes, watch and photograph the last trainload of pellets leaving LTV Steel Mining Co. on Friday morning.

Last train rolls away from LTV

This news article features former Erie employees watching the last trainload of pellets to Taconite Harbor.

Last carload of Erie pellets with broom "clean sweep" symbol.

Prospectus for LTV Steel Mining Company

People
A highly skilled workforce of over 1,400

Property
73,000 acres of surface and mineral lands

Plant
Includes a crusher, concentrator and pelletizer

Power
A power plant with a total demonstrated capacity of 225 megawatts

Port
A 2,234-foot-long shipping pier at Taconite Harbor, Lake Superior

Plus Railroad
Cars, locomotives and a 74-mile mainline railroad that connects the mine and plant with the port

LTV Steel Mining Company, Hoyt Lakes, Minnesota

This brochure describes Erie facilities after the closure announcement.

Erie shovel being moved to the new owner.

DM&IR transports Erie locomotives to new owners, ca. 2003.

Empty Stockpile.

Erie Pellet Plant being dismantled in 2007.

MANAGEMENT CHANGES

Management organizations change over time. The reasons for change include shifting objectives as an organization goes from startup to routine operations, new technologies, changes in management philosophy, and owner directives.

Leonard Johnston, Works Manager 1957–1961

Except for a startup period, Erie operated under a traditional mine management structure for most of its history. At the top level was the Works or General Manager. The next level down were the operating department Superintendents, each with an Assistant Superintendent. Below the Assistant Superintendent were the General Foremen (GF) followed by Assistant General Foreman (AGF). The next level of management was the frontline Foreman who had direct contact with the operating and maintenance working crews. These were all salaried non-union positions.

At startup of the Commercial Plant, the management structure was designed to deal with the anticipated challenges of startup and reaching normal operations. Erie's first Works Manager was Leonard Johnston, and the senior management was structured as shown on Figure 1. Maintenance positions (GF, AGF, and Foremen) were centralized under the Superintendent of Maintenance even if they were assigned to work in other departments.

By 1961 Erie's production reached design level and operations were stabilized. Bernard "Spike" Borgel was named Works Manager, and the management structure was rearranged as shown on Figure 2.

Bernard "Spike" Borgel, Works Manager 1961–1962

Figure 2

In 1962 John "Jack" Healy became Works Manager. While Healy was Works Manager, Erie's annual production capacity was expanded from 7.5 to 10.3 million tons. In spite of the added activity and additional workforce, the management structure remained the same.

John "Jack" Healy, Works Manager 1962–1969

In 1969 Clyde Keith was named Erie's General Manager (previously Works Manager). To better align resources with responsibilities, Maintenance was decentralized by reassigning maintenance positions (GF, AGF, and Foremen) to the operating department superintendents. The Superintendent of Maintenance continued to manage the General Shops and specialized service crews. During this period there were significant changes in computer technology and mine equipment, which

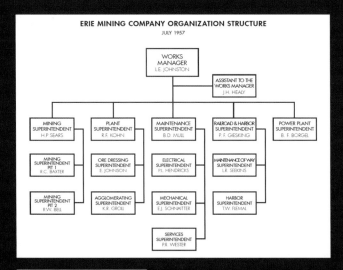

Figure 1

drove manpower reductions in the clerical and equipment operators staffing levels. This organization was still in effect in 1986 when George Lerick was named General Manager.

While Lerick was General Manager, LTV Steel became sole owner of Erie and Pickands Mather was acquired by Cliffs. These were significant changes resulting in a different management philosophy and cultural adjustments, but the management structure at Erie remained the same.

Rainald "Ray" von Bitter became General Manager in 1987, and soon changes to the organization were initiated. In response to a change in management philosophy and owner directives, organizational titles changed, more responsibility was delegated to lower management levels, and frontline supervision was reduced. Assistant Superintendents became Operating Engineers, GFs became General Supervisors, AGFs became Assistant General Supervisors, and Foremen became Supervisors. This coincided with the period of increasing employee participation through programs like LMPT and IPC.

Driven by additional focus on cost reduction, more organization changes occurred in the mid-1990s. Superintendents became Area Managers, Assistant General Supervisors and General Supervisors became Section Managers, and Supervisors became

Clyde Keith, General Manager 1969–1986

George Lerick, General Manager 1986–1987

Coordinators. The Operating Engineers positions were eliminated. This reduced five management levels to three.

When John "Jack" Toumi became General Manager in 1996, Erie was faced with many challenges owing to imports and increasing costs, which ultimately resulted in the announcement in May 2000 that Erie would close in mid-2001, and a scheduled decrease in production capacity began.

In the fall of 2000, Dennis Koschak was named General Manager and continued the orderly shutdown plan. During this period, the management structure remained the same, but as the plan was implemented, personnel reductions occurred. However, on December 29, 2000, LTV Steel filed for bankruptcy, and Koschak was instructed to cease Erie's operations immediately.

The table below shows the evolution of Erie's management structure at representative intervals from 1957 through 2000.

Rainald "Ray" von Bitter, General Manager 1987–1996

John "Jack" Toumi, General Manager 1996–2000

Dennis Koschak, General Manager 2000–2001

OPERATING DEPARTMENT STAFFING						
Works/General Manager	Johnston	Borgel/Healy	Keith/Lerick	von Bitter/Tuomi/Koschak		
	1957	1968	1983	1992		2000
Superintendent/Assistants	14/0	5/5	5/0	5/6	Area Mgr	5/0
General Foreman	na	19	18	15	Section Mgr	11
Assistant General Foreman	na	54	17	20		
Foreman	na	220	206	122	Coordinators	103

Chapter 11

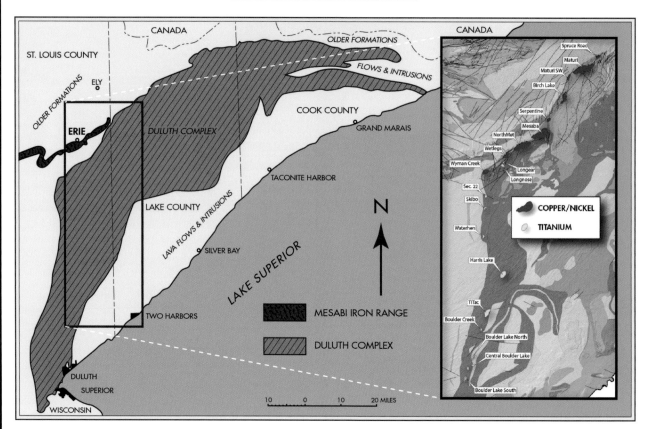

GENERALIZED GEOLOGY OF DULUTH COMPLEX IN NORTHEASTERN MINNESOTA

THE FUTURE OF MINING IN NORTHEASTERN MINNESOTA

The iron ore resource of the Mesabi Range has been known about from the 1860s, and since 1968, when taconite pellet production surpassed natural ore mining, most of the deposits are dedicated to the existing pellet producers. However, there are still areas that offer potential for iron ore development with the former Erie site being the largest. There are also tailing basins and lean ore stockpiles from depleted mines across the Mesabi Range that contain recoverable iron.

Starting in 2004 world iron ore prices steadily rose from about $38 per ton to a peak of $192 per ton in 2011 driven by industrial growth in Asia. But in 2015, prices fell to $37 per ton as the world economy slowed. The rising prices initially prompted investment in several iron ore projects using new technologies on the Mesabi Range, but when prices dropped their products were not competitive and the projects shut down.

In addition to iron ore, northeastern Minnesota is rich in other minerals contained in the Duluth Complex, a geological formation lying immediately

Minnesota Power wind turbines at Taconite Ridge Wind Farm.

south of the eastern Mesabi Range. The Duluth Complex is one of the largest undeveloped copper/nickel resources in the world and contains substantial amounts of cobalt, silver, and gold as well as platinum group minerals (PGMs), mainly platinum and palladium. The area also has known deposits of titanium. The possibility exists that other valuable deposits and minerals will be found in unexplored areas associated with the Duluth Complex.

As demand for these strategic metals continues to grow domestically and globally, the Duluth Complex minerals have the potential to bring great economic opportunity to Minnesota. These metals are critical for a sustainable future including construction, communications, power distribution, national defense, medicine, and renewable green energy. Development of the Duluth Complex minerals would support the domestic economy, boosting job creation, spurring growth, and producing metals necessary for the emerging green economy. Minnesota could become a world leader in the production of green energy metals used in wind turbines, hybrid and electric vehicles, batteries, and solar energy panels.

Erie's remaining facilities have the potential of processing taconite or the Duluth Complex minerals. Following Erie's closure, two companies began development at the former Erie location—Mesabi Nugget, LLC (Mesabi Nugget) and PolyMet Mining Corporation (PolyMet). Mesabi Nugget is a value-added iron (+95 percent iron content) project, and PolyMet is a copper/nickel, PGMs project.

MESABI NUGGET

Increasing steel production from EAFs created a market for value-added iron products. This resulted in an opportunity for value-added iron production on the Mesabi Range and fit well with the efforts of the state and Cliffs to use the former Erie site.

After an extensive review of potential technologies, the Kobe-Midrex iron-making process was selected. A pilot plant was constructed at Northshore Mining Company (formerly Reserve) where there was a ready supply of iron concentrate and space for the test equipment. The plant converted concentrate in a rotary furnace to a product with an iron content of 95 percent compared to a typical pellet of 65 percent. The product was called an "iron nugget"— a small irregularly shaped lump of iron.

Iron nuggets produced from a rotary furnace.

In 2006, Indiana-based Steel Dynamics Inc. (SDI), Cliffs, Kobe Steel, and Ferrometrics announced plans to construct a full-scale commercial iron nugget plant at the former Erie Area 1 mine location. Ownership of the project was restructured in 2007 when SDI (81 percent) and Kobe Steel (19 percent) formed Mesabi Nugget and announced the construction of a $235 million 500,000 ton per year iron nugget facility.[1] The State of Minnesota supported Mesabi Nugget's investment with $16.5 million in IRRRB financing and a $10 million loan.[2] The initial project did not include mining and concentrating taconite but instead relied on receiving concentrate from other sources. Mesabi Nugget's production was to be shipped to SDI's EAF plants in Indiana. Some five hundred workers were employed during the eighteen-month construction period.[3] Mesabi Nugget employed about a hundred workers and was the world's first commercial iron nugget plant.

At various times, the iron nugget plant processed concentrate from Northshore Mining Company, Magnetation LLC (Magnetation), and Mining Resources LLC (Mining Resources), a joint venture of SDI (80 percent) and Magnetation (20 percent), all delivered by truck. Mesabi Nugget provided a needed boost for the Mesabi Range and an affirmation of the industrial potential of the former Erie site.

Mesabi Nugget facility with Erie plant buildings in upper right.

Railcars each contain 100 tons of iron nuggets destined for SDI's EAF plants.

In 2008, Mesabi Nugget announced Phase II of the project and started the environmental review process by submitting an Environmental Assessment Worksheet (EAW). Phase II plans anticipated mining taconite from the former Erie Mine Areas 6, 9, and 2WX and producing about three million tons per year of iron concentrate in a new concentrator. One million tons of concentrate would be delivered to the iron nugget plant under construction and two million tons to be shipped to other facilities.

ENVIRONMENTAL REVIEW PROCESS

In the 1950s, when Erie was constructed, new mining projects were required to apply for only a few state-issued permits, and no formal environmental review process was conducted. Today, however, environmental regulations tightly control how mines are permitted, designed, operated, and closed. Financial assurance is required to guarantee reclamation and closure performance. All mining projects now start with a formal environmental review.

In 1970, the federal government enacted the National Environmental Policy Act (NEPA), which mandated an environmental review for a project that required federal permits. Minnesota formalized its environmental review process in 1973 by passing the Minnesota Environmental Policy Act (MEPA).

These federal and state laws define the types of projects that require environmental review and the scope of the review. Mining projects typically have significant environmental impacts, and before permits can be issued for land disturbances, water discharges, and air emissions, an Environmental Impact Statement (EIS) is required. An EIS is a document that describes a project, presents alternatives (including not to proceed with the project), and identifies potential environmental and social impacts associated with the project and alternatives.

In Minnesota, the Minnesota Pollution Control Agency (MPCA) issues water discharge and air emission permits, and the Minnesota Department of Natural Resources (MDNR) issues permits to mine as well as water appropriations permits. The United States Army Corps of Engineers (USACE) issues permits to fill or drain wetlands, and much of northeastern Minnesota's topography consists of marshes, bogs, swamps, streams, and shallow lakes (i.e., wetlands). Collectively, this means that a mining project in northeastern Minnesota requires actions by federal and state agencies and an EIS that must meet both federal and state requirements.

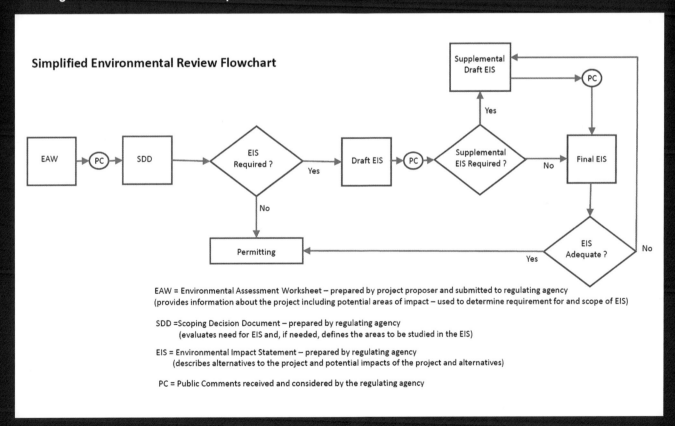

Simplified Environmental Review Flowchart

EAW = Environmental Assessment Worksheet – prepared by project proposer and submitted to regulating agency (provides information about the project including potential areas of impact – used to determine requirement for and scope of EIS)

SDD =Scoping Decision Document – prepared by regulating agency (evaluates need for EIS and, if needed, defines the areas to be studied in the EIS)

EIS = Environmental Impact Statement – prepared by regulating agency (describes alternatives to the project and potential impacts of the project and alternatives)

PC = Public Comments received and considered by the regulating agency

The review is initiated when the company proposing a project submits an Environmental Assessment Worksheet (EAW) that describes the project and presents the potential environmental, social, and economic impacts of the project to the appropriate regulatory agency. The agency reviews the EAW, conducts public meetings to present the project and potential impacts, receives public comments, considers those comments, and issues a Scoping Decision Document that serves as a blueprint for the EIS.

Typically, there is a formal agreement among the various agencies that a joint federal/state EIS will be prepared. The agreement defines which agencies that will lead the preparation of the EIS and the parties that will participate by providing input and comment in their areas of knowledge.

The lead agencies select an independent consultant, with expertise in the aspects of the project and the NEPA/MEPA process, to prepare a Draft EIS (DEIS) under the direction of the lead agencies. The company participates in the development of the DEIS, providing information as requested by lead agencies. A major aspect of the DEIS preparation process is to identify and evaluate alternatives that may lead to changes in the project. The lead agencies review the DEIS, conduct additional public meetings to present the project and potential impacts, receive public comments, and respond to those comments.

If public comments raise a significant new issue or if new information becomes available, a Supplemental DEIS (SDEIS) may be required and would go through the same procedure as the original DEIS. Once the DEIS (or SDEIS) process has been successfully completed, the lead agencies issue a Final EIS (FEIS) and determine the review to be adequate, which closes the review process.

The company can then submit applications for the permits needed based on the project as defined by the FEIS. The permitting agencies use the information gathered in the FEIS to develop draft permits containing specific conditions and limits. Once all permits have gone through another review process, including public comment periods, the final permits are issued.

The MDNR, MPCA, USACE, and other state and federal agencies will enforce the regulations protecting the state's natural resources and ensure that all permit requirements are met.

Major PolyMet permits issued by MDNR.

In 2015, SDI announced it was terminating the environmental review process for Phase II and placing Mesabi Nugget and Mining Resources on extended shutdown status because the Mesabi Nugget product was not competitive with current market prices.

MAGNETATION

Another new company that used the mineral resources of the Mesabi Range was Magnetation, a joint venture of Magnetation Inc. (50.1 percent) and AK Steel Corporation (49.9 percent). Magnetation Inc. developed a patented process to recover high-quality iron concentrate from tailing generated by natural ore beneficiation plants. Magnetation built their first plant at Keewatin in 2008 and eventually added iron recovery facilities at Taconite, Coleraine, and Chisholm (the joint venture Mining Resources facility) and a pellet plant in Indiana.

Aerial view of a Magnetation plant on the Mesabi Range.

Following start-up in 2008, Magnetation expanded over a seven-year period to a company with five hundred employees and $1 billion in assets. Magnetation shipped product to Mesabi Nugget, their pellet plant in Indiana, and other customers as far away as Mexico. However, due to decreasing global iron ore prices, Magnetation was not competitive and filed for bankruptcy in 2015. By the summer of 2016, it had shut down its plants in Minnesota and Indiana.[4] Magnetation's assets were subsequently sold out of bankruptcy.

MINNESOTA STEEL

The long-held vision to build Minnesota's first steel mill at the mine and by doing so add more value to the ore mined on the Mesabi Range took a step toward reality in 2005 when Minnesota Steel Industries LLC (MSI) announced plans to build a massive steel-making complex near Nashwauk. Coming after the closure of Erie, the proposed project won widespread state and local government support.

MSI was formed as a wholly owned subsidiary of the J.M. Longyear heirs and the R.M. Bennett heirs. Since the early 1890s, the Longyear and Bennett families had been partners in the development of Minnesota's iron ore industry and owned ore reserves near the project. MSI proposed to reactivate the former Butler Taconite mine and tailings basin area, which was active from 1967 until 1985 when the mine was closed and the facilities dismantled. MSI's project would combine taconite mining, ore processing, pelletizing with DRI production, and steel making into an integrated facility to provide steel for the domestic and world markets. In addition to the construction of new facilities, including crusher, concentrator, pellet plant, DRI plant and a complete steelmaking facility would be built. The MSI process envisioned producing finished steel from taconite pellets in forty-eight hours and would achieve efficiencies by having a continuous flow of materials at higher temperatures throughout the process, eliminating multiple transportation and handling steps. MSI initially planned to produce 2.5 million tons of steel slabs annually for direct shipment or for conversion to hot rolled coils on site. In general, about 3.4 tons of taconite ore would be converted to 1 ton of finished steel product.[5] Employment at MSI was expected to be about 700.[6]

From 2005 to 2007, an environmental review of the MSI project was conducted, and in August 2007 permits were issued. In October 2007, Essar Steel Minnesota LLC (Essar) purchased MSI and announced that it would immediately invest $1.65 billion to build the facility. The project received strong support from the State of Minnesota including a $40 million state bonding initiative, $11 million in supplemental appropriations, a $14.9 million grant, and $6 million in publicly subsidized project development loans.[7]

Pellet Plant under construction.

On September 19, 2008, Essar started construction. IRRRB Commissioner Sandy Layman said, "This project marks the beginning of a new value-added industry on the Iron Range that will generate tremendous economic benefits for our communities, schools, businesses and the State."[8]

However, almost immediately, the project suffered from insufficient corporate funding, and construction was interrupted numerous times because contractors were not being paid.

In 2011, Essar approached MDNR with modifications to the originally proposed project and sought to increase pellet production from the 3.8 million tons per year originally permitted to 6.5 million tons per year so that Essar could provide pellets to the company's steel mill in Canada. The proposed modification did not change Essar's plans to produce direct reduced iron pellets or steel in Minnesota but reduced the project life from twenty years to fifteen.

In 2016, Essar, which had already spent $1.8 billion on the project, suspended construction on the partially completed facility. At the time the company owed $66 million to the State of Minnesota and nearly $50 million to vendors and contractors.[9] As a result Essar filed for Chapter 11

Construction at the plant site was halted several times.

New taconite plant under construction.

Bankruptcy halted construction.

bankruptcy protection. Because Minnesota officials had no confidence that Essar could carry the project to completion and to protect the state's mineral interests, Essar's state mining leases were terminated just prior to the bankruptcy.

In late 2017, Essar's assets were sold out of bankruptcy to Mesabi Metallics Company LLC (Mesabi Metallics) and the state's mining leases transferred to Mesabi Metallics, but as of 2019 construction had not restarted. Estimates indicated that it would cost another $1.3 billion to complete the mine, concentrator, and pellet plant construction, and then another $650 million to build the DRI plant. If completed, the project would be Minnesota's most expensive single private construction project ever, totaling more than $3.7 billion.

DULUTH COMPLEX MINERAL POTENTIAL

Copper, nickel, and PGMs are essential to today's green economy, providing materials needed for catalytic converters, hybrid vehicles, and wind turbines. These metals are also critical to the manufacture of electrical equipment, electronics, piping, and jet engines. In 2018 the United States imported a large portion of the strategic metals that are found in the Duluth Complex, specifically—nickel, 100 percent; platinum, 79 percent; palladium, 60 percent; and copper, 40 percent.

The Duluth Complex in northeastern Minnesota is one of the world's most significant undeveloped mineral resources, containing the second-largest amounts of copper and PGMs and third-largest amount of nickel. The Duluth Complex was

formed by a massive volcanic intrusion about 1.5 billion years after the Biwabik Iron Formation was deposited. It generally extends from Duluth along Lake Superior and north to the iron formation near Erie and northeast beyond Ely. At least nine areas generally located along the northern edge of the Duluth Complex have been explored and are rich in copper, nickel, and PGMs.

EXPLORATION IN THE DULUTH COMPLEX

In the 1950s and 1960s, many mining companies began diamond drilling the Duluth Complex in northeastern Minnesota near Babbitt. These initial results were promising, and in 1966, Minnesota opened state-owned lands for copper/nickel exploration. More than thirteen hundred exploration holes were drilled, and two test shafts were sunk. However, from 1974 to 1978, exploration on state lands was suspended while the state conducted a $4.3 million Regional Copper-Nickel Study that was intended to evaluate the potential social, economic, and environmental impacts of development of the Duluth Complex minerals.[10] The study made significant contributions to the state's knowledge of copper/nickel mineral development but, following the direction of the Minnesota Legislature, presented only technical findings and not policy recommendations.[11] Exploration on state lands resumed in 1982.

PGMs were first discovered at the Birch Lake copper/nickel deposit in 1985, which significantly increased the value of the deposit because metals from these minerals sell for hundreds of dollars per ounce. PGMs have since been found in other Duluth Complex copper/nickel deposits.

POLYMET

In 1998, PolyMet, a Canadian mining development company, focused on exploring an ore body located between the former Reserve taconite mine and Erie's railroad and developing a metallurgical process that would recover all the metal values from the deposit. Past efforts were focused on recovering only copper and nickel concentrates.

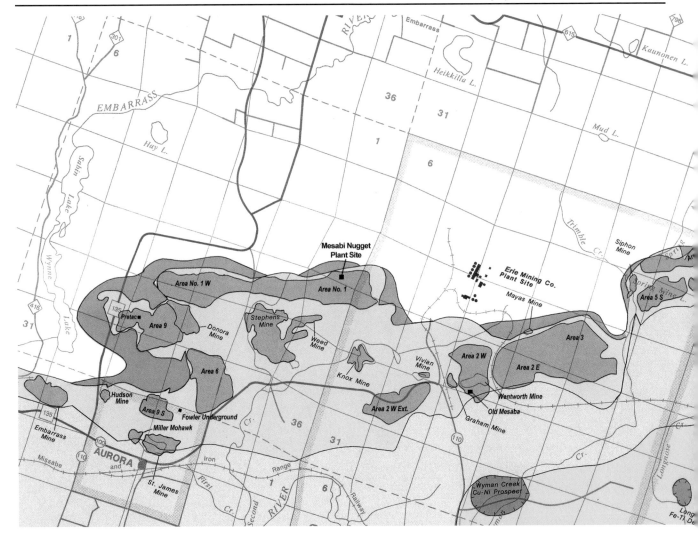

Map shows iron mining activity and mineral deposits in the northern portion of the Duluth Complex near Erie.

By 2000, PolyMet had developed a process to concentrate all the minerals and a separate hydrometallurgical process that included a patented PGMs recovery step. PolyMet envisioned building a new plant and tailings basin; however, capital cost estimates were high, and the project was put on hold.

In early 2004, PolyMet secured an option to purchase portions of Erie including the Coarse Crusher, Fine Crusher, Concentrator, and Tailing Basin. PolyMet announced its intention to become the first company to mine copper, nickel, platinum, palladium, cobalt, and gold from the Duluth Complex.[12] PolyMet's project, called NorthMet,

was designed to process 32,000 tons of ore per day and would cost $380 million. The revised plan included developing a mine, reusing significant portions of Erie's railroad, Coarse Crusher, Fine Crusher, Concentrator, Tailing Basin and support facilities, and constructing a new flotation building and hydrometallurgical plant.[13]

In 2005, PolyMet initiated the environmental review process by submitting an Environmental Assessment Worksheet (EAW). This began the longest and most expensive environmental review in Minnesota to date. State and federal regulators agreed to perform a joint environmental review, which was to be led by the MDNR and United States Army Corps of Engineers (USACE) with the participation of the MPCA and three local

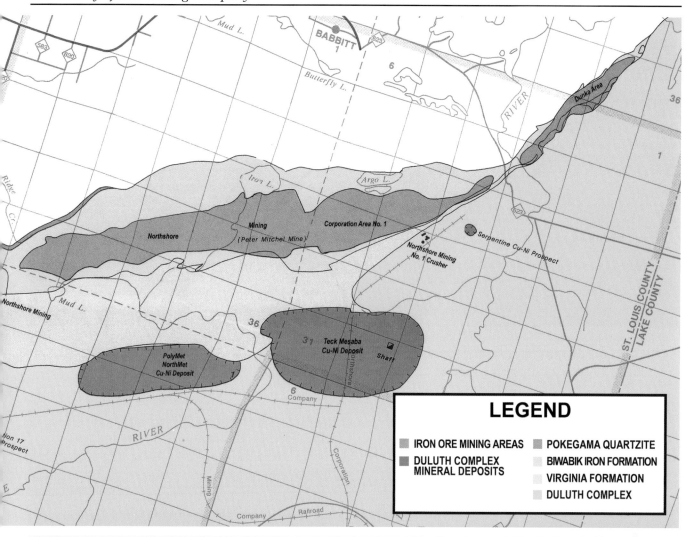

LEGEND

- IRON ORE MINING AREAS
- DULUTH COMPLEX MINERAL DEPOSITS
- POKEGAMA QUARTZITE
- BIWABIK IRON FORMATION
- VIRGINIA FORMATION
- DULUTH COMPLEX

View of Erie facilities owned by PolyMet.

Proposed new PolyMet processing facilities (dark red) at Erie.

Native American bands. The Draft Environmental Impact Statement (DEIS) was completed in 2009. Subsequently, state and federal agencies determined additional review was needed and a Supplemental Draft Environmental Impact Statement (SDEIS) was required. The U.S. Forest Service became one of the lead agencies, and the U.S. Environmental Protection Agency became a participant. The SDEIS was completed in 2013, and the Final Environmental Impact Statement (FEIS) was published in 2015. There were several significant changes to the project during the ten-year environmental review period, including segregating the waste rock from stripping, collecting and treating all water seeping from the Tailing Basin, and shipping of concentrates instead of producing final products on site.

Following completion of the FEIS, PolyMet entered the next phase, developing the permit applications. Permits are required from various agencies authorizing specific activities related to the project. Each permit has its own applicable requirements and processes. In 2016, PolyMet submitted permit applications to the MDNR (Permit to Mine, Water Appropriations, Dam Safety), the MPCA (Air Emissions, Water Discharge), and the USACE (Wetlands).

Minnesota has very rigorous permitting standards and strictly enforces environmental statutes and regulations. The State Permit to Mine evaluates details of the proposed mine plan and includes financial assurance provisions, requiring the company to set aside funding to ensure that all environmental liabilities are fully covered in the event of a PolyMet bankruptcy. All of the various permits must be received before the project can proceed. By 2018, the permitting process was nearly complete.

TWIN METALS

In 2005, another Canadian mining company, Wallbridge Mining Company, Limited (Wallbridge) created Duluth Metals Limited (Duluth Metals) for mineral exploration and project development in northern Minnesota. By 2010, Duluth Metals had defined one of the world's largest undeveloped PGMs, copper and nickel deposits, which it began developing through Twin Metals Minnesota LLC (TMM), a joint venture partnership with South American copper producer Antofagasta PLC (Antofagasta). In 2011, TMM effectively doubled its Minnesota mineral and land assets by acquiring neighboring Franconia Minerals Corporation, and in 2015, Antofagasta purchased the remaining interests in Duluth Metals, and TMM became a wholly owned subsidiary. The TMM project covers approximately 32,000 acres and has control of 40,000 acres of land/mineral interests in the Duluth Complex.

TMM plans to process approximately 20,000 tons of ore per day from an underground mine at a concentrator on a 100-acre, company-owned site approximately one mile south of the underground mine near the north end of Birch Lake. Underground mining operations would allow for belowground storage of some waste rock and tailing and reducing the impact of mining activities on the surrounding land. The estimated $2 billion TMM Project would employ approximately 650 people. TMM expects to eventually submit a formal proposal, which will begin the rigorous and thorough environmental review of the project by multiple state and federal agencies.

New TMM headquarters located in Ely.

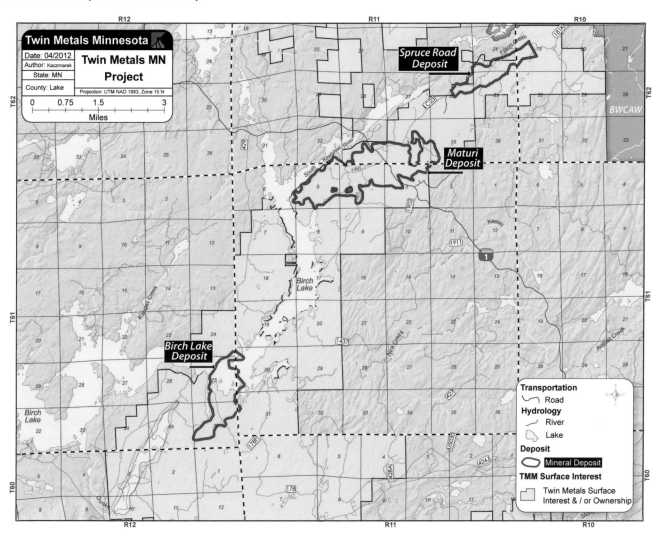

Map of TMM deposits and land holdings.

COPPER, NICKEL, PGMS EXPLORATION

In addition to PolyMet and TMM, other companies are actively exploring the Duluth Complex for copper, nickel, PGMs, and other minerals. Between 2011 and 2018, DMC USA LLC, Encampment Minerals, HTX Minerals, Kennecott Exploration Co., Minerals Processing Corp., MMG USA, Prime Meridian Resources, and Teck American Inc. (Teck) had active exploration drilling programs in the Duluth Complex and other areas of northern Minnesota.[14] Teck, a subsidiary of Canadian-based Teck Ltd., holds mineral leases on the largest known copper/nickel deposit, the Mesaba deposit, which lies between the PolyMet's planned NorthMet mine and TMM's Birch Lake deposits.

TITANIUM

The presence of titanium was first discovered in northeastern Minnesota in the late 1800s. In 1958, ilmenite (titanium-iron oxide) deposits, located along the western edge of the Duluth Complex just east of Hoyt Lakes, were identified and are estimated to be the largest high-grade ilmenite deposits in North America. In the 1990s, other deposits were also discovered in the southern part of the Duluth Complex during exploration for copper and nickel.

Titanium oxide produced from the ilmenite is the predominant white pigment used in paints, paper, and plastics. In addition, titanium is essential in aerospace, military, and medical applications.

The presence of impurities reduces the value of Minnesota's ilmenite ore to the point where it was not profitable to mine. However, in 2017, following a $600,000 grant from the IRRRB and the University of Minnesota, research conducted by the University of Minnesota's Natural Resources Research Institute (NRRI) and a Canadian research firm successfully developed a process to remove the impurities from the ilmenite and produce a pigment-grade titanium dioxide in a pilot plant.

Erie's facilities, a birthplace of Minnesota's taconite industry, may one day process other important minerals.

ERIE'S VISION CONTINUES

The story of Erie began with the discovery of the hard, low iron content rock called taconite in northeastern Minnesota in 1865. The taconite formation extended for 120 miles and contained the high-grade natural ore deposits that were first mined in 1892 and made the Mesabi Range famous. In 1922, Mesabi Iron made the first commercial attempt to mine and process taconite near Babbitt. Mining the hard rock and recovering the fine-grained iron particles was challenging, and the project was financially unsuccessful.

However, it was realized that Minnesota's natural ores were being rapidly depleted, and that the vast deposits of taconite would have to be mined and processed if the United States was to supply its own iron ore to its steel industry. Pickands Mather's leaders recognized this and in 1930 began investigating taconite's potential by initiating taconite exploration and participating in research. They envisioned that American ingenuity and perseverance would find ways to unlock the valuable iron from taconite and build a whole new iron mining industry that would keep the nation independent and self-sufficient in this critical raw material for years to come.

In 1940, Pickands Mather began the move from vision to reality by forming Erie and establishing the Hibbing Lab to develop an economically viable taconite process. This effort resulted in the construction of PreTac in 1948 where it was demonstrated that a taconite plant designed using full-scale equipment could be continuously and successfully operated. The equipment, process, and operating procedures were proven, and in 1953 construction of the Erie Commercial Plant, the world's largest, began.

To produce the 330 million tons of pellets for its owners, the innovative, skilled, hardworking employees of Erie overcame many challenges resulting in improved equipment design, new technology, and procedures that have been applied throughout the mining industry. In addition, Erie contributed to the overall economy by paying taxes, supporting satellite businesses, and providing good wages, training, and opportunities for generations of employees, who established lasting communities with many social and recreational opportunities.

Erie and its dedicated employees demonstrated that, with optimism toward the future, the journey from vision to reality can be accomplished. But as shown by the attempts of Mesabi Nugget, Magnetation, and Minnesota Steel to expand Minnesota's iron ore industry that goal is not easily achieved. The vision to develop the Duluth Complex minerals is not without its challenges. If the efforts of PolyMet, TMM, and others toward making their visions a reality are successful, a new industry will emerge that will make Minnesota a world leader in providing essential metals following the path of Erie Mining Company that brought "New Life for Minnesota's Iron Range."

IN HONOR AND IN MEMORY OF AND OTHER DONORS

As part of the Erie Mining History project, individuals and organizations who had a special connection to Erie were offered the opportunity to recognize family members, friends, or associates who either worked at or provided services to Erie or were part of the local community. In the following section, those honored or memorialized are shown in bold text, below the name(s) of those donating to fund the project at one of four contribution levels: Iron ($5,000 and greater), Taconite Pellet ($2,000 to $4,999), Concentrate ($500 to $1,999), or Taconite Ore (less than $500).

IRON LEVEL CONTRIBUTIONS

Al and Erika Hodnik
In Memory of
Paul Bajda

Patricia Barnes, Daniel DeVaney,
Nancy Hegelheimer
In Memory of
Fred DeVaney

Al and Erika Hodnik
In Memory of
Frank Hodnik

Al and Erika Hodnik
In Memory of
Frank Kermouner

Brian Maki
In Memory of
Vern and Barbara Maki
(Hoyt Lakes Mudders)

The Hoyt Family
In Memory of
Elton Hoyt 2nd and Elton Hoyt III

OTHER CONTRIBUTORS

Barr Engineering Co.
Canadian National Railway Co.
Cleveland-Cliffs, Inc.
William E. and Mary F. Conway
Dyno Nobel Inc.
Hallett Dock Company
Ronald and Joyce Hein
Industrial Lubricant Company
Krech Ojard & Associates, Inc.

Mars Supply
Mielke Electric Works Inc.
Minnesota Power Foundation
MN Legacy Grant (via Ely-Winton
Historical Society)
Pickands Mather Group
PolyMet Mining
Steel Dynamics, Inc.
The Interlake Steamship Company

TACONITE PELLET LEVEL CONTRIBUTIONS

Lila Klaras and Family
In Memory of
Robert C. Klaras

Elaine Melby-Moen
In Memory of
Gordon Melby Sr. and Gordon Melby Jr.

Jim Scott
In Honor of Electrical Mentors
Ed Prinkkila, Al Harris, Les Deppe, Vern Dahl, Gordon Kindberg, John McLean and Ted Williams

Laurie and Joe Eichelberger
In Memory of
Telford "Ted" and Audrey Williams

OTHER CONTRIBUTORS

Deborah and Roger Anderson
KeyBank Foundation
Robert McInnes

Northeast Technical Services, Inc.
Robert L. Oldenburg
Road Machinery & Supplies Co.

CONCENTRATE LEVEL CONTRIBUTIONS

John Nyhus
In Honor and Memory of
**Adrian "Ace" Barker, Don Markwardt,
Gil Menuey**
Restarting the Frozen Tailing Thickeners

Their Children
In Honor of
**Dr. Richard Barnes and
Mrs. Patricia DeVaney Barnes**

Billy Bauman
In Memory of
William S. "Bill" Bauman

Paul, Bruce & Ralph Berge
In Memory of
O. T. and Bernice Berge

Charles Farrell
In Memory of
Sue and Bill Farrell

The Forsman Family
In Memory of
Elmer Forsman

Mike and Marilyn Healy, Grace Healy Shields,
Jane Healy Bradford and Rick Bradford
In Memory of
John H. "Jack" Healy

Larry Osvold
In Honor of
Ronald L. Hein

Kathleen, Jennifer, and Elizabeth Hein
In Memory of
Mabel Virginia Hein

Tim Lerick, Cindy Lerick, Anne Lerick Csargo,
and Keith Lerick
In Memory of
George E. Lerick

Tanner & Kari Hein
In Memory of
Fran Lindholt

Tanner & Kari Hein
In Honor of
Virg Lindholt

Lynn and Tom Niemi
In Memory of Suppliers
**McKenzie Machine Company
Gillespie Machine Company
Danielson's Machine Company**

Greg and Barb Walker
In Honor of
Our Fathers - Taconite Miners

Ed Prinkkila Family: Ellen, Mary Ann, Lee
In Memory of
Edward E. Prinkkila

Wife, Johanna and their children: Sharon,
Rhonda, Ray Frank, Roland, Lorna,
Rodger, Melanie, Joni and Jonathan
In Memory of
Ray "Shifty" Schaefbauer

The Shields Family
In Memory of
Neil E. Shields

Joe Welch Equipment Company
In Honor of
Jerry and Betty Welch

Patricia D. Whaley
In Memory of
Henry P. Whaley

OTHER CONTRIBUTORS

JoAnne Coombe
Edwards Oil Inc.
Fort & Company, PA
GPM, Inc.
Hoyt Lakes Chamber of Commerce
International Union of Operating Engineers
Local No. 49
Komatsu Mining Corp.

Clyde and Cathy Nelson
Essential Health Northern Pines Medical Center
RMS TriTec, Inc.
Tufco, Inc.
Twin Metals MN LLC
Greg and Barb Walker
Henry and Sarah Wheeler Historical
Awareness Fund

TACONITE ORE LEVEL CONTRIBUTORS

Donald, Kim and Cheryl Alguire
In Honor of
The Alguire Family

SOAR
(Steelworker Organization of Active Retirees)
Chapter 33-4
In Honor and Memory of
All Erie employees

Donald J. Purkat
In Honor of
All PM and Erie Employees

David Hamalainen
In Memory of
All the great people with whom I worked

Edward and Anita Alto
In Memory of
Norman Alto

Jim and Kathy Anderson and Jean Mann
In Memory of
Eugene G. Anderson

Janice and George Brown, Karoline Anderson,
Bonnie and Larry Soular,
Steve and Janet Anderson
In Memory of
Nels Anderson

Marion Anderson
In Memory of
Orlyn "Orlie" Anderson

Butch and Pat Hakala
In Memory of
Frank L. Anzelc

Bill Armstrong
In Honor of
Bill Armstrong Family

The Arola Family
In Memory of
Paul E. Arola

Patty Axelsen and Cheryl Axelsen Jones
In Memory of
Ralph Axelsen
(Electrician 1957–1986)

The Bakka Family
In Memory of
Clemens Bakka

The Barker Family
In Memory of
Adrian "Ace" Barker

Rosalyn Barker
In Memory of
Dave Barker

Dona Basso
In Memory of
John Basso

John P. Baxter
In Memory of
**Bob Baxter, Milt Hall, Harold Flann, Fred
Lofquist, Bill Koski, and Lila Maki**

Kathy and Ron Beise
In Memory of
Gary Beise

Kathy and Ron Beise
In Memory of
Russell Beise

Carl Parin
In Honor of
Kenneth Berens

Bill and Virginia Moraski
In Memory of
Rudolph "Rudy" Beloy

Dan and Heidi Furry
In Memory of
Joe and Maria Bradach

The Burich Family
In Memory of
Robert Burich

Roy E. and Viva Kuitunen
In Memory of
Winston W. Cadwell and Onni W. Kuitunen

Marie Carleton White
In Memory of
Robert P. Carleton (Locomotive Foreman)
and Beverley A. Carleton (Labor)

Jane Carlson
In Honor of
Jim Carlson Family

Brian Chapman and Donna Chapman
In Memory of
Donald "Moose" Chapman

Mary, Liam and Elizabeth Conger
In Honor of
William "Bill" Conger

Diane Darbo Sandvig
In Memory of
Cleve Darbo

The Paul Stark Family
In Memory of
Maynard Desjardin

Teresa and Sarah Fredrickson
In Memory of
**Jerome Deutsch, Richard Fredrickson, and
Raymond Fredrickson**

Ben and Taylor Dickinson
In Honor of
Sam Dickinson

Joe Sokoloski
In Memory of
Betty and Orlin Ekeroth

Carol Ellis
In Memory of
John "Jack" Ellis

Peter Esala
In Memory of
Sulo M. Esala

Roberta, Jill, and Lisa Farrell
In Memory of
Robert H. Farrell

Alan Fazio
In Memory of
Joseph and Carol Fazio

Lois Ferguson
In Memory of
Eugene Ferguson

Larry and Teresa Lehtinen
In Honor of
Jim Flanagan
(Instrument Repairman)

Paul Flann, Linda Nelson, and Anita Shontz
In Memory of
Harold Flann

Carol Bowman
In Memory of
Thomas J. Flatley

Dan and Heidi Furry
In Memory of
Charles and Lorraine Furry

Jeanette Washburn
In Memory of
Paul P. Gaul

Dennis and Donna Peterson
In Honor of
Joseph Glatch Family

The Guy Girls
In Honor of
Jean and Jack Guy

The Guy Girls
In Honor of
Jean Guy and the Fabric & Craft Shop

Butch and Pat Hakala
In Memory of
Wayne N. Hakala

David R. and Melaine Hamalainen
In Honor of
David B. Hamalainen

Edward and Anita Alto
In Memory of
Melvyn "Doc" Halliday

Michael and Marilyn Healy
In Memory of
Jack and Betty Healy

Ronald Hein Family
In Memory of
Dale Lee Hein

Robert and Shannon Hill
In Memory of
Auno J. Hill

Robert and Shannon Hill
In Honor of
Gordy Hill

Jeff and Terrie Hockin
In Memory of
E. Bruce Hockin

Mick and Marie Hogan
In Memory of
Don and Mary Joyce Hogan

Jim and Mary Koepke
In Memory of
Gerald Holmes

Dennis Holst
In Honor of
Bruce Holst

Dennis Holst
In Honor of
David Holst

Dennis Holst
In Honor of
David G. Holst

Dennis Holst
In Honor of
Deane Holst

Dennis Holst
In Honor of
Dennis Holst

Dennis Holst
In Honor of
Donald Holst

Dennis Holst
In Honor of
John Holst

Tasha Rostvit, Raylon Honkola,
and Barrett Honkola
In Memory of
Rodney Honkola

Leonard and Dolores Hotakainen
In Memory of
William and Helga Hotakainen

Lauren and Linda Jallen
In Memory of
Selmer B. Jallen

Jim and Nancy Janzig
In Honor of
The Janzig Family

Jamie L. Brown
In Memory of
Everett L. Jenkins

Pat, Mike, and Mark Johnson
In Honor of
Ralph G. Johnson

The Johnson Family
In Memory of
Ronald M. Johnson

Evelyn E. Johnson
In Honor of
Walter E. Johnson

Micheal P. Jokinen and Alan L. Jokinen
In Memory of
Paul G. Jokinen

Elaine Jurkovich
in Loving Memory of
Greg Jurkovich

Vivian Williams
In Memory of
Ervin G. Kahtava

Terry and Mary Roses
In Memory of
Mike Karich

Perry Roberts
In Memory of
Ernie H. Keil

Their Family
In Honor of
Clifford and Beverly Kippley

SOAR
(Steelworker Organization of Active Retirees)
Chapter 33-4
In Memory of
Eldon Kirsch

Jim and Mary Koepke
In Memory of
Donald Koepke

Ralph G. Johnson
In Memory of
Terry Koivisto

Ralph G. Johnson
In Memory of
John Kowalski

Bill and Linda Larson and Bob and Collene Finc
In Memory of
John Krezel

Wayne and Marlene Kuitunen
In Honor of
Elmer A. Kuitunen and Oliver O. Omlid

Art Lee Jr.
In Memory of
Arthur E. Lee

Linda C. Lee and Family
In Memory of
Owen F. Lee

Robert Lehto Family
In Memory of
Robert Wilho Lehto

Donna LeMay Pluskwik
In Honor of
Donald B. LeMay
(LTV Steel)

JoAnne Musich
In Honor of
Richard "Dick" LeMoine and Tom Musich

Ralph G. Johnson
In Memory of
Dave Liimatta

Jim & Jennifer Swedberg
In Honor of
Virgil & Frances Lindholt

Ardell "Art" Thoreson
In Honor of
Locomotive Maintenance Department

The Loe Family
In Memory of
Terry Loe

Karen (Loken) Rebb
In Memory of
Glen and Vivian Loken
(Loken's Bakery & Coffee Bar)

William Lopac Family:
Anne, Lori, John, Todd, Joey
In Memory of
William J. Lopac

Mary Mackey and Family
In Memory of
John Mackey

Charlie, Gail, Jayne Mahovlich
In Memory of
Charlie Mahovlich
(Maintenance Foreman, General Shops)

Don and Carole Babich Majerle
In Memory of
Tony and Mary Majerle

Cindy and Paul Hayden
In Memory of
Jim Marshall

Tracy and Tom Welch and
Dawn and Owney Koski
In Memory of
John "Jack" and Virginia Marvel

Chuck and Bob Mattson
In Memory of
Herbert Mattson

Catherine Maxwell
In Memory of
Samuel Maxwell
(Husband)

Mike McGinnis
In Memory of
Donald McGinnis

McNulty Family
In Memory of
Boyd and Inez McNulty

The Meckola Family
In Memory of
Herbert Meckola

Merrie L. Healy
In Memory of
Gordon S. Melby Jr.

Merrie L. Healy
In Memory of
Gordon S. Melby Sr.

Martina, Mark, Tim, Tony, and Paul Michals
In Memory of
Bernard Michals

Thomas, Anthony and Bernard Michels
In Memory of
George Michels

Theresa Miklausich
In Memory of
Robert Miklausich

Mike, George, and Bill Mohar
In Memory of
Frank Mohar

The Monson Family
In Memory of
Russell Monson

The Howard Monsrud Children
In Honor of
Howard B. Monsrud

Bill and Virginia Moraski
In Memory of
Jack Moraski

Bill and Virginia Moraski
In Memory of
Jim Moraski

Daniel and Anne Moravitz
In Memory of
James Moravitz

Linda Myklebust
In Memory of
Arthur and Lillian Moscatelli

Gregory and Suzanne Niemi
In Memory of
Leonard Niemi

The O'Donnell Family
In Memory of
Gerald O'Donnell

The Family of Clayton Okstad Sr.
In Memory of
Clayton Okstad Sr.

Violet V. Olson and Chris Sandvig
In Memory of
Harold K. Olson

Ralph G. Johnson
In Memory of
Kenny Olson

Earl and Marcia Wilkins
In Memory of
Jack Oman

Flossy Opitz
In Memory of
Sam Opitz

Larry and Shonna Orso
In Memory of
Louis Orso

Tom and Tracy (Ostby) Baldrica
In Memory of
Walter "Bob" Ostby

Bob Paavola Family
In Memory of
Elmer and Muriel Paavola

Carl Parin
In Honor of
Ronald Parin

Carl Parin
In Memory of
William Parin

Robin and David Chrisinger
In Memory of
Ernie Pavlisich
In Honor of
Robert Pavlisich

Frank A. Planton Family
In Honor of
Frank A. Planton
(42 years)

Caron Porthan, John Porthan, and
Lisa Porthan Carson
In Memory of
Sheldon Porthan

Richard Poupard's Children
In Honor of
The Poupard Family

Edward and Anita Alto
In Memory of
Larry Powell Sr.

Donald J. Purkat
In Memory of
Anton (father) and Cyril A. (brother) Purkat

Angela Radniecki and Family
In Memory of
Dean Radniecki

Shirley Randall
In Memory of
Don Randall

James, Wendy, and Anna Rauzi
In Memory of
Dominic C. Rauzi
(Assistant General Foreman)

Brian and Cyndee Forsman, Tony and
Sandy Addy, and John Rent
In Memory of
The Leonard Rent Family

The Ritala Family
In Memory of
Robert Ritala

Kurt Jopke
In Memory of
Ron Rolando

Connie Krtinich
In Memory of
Vernon Rolfson

Cheri Lemberg, Chris Green, Corrie Odland,
Michelle Bedard, and Family
In Honor of
Gary Ruckdaschel

Arthur R. Ruohonen
In Memory of
Arthur A. Ruohonen

Gary Saatela
In Memory of
Einard Saatela

Sharon Sainio Erickson
In Memory of
Lauri P. Sainio

Kitty
In Memory of
Darwin Oscar Salo

Mary Jo Salo and Family
In Memory of
Ronald E. Salo

Bryan and Teresa Sandnas
In Memory of
Clarence C. Sandnas

Dennis Sandstrom
In Honor of
David A. Sandstrom,
(St. Louis County Mine Inspector)

Dennis and Rosie Sandstrom
In Memory of
Jack Sandstrom
(AGF Mining Services)

The Sandvig Family
In Honor of
Morris E. Sandvig

The Children of Paul G. Schweiger
In Memory of
Paul G. Schweiger

Mike Servaty and Sue Bowman
In Memory of
Arnold Servaty

Family of Ronald Setniker
In Memory of
Ronald Setniker

Erie History Project Team
In Memory and Honor of
Frank Settimi

Ronald Hein
In Honor and Memory of
Frank Settimi

Gregory Skalko
In Memory of
John Skalko

Gregory Skalko, Carol Skalko, Susan Malevich,
and Barb Skalko Kern
In Memory of
Steve Skalko

The Skubic Family
In Memory of
John F. Skubic

Ed Casey, Jim Kozar, Elroy Rafferty
In Memory of
Joe Smilanich

The Family of Kenneth Smith
In Honor of
Kenneth Smith

Sharon M. Lakso
In Memory of
Rudy & Mary Smolich

SOAR
(Steelworker Organization of Active Retirees)
Chapter 33-4
In Honor of
SOAR Chapter 33-4 Members

Jim and Sue Sowers
In Memory of
Leonard Sowers

The Sprink Family
In Honor of
LeRoy Sprink

Dorothy and R. J. Stanek
In Memory of
Ronald Stanek

Kathy Sterk
In Honor of
Mike Sterk

Virginia Area Historical Society
In Honor of
Mike Sterk

The Stiles Family Children
Dick, Ray, Sandy, Gale, John, and Mary
In Memory of
Chuck and Olive Stiles

Greg and Jocelyn Stoch
In Memory of
E. G. Stoch

Mary, Maria, and Allan Strand
In Memory of
Steven Allan Strand

The Studnek Family
In Honor of
Edward and Maria Studnek

Rustlyn Sturgis and Family
In Memory of
James Sturgis

John T. and Lorraine Sullivan
In Memory of
Thomas J. Sullivan
(a 38-year employee)

Pat Surla
In Memory of
Joe Surla

Judy Thomas Malmberg
In Memory of
Clyde and Gudrun Thomas

Tony and Tina Thoreson
In Honor of
Ardell Thoreson

The Toms Family
In Memory of
Philip K. and J. Beryl Toms

Bob and Dottie Morton
In Honor of
Dave Trach with gratitude for his
many years of dedicated service
to his Local Union and Fellow Workers

Linda Tyssen
In Honor of
Gerry Trunzo

Kathryn (Venaas) Oliver
In Memory of
Burton K. Venaas

Mary Palcich Keys
In Memory of
Jerry Verrant

Louis Vesel, Joy Hill, and Melissa Reek
In Memory of
Bryan Vesel

Joy Hill and Melissa Reek
In Honor of
Louis J. Vesel

Carl and Pat Christmann
In Memory of
George C. Watts and Bernard "Spike" Borgel

Jane Wertanen
In Honor of
Alvin Wertanen

Margaret Batteen, Joan Lien,
Jeanette Westbrook, Jim Westbrook,
and Virginia Westbrook
In Memory of
Katherine and Charles Westbrook

Jessie Erickson, Sandra Fladeland, Ann Vreeland,
and Nancy Fladeland
In Honor of
James Westbrook

Pat and Ralph Johnson
In Memory of
Hugh F. Whitcraft

Ronald Hein
In Honor and Memory of
Telford "Ted" Williams

His Family
In Memory of
Telford Alan Williams

Hoyt Lakes Water Carnival Committee
In Memory of
Telford Alan Williams

Kelly and Bill Merchant
In Honor of
Telford Alan Williams

Matt & Sarah Royseth
In Memory of
Ted Williams

T. Alan Williams
In Honor of
Telford Williams

The Dunder Family
In Memory of
Telford and Audrey Williams

Roger and Jan Hull
In Memory of
Telford and Audrey Williams

Margaret and Julie Joynes
In Memory of
Telford and Audrey Williams

Barbara and Larry Sommer
In Memory of
Telford and Audrey Williams

John and LuAnn Vassar, Marilyn Hamilton,
Dean and Dawn Mooney, and Joan Wallis
In Memory of
Telford and Audrey Williams

Vivian Williams
In Memory of
Ernest E. Williams

Gary Witzman
In Memory of
Roman and Ron Witzman

Arvin Zilmer's Family
In Honor of
Arvin Zilmer

The Family of John Zins
In Memory of
John Zins

ANONYMOUS IN MEMORY OR HONOR OF

Ron Carpenter

Al Cochran

Dick Cooney

Paul Fontecchio

Robert Irmen

Arno Keller

Jerry Kohrt

Ron Leonzal

Toivo Maki

Bob Miklausich

John Reigle

John Smolich

Erv Stoch

John Sullivan

Greg Walker

OTHER CONTRIBUTORS

David C. Carlson

Kathleen Hein

Roger and Jeanette Hull

IDEA Drilling, LLC

James and Nancy Janzig

Bradley C. Jenson, CFP

Mary Whaley Kiefer

William D. Kirsch

L & M Radiator, Inc.

Arthur M. Lee

Tom and Lynn Niemi

Tom Novak

Larry Osvold

Stephen & Carole Quaife

Elroy and Judy Rafferty

Eugene and Mary Lou Voelk

Ziegler CAT

GLOSSARY
TECHNICAL TERMS AND COMPANY NAMES

Term/Company	Usage in This Book
Accounting	Erie staff department responsible for preparing budgets, tracking costs and paying bills (payroll and accounts payable).
Additive Plant	Erie Plant Site building that housed unloading, preparation, storage and handling facilities for commodities added to the process such as bentonite added in balling and flocculants added to thickeners.
Administration Building	Constructed outside of restricted mine and plant areas to provide offices for staff departments, dispensary and the General Manager's Office.
Agglomerating	Erie operating department responsible for pelletizing iron ore concentrate, incorporating concentrate storage, filtering, balling, indurating and pellet handling and storage.
Agglomeration	The process of binding together small particles to form larger clusters.
Anaconda	Anaconda Copper Mining Company: Contracted to design and supervise construction of the Commercial Plant.
Area 1 Shops	Erie mine maintenance facility that initially served western mining area (Area 1) and was later expanded to perform the maintenance on all large mining equipment.
Area 2 Shops	Erie mine maintenance facility that initially served eastern mining area (Area 2) and provided service for mine locomotives.
Armco	Armco Steel Corporation: 50 percent owner of Reserve.
Arrowhead	Arrowhead Constructors (Winston Bros. Company, C. F. Lytle Company, Green Construction Company, Donovan Construction Company, and Missouri Valley Constructors, Inc. joint venture): Contracted to construct Mainline Railroad subgrade.
Ball Mill	A Grinding Mill that uses hardened alloy steel balls as media. Erie's second stage of grinding and its regrind mills were Ball Mills.
Balsam Junction	Erie railroad location (MP 3.7) where trains carrying ore from the Dunka Mine were switched from the Mainline Railroad track to the Marshalling Yard.
Beneficiation	The process of improving the grade (iron content) of an ore by removing impurities through concentrating using screening, gravity, flotation or magnetic separation.
Bethlehem	Bethlehem Steel Corporation: Initial partner in Erie (45 percent).
Biwabik Iron Formation	Iron formation found in northeastern Minnesota, a sedimentary deposit averaging about 1-1/2 miles wide and extending roughly 120 miles in length and varying in thickness from 500 feet to 700 feet, consisting of four layers, the Upper Slaty, Upper Cherty, Lower Slaty and Lower Cherty.
BLA	Basic Labor Agreement: The agreement between the USWA and steel companies that negotiated basic wages and benefits at the national level.
Blast Pattern	1) The design of a blast that specifies the location and depth of individual drill holes. 2) The area in the mine where holes were drilled into rock in which explosive were placed and detonated to break up the rock so that it could be loaded into ore cars or trucks and ultimately delivered to the Coarse Crusher.
Bond Holders	Entities that purchased Eire's first mortgage bonds: Aetna Life Insurance Company, Chemical Corn Exchange Bank, Connecticut General Life Insurance Company, The Equitable Life Assurance Society of the United States, Metropolitan Life Insurance Company, New York Life Insurance Company, The Northwestern Mutual Life Insurance Company, Provident Mutual Life Insurance Company of Philadelphia, Sun Life Assurance Company of Canada and Bethlehem.
Briquetting	Agglomeration method that uses mechanical pressure and a binder to mold fine particles into small brick-like blocks (briquettes).
Bunker C	Heavy tar-like fuel oil (No. 6 oil) originally used to fuel Erie's shaft furnaces.

Term/Company	Usage in This Book
C-424	ALCO Century-424: Locomotive model used at Erie primarily for Dunka Mine to Plant Site ore haul on the Mine Railroad.
CDP	Career Development Program: A company/union agreed-to program available to Erie employees that provided the opportunity to obtain post-secondary education and vocational skills.
CE	Combustion Engineering: Manufacturer of the steam generating equipment at the Power Plant.
Certificate of Necessity	Awarded by the Defense Production Administration to permit Erie to produce up to 10.5 million tons of pellets each year. Also carried provisions allowing an accelerated tax depreciation write-off on up to $298 million of the construction costs.
Cliffs	Cleveland-Cliffs Inc.: Iron ore mining and management company—acquired Pickands Mather in 1986 and assumed management of Erie—acquired Erie's non-mining assets in 2001.
Coarse Crusher	Erie Plant Site building that housed railcar dumping into two parallel crushing lines each consisting of one 60" gyratory primary crusher and four 36" gyratory secondary crushers and discharging to 60" wide conveyors that fed the Coarse Ore Bins.
Coarse Ore Bins	Erie ore storage facility in the Fine Crusher that received crushed ore from the Coarse Crusher and fed fine crushing lines.
Colby Lake	Source of new water for the Plant Site.
Cook	George F. Cook Construction Co.: Contractor that constructed PreTac.
Commercial Plant	Erie's iron ore processing facility with a design based on the work done at the Lab and PreTac intended to produce a commercially acceptable pellet.
Concentrate	Finely ground iron-bearing particles that remain after separation from silica and other impurities in the ore.
Concentrator	Erie Plant Site building that originally housed twenty-seven parallel mill lines, each consisting of one rod mill, one ball mill, cyclones and three stages of magnetic separation (rougher, cleaner, finisher) fed by the Fine Ore Bins. Concentrate was pumped to the Pellet Plant and tailing to the Tailing Basin. Expanded to thirty-six mill lines in 1967. Regrind Mills and Fine Screening added in 1967–1971. Two mill lines were removed, and flotation added in 1987.
Contracting Out	Having non-Erie employees working at Erie or vendors fabricating items used at Erie.
Control Tower	Taconite Harbor Dock structures (A and B) from which ore boat loading was controlled.
Cramer Tunnel	1,860-foot-long railroad tunnel, cut through a solid rock hill located about ten miles west of Taconite Harbor.
Crusher	Mineral processing equipment that reduces the size of ore. Crushers break the ore by compressing it so that it fractures into smaller pieces.
CTC	Centralized Train Control: A train control system that was implemented on a section of Erie track used jointly by the Mine Railroad (Dunka Mine ore) and Mainline Railroad.
Cyclone	Mineral processing equipment that separates ore particles based on size—slurry is pumped into the cyclone and a vortex is created within the cyclone separating particles by size—smaller lighter particles flow upward to the overflow and larger heavier particles flow downward to the underflow.
Davis Tube	Davis Tube Magnetic Separator: An instrument invented by E. W. Davis that provided a quick and easy method for determining the amount of iron that could be recovered from taconite.
Defense Production Administration	Established by the federal government on January 3, 1951, with the mandate to oversee the nation's defense production program, which included materials production, setting of production quotas, and establishing the mix of defense and civilian production.
DEIS	See EIS.
Demonstration Plant	Facility using full-scale process equipment to attempt to prove the commercial feasibility of a process.
Diamond Shamrock	Diamond Shamrock Corporation: A shipping, chemical manufacturing, and oil refining company that owned Pickands Mather from 1969 to 1972.

Term/Company	Usage in This Book
Dispensary	Erie on-site medical facility that provided routine annual physicals and emergency service. Staffed by the East Range Clinic.
Diversion Works	Erie facility that regulates the flow of water between Colby Lake and Whitewater Reservoir.
Dock	Erie Taconite Harbor facility that could hold 100,000 tons of pellets delivered by rail from the Plant Site and load those pellets into ore boats for delivery to steel mills.
Dravo	Dravo Corporation: Contracted to construct the Taconite Harbor Dock.
DRI	Direct Reduced Iron: A value added iron product (i.e. +95 percent iron content) that can be used in Electric Arc Furnaces (EAFs).
Drill Core	Rock sample obtained from exploration drills that have a hollow bit and stem.
DM&IR	Duluth Mesabi and Iron Range Railway: Provided rail service to PreTac and the Erie Commercial Plant.
Duluth Complex	Geological formation of igneous rock in northeastern Minnesota containing copper, nickel, cobalt, and PGMs.
Dunka Junction	Erie Mainline Railroad location (MP 9.4) where Mainline Railroad and Dunka Mine tracks meet.
Dunka Mine	Mining Area 8 located twenty-two miles east of the Plant Site with its own shop facility and two Loading Pockets. Supplied higher grade ore from 1965 to 1994.
EAF	Electric Arc Furnace: A steelmaking process that uses electric current to melt scrap iron or value added iron products instead of iron ore pellets.
EAW	Environmental Assessment Worksheet: First step in the environmental review process—describes the project and presents the potential environmental, social and economic impacts—for mining projects it determines the scope of the EIS.
EIS	Environmental Impact Statement: Describes a project, presents alternatives (including not to proceed with the project) and studies potential environmental and social impacts associated with the project and alternatives. The process starts with a preparation Draft EIS (DEIS) followed by a Supplemental DEIS and then a Final EIS (FEIS).
Empty Tracks	Railroad tracks that received empty pellet trains returning from Taconite Harbor.
ENA	Experimental Negotiating Agreement: An agreement between the USWA and steel companies to resolve basic steel issues by binding arbitration rather than nationwide steel strike.
Erie	Erie Mining Company: Formed in 1940 by Pickands Mather, Bethlehem, Interlake and Youngstown to find a way to use taconite.
Essar	Essar Steel Minnesota LLC: Purchased MSI in 2007 and started construction of a steelmaking complex near Nashwauk, MN in 2008—filed for bankruptcy in 2016 without completing the project.
Evergreen	Evergreen Trailer Park: Temporary housing for construction workers and early Erie employees near the Plant Site from 1953 to 1958.
F9	EMD (Electro-Motive Division of General Motors Corporation) F9: Locomotive model used at Erie primarily for Mainline Railroad.
FEIS	See EIS.
Filter	Mineral processing equipment that removes most of the water from a process stream and leaves the solids.
Fine Crusher	Erie Plant Site building that housed six parallel crushing lines consisting of one standard cone crusher followed two shorthead cone crushers fed by the Coarse Ore Bins and discharging to 60"-wide conveyors that fed the Fine Ore Bins. Expanded to seven lines in 1967.
Fine Ore Bins	Erie ore storage facility in the Concentrator that received crushed ore from the Fine Crusher and fed the rod mills.
Fired Pellets	Final Pelletizing Plant product—Green Balls of taconite concentrate hardened by heating in the pelletizing process to become taconite pellets.
Flotation	Concentration method that uses air bubbles that attracts a mineral in an ore slurry to float fine particles of that mineral to the top.

Term/Company	Usage in This Book
Flowsheet	A schematic diagram of processing equipment and conveyance systems (conveyors/chutes/bins for solids and pipes/pumps/tanks for liquids) intended to depict a specific process.
Fluxed Pellets	A type of pellet that include a small percentage of finely ground limestone, which permits more efficient melting in the blast furnace. Starting in 1987, Erie attempted to produce fluxed pellets in two shaft furnaces but was unable to stabilize operation to allow full plant conversion.
Foley	Foley Constructors of Minnesota, Inc. (Foley Brothers, Pleasantville, NY, and Foley Brothers, St. Paul, MN, joint venture): The general contractor for original construction at the Plant Site and Power Plant.
Galbreath	John W. Galbreath & Company: Contracted to manage the construction of Hoyt Lakes and the Taconite Harbor townsite.
General Shops	Erie Plant Site building that included Blacksmith Shop, Car Shop, Electric Shop, Instrument Shop, Locomotive Shop, Machine Shop, Weld Shop, etc.
Gibson	Gibson and Roberts, Inc: Contracted to bore the Cramer Tunnel.
Grade	1) The mineral content in the ore—low grade means low mineral content. 2) The slope of a road or railroad track. 3) The path that a railroad track follows.
Grate-Kiln Machine	Equipment that performs the heating step of pelletizing. Green balls are fed onto a moving grate where they are dried, partly hardened and discharged into a heated rotating kiln to complete the hardening and produce fired pellets.
Green Balls	Soft balls of taconite concentrate formed in the pelletizing process by an inclined rotating drum or disk that are hardened by heat to become taconite pellets.
Grinding Mill	Mineral processing equipment that reduces the size of ore. A large horizontal rotating cylinder containing hardened alloy steel rods or balls as grinding media. The tumbling action of the media breaks the ore. Ball Mills can grind ore into finer particles than a Rod Mill.
Harrold	J. D. Harrold Company: Constructed first 200 houses in Hoyt Lakes.
Heating Plant	Erie building that housed the equipment that provided hot water for heating and compressed air to other Plant Site buildings.
Hinsdale	Location of Erie railroad's interchange with the outside railroad—originally DM&IR.
HBI	Hot Briquetted Iron: A value-added iron product (i.e. +95 percent iron content) that can be used in EAFs.
Hot Metal	In steelmaking, the molten iron that is produced by a blast furnace from iron, coke and limestone.
Hot Relief	Paying equipment operators fifteen minutes overtime per shift to be relieved at the equipment rather than being transported to and from the mine reporting buildings at shift change.
Hovland	Hovland Trailer Park: Temporary housing for Taconite Harbor construction workers.
Hoyt Lakes	New town constructed as part of Erie's commercial project.
Hy-Rail	Highway vehicle that has guide wheels for rail operation used for track inspections and to transport track maintenance crews and equipment.
Industrial Engineering	Erie staff department that performed economic assessment of capital projects, evaluated wear part life, performed time studies and calculated incentive pay.
Industrial Relations	Erie staff department that hired and trained employees, maintained employee records, and coordinated labor-management relations.
IPC	Integrated Process Control: The LTV Steel corporate-wide quality management program that was implemented at Erie. It increased employee involvement in the process by promoting individual action within agreed operating procedures with the objective of reducing variability and improving the process.
Interlake	Interlake Iron Corporation: Initial partner in Erie (10 percent).
Interlake Steamship	Interlake Steamship Company: Formed by Pickands Mather in 1913—became a privately held company in 1987—Great Lakes bulk carrier operator. Delivered first load of coal to Taconite Harbor and transported the first and last load of pellets from Taconite Harbor.

Term/Company	Usage in This Book
IRRRB	Iron Range Resources and Rehabilitation Board: State agency intended to diversify the economy of northern Minnesota. Initiated a program to help fund major projects at taconite producers, including Erie's Super Pocket and magnetic separator upgrades.
Jig Concentrator	Mineral processing equipment that separates ore particles in a process stream based on their density.
JPM-1	First commercial jet piercing drill developed by Erie and Linde and field proven at PreTac.
J&L Steel	Jones and Laughlin Steel Corporation: Component of LTV Corporation acquired Youngstown with its 35 percent ownership of Erie in 1978.
Kiewit	Peter Kiewit Sons: Contractor that performed earthwork (overburden stripping, site clearing and railroad grade) at PreTac, site preparation at the commercial plant and Hoyt Lakes, and breakwater and railroad construction at Taconite Harbor.
Knox	Erie railroad location that was the start on the Mainline Railroad (MP 0).
Kuhn, Loeb & Co	Kuhn, Loeb & Co.: Investment firm that arranged for sale of bonds to finance Erie commercial plant construction. *See* Bond Holders.
Lab	Erie Research Laboratory also called Erie Lab, Hibbing Laboratory, Pickands Mather Laboratory, Cliffs Research Laboratory: Established in 1940. Closed in 2001.
Linde	Linde Air Division of Union Carbide: Developed jet piercing drill and supplied oxygen to Erie produced at an on-site Oxygen Plant.
Link Belt	Link Belt Corporation: Provided Erie's pellet stacking system, which was at the time the world's largest conveyor belt stacking machine for stockpiling, and ore boat loading system.
LMPT	Labor Management Participation Team: A voluntary program that encouraged involvement of employees in problem solving and process improvement.
Load Tracks	Railroad tracks that received loaded pellet cars to be assembled into trains for shipment to Taconite Harbor.
Loading Pocket	A facility that receives ore from mine haulage trucks, stores and transfers the ore into railcars.
Local Agreement	Labor agreement between Erie and LU 4108 agreed to by those parties.
Local Issue	A labor issue specific to Erie and LU 4108.
Low Grade Ore Stockpiles	Storage sites at a mine for material that is not economic at the time of mining, but may become worthwhile in the future.
Lower Cherty	Layer in the Biwabik Iron Formation—generally ore—average 120 feet thick at Erie.
Lower Slaty	Layer in the Biwabik Iron Formation—generally waste rock.
LTV Steel	LTV Steel Corporation: Bankruptcy in December 2000 resulted in immediate closure of LTVSMC (Erie) and liquidation of LTV Steel.
LTVSMC	LTV Steel Mining Company: Subsidiary of LTV Steel—the new name of Erie when LTV Steel acquired 100 percent ownership of Erie.
LU 4108	Local Union 4108: USWA local which represented Erie's union employees.
Magnetation	Magnetation LLC (Magnetation Inc. and AK Steel Corporation joint venture): Built three plants on the Mesabi Range to recover iron by processing natural ore tailing. The plants operated from 2008 to 2016.
Magnetic Separator	Mineral processing equipment that separates ore particles in a process stream based on their magnetic properties.
Magnetic Survey	Measurements of the earth's magnetic field used to explore for magnetic iron deposits.
Mainline Railroad	Erie rail equipment and track that was used to transport pellets from the Plant Site to the Dock at Taconite Harbor.
Maintenance	Erie operating department that performed equipment service, repair and rebuilding functions.
Marshalling Yard	Erie railroad facility where the thirty-six-car trains from the Dunka Mine were divided into two eighteen-car trains for delivery to the Coarse Crusher.

Term/Company	Usage in This Book
Materials Management	Erie staff department that provided purchasing functions.
Mesaba	First incorporated village on the eastern Mesabi Range—location of natural ore mines and taconite deposits that became part of Erie.
Mesabi Iron	Mesabi Iron Company: Operated first taconite mine and plant near Babbitt that produced iron sinter product from 1922 to 1924—was not commercially successful. Nearly thirty years later the facilities served as a demonstration plant for Reserve.
Mesabi Metallics	Mesabi Metallics Company LLC: Purchased Essar Steel in 2017.
Mesabi Nugget	Mesabi Nugget LLC (SDI/Kobe Steel joint venture): Acquired Erie Areas 1, 2WX, 6 and 9 from Cliffs and constructed and operated a value-added iron plant that processed iron concentrate from external sources (Reserve, Magnetation, Mining Resources) from 2009 until 2015 when operations were suspended.
Mesabi Range	Largest of Minnesota's three major iron ranges (Mesabi, Vermilion and Cuyuna). Erie mined on the eastern Mesabi Range.
Mesh	Mesh number is the number of screen holes per linear inch in a screen. A higher mesh number means a smaller particle will pass through the screen.
Mine Engineering	Erie staff department that developed long- and short-term plans for mining, kept records and provided reports of all materials mined and provided all surveying services.
Mine Railroad	Erie rail equipment and track that was used to transport ore from direct loading shovels or Loading Pockets to the Coarse Crusher.
Mineral Processing (or Ore Dressing)	To upgrade or beneficiate low grade ore by separating the target mineral and removing impurities from the rock.
Mining	Erie operating department that performed stripping, drilling, blasting, loading and hauling functions.
Mining Area	One of twelve mining locations at Erie (1, 1W, 2, 2W, 2WX, 3, 5N, 5S, 6, 8, 9N and 9S). Some had facilities where employees could take lunch and wash up and where mine equipment was parked. Mining Area 8 was also called the Dunka Mine.
Mining Resources	Mining Resources LLC (SDI and Mangnetation joint venture): Built a plant at Chisholm, MN, to supply Mesabi Nugget with iron concentrate recovered by processing natural ore tailing. The plant operated from 2011 to 2015.
MDNR	Minnesota Department of Natural Resources: State agency that issues mining and water appropriations permits and regulates associated activities.
MPCA	Minnesota Pollution Control Agency: State agency that issues water discharge and air emission permits and regulates associated activities.
MP&L	Minnesota Power & Light: Utility that provided electric service to PreTac and the Erie commercial plant—acquired Erie's non-mining assets in 2001.
Moore-McCormack	Moore-McCormack Company: An operator of ocean-going vessels—owned Pickands Mather from 1972 to 1986.
MSI	Minnesota Steel Industries LLC: Announced plans for a steelmaking complex near Nashwauk, MN, in 2005—purchased by Essar in 2007.
Murphy City	Erie facility located at the intersection of State Highway 1 and the Mainline Railroad—was a railroad construction headquarters and later a base for track maintenance.
Nodulizing	Agglomeration method wherein the fine particles are passed through inclined rotary kiln heated by gas or oil. The rotation of the kiln causes the particles to clump together and the heat in the kiln cause them to harden into irregular shapes.
NOLA	Neutron On Line Analysis: A system pioneered at Erie that measured silica in the ore as trains were dumped at the Coarse Crusher. Recognized in 1972 by the Minnesota Society of Professional Engineers as being one of the state's best engineering projects.
Oglebay Norton	Oglebay Norton and Company: A mine management and operating company that acquired the assets of Mesabi Iron and organized Reserve.

Term/Company	Usage in This Book
OIMC	Oliver Iron Mining Company: Iron mining subsidiary of U.S. Steel—was the largest producer of natural ore on the Mesabi Range.
Old Ad	Old Administration Building: TCC headquarters—later used as offices for Erie's Maintenance, Mining and Industrial Relations (Training) Departments.
Ore	Rock that has enough mineral content to be mined and processed to recover the targeted mineral for economic benefit. In taconite ore the iron content ranges from 25 percent to 35 percent with most of the remaining rock being silica.
Ore Dressing	Erie operating department that performed crushing, grinding, separation and tailing management functions to produce a concentrate.
Overburden	Sand, dirt, muskeg and boulders that must be removed to access the ore body.
Parsons-Jurden Corporation	Company contracted in 1965 to design and construct Erie's $50 million expansion, which increased annual production capacity to 10.3 million tons and was completed in 1967.
Partridge Lakes Development	Original name for Hoyt Lakes.
Pellet Loading Pocket	Erie Plant Site building that received pellets from the Pelletizing Plant and transferred them to railcars or Pellet Stockpile.
Pellet Stockpile	Erie Plant Site facility that accumulated pellet production awaiting shipment. The stockpile was reclaimed by shovel or front end loader into railcars for shipment to Taconite Harbor.
Pelletizing	Agglomeration method wherein fine particles are rolled into uniformly size balls and hardened by heating. For magnetic taconite, this process results in a chemical change that generates heat and makes the iron non-magnetic.
Pelletizing Plant	Erie Plant Site building that housed twenty-four parallel pelletizing lines each consisting of two filters, one balling drum and one furnace. The lines were fed from the Concentrate Storage Tanks and discharged hardened (fired) pellets to the Pellet Loading Pocket. Expanded to twenty-six lines in 1959 (G section) and twenty-seven lines in 1967 (H Section).
PGMs	Platinum Group Minerals: Minerals that contain the Platinum Group Elements—platinum, palladium, iridium, osmium, rhodium and ruthenium.
Pickands Mather	Pickands Mather & Co.: A mine management, Great Lakes shipping and operating company that organized, developed, managed and operated Erie—acquired by Cliffs in 1986.
Pilot Plant	A test facility using smaller than full scale equipment operated to generate information about the behavior of a process for use in larger facilities.
Plant Engineering	Erie staff department that provided civil, mechanical and electrical engineering services including drafting.
Plant Reservoir	Erie Plant Site facility that held ten million gallons of water for process, potable and fire protection that was supplied from Colby Lake.
Plant Site	Erie facilities near Hoyt Lakes including Commercial Plant, Tailing Basin, shops, pellet handling and storage.
Plant Switching	Erie rail equipment and track that was used to move railcars to and from the Hinsdale interchange, and to and from locations within the Plant Site.
PolyMet	PolyMet Mining Corporation: Acquired Erie's Plant Site and Tailing Basin from Cliffs and initiated the environmental review and permitting for a project to mine and process copper/nickel/PGM ore from the Duluth Complex.
Power Plant	1) Erie coal-fired electric generating facility located at Taconite Harbor with two 75 MW units. A third 75 MW unit was added in 1967. 2) Erie operating department that performed power generation and energy management functions.
PPE	Personal Protection Equipment: Hard hats, safety glasses, hard toe shoes, gloves, ear protection, respirators and protective clothing worn by employees.
PreTac	Erie Preliminary Taconite Plant: Commercial scale 200,000 ton per year taconite plant located three miles north of Aurora. Built to optimize the process and equipment for the Commercial Plant. It was the world's only commercial taconite plant from mid-1948 to mid-1952 and operated until 1958.

Term/Company	Usage in This Book
Process Development	Erie staff department that coordinated activity with the Hibbing Lab and provided quality control and process improvement services.
Public Relations	Erie staff department that provided internal communications to employees and coordinated official communications with the public and government officials.
Railroad and Harbor	Erie operating department that performed pellet transport to and coal transport from Taconite Harbor and ore boat loading and coal boat unloading functions.
Republic	Republic Steel Corp.: 50 percent owner of Reserve.
Reserve	Reserve Mining Company: Formed based on the assets of Mesabi Iron in 1939 by Oglebay Norton. Started construction of mine at Babbitt and plant at Silver Bay in 1950. Armco and Republic 50/50 owners.
Roasting	An initial step in a two-stage iron ore separation method, in which heat is applied to a non-magnetic ore to make the iron magnetic so that it can be separated magnetically from impurities.
Rod Mill	A Grinding Mill that uses long hardened alloy steel rods as media. Erie's first stage mills were Rod Mills.
RS-11	ALCO (American Locomotive Company) RS-11: Locomotive used at Erie primarily for Mine Railroad.
S-12	Baldwin (Baldwin-Lima-Hamilton Corporation) S-12: Locomotive used at Erie primarily for Plant Switching.
Safety	Erie staff department that managed the accident prevention program, security, fire brigade, industrial hygiene, dispensary and personal protection. Coordinated safety inspections by federal and St. Louis County inspectors and conducted joint Union/Management safety and housekeeping inspections.
Scholes	T.F. Scholes, Inc.: Contracted to construct the Mainline Railroad track.
Screen	Mineral processing equipment that separates ore particles based on size—smaller particles fall through the screen openings and larger particles move across the screen.
Screw Classifier	Mineral processing equipment that separates particles in a slurry based on size. The larger, heavier particles settle out and are pulled by a rotating screw up an inclined trough to the discharge. Smaller, lighter particles flow over the back of the trough.
SDI	Steel Dynamics Inc: EAF-based steelmaker that was a partner in Mesabi Nugget and Mining Resources.
Shaker Table	Mineral processing equipment that separates ore particles based on their density. An ore slurry flows onto a tilted vibrating table with diagonal grooves or riffles. Particles of different sizes and density will collect in different riffles and be guided off the table and be collected.
Sintering	Agglomeration method during which fine particles are heated to fuse the particles together and form large irregular shapes to facilitate handling and further processing.
Skillings	*Skillings Mining Review*: A weekly mining industry trade magazine established in 1912.
Slurry	Moving mixture of water and solids.
Snake Trail	Local name for CHWxxx, the initial access road from Aurora to the Plant Site.
Snare	Frederick Snare Corp.: Contracted for design of Dock facilities.
Spiral Concentrator	Mineral processing equipment that separates fine ore particles based on their density. An ore slurry flows downward in a vertical spiral. The heavier ore particles move to the center of the spiral and the lighter particles move to the edge of the spiral where they are collected separately.
Stacker	Erie Plant Site rail-mounted conveyor system that transported pellets to the Pellet Stockpile.
Stelco	Steel Company of Canada: Partner in Erie commercial project (10 percent)
Stripping	Mining activity that removes the overburden (surface) and rock covering the ore.
Super Pocket	A Loading Pocket with almost twenty times the storage capacity and three times the railcar loading rate as compared to Erie's original Loading Pockets.
Surface	Surface Combustion Corporation: Designed Erie vertical shaft pelletizing furnaces.

Term/Company	Usage in This Book
Taconite	A very hard, abrasive gray-black rock that contains about 30% iron in the form of magnetite—a magnetic iron mineral. Term first used in 1891 by Minnesota state geologist, Newton H. Winchell, to describe the rocks of the Biwabik Iron Formation.
Taconite Amendment	Minnesota amendment passed in 1964 intended to stimulate further investments in the taconite industry by ensuring that the industry would be taxed fairly. Passage spurred new plant construction and expansion of existing plants including Erie.
Taconite Harbor	Erie facilities at Two Islands on the shore of Lake Superior—Power Plant, Dock, harbor and townsite.
Tailing	Small rock particles containing little or no magnetic iron, which are removed during concentration. Most of the separation is done with magnetic separators.
Tailing Basin	Erie Plant Site area for storing tailing. The solids settled and were stored in the basin and the water returned to the Concentrator for reuse. Silica is the main mineral constituent of Erie's tailing which totaled about two-thirds of the ore mined.
TCC	Taconite Contracting Corporation: Formed by Erie's partners to manage construction of the commercial project.
Thickener	Mineral processing equipment that reduces the amount of water in a slurry—large tank where most of the solids settle to the bottom and are removed and the overflow is collected and recycled.
Trackmobile	Vehicle designed for railcar movement that can travel on rails or roads. Used at Erie to pull pellet cars through the Pellet Loading Pocket and for railcar movement at the General Shops and Additive Plant.
Traveling Grate Machine	Equipment that performs the heating step of pelletizing. Green balls are fed onto a moving grate where they are dried and hardened to produce fired pellets.
TRC	Taconite Recreational Club, Inc.: Recreational organization for employees and their families formed by Erie employees.
Tripper Car	A conveyor belt machine that travels on rails above material storage bins that transfers the material from the conveyor belt into the bins.
Trommel	Mineral processing equipment that separates based on size—a screen attached to rotating equipment. Smaller objects pass through the screen openings and larger objects are carried to the end of the device. At Erie, a balling drum trommel separates small green balls for recycling as seed balls.
Trow	Erie railroad location (MP 42) where there was a siding where full-length trains could pass. Named in honor of Conrad Trowbridge, Manager of Railroad and Harbor Construction.
United	United Engineers and Constructors, Inc: Contracted to erect the Power Plant and began construction in the spring of 1955.
Upper Cherty	Layer in the Biwabik Iron Formation—generally ore—average 175 feet thick at Erie.
Upper Slaty	Layer in the Biwabik Iron Formation—generally waste rock.
USACE	United States Army Corps of Engineers: Federal agency that issues permits for harbor dredging and draining or filling wetlands, and regulates associated activities.
USWA	United Steelworkers of America: International union to which Erie's local union was affiliated.
U. S. Steel	U.S. Steel Corporation.
Vertical Shaft Furnace	Equipment that performs the heating step of pelletizing. Green balls are fed into the top of the furnace and move downward against an ascending flow of hot gases, which first dry and then harden the green balls into fired pellets that exit the bottom of the furnace. Erie pioneered the use of vertical shaft furnaces.
Waste Rock	Rock does not have enough mineral content to be ore but must be removed to access ore.
Westinghouse	Westinghouse Electric Corporation: Provided the steam-driven turbines and electric generators at the Power Plant.
Whitewater Reservoir	Erie facility that stored water for plant use.
Youngstown	Youngstown Sheet and Tube Corporation: Initial partner in Erie (35 percent).

The figures on the following pages show the planned equipment layout in Erie's original main processing plant buildings—Coarse Crusher, Fine Crusher, Concentrator, and Pelletizing Plant.

Figure G-1 shows the Coarse Crusher building looking east. Railcars dumped ore into the 60-inch primary crusher and then the ore was split to feed four 36-inch secondary crushers (two of the secondary crushers are located behind the two shown). The "inch" dimension indicates the largest size of ore that can be handled by the crusher. The Coarse Crusher reduces the size of the ore from 60 inches across to 6 inches or less.

Figures G-2 and G-3 show the Fine Crusher building looking east and down (plan view), respectively. G-2 shows one of two trippers (one is located behind the one shown) that distribute coarse ore along the bins, three of the six fine crushing lines (three are located behind the three shown) each with a single standard crusher feeding two shorthead crushers and the conveyor that collects the fine ore from the shortheads. The Fine Crusher reduces the size of the ore from six inches to smaller than three-fourths of an inch. G-3 shows the six fine crushing lines with the tripper cars and bins between as well as the Repair Bay at the left.

Figures G-4 and G-5 show the Concentrator building looking south and down (plan view), respectively. G-4 shows one of two traveling trippers (one is located behind the one shown) that distribute fine ore along the bins, one of the twenty-seven mill lines (twenty-six are located behind the one shown) each with a single rod mill feeding a single ball mill, the three sets of magnetic separators, and the pipes and pumps that move the concentrate and tailing throughout the plant. G-5 shows the twenty-seven mill lines with the tailing thickeners at the bottom and the Repair Floor in the center.

Figures G-6 and G-7 show the original Pelletizing Plant building looking south and down (plan view), respectively. G-6 shows two of twelve thickeners (ten are located behind the two shown) that feed thickened concentrate to the filters and four of the twenty-four furnace lines (twenty are located behind the four shown) each with two filters, a single balling drum, and a single furnace. G-7 shows the twenty-four furnace lines with the concentrate storage tanks running down the center of the plant.

Figure G-8 shows an early conceptual layout of the Plant Site. The actual construction varied significantly as the design was refined—the Pelletizing Plant's shape and orientation changed, and the Oxygen Plant, Employment Office, and Main Office were relocated to the south. Note that the Coarse Crusher is labeled Primary Crushing Plant; the Fine Crusher is labeled Secondary Crushing Plant. The lighter lines indicate potential expansion of the Secondary Crushing Plant and Concentrator.

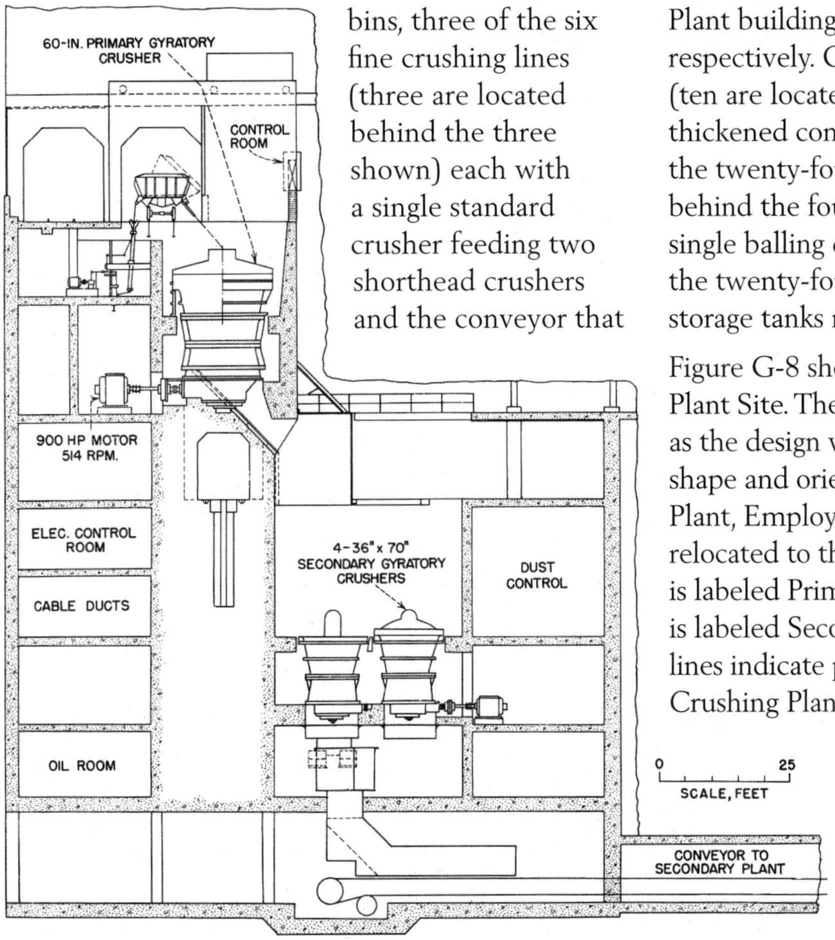

Figure G-1 Coarse Crusher Building Looking East
The coarse crushing line shown became the South Coarse Crusher when the second line (North) was added to the left.

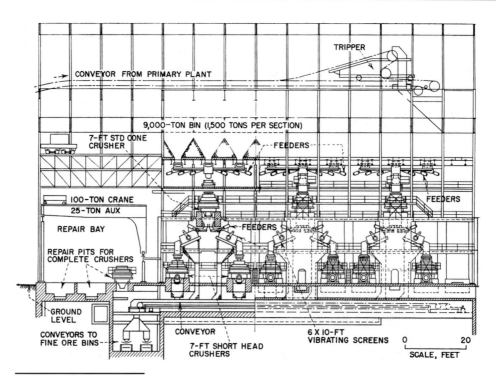

Figure G-2 Fine Crusher Building Looking East

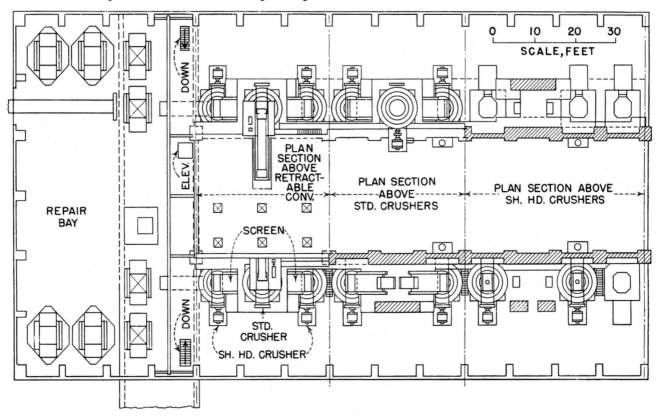

Figure G-3 Fine Crusher Building Looking Down
The three fine crushing lines at the top are E1 to E2 starting at the Repair Bay. Those at the bottom are W1 to W3. The expansion added W4 to the right of W3.

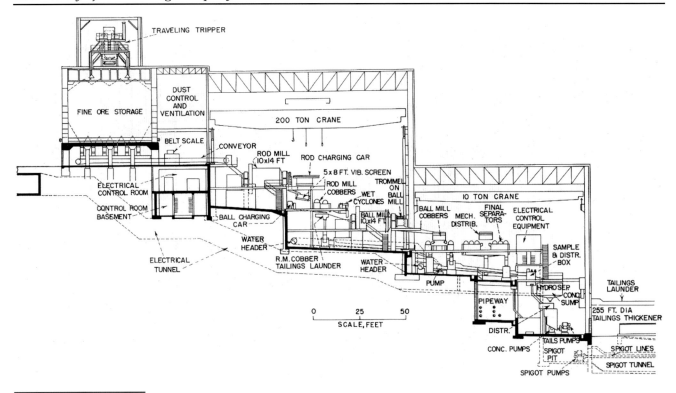

Figure G-4 Concentrator Building Looking South

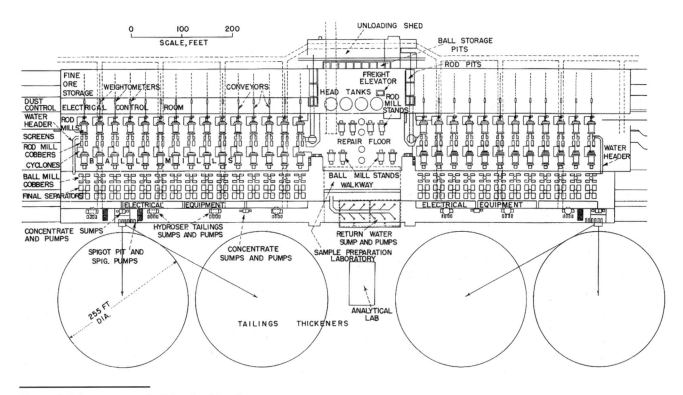

Figure G-5 Concentrator Building Looking Down
The twelve mill lines to the right of the Repair Floor are 1S to 12S. The fifteen to the left are 1N to 15N. The expansion added 16N to 24N to the left of 15N.

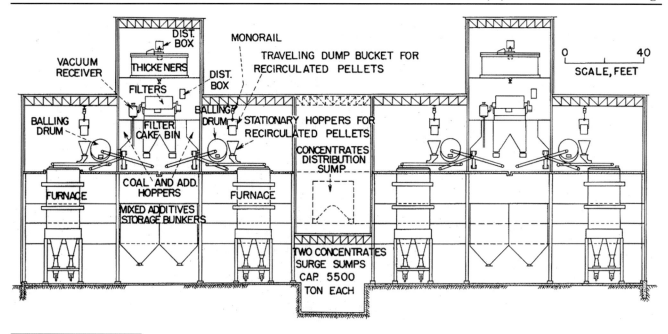

Figure G-6 Pelletizing Plant Building Looking East

ERIE MINING COMPANY

ORIGINAL 24 FURNACE AGGLOMERATING PLANT
OPERATING FLOOR PLAN GENERAL ARRANGEMENT

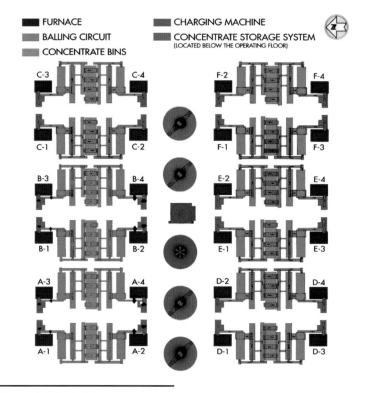

Figure G-7 Pelletizing Plant Building Looking Down
Original twenty-four furnaces with added furnaces G-1, G-2, and H-1
not shown

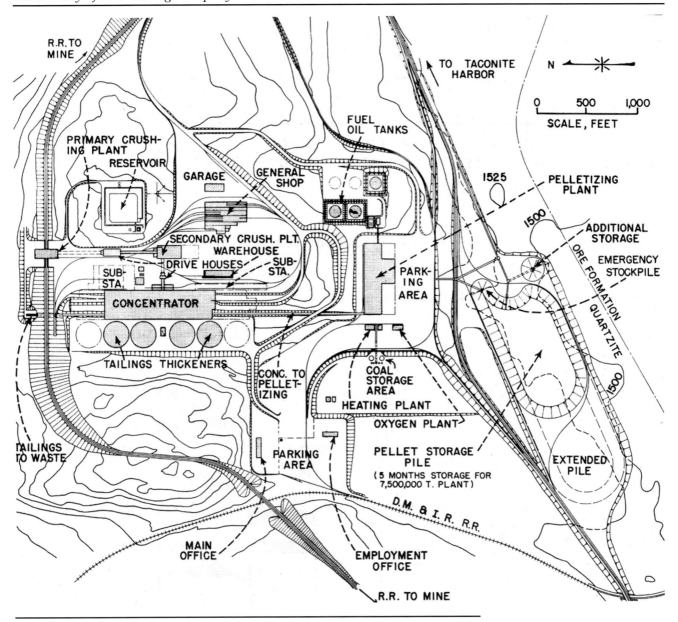

Figure G-8 Conceptual Plant Site Layout
The actual construction varied significantly as the design was refined—the Pelletizing Plant's shape and orientation changed, and the Oxygen Plant, Employment Office, and Main Office were relocated to the south. Note that the Coarse Crusher is labeled Primary Crushing Plant; the Fine Crusher is labeled Secondary Crushing Plant. The lighter lines indicate potential expansion of the Secondary Crushing Plant and Concentrator.

LIST OF ORAL HISTORY INTERVIEWEES

The following people contributed their personal stories through Oral History Interviews which were a significant part of the research effort for writing this book. A transcription of their interviews and a digital voice recording are located at:

1. St. Louis County Historical Society in Duluth, MN
2. The Iron Range Research Center at the Minnesota Discovery Center in Chisholm, MN
3. The Public Libraries in Hoyt Lakes, Aurora, and Ely, Minnesota

Using the access instructions included on page 338 of this book, you can find a link to a text copy of the interviews.

Akins, Dorothy	Postmistress, U.S. Post Office, Hoyt Lakes, MN
Anderson, Virginia	Buyer, Purchasing
Armstrong, Bill / Ruth	Operation Foreman, Ore Dressing / Spouse
Baland, Jerry	Supervisor, Public Affairs
Barker, Adrian "Ace"	General Foreman, Ore Dressing
Barker, James R.	Chairman – Interlake Steamship and MORMAC Marine Group
Barkley, Tom	General Foreman, Drilling and Blasting
Barnes, Patricia	Spouse of Dr. Richard Barnes
Barteck, Ron	Assistant General Foreman, Rebuild Shop
Bartholomew, Robert "Bart"	Millwright (Welder) and Union Representative
Bauerkemper, Joseph	Professor of Indian Studies U of M Duluth
Bentley, Marlene	Director of Nurses, White Community Hospital
Braaten, Al	Shovel Operator, Mining
Buell, Doug	Mining Engineer, Mine Engineering
Burich, Rebecca	Secretary to the General Manager
Bymark, John	Research Engineer, Hibbing Lab
Carlson, Dave	Electrical Supervisor, Harbor
Casey, Ed	Railroad Car Repairman, Maintenance and Union Representative
Chance, Mayo	Millwright (Welder) and Union Representative
Cicak, Tony (Anton)	Operations Supervisor, Power Plant
Conway, Bill	Vice President, Pickands Mather, Cleveland, OH
Cooper, Dick	Quality Manager, Iron Producing, LTV, Cleveland, OH
Day, Don	Section Manager, Safety and Benefits
DeGrio, Ralph	Electronic Repairman, Electric Shop
DeVaney, Dan	General Foreman, Ore Dressing (Tailing Basin)
Dorn, Ed / Virginia	Crane Operator, Hoyt Lakes Police Officer / Small Business Owner
Dorn, Steve	Senior Coordinator, Training
Doyea, Karen	Owner, "The Mart" Hardware Store in Hoyt Lakes
Ebnet, David	Millwright (Plumber) and Union Vice-President
Eden, Corinne	Millwright (Maintenance Mechanic) and LMPT Facilitator

Evers, Joel — Section Manager, Mining
Flanagan, John — Maintenance Foreman, Agglomerating
Francisco, Larry — Locomotive Electrician, Locomotive Shop
Gardner, David — Public Relations Manager
Gerlach, Bruce — Area Manager, Crusher and Maintenance
Gervais, Ron — Master Trackman-Towerman-Water Tester, Harbor
Godwin, Shirley — Heavy Equipment Operator
Gramstrup, Jessie — Concentrate Attendant, Ore Dressing
Gramstrup, LeRoy — Millwright (Maintenance Mechanic)
Grivette, Barry — Operations Coordinator, Mining
Gruden, Frank — Millwright (Welder)
Hakala, Wayne — Millwright (Maintenance Mechanic)
Hansen, Gary — Supervisor, Power Plant
Haveri, Darwyn — Mechanical Supervisor, Harbor
Healy, Merrie — Hoyt Lakes Resident
Healy, Mike — Industrial Hygienist, Safety
Hein, Ronald — Director, Organizational Development
Hestitune, Dan — Division Manager, U.S. Steel Minntac
Hirsch, Leonard — Lab Technician, Hibbing Lab
Hockin, Charlotte — Spouse of Bruce Hockin, Industrial Engineer
Hodnik, Al — President and CEO, ALLETE Corporation
Hoechst, Ron — Millwright (Maintenance Mechanic) and LMPT Facilitator
Hogan, Mike — Operations Coordinator, Railroad
Hudy, Robert — General Foreman Operations, Agglomerating
Hull, Roger — Superintendent, Ore Dressing
Jallen, Lauren — Section Manager, Agglomerating
Janzig, Jim — Controller, Raw Materials, Flat Roll Finance, LTV Steel
Johnson, Harry — Turbine Attendant, Power Plant
Johnson, Mike — Area Manager, Agglomerating
Johnson, Wallace "Wally" — Employment Supervisor, Industrial Relations
Jones, Dannie — Instrument Repairman, Power Plant
Karish, Bob — Millwright (Maintenance Mechanic)
Kemppainen, John — Millwright (Maintenance Mechanic)
Kiesel, Richard — Research Engineer, Hibbing Lab
Kopp, Marvin — Mobile Crane Operator, Maintenance
Koski, Roy — Mechanical Supervisor, Maintenance
Kozar, Jim — Shovel Operator, Mining and Union President
Kurpius, Jerome (Jerry) — Electrical General Foreman, Maintenance
Lakso, Sharon — Secretary, Steelworkers Union Local 4108
Leciejewski, Val — Track Maintenance, Mainline Railroad
Lehtonen, Art — Training Coordinator, Agglomerating
Lenich, Tom — Section Manager, Process Development
Lenk, Larry — Electrician, Ore Dressing
Lesar, Barry — St. Louis County Mine Inspector
LeTourneau, Tom — Assistant General Foreman, Agglomerating
Maki, Paul — Apprentice Instructor (Welding), Training

Maki, Sylvia	Director of Nurses, White Community Hospital
Markwardt, Don	Assistant Superintendent Ore Dressing
Mattson, Chuck	Area Manager, Human Resources
McGinnis, Mike	Section Manager, Labor and Personnel Relations
McInnes, Robert	President, Pickands Mather
Michels, Tom	Millwright (Maintenance Mechanic) and Union Representative
Mobilia, Richard	Millwright (Welder)
Moen, Elaine Melby	Hoyt Lakes Resident
Monson, Russell	Maintenance Foreman, Ore Dressing
Moraski, Bill	Section Manager, Agglomerating
Morrin, John	Grand Portage Tribal Council Member
Nelson, Clyde	Resident Controller, Accounting
Niemi, Lynn	Senior Accountant, Accounting
Niemi, Tom	Area Manager, Power Plant & Railroad
NRRI	Geologists, Natural Resources Research Institute, Duluth, MN
Don Fosnacht	
George Hudak	
Dean Peterson	
Nygard, Harland	Maintenance General Foreman, Mining
Nyland, Gerald "Jerry"	Assistant General Foreman, Agglomerating
Ohman, Jim, Jon	Evergreen Trailer Park Residents
Okstad, Clayton, Sr.	Maintenance Foreman, Locomotive Shop
Oldenburg, Robert	Legal Consul, Pickands Mather
Overby, Ken	Tire Repairman, Mining
Paavola, Robert "Bob"	Maintenance Coordinator, Ore Dressing and IPC Coordinator
Paavola, Gary	Automotive Maintenance Instructor, Training
Palm, Mike	Electrician, Mining
Pederson, Russ	Buyer, Purchasing
Perala, Mike	Section Manager, Mining and Agglomerating
Peters, Edward	Mining Engineer, Mine Engineering
Peterson, Glenn	Section Manger, Process Development
Petrich, Joe	Operations General Supervisor, Ore Dressing
Plevell, John	Warehouse Issue Clerk, Accounting
Plichta, Bill	Mechanical Engineer, Maintenance
Pospect, Marlene	Mayor of Hoyt Lakes – Marketing Director IRRRB
Prest, Jim	Legal Consul, Pickands Mather Duluth District Office
Pullar, Leo	Locomotive Engineer, Railroad
Purkat, Don	Warehouse, Receiving and Issue
Quaife, Steve	Tractor Operator, Harbor and Union Representative
Rafferty, Elroy	Production Truck Driver, Mining and Union Representative
Rollins, Gerald (Curly)	Maintenance Foreman, General Shop
Ruckdashel, Gary	Mining Engineer, Mine Engineering
Rude, Richard	Production Truck Driver, Mining
Salo, Mike	Maintenance General Foreman, Railroad
Sandvig, Bill	Control Room Operator, Ore Dressing
Saumer, Eugene	Maintenance Foreman, General Shop

Schaefbauer, Ray   Locomotive Mechanic, Locomotive Shop
Schroeder Area Hist Soc   Panel Discussion with Charlie Tice,
Scott, Jim   Area Manager, Technical Services
Seme, Jim   Assistant General Foreman, Rebuild Shop
Settimi, Frank   Superintendent, Agglomerating
Skelton, Mark   Mayor of Hoyt Lakes
Smith, Reed   Railroad Car Repairman, Maintenance
Snetsinger, Jerry   Maintenance Foreman, General Shop
Soular, Pat   Section Manager, Accounting
Stauber, Jim   Senior Coordinator, Safety
Stauber, Jim (Mesabi Miner) Senior Coordinator, Safety
Stead, Malcolm   Millwright (Maintenance Mechanic)
Sterk, Mike   Area Manager, Mining
Stewart, Tom   Millwright (Welder)
Tice, Charlie   Operations Section Manager, Harbor
Tossava, Jim   Blaster, Mining
Walker, Greg   Assistant General Manager
Wahlgren, Terry   IPC Manager, General Manager's Office
Watson, Kristine   Regrind Attendant, Agglomerating
Watson, Pat   Locomotive Mechanic, Locomotive Shop
Weiberg, Carol   Plant Oiler, Ore Dressing
Welch, James   Owner, Hoyt Lakes Drug and Variety Store
Westbrook, Jim   Millwright (Welder)
Whaley, Pat   Spouse of Henry Whaley, Pickands Mather Vice President
Wilkins, Earl   Section Manager, Plant Engineering
Williams, Ted   Superintendent, Maintenance
Winkelaar, Karel   Coordinator, Agglomerating
Youngman, Dave   Forester, Mine Engineering
Zilmer, Arvin   Locomotive Engineer, Railroad

INFORMATION LINK
TO THE ERIE MINING COMPANY HISTORY PROJECT

Research Database, Oral History Transcriptions and the Educational Package

Documents, Engineering Drawings and Maps, Photos and Oral History Interview Transcriptions gathered during the development of this book have been preserved and organized via the Erie Mining History Project Digital Archive. To explore the Archive please visit St. Louis County Historical Society website's News and Resource tab, at **www.thehistorypeople.org/news-and-resources**, and click on the ***Erie Mining History Project Digital Archive*** featured post.

The copyright and related rights status of the research documents contained in the research database has been reviewed; however, we are unable to make a conclusive determination as to the copyright status of each Item. Please refer to the organization that originated the documents for more information. Your use of the documents is only permitted by the copyright and related rights legislation that apply.

An Educational Package based on this book has been developed and is available free of cost to educators and their students. For more information about this Educational Package contact the Iron Mining Association of Minnesota (IMA) by Email at **info@taconite.org.**

CREDITS
FOR PHOTOS, MAPS, AND CHARTS

Unless noted below all photos/illustrations are from Erie files located at the Minnesota Discovery Center, the Hoyt Lakes Public Library, and the Iron Range Historical Society, as well as various personal collections including those of Anne Libbey Clayton, Ron Hein, S. Ward Huntley, Tom Michels, Frank Settimi, and Dave Youngman.

CHAPTER ONE	
Arthur d'Arazien Industrial Photographs, ca. 1930–2002, Archives Center, National Museum of American History.	Page 15 lower left
Doug Buell	Page 30 upper left
Iron Range Historical Society	Page 18 upper left, Page 29, Page 36, Page 37, Page 31 middle left
Krech Ojard & Associates, Inc.	Page 15 middle right, Page 16, Page 19, Page 20 top, Page 20 middle, Page 20 bottom, Page 22 top, Page 22 bottom, Page 30 bottom, Page 32 top, Page 33, Page 34 top, Page 34 middle left
Library of Congress	Page 18 middle left
Minnesota Historical Society	Page 34 lower right
Mike Sterk Collection	Page 31 lower left
Michigan Technological University – Industrial Archeology Image Archive	Page 15 lower right
Postcard	Page 24
Tom Novak Collection	Page 23 top
Tom Niemi	Page 18 upper right, Page 18 middle upper right, Page 18 middle lower right, Page 18 lower right
Lake Superior Maritime Collection – University of Wisconsin Superior	Page 27 middle left
Vein of Iron: The Pickands Mather Story (Cleveland: The World Publishing Company, 1958)	Page 17
CHAPTER TWO	
Pioneering with Taconite (St. Paul: Minnesota Historical Society, 1964)	Page 45
Skillings Mining Review	Page 38
CHAPTER THREE	
Krech Ojard & Associates, Inc.	Page 49, Page 53 bottom, Page 54 top
Pioneering with Taconite (St. Paul: Minnesota Historical Society, 1964)	Page 61
Vein of Iron: The Pickands Mather Story (Cleveland: The World Publishing Company, 1958)	Page 54 bottom left

CHAPTER FOUR	
Krech Ojard & Associates, Inc.	Page 62, Page 63 bottom
Pioneering with Taconite (St. Paul: Minnesota Historical Society, 1964)	Page 64

CHAPTER FIVE	
Doug Buell	Page 96 bottom, Page 126 lower left
Doug Buell Collection	Page 96 middle right
Krech Ojard & Associates, Inc.	Page 93 bottom, Page 100 top, Page 101 top, Page 105, Page 129
Tom Niemi	Page 115 middle right, Page 128
Insurance by North America	Page 106

CHAPTER SIX	
Doug Buell	Page 151, Page 168 top, Page 173 middle left, Page 176 upper left, Page 176 upper right, Page 176 middle left
Doug Buell Collection	Page 179 upper left
David Schauer	Page 131 upper right
Krech Ojard & Associates, Inc.	Page 137 bottom, Page 141, Page 145 bottom, Page 155 bottom, Page 163
Mike Sterk Collection	Page 160
Tom Novak Collection	Page 132 lower right, Page 133 upper left
Tom Niemi	Page 166 lower left, Page 176 lower right

CHAPTER SEVEN	
Doug Buell	Page 181 second from top, Page 181 second from bottom, Page 181 bottom, Page 182 middle, Page 183 lower right, Page 184 top, Page 184 middle, Page 185 lower right, Page 186 top, Page 186 middle, Page 186 bottom, Page 187 upper right, Page 187 middle left, Page 187 lower left, Page 191 lower left, Page 191 middle right, Page 194 bottom, Page 195 middle left, Page 195 middle right, Page 195 bottom, Page 197 middle right, Page 197 bottom, Page 198 top, Page 198 lower right, Page 199 upper left, Page 199 middle left, Page 199 lower right, Page 201 middle right, Page 202 upper left, Page 202 upper right, Page 203 middle left, Page 205 top, Page 212 lower left, Page 223 upper right, Page 223 bottom
Doug Buell Collection	Page 184 bottom, Page 213 lower left
Krech Ojard & Associates, Inc.	Page 182 bottom, Page 192–193 bottom, Page 210 top, Page 218 top
Lake Superior Railroad Museum	Page 187 lower right
S. Ward Huntley	Page 212 lower right

Tom Niemi	Page 182 top, Page 191 upper right, Page 191 lower right, Page 194 upper left, Page 194 upper right, Page 194 middle left, Page 194 middle right, Page 195 upper left, Page 195 upper right, Page 196 lower left, Page 196 upper right, Page 200 lower left, Page 200 upper right, Page 200 middle right, Page 200 lower right, Page 204 upper left, Page 204 lower left, Page 204 upper right, Page 210 lower right, Page 211 lower left, Page 211 lower right, Page 215 upper right, Page 219 bottom, Page 224 upper left, Page 224 bottom, Page 225
WABCO	Page 185 upper right

CHAPTER EIGHT

Krech Ojard & Associates, Inc.	Page 227
Tom Michels	Page 233
Internet	Page 239 middle right

CHAPTER NINE

Robert Barthomhew	Page 259 lower left, Page 259 middle right, Page 259 middle left, Page 259 lower right, Page 262 top, Page 262 middle, Page 262 bottom
Belle Storbeck	Page 268
Doug Buell	Page 261 middle right, Page 261 lower left, Page 274 middle right
Essentia Health	Page 261 lower right
Iron Range Historical Society	Page 274 middle left, Page 274 lower left, Page 274 lower right
Krech Ojard & Associates, Inc.	Page 251 lower left
Tom Niemi	Page 264 top, Page 271 upper right
Virginia Anderson	Page 272 upper left, Page 272 upper right

CHAPTER TEN

Doug Buell	Page 286 upper left, Page 286 upper right, Page 286 middle upper right, Page 286 middle lower right, Page 286 lower right, Page 290 upper right, Page 290 lower right, Page 292 bottom, Page 293 bottom, Page 293 top
Duluth News Tribune	Page 283 middle left, Page 290 middle right
Jim Scott	Page 282 upper left
Mesabi Daily News	Page 281 middle right, Page 283 lower left
Mike Sterk Collection	Page 281 upper left, Page 282 lower right, Page 291
Mrs. Sam Maxwell	Page 292 top
Tom Niemi	Page 281 lower left, Page 284 lower left, Page 284 lower middle, Page 284 upper right, Page 284 lower right, Page 289 lower right, Page 295 bottom
Ron Hein	Page 294 lower left, Page 294 middle right

CHAPTER ELEVEN	
Doug Buell	Page 298 lower right
Jim Scott	Page 299
Krech Ojard & Associates, Inc.	Page 304–305 top
PolyMet Mining Corp.	Page 305 bottom, Page 306
Steel Dynamics, Inc.	Page 298 left
Internet	Page 297 lower right, Page 298 upper right, Page 300, Page 301, Page 302 upper left, Page 302 bottom, Page 302 middle right, Page 303, Page 304 middle left, Page 307 upper left, Page 307 bottom
Allete, Inc.	Page 297 top
Krech Ojard & Associates, Inc. with Inset provided by University of Minnesota Duluth's Natural Resources Research Institute	Page 296
GLOSSARY	
Engineering & Mining Journal	Page 328, Page 329 top, Page 329 bottom, Page 330 top, Page 330 bottom, Page 331 top, Page 332
Krech Ojard & Associates, Inc.	Page 331 bottom
GATEFOLD	
Cleveland-Cliffs Inc.	Page G-8 upper right, Page G-8 upper left, Page G-8 middle lower right
Doug Buell	Page G-5 upper middle, Page G-6 lower left, Page G-6 upper right, Page G-6 lower right
Hanna Mining Company	Page G-8 lower right
Skillings Mining Review	Page G-3 one down left
Tom Niemi	Page G-6 top second from left, Page G-6 middle right
Vein of Iron: The Pickands Mather Story (Cleveland: The World Publishing Company, 1958)	Page G-3 lower middle
Internet	Page G-8 middle upper right, Page G-8 middle left, Page G-8 lower left
OTHER	
Doug Buell	Page 11
Krech Ojard & Associates, Inc.	Front Inside Cover, Back Inside Cover
Thomas Leonard Studio	Page 7 left
Ted Williams	Page 7 right

GENERAL INDEX

NAMES INDEX

NOTES

CHAPTER 1

1. George M. Schwartz and George A. Thiel, *Minnesota's Rocks and Waters* (Minneapolis: University of Minnesota Press, 1963), 242.
2. Ibid., 244–250.
3. John W. Gruner, *Taconites of the Mesabi Range Minerals Processing*, November 1966, *14*.
4. Grace Lee Nute, *Lake Superior* (New York: Bobbs-Merrill Co., 1944), 109
5. Stephen Royce, "Geological Description of the Mesabi Range Taconite," *Skillings Mining* Review, November 24, 1945.
6. William E. Lass, *Minnesota, A History* (New York: W.W. Norton and Co., Inc., 1977), 208.
7. Timothy J. LeCain, "The Biggest Mine," *Invention and Technology* (Winter, 2001): 14-1.
8. Donald C. Wright, "Developing the First Taconite," *Lake Superior Magazine* (May–June 1987): 61.
9. Ibid.
10. Ibid., 64–65
11. Donald C. Wright, "The Mesabi Iron Company, Taconite Pioneer," *Range History* (June 1984): 3.
12. Ibid., 6
13. Ibid., 7
14. Marvin G. Lamppa, *Minnesota's Iron Country: Rich Ore, Rich Lives* (Lake Superior Port Cities, 2004)

CHAPTER 2

1. Terry S. Reynolds and Virginia P. Dawson, *Iron Will: Cleveland-Cliffs and the Mining of Iron Ore, 1847–2006* (Detroit: Wayne State University Press, 2011), 165.
2. "The Research Lab," *PM Producer*, March 1954, 3.
3. "Facilities to Experiment with Low Grade Iron Ore," *Skillings Mining Review*, n.d., 1943.
4. AJG to A.D. Chisholm, Typewritten Report on Operations of the Erie Mining Company, January 1 to September 1, 1943, 1.
5. Ibid., 4–5.
6. Ibid., 5.
7. Dan DeVaney interview by Barbara Sommer, April 1, 2015.
8. AJG to A.D. Chisholm, Typewritten Report on Operations of the Erie Mining Company, January 1 to September 1, 1943, 5–6
9. Ibid., 6
10. Ibid., 7
11. Walter Havighurst, *Vein of Iron: The Pickands Mather Story* (Cleveland: The World Publishing Company, 1958), 207.
12. Ibid., 207–208.
13. E.W. Davis, "Iron Ore for the Future," Copyright 1949 by Electric Machinery Mfg. Company, 2.
14. E.W. Davis, *Pioneering with Taconite* (St. Paul: Minnesota Historical Society, 1964), 109–110.
15. "U.S. Steel Studies Low Grade Iron Ore," *Skillings Mining Review*, n.d., 1943.
16. "Oliver Iron Names I.J. W. Johnston as Concentration Engineer," "Oliver Research Laboratory to Be Ready Soon," *Skillings Mining Review*, n.d., 1945.

17. R.L. Bennett, R.E. Hagen, and M.V. Mielke, "Nodulizing Iron Ores and Concentrates at Extaca," *Skillings Mining Review*, October 17, 1953, 1.
18. Fred D. DeVaney, "The Iron Ore Story of the Upper Great Lakes—Past and Future," paper delivered to the Minnesota Chapter, American Institute of Mining Engineers, summarized in *Skillings Mining Review*, January 30, 1971, 4.
19. "Hibbing, Minn. Research Laboratory Devoted to Taconite Industry to Close Down," *Duluth News Tribune*, August 29, 2001.
20. "Fred DeVaney Retires after 23 Years," *PM Producer*, January 1966, 1.
21. "Personal Mention," *Skillings Mining Review*, January 3, 1970, 1.
22. "Minnesota A.I.M.E. and Mining Symposium," *Skillings Mining Review*, February 10, 1973, 20.

CHAPTER 3

1. *Aurora, Minnesota, The First Century, 1903–2003*, 88–89
2. Walter L. Thomte, "The Story of Erie Mining Company," *Mining Engineering* (May 1963): 1.
3. "P.M. & Co. to Erect Plant to Make Iron Concentrate from Taconite," *Skillings Mining Review*. January 25, 1947, 1.
4. Ibid.
5. "Erie Mining Co. Lets Contract for First Taconite Mining," *Skillings Mining Review*, n.d., 1947.
6. "Two Taconite Ore Projects Scheduled for Hearings," *Skillings Mining Review*, n.d., 1947.
7. E.W. Davis, *Pioneering with Taconite* (St. Paul: Minnesota Historical Society, 1964), 118.
8. "Erie Preliminary Taconite Plant Charges to Various Accounts Based Upon Flowsheet Dated Oct. 11, 1947 Corrected to March 15, 1948," 2.
9. "Erie Mining Co. Continues Taconite Research on Mesabi Iron Range," *Skillings Mining Review*, October 22, 1949, 1.
10. Ibid.
11. Ibid.
12. Ibid.
13. Frank Settimi interview by Barbara Sommer, March 31, 2015.
14. "Teamwork on Taconite," *Engineering and Mining Journal*, March 1955, 91.
15. Dan DeVaney interview by Barbara Sommer, April 1, 2015.
16. Ibid.
17. Fred D. DeVaney, "The Concentration and Pelletizing of Taconite, Part I,) *Mineral Processing*, November 1966, 28.
18. Joe Calaman, "History of the Technological Development of the Linde JPM-1 Jet Piercing Machine and Its Impact on the Startup and Growth of the U.S. Taconite Industry," *Range History*, September 1988.
19. Ibid.
20. Ibid.
21. Ibid.
22. Ibid.

23. E. W. Davis, "Iron Ore for the Future," Copyright 1949 by Electric Machinery Mfg. Company, 4.
24. Ibid., 5.
25. Fred D. DeVaney, "The Concentration and Pelletizing of Taconite, Part II," *Mineral Processing*, December 1966, 17.
26. Bill Beck and C. Patrick Labadie, *Pride of the Inland Seas*, 179.

CHAPTER 4
1. Einar W. Karlstrand, "Erie Taconite Finance Plan Is Completed, *Duluth News-Tribune*, n.d., December 1953.
2. Ibid.
3. "Erie Mining to Sell $207 Million Issue for Taconite Project," *Wall Street Journal*, December 4, 1953, 15.
4. Einar W. Karlstrand, "Erie Taconite Finance Plan Is Completed, *Duluth News-Tribune*, n.d., December 1953.
5. Ibid.
6. Taconite Contracting Corporation, Annual Report, 1954, 1.
7. "New Industry for the Iron Range," *Excavating Engineer*, May 1957, 8.
8. Taconite Contracting Corporation, Annual Report, 1954, 1-2
9. Walter Havighurst, *Vein of Iron: The Pickands Mather Story* (Cleveland: The World Publishing Company, 1958), 209-210
10. "New Industry for the Iron Range," *Excavating Engineer*, May 1957, 8.
11. Taconite Contracting Corporation, Annual Report, 1954, 2.
12. Ibid., 3
13. Walter Havighurst, *Vein of Iron: The Pickands Mather Story* (Cleveland: The World Publishing Company, 1958), 210.
14. Taconite Contracting Corporation, Annual Report, 1954, 2.
15. "Erie Mining Co. Taconite Development," *Skillings Mining Review*, September 3, 1955, 2.
16. "TACONITE," *The North America FIELDMAN*, Vol. 14, No. 7, August/September 1957.
17. Dan DeVaney interview by Barbara Sommer, April 1, 2015.
18. Ibid.
19. Ray Schafebuaer interview by Ron Hein, March 22, 2016.
20. Dan DeVaney interview by Barbara Sommer, April 1, 2015.
21. Harry Johnson interview by Tom Niemi, April 12, 2016.
22. Gary Hansen interview by Tom Niemi, March 22, 2016.
23. Ron Gervais interview by Tom Niemi, May 11, 2016.
24. "New Taconite Railroad Crosses Famous Manitou River," *Skillings Mining Review*, n.d., 1955.
25. "Lay Taconite Railroad," *Excavating Engineer*, May 1957, 35–37.
26. "Digging into the Past" *LTV Times*, n.d., 3.
27. Ted Williams interview by Barbara Sommer, May 4, 2015.
28. David Carlson interview by Tom Niemi, April 12, 2016.
29. Ron Gervais interview by Tom Niemi, May 11, 2016.
30. C. M. White, in Hearings before the Subcommittee on the Study of Monopoly Power, Committee on the Judiciary, U.S. House of Representatives (19 April 1950), No. 14, part 4A, 205–247.
31. Ibid.
32. Defense Production Act of 1950, Public Law 774, 81st Congress (8 September 1950), 64 Stat. 798, 50 U.S.C. sect. 2061–2166.
33. Ibid.
34. "Taconite Boom," *Time* magazine, April 28, 1952, 92–94.
35. Ted Williams interview by Barbara Sommer, May 4, 2015.
36. Ibid.
37. News item, *Skillings Mining Review*, n.d., 1955.

CHAPTER 5
1. "The Taconite Project of Erie Mining Company," *Excavating Engineer* magazine, May 1957.
2. Walter L. Thomte, "Mining Methods at Erie Mining Company," 1963 AIME Technical Symposium, Duluth, Minnesota, 6.
3. Ibid.
4. Doug Buell interview by Ron Hein, June 10, 2016.
5. Walter L. Thomte, "Mining Methods at Erie Mining Company," 1963 AIME Technical Symposium, Duluth, Minnesota, 6.
6. Tom Barkley interview by Ron Hein, June 2, 2016.
7. Jim Tossava interview by Ron Hein and Elroy Rafferty, March 16, 2016.
8. Joel Evers interview by Ron Hein, June 28, 2016.
9. Harland Nygard interview by Ron Hein, March 15, 2016.
10. Mike Hogan interview by Tom Niemi, November 5, 2015.
11. Doug Buell, "Erie Mining: Part I—Mine Railroad," *Ore Extra*," v.15, no.2, Fall 2002, 23.
12. Walter L. Thomte, "Mining Methods at Erie Mining Company," 1963 AIME Technical Symposium, Duluth, Minnesota, 4.
13. Joel Evers interview by Ron Hein, June 28, 2016.
14. Fred D. DeVaney, "The Concentration and Pelletizing of Taconite—Part III," *Minerals Processing*, December 1966, 19.
15. Dan DeVaney interview by Barbara Sommer, April 1, 2015.
16. Doug Buell interview by Ron Hein, June 10, 2016.
17. Adrian "Ace" Barker interview by Dan DeVaney, February 22, 2016.
18. Frank Settimi interview by Barbara Sommer, March 31, 2015.
19. Art Lehtonen interview by Ron Hein, May 3, 2016.
20. "Part of Pellet Handling System on Mesabi Range," *Link-Belt News*, July 1959, 1.
21. Gerald "Curly" Rollins interview by Ron Hein, July 27, 2016.
22. Ken Overby interview by Tom Michels, January 13, 2016.
23. Ted Williams interview by Barbara Sommer, May 4, 2015.

24. Ibid.
25. Dan DeVaney interview by Barbara Sommer, April 1, 2015.
26. Ibid.
27. Ibid.
28. Ted Williams interview by Barbara Sommer, May 4, 2015.
29. Gary Paavola interview by Ron Hein, June 3, 2016.
30. Ron Hoechst interview by Jim Westbrook, July 26, 2016.
31. Malcolm Stead Jr. and Myra Stead interview by Jim Westbrook, November 10, 2015.
32. Robert "Bart" Bartholomew interview by Ron Hein, June 20, 2016.
33. Jim Westbrook interview by Ron Hein, July 22, 2016.
34. Greg Walker interview by Barbara Sommer, November 24, 2015.
35. Darwyn Haveri interview by Ron Hein, July 28, 2015.
36. Corinne "Petey" Eden interview by Lynn Niemi and Tom Michels, June 3, 2015.
37. Lynn Niemi interview by Tom Niemi, June 10, 2015.
38. Ibid.
39. Roger Hull interview by Barbara Sommer, May 4, 2015.
40. Doug Buell, "Erie Mining Part 1—Mine Railroad," *Ore Extra*, v.15, no.2, Fall 2002.
41. Ibid.
42. Richard Rude interview by Elroy Raferty, March 11, 2015.
43. Mike Hogan interview by Tom Niemi, November 5, 2015.
44. Ibid.
45. Gerald "Curly" Rollins interview by Ron Hein, July 27, 2016.
46. Tom Niemi interview by Lynn Niemi, May 5, 2015.

CHAPTER 6

1. Peter J. Kakela, "Iron Ore: From Depletion to Abundance," *Science*, v.212, April 1981, 132–136.
2. "Railroad and Truck Haulage Methods Discussed by Panel," *Skillings Mining Review*, December 19, 1970, 19.
3. "99 A.I.M.E. Annual Meeting Held Feb. 15–19," *Skillings Mining Review*, March 28, 1970, 8.
4. Ibid.
5. "Railroad and Truck Haulage Methods Discussed by Panel," *Skillings Mining Review*, December 19, 1970, 19.
6. Henry P. Whaley, "The Story of Erie Mining Company: The Milling Process," *Mining Engineering*, May 1963, 5.
7. Ibid.
8. Erie Mining Company, "The Story of Erie Mining Company," January 1969, p. 14.
9. Ibid.
10. Henry P. Whaley, "Milling Methods at Erie Mining Company," AIME 1963.
11. Vernon Daughney Mining Memories 50 Years.
12. Frederick P. Morawski, "The Story of Erie Mining Company: The Pelletizing Process," *Mining Engineering*, May 1963.
13. Ibid.
14. Frederick P. Morawski, "The Story of Erie Mining Company: The Pelletizing Process," *Mining Engineering*, May 1963.
15. Ted Williams interview by Barbara Sommer, May 4, 2015.
16. Ibid.
17. Frank Settimi interview by Barbara Sommer, March 31, 2015.
18. Ibid.
19. Ibid.
20. Fred D. DeVaney, "The Concentration and Pelletizing of Taconite—Part III," *Minerals Processing*, December 1966, 19, 20.
21. Babcock Wilcox-Steam, 5 Printing, 37 Edition.
22. Fred D. DeVaney, "The Concentration and Pelletizing of Taconite—Part II," *Minerals Processing*, December 1966, 20.
23. Ibid., 20.
24. C.D. Keith, A.J. Carlson, W.H. Tuttle, and H.R. Peterson, "Fine Screening Operations at Erie Mining Co. and Other Pickands Mather & Co. Properties," *Skillings Mining Review*, April 3, 1971, 1, 8–10.
25. "Erie Mining Company reaches 200 million ton production mark," *Erie Times*, Fall 1981.
26. IRRRB Biennial Report, 1962–1964, 1–2.
27. Fred D. DeVaney, "The Concentration and Pelletizing of Taconite—Part III," *Minerals Processing*, January 1967, 23.
28. Ling-Tempco-Vought, Inc. Annual Report 1969.

CHAPTER 7

1. Tom Niemi interview by Lynn Niemi, May 5, 2015.
2. Doug Buell, "Erie Mining: Part II," *Ore Extra*," vol. 15, no. 3, Winter 2003, 16.
3. Ibid., 21.
4. Doug Buell, "Erie Mining: Part I—Mine Railroad," *Ore Extra*, vol. 15, no. 2, Fall 2002, 21.
5. Doug Buell, "Erie Mining: Part II," *Ore Extra*, vol. 15, no. 3, Winter 2003, 16.
6. Robert "Bart" Bartholomew interview by Ron Hein, June 20, 2016.
7. Ron Gervais interview by Tom Niemi, May 11, 2016.
8. Tom Niemi interview by Lynn Niemi, May 5, 2015.
9. Mike Salo interview by Tom Niemi, December 8, 2015.
10. "Iron Horses Hibernate," *PM Iron News*, January 1957, 8.
11. Ibid.
12. Ibid., 9.
13. "Mining Railroad Winterizing Program," September 27, 1963, Henry J. Whaley Papers, IRRC, Box 1.
14. Doug Buell, "Erie Mining: Part II," *Ore Extra*, vol. 15, no. 3, Winter 2003, 16.
15. Darwyn Haveri interview by Ron Hein, July 28, 2015.
16. Ibid.
17. Ibid.
18. Ibid.
19. Ted Williams interview by Barbara Sommer, May 4, 2015.
20. Ron Gervais interview by Tom Niemi, May 11, 2016.
21. Ibid.
22. Gary Hansen interview by Tom Niemi, March 22, 2016.
23. Doug Buell, "Erie Mining: Part II," *Ore Extra*, vol. 15, no. 3, Winter 2003, 21.
24. Doug Buell, "Erie Mining: Part II," *Ore Extra*, vol. 15, no. 3, Winter 2003, 25.
25. "Automatic Car Dumping Apparatus," U.S. Patent 3080075A, March 5, 1963, https://www.google.ch/patents/US3080075.
26. "Taconite Harbor, Where the Best Searches for Ways to Get Better," *PM Iron News*, August 1960, 3.
27. Tom Niemi interview by Lynn Niemi, May 5, 2015.
28. Doug Buell, "Erie Mining: Part II," *Ore Extra*, vol. 15, no. 3, Winter 2003, 16.
29. "Dockmen: Link Between Land and Lake," *PM Iron News*, n.d.
30. "Bethlehem Steel Corp.'s New *mv. Stewart J. Cort*," *Skillings Mining Review*, June 17, 1972, 1.
31. "Super Ore Carrier Arrives at Taconite Harbor," *Erie Times*, May 1972.
32. Ibid.
33. Mike Salo interview by Tom Niemi, December 8, 2015.
34. Doug Buell, "Dinosaurs on the Iron Range," *PM Iron News*, April 1993, 3.
35. Ibid.
36. Ibid.
37. *Skillings Mining Review*, July 3, 1954.

CHAPTER 8

1. Jim Kozar interview by Tom Michels, February 8, 2016.
2. Ibid.
3. Ted Williams interview by Barbara Sommer, May 4, 2015.
4. *New York Times*, December 12, 1977.
5. Glenn Peterson interview by Ron Hein, February 9, 2015.
6. Jim Kozar interview by Tom Michels, February 8, 2016.
7. Tom Michels interview by Jim Westbrook, July 9, 2016.
8. Ed Casey interview by Tom Michels, February 9, 2016.
9. Tom Niemi interview by Lynn Niemi, May 5, 2015.
10. Jim Kozar interview by Tom Michels, February 8, 2016.
11. David Ebnet interview by Tom Michels, November 25, 2015.
12. 1993 BLA, pp. 180–181.
13. Greg Walker interview by Barbara Sommer, November 24, 2015.

CHAPTER 9

1. Taconite Contracting Corp., Annual Report 1954.
2. Erie Mining Company, "Erie Mining Company Offers Challenging Careers in Taconite Development."
3. Carol Weiberg interview by Lynn Niemi, October 13, 2015.
4. Dan DeVaney interview by Barbara Sommer, April 1, 2015.
5. Draft Report—"Community Profiles of Eight East Range Communities"—Minnesota Legislative Reference Library MN Legislature.
6. Elaine Melby-Moen interview by Ron Hein, March 3, 2015.
7. Hoyt Lakes 50 Year Anniversary 1955–2005, 8.
8. Ibid., 16.
9. "Hoyt Lakes Mudders recall its beginning," *Mesabi Daily News*, September 24, 1989.
10. *Hoyt Lakes 50 Year Anniversary 1955–2005*, 73.
11. Telephone interview with Patrick McGauley, Naples, Florida, February 9, 2016.
12. Hoyt Lakes 50 Year Anniversary 1955–2005, 51.
13. Ted Williams interview by Barbara Sommer, May 4, 2015.
14. Ibid.
15. "Open House Featured New 33-Cubic-Yard Shovel," *LTV Steel Mining Company Times*, September 1992, 1, 8.
16. Ibid.
17. Merrie Healy, "Community Assessment of Hoyt Lakes, Minnesota," 1984, 31.
18. "The Young Kid: The Birth of Hoyt Lakes," *Mesabi Daily News*, June 24, 1997.
19. Ed Casey interview by Tom Michels, February 9, 2016.
20. Duane Ramfjord, "The Building of Giant's Ridge," *Home Town Focus*, February 10, 2017.

CHAPTER 10

1. Minnesota Department of Revenue, "History of Minnesota Taconite Production," 1998.
2. Beck and Labadie, *Pride of the Inland Seas*, 239.
3. Greg Walker interview by Barbara Sommer, November 24, 2015.
4. "LTV Corp. Files for Bankruptcy; Debt Is $4 Billion," *The New York Times*, July 18, 1986.
5. Minnesota Department of Revenue, "History of Minnesota Taconite Production," 1998.
6. Ibid.
7. Jim Kozar interview by Tom Michels, February 8, 2016.
8. Ed Casey interview by Tom Michels, February 9, 2016.
9. "Walker Addresses Kiwanis Club," *LTV Steel Mining Company Times*, July 1993, 1.
10. "LTV Mine Closing: What Does It Mean?" *Skillings Mining Review*, November 18, 2000.
11. "LTV Steel Announces Intention to Close Minnesota Iron Mining Operation," LTV Corp. Press Release, May 24, 2000, 1.
12. Ibid.
13. Ibid.
14. "LTV Announces Intention to Close Mine," *LTV Steel Mining Company Times*, July 2000, 1–2.
15. Jim Janzig interview by Ron Hein, August 24, 2015.
16. "LTV Steel Announces Intention to Close Minnesota Iron Mining Operation," LTV Corp. Press Release, May 24, 2000, 1.
17. Ibid.
18. Ibid.
19. Paul Maki interview by Ron Hein, September 4, 2015.
20. Eugene Saumer interview by Jim Westbrook, October 23, 2015.
21. Mike McGinnis interview by Ron Hein, August 25, 2015.
22. Mike Johnson interview by Ron Hein, September 2, 2016.
23. Joel Evers interview by Ron Hein, June 28, 2016.
24. Mike Sterk interview by Barbara Sommer, February 24, 2016.
25. Bruce Gerlach interview by Ron Hein, August 3, 2016.
26. Ibid.
27. Jim Scott interview by Barbara Sommer, February 24, 2016.
28. Trico Steel Company, www.ltvsteel.com.
29. Marlene Pospeck interview by Lynn Niemi, May 28, 2015.
30. LTV Steel Mining Company, "Weekly Management Report," January 10, 2001.
31. Dennis Koschak, "Notice to All Employees," January 3, 2001.
32. Paul Maki interview by Ron Hein, September 4, 2015.
33. Corinne "Petey" Eden interview by Lynn Niemi and Tom Michels, June 3, 2015.
34. Dennis Koschak, "Dear LTVSMC Salaried Employee," February 8, 2001.
35. James Welch interview by Tom Niemi, January 13, 2016.
36. Becky Burich interview by Ron Hein, August 8, 2016.
37. Lee Bloomquist, "Last train rolls away from LTV," *Duluth News-Tribune*, June 23, 2001.
38. Brian Hiti interview by Bill Beck, Eveleth, Minnesota, February 9, 2016.
39. "Paul Wellstone Memorial and Historic Site," https://brucemineincident.wordpress.com/related-places-of-interest-2/paul-wellstone-memorial-and-historic-site/.

CHAPTER 11

1. "Mesabi Nugget Timeline," *RangeView*, Winter 2007–2008, 7.
2. Sandy Layman, "Dear *RangeView* Readers," *RangeView*, Winter 2007–2008, 2.
3. "State financing approved for Mesabi Nugget," *RangeView*, Winter 2007–2008, 1.
4. "Company bids on former Magnetation sites," *Duluth News-Tribune*, May 22, 2019.
5. MDNR Web Page https://www.dnr.state.mn.us/input/environmentalreview/minnsteel/index.html.
6. "Minnesota Steel project nears reality," *RangeView*, Fall 2007, 3.
7. Ibid.
8. "A new era in Minnesota mining," *RangeView*, Fall 2008, 1.
9. John Myers, "Essar Steel Minnesota files for bankruptcy as Dayton pulls mineral leases," *Duluth News-Tribune*, July 8, 2016.
10. Minnesota Geological Survey: "Geology and Mineral Potential of the Duluth Complex and Related Rocks of Northeastern Minnesota."
11. State Planning Board: "The Minnesota Regional Copper-Nickel Study 1976–1979 Volume 1 Executive Summary."
12. "Polymet: a mining venture about to be reborn," *RangeView*, Spring 2008, 1.
13. Ibid.
14. MDNR Web Page https://www.dnr.state.mn.us/lands_minerals/exploration.html.

ERIE MININ

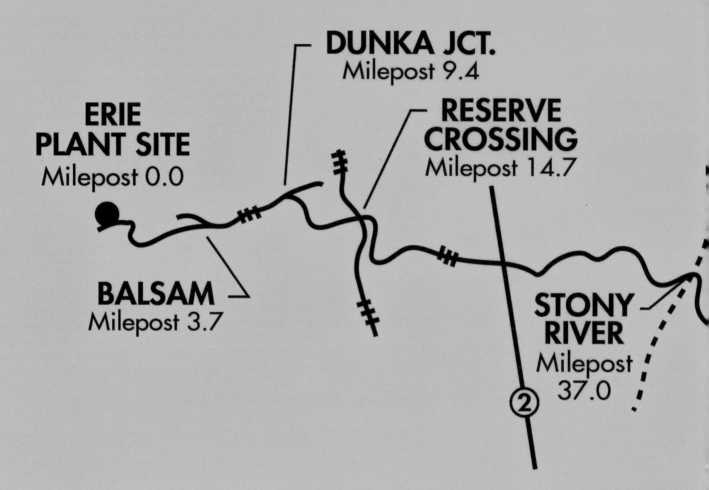

ERIE PLANT SITE
Milepost 0.0

DUNKA JCT.
Milepost 9.4

RESERVE CROSSING
Milepost 14.7

BALSAM
Milepost 3.7

STONY RIVER
Milepost 37.0

②

TACONITE MINING & PROCESSING FLOWCHART

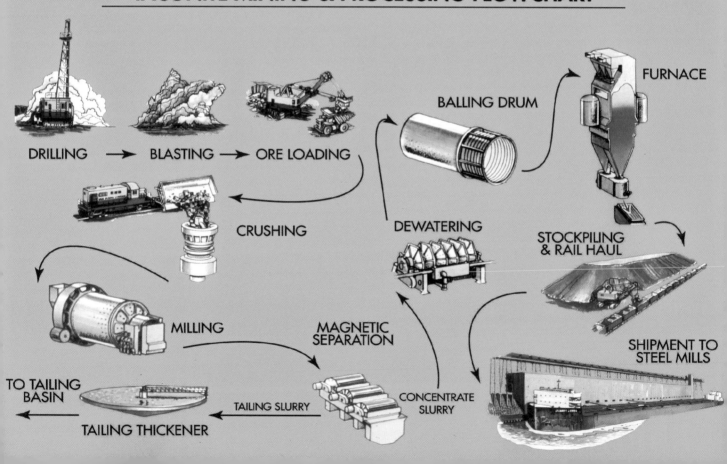

DRILLING → BLASTING → ORE LOADING

CRUSHING

MILLING

TO TAILING BASIN

TAILING THICKENER

TAILING SLURRY

MAGNETIC SEPARATION

CONCENTRATE SLURRY

DEWATERING

BALLING DRUM

FURNACE

STOCKPILING & RAIL HAUL

SHIPMENT TO STEEL MILLS